Social Security in the 21st Century

ERIC R. KINGSON AND JAMES H. SCHULZ
Editors

New York   Oxford
OXFORD UNIVERSITY PRESS
1997

OXFORD UNIVERSITY PRESS

Oxford   New York
Athens   Aukland   Bangkok   Bogotá   Bombay
Buenos Aires   Calcutta   Cape Town   Dar es Salaam   Delhi
Florence   Hong Kong   Istanbul   Karachi
Kuala Lumpur   Madras   Madrid   Melbourne
Mexico City   Nairobi   Paris   Singapore
Taipei   Tokyo   Toronto

and associated companies in

Berlin   Ibadan

Library of Congress Cataloging-in-Publication Data

Social Security in the 21st century /
edited by Eric H. Kingson and James H. Schulz
p.   cm.
Includes bibliographical references and index.
ISBN 0-19-510424-2. — ISBN 0-19-510425-0 (pbk.)
1. Social Security—United States.
2. Social security—United States—Forecasting.
3. Twenty-first century—Forecasts.
I. Kingson, Eric R.   II. Schulz, James H.
HD7125.S59923   1996   368.49390097301—dc20   95-26367

3 5 7 9 8 6 4 2
Printed in the United States of America
on acid-free paper

Contents

Foreword

Social Security is one of our most important programs. In 1995, $332.6 billion were paid in benefits to 43.4 million people. An estimated 141 million people paid contributions on their earnings, yielding $359.0 billion in payroll tax revenues.

For many workers, their Social Security contribution was larger than their income tax liability. In 1992, 63 percent of aged families received 50 percent or more of their income from Social Security (or, more precisely, from the Old-Age, Survivors, and Disability Insurance program). Together with Medicare, Social Security makes an enormous difference in the everyday lives of Americans. Few government initiatives have received such widespread public support. But Social Security is also the source of much misunderstanding and periodic heated debate. As the economy changes and the baby boomers age, the nation is again assessing various approaches to adapting Social Security. This book, written by an interdisciplinary group of experts, provides students, policymakers, university faculty, journalists, and the reading public with the tools necessary to participate in this new debate.

The impetus for this book came from the National Academy of Social Insurance, an institution that was created in 1986 to encourage research, understanding, and sound policy for the nation's social insurance programs. This academy is made up of social insurance experts who come from a variety of disciplines and professions including actuarial science, economics, health policy, history, law, medicine, philosophy, political science, public administration, social work, and sociology. Some also come with distinguished public- and private-sector careers in the development and administration of many of the nation's social insurance, private pension, and health financing systems.

Recognizing the need for an up to date and comprehensive social security book, the board of the academy selected two of the nation's leading experts to undertake the project and appointed an advisory committee to help them plan it. The academy left Kingson and Schulz free to organize the collection as they saw best. Naturally, the editors called on academy members for contributions and to help with formal reviews of the chapters. The board of the academy also reviewed the final product for quality and balance and was very pleased with what it saw.

There are a variety of types of essays in this collection, in order to cater to a variety of different interests in Social Security. To run quickly through the list, in chapter 1, Lawrence Thompson and Melinda Upp explain why there is a case for gov-

ernment intervention in the provision of income to the elderly and contrast the social insurance approach (using a universal government program) with alternatives
of employer or individual mandates, tax expenditures, and a means-tested approach.
In chapter 2, Edward Berkowitz reviews the history of social insurance, dividing
the past into four periods: the pre-1935 struggle for political legitimacy, the 1935–50
fight for survival, the 1951–72 period of expansion, and the post-1972 period of re-
sponses to issues about cost. Chapter 3, written by the editors, reviews the arguments against means-tested alternatives to the universal nature of Social Security.
In Chapter 4, Marilyn Moon lays out different contexts for evaluating the question
of whether Social Security benefits are too high or too low. In Chapter 5, Yung-
Ping Chen and Stephen Goss describe the relationship between OASDI taxes paid
and benefits received, in terms of both empirical experience and hypothetical earnings histories. They give a guide to the sizable literature on this subject. In Chapter
6, Karen Holden describes the changes that have occurred in the work and family
roles of women and the appropriateness of the current structure of benefits as they
affect women. In Chapter 7, Jerry Mashaw enumerates the concerns that lead to the
provision of income for the disabled and the dilemmas posed in reforming disability policy. In Chapter 8, Jill Quadagno and Joseph Quinn examine what is known
about how the financial factors in both Social Security and private pensions affect
the timing of retirement. In Chapter 9, Edward Gramlich looks more broadly at how
Social Security affects the economy, considering individual incentives, capital accumulation, and the issue of competitiveness. In Chapter 10, Barry Bosworth explores the implications of investing part of the Social Security Trust Funds in private securities. In Chapter 11, Virginia Reno and Robert Friedland report and analyze
survey findings on public knowledge of, support for, and confidence in Social
Security. In Chapter 12, Theodore Marmor, Fay Cook, and Stephen Scher question
claims of generational conflict over Social Security, contrasting the approaches to
policy inherent in a social insurance concept with that of a residualist safety net
concept. In Chapter 13, Robert Myers discusses the actuarial status of Social Security
and its relationship to public confidence in it.

One of the virtues of this book is the presence of three chapters by commentators who were invited to read the other chapters, add missing pieces, and voice disagreement with any of the stated conclusions. These chapters—by Michael Hurd,
Dwight Bartlett, and Stanford Ross—comment on a number of features including
the windfall gains to start-up generations, the complications in the treatment of single earners and of one- and two-earner couples, the lack of certainty in actuarial
projections, and the legal foundations and administrative structure that have engendered the supportive political culture for Social Security.

The final two chapters focus on the future and issues of reform. Eugene Steuerle
lays out principles for reform and explores a number of issues including delays in
both the normal and the early entitlement age. He also identifies reforms to avoid.
Robert Ball (with Thomas Bethell) suggests a different approach to principles, presents a reform package to restore actuarial balance, and discusses a wide range of
alternatives including some that he thinks it best to avoid.

The editors and authors have worked long and hard in putting together this excellent volume. It will help students interested in learning about this central feature
of American life. It will be a useful resource for university faculty who want to ex-

plore Social Security policy questions with their students. Policymakers, journalists, and other participants in the Social Security policy arena will be similarly pleased to find an understandable book written by an eminently qualified group of authors.

As an economist who studies Social Security, I recognize that the projected "actuarial imbalance" in Social Security requires that changes be made. By starting the discussion and debate long before financial crisis occurs, we can hope to have a smooth adjustment of Social Security. Recognizing the wide impacts Social Security has, I am concerned that this adjustment reflect its many important effects, balancing its somewhat conflicting goals. As a citizen, I am eager to see this debate conducted with understanding and intelligence. This book will enlarge the community of the well informed and enhance the quality of this debate; it should be of interest to all who seek a reasoned and balanced overview of the choices that will shape Social Security.

PETER A. DIAMOND

Paul A. Samuelson Professor of Economics,
Massachusetts Institute of Technology
and President, National Academy of Social Insurance

Preface

This book provides the basic facts and an understanding of the various complexities surrounding Social Security, that is, the United States' Old-Age, Survivors, and Disability Insurance program. In reading this book, we hope that our colleagues in educational institutions, their students, journalists, policymakers, and the general public will find many of their questions and concerns answered.

This is a time when many people are asking questions about the future of Social Security. We believe that it is especially important that the asserted "facts," the various opinions, and ultimately the decisions arising from the ensuing discussions and debates be based on a sound understanding of current policy issues and choices. Thus, as most of the chapter headings imply, the main part of this book is built upon the many questions that have been raised about how Social Security operates and what its impact is on both individuals and the American political economy. We have asked experts to address each issue area, to examine the questions in depth, and to provide answers where possible.

No other government program has larger receipts or expenditures. Between its inception and 1994, $4.6 trillion was paid into Social Security. The benefits that were paid out over this same period equaled $4.2 trillion, the excess accumulating in the program's trust funds. Revenues were about $405 billion in 1995, and expenditures were $340 billion.

Social Security is not just a program for old people. It was designed to help deal with economic insecurity that threatens individuals and their families *over the life-span*. Supporters point out that Social Security raises individual well-being and strengthens family and community life. It does this by providing widespread and meaningful protection against income losses that can accompany the disability, death, or old age of working persons.

In stark contrast, its harshest critics often call Social Security a "Ponzi scheme" or a "chain letter." They argue that it threatens the welfare of younger generations as a result of declining "rates of return" and fiscal problems that they think threaten the sustainability of its benefit promises. Hence, some now argue, for example, that Social Security should no longer be universal—calling for denial of some benefits to those with very high incomes.

Supporters recognize the future financial strains on Social Security imposed by the demographic and economic changes occurring over time. But many think that, as in the past, the program can readily adjust through a combination of modest changes, including some benefit reductions and/or tax increases. Many critics argue, in contrast, that Social Security is clearly overextended and that the aging of the "baby-boom" cohorts will require a major overhaul of the program. They also think that Social Security introduces numerous distortions into the economy, including savings and work disincentives. And some people reject the argument that Social Security is a "self-financed program," arguing instead that its spending should be examined as part of each year's budgetary process.

Not surprisingly, the public is confused. On the one hand, opinion polls consistently show strong support for Social Security across virtually all socioeconomic groups. On the other hand, these same polls show that the public, especially the young, is very worried that the program will not pay promised benefits. In fact, many people fear that the program will not even be there when they retire. Others think that the benefits will not be adequate. Still others are concerned that, because of their age, race, or sex, they will not be treated fairly under the rules of the program. All these concerns are voiced frequently in university classrooms, by the media, and in the halls of Congress.

Unquestionably, today's students, citizens, and policymakers will be called upon in the future to make decisions that will determine the shape of Social Security for generations to come. University faculty will need to acquaint their students with the complexities surrounding many programmatic issues and policy options. Journalists and broadcast commentators will continue to cover Social Security policy debates. And, without doubt, policymakers will need to make numerous decisions about the financing, adequacy, and fairness of the program.

An informed policy debate requires knowledgeable participants. Unfortunately, there is reason to believe that the prerequisites for such debate are sadly lacking. Surveys indicate that, among both professionals and laypeople, little is known about Social Security beyond the basic facts of coverage and benefit categories and the need for increased sources of funding in future years if benefits are not to be cut sharply.

Failure to understand the programs's history, the principles upon which it is based, the facts surrounding policy issues, and the nature of the choices that can be made opens the door to misunderstanding and misinformation. For example, few people understand *why* and *how* the program seeks to target benefits to low-income persons while simultaneously providing a "floor of protection" for middle-income (and even upper-income) people. Few understand the differences between private insurance and the social insurance approach to economic welfare. And few understand the difference between "pay-as-you-go" and partial advance funding.

Yet these are but a few of the concepts that must be mastered to participate fully in Social Security policy discussions. In addition, there are numerous contemporary issues that must be examined. These include questions regarding economic effects, affordability, impact on the federal deficit, fairness to various groups, benefit adequacy, changes in disability policy, and generational equity.

This book is not a technical book for experts in the fields of private and public pensions. Rather, it is a book for people who know very little about pensions but who would like to get a comprehensive overview of contemporary Social Security issues. The authors of the chapters in the book, almost all members of the National Academy of Social Insurance, have been asked to speak in a clear and authoritative voice but to also give a balanced, scholarly treatment to each topic. They were asked, moreover, to avoid technical jargon.

Each of the authors is a recognized expert in the field of Social Security. While broadly supportive of the social insurance approach, the authors provide a wide range of views with regard to problem definition and preferred policy solutions. For example, some authors would rely heavily on payroll tax increases to address projected long-term financing problems; others would rather emphasize benefit reductions. As editors, we have purposely sought to provide the reader with different points of view through the selection of authors, the use of a peer review process to give authors feedback (see the acknowledgments), and the inclusion of three shorter "reactor chapters" that provide comments on the main chapters.

The book is divided into four parts. There is a short overview section at the beginning. This provides the reader with general information on various approaches to dealing with economic insecurity; social insurance principles are introduced and a historical review of programmatic Social Security developments is presented. The main part of the book discusses the most frequently asked questions about Social Security. This is followed by three reactor chapters; these authors were given prepublication copies of the "issues chapters" and asked to react, extend upon, and/or critique them. Finally, the book ends with two chapters that take a more integrative view of the issues and look to the future.

Readers will immediately notice that the book focuses primarily on Social Security disability, survivors', and old-age pensions. Health issues and the Medicare and Medicaid programs were explicitly omitted from the main scope of the book (although some chapters briefly discuss them). To address the many additional (and often very different) issues the health area raises would have made the book unacceptably long. Similarly, other programs were also omitted (e.g., unemployment insurance and the Supplemental Security Income program).

The first American Social Security benefit ever paid was $22 a month and was received by Miss Ida Fuller, a retired law firm secretary, in early 1940. Miss Fuller (who died in 1975) lived to be over 100, paid into the program less than $100 in payroll taxes, and over the years received about $21,000 in Social Security benefits. To some, the nearly $21,000 "bonanza" received by Ida Fuller is illustrative of the flawed financial base upon which Social Security was originally built. To others, these early "windfall gains" may have been appropriate during the program's start-up, but they now urge us to think about radical changes to the program. And to others, Ida Fuller's benefits are illustrative of a nation collectively responding to the needs of the time, through a program that has been continually changing and adapting over the years to new social and economic conditions.

We hope that after you read this book, you will have an informed opinion on this and many other issues related to Social Security.

Eric R. Kingson

James H. Schulz

Acknowledgments

This book is the result of the efforts of many individuals—authors, reviewers, and advisors, alike—and of the support provided by three organizations: The National Academy of Social Insurance, Brandeis University, and Boston College. As editors, we wish to express our appreciation to those who contributed their ideas, time, and insights.

We owe a big debt of gratitude to the National Academy of Social Insurance, especially its board of directors. The academy identified the need for this book and provided support and consultation throughout its writing. As a nonpartisan policy research organization, the academy seeks to provide a forum for the exploration of a broad range of ideas related to the field of social insurance, seeking to promote an understanding of policy and program issues among policymakers, researchers, and the general public. Its board encouraged us to draw upon its membership of over 400 experts in the fields of social insurance and health-care financing to produce a book that would provide an accessible, in-depth overview of Social Security pension issues. At every stage, Pamela Larson, the executive vice-president of the academy, assisted effectively with the coordination of the academy's contributions to the book.

Members of the academy-convened advisory committee to the book were Professors Edward Berkowitz, Yung-Ping Chen, Theda Skocpol, and John Williamson. This committee assisted with developing the book's primary objective, the topics to be covered, and the structuring of the peer review process. Members of the committee also wrote or reviewed various chapters. We are grateful for all their help.

We extend thanks to the chapter authors for their excellent work and collegiality throughout the production process. And we greatly appreciate the work of other members of the academy who served as peer reviewers for various chapters. Their reviews provided the authors and us with excellent questions to consider, errors to be addressed, and many recommended changes. The final product was much stronger as a result of their efforts. The reviewers were: Emily S. Andrews, G. Larry Atkins, Robert M. Ball, Merton C. Bernstein, Robert H. Binstock, Gary Burtless, Robert L. Clark, Fay Lomax Cook, Renato A. DiPentima, Richard S. Foster, Robert J. Lampman, Mark H. Leff, Robert J. Myers, John L. Palmer, Joseph F. Quinn, Dallas Salisbury, Bruce Schobel, John Trout, John B. Williamson, and Howard Young.

Margaret Stubbs at Brandeis University has our deep appreciation for her many contributions in preparing the manuscript for final submission. This task would have been immeasurably more difficult to accomplish without her efforts and strong commitment to providing a highly professional final product.

Brandeis University's Florence Heller Graduate School for Advanced Studies in Social Welfare provided secretarial and other important support for the book. We appreciate the assistance provided by Brandeis University and the Boston College Graduate School of Social Work, both of which supported our work as editors in a variety of ways.

For the record, we note that the views presented in this book are those of the authors and not necessarily representative of any organization to which they may belong. Similarly, as editors with sole responsibility for the selection of authors and for the final approval of manuscripts for publication, we hasten to add that our decisions are not the decisions that might have been made by other members of the National Academy of Social Insurance or of any other organizations with which we are affiliated. Of course, we take responsibility for any errors that may have occurred in the editorial process.

Finally, a personal note—we must confess that when we started this project we did not really know what a gigantic undertaking it would turn out to be. As with any large task of this sort, there were many unanticipated problems and delays. But having now completed the task, we are pleased with the results, an outcome that would not have been possible without the on-going patience (though perhaps tried at times), support, and humor of our families. To them, our final word of thanks.

Contributors

Robert M. Ball is a consultant on Social Security, health, and welfare policy to many organizations and elected officials. From April 1962 to March 1973, he was U.S. Commissioner of Social Security, serving under presidents Kennedy, Johnson, and Nixon. He was a member of the 1982–83 National Commission on Social Security Reform, a Visiting Scholar at the Center for the Study of Social Policy, and a Senior Scholar at the Institute of Medicine. His numerous writings include the books *Pensions in the United States, Social Security: Today and Tomorrow,* and *Because We're All in This Together.* He was a member of the 1994 Advisory Council on Social Security and has served as both member or staff on many other advisory councils. A founding member of the National Academy of Social Insurance, he chaired its board of directors from 1986 to 1996.

Dwight K. Bartlett, III is Maryland Insurance Commissioner. He served as Chief Actuary of the U.S. Social Security Administration from 1979–81. He then became president of Mutual of American Life Insurance Company (until 1989). He has been a visiting executive professor at the Wharton School, University of Pennsylvania, and a principal of Barlett Consulting Services, Inc. He is a founding member and former board member of the National Academy of Social Insurance and a Fellow of the Society of Actuaries.

Edward D. Berkowitz is Professor of History and Chair of the History Department at George Washington University. His many writings on social security include the books *America's Welfare State* and *Mr. Social Security: The Life of Wilbur J. Cohen.*

He has also written widely on disability policy, including the book *Disability Policy: America's Programs for the Handicapped*. He is a founding member of the National Academy of Social Insurance and was the academy's first Visiting Scholar.

Thomas N. Bethell is a Washington, D.C., writer and editor who has produced reports on policy issues ranging from occupational safety and health and rural economic development to health-care reform and the future of Social Security. He previously worked with Robert M. Ball on *Because We're All in This Together*, a book on long-term care published by the Families USA Foundation.

Barry Bosworth is a Senior Fellow in the Economic Studies Program at the Brookings Institution, where he has been since 1971. He has also held positions as Director of the President's Council on Wage and Price Stability (1977–79), visiting lecturer at the University of California (1974–75), and assistant professor at Harvard University (1969–71). His research has concentrated on issues of capital formation and saving behavior. A founding member of the National Academy of Social Insurance, his books include *Can America Afford to Grow Old* (with H. Aaron and G. Burtless), *Tax Incentives and Economic Growth, Saving and Investment in a Global Economy, The Chilean Economy: Policy Lessons and Challenges* (edited with R. Dornbush and R. Laban), and *The New Gatt: Implications for the United States* (edited with S. Collins).

Yung-Ping Chen holds the Frank J. Manning Eminent Scholar's Chair in Gerontology at the University of Massachusetts, Boston. He was a delegate to the 1971, 1981, and 1995 White House Conference on Aging and consultant to the staff of these conferences. He served on the Panel of Actuaries and Economists of the 1979 Advisory Council on Social Security. He is a Fellow of the Gerontological Society of American (GSA) and was chair of the GSA's Economics of Aging Formal Interest Group (1992–1993) and editor of the Interest Group's Newsletter (1988–93). A founding member of the National Academy of Social Insurance (and its Visiting Scholar in 1989), his books include: *Social Security in a Changing Society, Checks and Balances in Social Security,* and *Choices and Constraints: Economic Decisionmaking*.

Fay Lomax Cook is Professor of Education and Social Policy and acting director of the Center for Urban Affairs and Policy Research at Northwestern University. She served as a scientific consultant to the congressionally mandated Task Force on Aging Research, was a member of the North American Program Committee for the 1993 International Congress of Gerontology, and was a Visiting Scholar at the Russell Sage Foundation. A member of the National Academy of Social Insurance, her publications include *Who Should Be Helped? Public Support for Social Services; The Journalism of Outrage: Investigative Reporting; Agenda Building in America;* and *Support for the America Welfare State: The Views of Congress and the Public*.

Robert B. Friedland is director of the National Academy on Aging. Previously he was research director for the National Academy of Social Insurance. He has also been Chief Economist for Maryland's Medicaid Program, Senior Research Associate at the Employee Benefit Research Institute, director of the Public Policy Institute for the American Association of Retired Persons, Senior Policy Analyst with Project HOPE's Center for Health Affairs, and staff member of the U.S. Bipartisan

Commission on Comprehensive Health Care. A member of the National Academy of Social Insurance, his many writings include the book *Facing the Costs of Long-Term Care,* which received the 1992 Elizur Wright Award from the American Risk and Insurance Association.

Stephen Goss is the Acting Deputy Chief Actuary for Long-range Actuarial Estimates in the U.S. Social Security Administration (SSA). He has been with the Office of the Actuary, SSA, since 1974. He is an associate member of the Society of Actuaries and a member of the National Academy of Social Insurance. He has written numerous papers and has conducted actuarial studies on a broad range of Social Security issues.

Edward Gramlich is Dean of the School of Public Policy and Professor of Economics and Public Policy at the University of Michigan. He served as deputy and then acting director of the Congressional Budget Office, on the staffs of the Federal Reserve Board of Governors and the Office of Economic Opportunity, as a Fellow of the Brookings Institution, and as Staff Director of the Economic Study Commission for major league baseball. His widely regarded textbook on benefit-cost analysis is now in its second edition. He has written many other books and articles in the areas of budget policy, income redistribution, fiscal federalism, the economics of professional sports, and Social Security. He is a member of the National Academy of Social Insurance and in 1994 was appointed Chair of the Advisory Council on Social Security.

Karen Holden currently holds joint appointments in the Robert M. LaFollette Institute of Public Affairs and the Department of Consumer Science at the University of Wisconsin. She is also associate director of the LaFollette Institute, on the Executive Committee of the Institute for Research on Poverty, and a member of the Steering Committee for the Center for Demography and Ecology (all at the University of Wisconsin). A member of the National Academy of Social Insurance, her research focuses on social and private insurance issues. She has written many books and articles on public policy issues relating to the economic welfare of the elderly, especially widows, and on the role of government in shaping pension choices.

Michael Hurd is Professor of Economics at the State University of New York at Stony Brook, Senior Economist at the Rand Corporation, and Research Associate at the National Bureau of Economic Research. His research interest is the economics of aging, particularly in saving behavior and how it interacts with Social Security and the pension system. He is a senior investigator on the Health and Retirement Survey and one of the Principal Investigators on the Survey of Asset and Health Dynamics Among the Elderly. A member of the National Academy of Social Insurance, his numerous publications include "The Annuity Value of Social Security" and "Research on the Elderly: Economics Status, Retirement, and Consumption and Saving."

Eric R. Kingson is Associate Professor of Social Policy at Boston College. A member of the board of directors of the National Academy of Social Insurance (1986–1996), he served as an advisor to the 1982–83 National Commission on Social Security Reform and to the 1994 Bipartisan Commission on Entitlement and Tax Reform. He directed the Emerging Issues Program of the Gerontological Society of America. His publications include many articles addressing Social Security policy, the generational equity debate, and the aging of the baby-boom cohort. He is the primary author of *Ties That Bind: The Interdependence of Generations* (with B. Hirshorn and J. Cornman) and *Social Security and Medicare: A Policy Primer* (with E. Berkowitz).

Theodore R. Marmor is Professor of Public Policy and Management at Yale University. At Yale since 1979, he previously taught at the universities of Wisconsin, Minnesota, and Chicago. He specializes in the modern welfare state, with an emphasis on medical care and health issues. He is a Fellow of the Canadian Institute of Advanced Research, a member of the Institute of Medicine, and a founding member of the National Academy of Social Insurance. His books include *Understanding Health Care Reform* and *America's Misunderstood Welfare State: Persistent Myths, Continuing Realities* (with J. Mashaw and P. Harvey).

Jerry L. Mashaw is Sterling Professor of Law and professor at the Institute for Social and Policy Studies at Yale University. He previously served on the law faculties of Tulane and the University of Virginia. He has written many publications on administrative law, regulation, and social welfare policy. He is a member of the American Academy of Arts and Sciences and a founding member of the National Academy of Social Insurance. His most recent publications include *America's Misunderstood Welfare State: Persistent Myths, Continuing Realities* (with T. Marmor and P. Harvey) and *The Struggle for Auto Safety*.

Marilyn Moon is Senior Fellow in the Health Policy Center of the Urban Institute. Prior to this position, she was Director of the Public Policy Institute, American Association of Retired Persons. She has also worked as a senior analyst at the Congressional Budget Office, as a consultant to the U.S. Bipartisan Commission for Comprehensive Health Care, and as an informal advisor to the Clinton campaign and health-care transition team. She has written extensively on health policy, public policy for the elderly, and income distribution, including occasional columns for the *Washington Post*. A member of the National Academy of Social Insurance and Public Trustee of the OASDHI Trust Funds, her most recent book is *Entitlements and the Elderly: Protecting Promises, Recognizing Realities* (with J. Mulvey).

Robert J. Myers is a member of the Prospective Payment Assessment Commission and an international actuarial consultant. He was Chief Actuary for the U.S. Social Security Administration (1940–70) and Deputy Commissioner (1981–82). He was also executive director of the National Commission on Social Security reform, chairman of the Commission on Railroad Retirement Reform, and a member of the Commission on the Social Security "Notch" Issue. He is president of the International Fisheries Commissions Pension Society, a founding member of the National Academy of Social Insurance, and a consultant on Social Security to the National Association of Life Underwriters and The Seniors Coalition. His hundreds of publications include the highly regarded text *Social Security*.

Jill Quadagno is Professor of Sociology at Florida State University, where she holds the Mildred and Claude Pepper Eminent Scholar's Chair in Social Gerontology. Previously she was a professor at the University of Kansas. She is an editor, or on the editorial boards, of several journals on aging and sociology. A member of the National Academy of Social Insurance, her most recent books are *The Color of Welfare* and *States, Labor Markets and the Future of Old Age Policy* (with J. Myles).

Joseph R. Quinn is Professor of Economics at Boston College. He has been a visiting professor at the Institute for Research on Poverty and the Economics Department, University of Wisconsin; the Graduate School of Public Policy, University of California at Berkeley; and the Department of Economics, the University of New South Wales in Australia. His research focuses on the economics of aging, with emphasis on the economic status of the elderly, the determinants of the individual retirement decision, and the patterns of labor force withdrawal among older Americans. A founding member of the National Academy of Social Insurance, his numerous publications include *Passing the Torch: The Influence of Economic Incentives on Work and Retirement* (with R. Burkhauser and D. Myers).

Virginia P. Reno is Director at the National Academy of Social Insurance. She served as Deputy Director for Social Security for the 1991 Advisory Council on Social Security and as Staff Director for the Social Security Policy Council at the Social Security Administration. In addition, she has been a LEGIS Fellow with the U.S. Senate Special Committee on Aging, Director of the Program Analysis Staff of the SSA Office of Research and Statistics, and Senior Advisor to the National Commission on Social Security Reform. A founding member of the National Academy of Social Insurance, she has authored many articles and reports on Social Security and related policy issues and has also directed the National Academy's Project on Disability Income Policy.

Stanford G. Ross is a Senior Partner in the law firm of Arnold & Porter. He has dealt extensively with public policy issues while serving in the U.S. Department of the Treasury, on the White House domestic policy staff, as Commissioner of Social Security, and as a Public Trustee of the Social Security and Medicare Trust Funds. He has taught law at the Georgetown, Harvard, New York University, and University of Virginia law schools and been a Visiting Fellow at the Hoover Institute. He has served as chairman of the American Bar Association Tax Section Committee on Social Security and provided technical assistance on pension and tax issues to various foreign countries, the International Monetary Fund, the World Bank, and the Organization for Economic Co-operation and Development. He was a founding member, director, and president (1990–92) of the National Academy of Social Insurance.

Stephen Scher teaches ethics and public policy at Yale School of Management. He previously taught at the Boston University schools of Medicine and Public Health and at Harvard Medical School. He was a Visiting Scholar at Yale Law School. His forthcoming book, *The Divisive Legacy of Bioethics: Beyond Dogma and Distrust*, will be published by Yale University Press in 1997.

James H. Schulz is Professor of Economics at Brandeis University and holds the Meyer and Ida Kirstein Chair in Aging Policy. He has previously worked at the Federal Reserve Board of Governors, the U.S. Bureau of the Budget, the University of New Hampshire, the University of Teheran, and the University of Melbourne. In recent years he has been consultant to the International Labour Office, the International Social Security Association, the United Nations, and the World Bank. He is a Fellow and past president of the Gerontological Society of America and a founding member of the National Academy of Social Insurance. Among his awards is receipt of the 1983 Robert W. Kleemeier Award for outstanding research in aging. His co-authored books include *Providing Adequate Retirement Income, The Economics of Population Aging, The Economic Status of Divorced Older Women,* and *When "Life-Time" Employment Ends.* He has also written *The World Ageing Situation, 1991* and *The Economics of Aging* (currently in its sixth edition).

C. Eugene Steuerle is a Senior Fellow at the Urban Institute and author of a weekly column in *Tax Notes.* He has served in various position in the U.S. Department of the Treasury, including deputy assistant secretary for Tax Analysis. He was a Federal Executive Fellow at the Brookings Institution and a Resident Fellow at the American Enterprise Institute. A member of the National Academy of Social Insurance, he is the author of many books, the most recent of which is *Retooling Social Security for the Twenty-First Century* (with J. M. Bakija).

Lawrence H. Thompson is a Senior Fellow at the Urban Institute. Prior to this he was Principal Deputy Commissioner in the U.S. Social Security Administration. He also served as Chief Economist and then Assistant Comptroller General in charge of the Human Resources Division of the U.S. General Accounting Office. He worked for nine years on income security issues in the U.S. Department of Health and Human Services, including holding the position of Associate Commissioner for Policy in the SSA. He is a founding member of the National Academy of Social Insurance and a member of its board. He has written numerous articles and policy reports addressing a wide range of Social Security and related social policy issues.

Melinda Upp is a senior policy analyst in the Office of Policy Analysis and Evaluation at the U.S. Social Security Administration. Previously she was on the staffs of the Office of Research and Statistics and the Office of Policy at the SSA. She has also worked at the U.S. Office of Economic Opportunity and as a newspaper editor. A member of the National Academy of Social Insurance, she has published a number of articles on Social Security issues.

PART I

An Overview of Social Security

CHAPTER 1

The Social Insurance Approach and Social Security

LAWRENCE H. THOMPSON AND MELINDA M. UPP

INTRODUCTION

Debate about reforming the Social Security system is taking place in several contexts, among them ensuring the financial stability of the Social Security program itself, improving rates of return for higher earners (and equity between couples with working and nonworking wives), and reducing overall federal spending, particularly spending on entitlements.[1] This chapter attempts to provide a framework for this debate. It begins with a discussion of the rationale for government intervention in providing pension income. Next, it suggests different forms that government intervention might take. Then it suggests specific objectives of government intervention and evaluates how well each form succeeds in achieving those objectives.

WHY GOVERNMENT INTERVENTION?

1. The Economic Need

As the United States shifted from an agrarian to an industrial society, the intergenerational family support structure weakened. The jobs created in the cities provided new opportunities but also major insecurities. The number of indigent aged persons grew rapidly, vastly exceeding the capacity of private charities. Employer-sponsored pensions were few and far between. Options for individual annuities were largely nonexistent.

In response to these changes and the Great Depression, President Roosevelt named the cabinet-level Committee on Economic Security (CES), which, within a very few months, wrote its report proposing the Social Security system. The result of this report, the Social Security Act of 1935, established the framework for the current United States social welfare system. Through it, the Congress created the Social

3

Security pension and the national unemployment insurance programs, as well as means-tested programs for aid to the aged and to widows with children. Equally important, in the process the Congress explicitly rejected several alternative approaches to constructing a social welfare system.

As Berkowitz (chapter 2) discusses in more detail, the actions in 1935 rejected a noncontributory, universal pension program—the Townsend plan—and the use of means-tested programs as the primary vehicle for income support for the aged. They affirmed that a social insurance approach should be used to provide the foundation for the social welfare system and that, in the long run, means-tested programs should serve only to fill gaps between the benefits provided by social insurance and some minimum income level.

From the beginning, the Congress intended that private provision should play an important role for the upper-income aged. Committee reports explained that Social Security was structured explicitly to pay proportionately more to lower-wage workers on the presumption that they would be relying almost exclusively on public programs for their income support while higher-wage workers could be expected to supplement their benefits from their own sources.[2]

The CES, which developed President Roosevelt's proposals, also articulated a vision for future development, which included enactment of universal contributory health insurance to be operated by the states under federal supervision. Arguments over national health insurance have continued off and on over much of the six decades since the release of the 1935 report. One of these episodes led to the second major debate over the structure of our social welfare system: the debate in the mid-1960s that culminated in the enactment of Medicare. As it had done in 1935, the Congress rejected extensive reliance on means-testing as a mechanism for financing health services for the aged and decided, instead, to provide basic protection through a program using the social insurance approach. A means-tested program (Medicaid) was created only for people with limited resources who required services not covered by Medicare.

2. Rationale for Government Intervention

Why was the intervention of the federal government necessary? Why not rely on voluntary private-sector approaches? Reasons include uncertainty about the future, adverse selection, intracohort income redistribution, protection against the imprudent, protection against myopia, and filialism. These are discussed in some detail next.

Uncertainty About the Future.   Individuals cannot know, and without knowing cannot provide for, their needs in retirement (or in the event of disability). And mistakes made in planning for retirement may not become apparent until they are irreparable. But it is impossible at the beginning of a work career to anticipate what lifetime earnings will be and thus what level of income will be needed to sustain a certain standard of living in old age. A young worker will not be able to anticipate the size or composition of his future family. He or she cannot know future health status, length of work career, or length of his or her lifetime.

Moreover, no one can know the level that inflation will be in the future, nor the returns or risks that would be associated with alternative forms of investment. There is fairly wide agreement among economists and politicians that the national government can provide the most effective protection against unanticipated inflation. It is relatively simple for a pay-as-you-go Social Security system to protect purchasing power of benefits: inflation tends to increase revenues at roughly the same rate as it increases benefits. It may be possible, in theory, for the private sector to offer similar protection (Bodie, 1982, pp. 47–64; Myers, 1979). But many believe some government intervention is necessary to provide inflation insurance, perhaps through the issuance of indexed bonds (Buchanan, 1968, pp. 386–395; Ferrara, 1982; Hobbs and Powlesland, 1975; Robertson, 1981; and Weaver, 1981).

Adverse Selection. Only the government can mandate participation. Without mandating, there is a tendency for "good risks" to opt out and "bad risks" to dominate programs (i.e., adverse selection). Because of the problem of adverse selection, the private sector cannot offer individual annuities that are actuarially fair.[3] Universal, mandatory group plans, like Social Security, can insure against the uncertainty of a long life more easily and more efficiently than can voluntary programs.

Intracohort Income Redistribution. A fundamental goal of social welfare policy since 1935 has been to ensure adequate protection against hardship (Brown, 1977). That is why Social Security replaces proportionately more of prior income of lower earners than of higher earners. Individuals and couples at the higher end of the income distribution can be presumed to be able to save for their own retirement to supplement public pensions. But only the government can effect the redistribution necessary to protect lower earners. Moreover, a program like Social Security can redistribute income on the basis of lifetime earnings, rather than current earnings. Current earnings, particularly those received close to retirement, may bear little or no relationship to the more relevant lifetime standard of living.

Protection Against the Imprudent. If society will support all aged and disabled members whose current incomes are inadequate, the imprudent need not save because they will be taken care of regardless of their lifetime earnings level. A mandatory public program can allow society to force the imprudent to shoulder their fair share of the burden of providing for the aged and the disabled (Musgrave, 1968).

Protection Against Myopia. If workers are myopic, in the absence of compulsion they undersave for retirement; a compulsory system can increase the welfare of society as a whole by correcting for individual myopia (Diamond,1977, pp. 275–298; Feldstein, 1977; Pechman, Aaron, and Taussig, 1968).

Filialism. Blinder (1988, pp. 17–40) has argued that one of the more compelling arguments for government intervention is to respond to the concerns of the young for the economic well-being of their elders. A compulsory government program provides for the sustenance of each older generation by institutionalizing intergenerational transfers, he argues, rather than relying on the individual generosity of the young.

CHARACTERISTICS OF POTENTIAL FORMS OF
GOVERNMENT RESPONSE

Most advanced societies rely on some combination of six approaches (or close variations) to structuring public income support programs:[4] social insurance, employer mandates, individual mandates, voluntary approaches (tax expenditures), means-tested programs, and universal programs.

The first approach we discuss is "social insurance." Many people use this term interchangeably with "Social Security," creating some confusion. Unfortunately, there is no consensus among either researchers or policymakers on the use of these terms. In the United States, the term "Social Security" is sometimes used to cover all national pensions, health, and social assistance programs; internationally, the term is often used in an even broader way. In this country, however, Social Security is most frequently used more narrowly to refer to Old-Age, Survivors, and Disability Insurance (OASDI), and social insurance is usually used as a more inclusive term to refer to OASDI, together with hospital insurance under Medicare and unemployment insurance, programs that share the characteristics discussed later. Although this book does not discuss unemployment insurance and does not give major attention to medical insurance issues, the term social insurance is often used in the book with reference to the approach upon which OASDI is based to protect citizens against identifiable risks. Thus, as used in this book, Social Security refers to OASDI, and social insurance refers to an approach to economic well-being that is inclusive of OASDI.

Social Security can be differentiated from other ways of providing social protection and social welfare. As just discussed, we call the key distinguishing characteristics of these programs the "social insurance approach." The characteristics that distinguish one type of these programs from another include whether participation is compulsory, the role of government, the nature of the financing mechanism, whether eligibility for benefits derives from contributions, whether benefit amounts are derived from contributions, the extent to which benefit criteria are specified in the law, and whether accounting is separate and there is an explicit long-range financing plan.[5] The interaction of these characteristics gives each type of program a unique set of attributes. The differences between social insurance and other social welfare approaches can be traced primarily to differences in the mix of these characteristics. In the sections that follow, the six types of government intervention will be defined according to these characteristics.

1. Social Insurance

The social insurance approach is the largest single element in, and the foundation for the social welfare systems of, most industrial countries. It grew out of voluntary insurance arrangements of the medieval European craft guilds, was institutionalized by European governments in the late nineteenth and early twentieth centuries, and soon spread from there to the Americas.

Today, programs based on social insurance are the largest component of the United States social welfare system. In 1992, social insurance expenditures came to $1,265.1 billion, accounting for almost half of social welfare spending by the public sector (Bixby, 1993). Major programs include the Old-Age, Survivors, and Disability Insurance program, Hospital Insurance (Medicare, part A), and Unemployment Insurance. Although there is no universally accepted definition, the social insurance approach is usually based on the following characteristics:

a. *Compulsory Participation.* For most persons, participation in social insurance programs is specified in the law. In some programs, a small minority may be allowed to choose whether to participate. For example, in the United States, governments were given the option of whether their employees would be covered by Social Security.[6] Religious clergy may choose whether to participate. However, participation now is mandatory for virtually all other United States workers. Compulsory participation eliminates the problem of adverse selection.

b. *Government Sponsorship (and Regulation).* Governments create and supervise social insurance programs, but do not necessarily manage them. The programs may be operated entirely by private sector institutions (for example, the German health and supplementary pension systems); by a combination of public agencies and private contractors (the Medicare model); or directly by a public-sector agency (the model used in the United States and most other Anglo-Saxon countries for operating their public pension programs). Where the private sector runs these programs, however, operations are tightly supervised by the public sector.

c. *Contributory Financing.* Most (sometimes virtually all) of the resources needed to run the program are raised through explicit contributions (payroll taxes) collected from the employer and the employee. A worker's contribution is usually a fixed percentage of his or her wage income.

d. *Eligibility Derived from Contributions.* Eligibility for benefits under social insurance programs rests, in part, on current or previous contributions by the individual, the individual's employer, or both. Frequently an individual's contributions also make family members eligible.

e. *Benefits Prescribed in Law.* Uniform sets of entitling events and schedules of benefits are developed, announced, and applied to all participants. Administrators of the program have little discretion in determining who should get benefits or how much they should get.

f. *Benefits Not Directly Related to Contributions.* Social insurance programs usually redistribute toward lower-wage workers or towards persons engaged in activities deemed to be socially desirable. In most public pension programs, including the United States Social Security program, benefits are scaled to previous earnings. Even then, as noted earlier, the lower-wage worker tends to get back proportionately more than the higher-wage worker, sometimes much more. Many social insurance plans also subsidize benefits for nonworking members of families of workers, for students, for members of the armed forces, for homemakers caring for children, and for others whose activities are deemed to be socially beneficial.[7]

g. *Separate Accounting and Explicit Long-Range Financing.* Social insurance contributions usually are earmarked to pay social insurance benefits. Governments typically keep separate accounts that permit comparisons of program receipts and program benefits, though they may also present financial information that integrates the social insurance programs with other government operations. Governments also typically develop an explicit plan showing that projected revenues are sufficient to finance projected expenditures for several years into the future (75 years, in the case of the United States Social Security program).

It must be noted, however, that full reserve financing is not required and, in fact, is relatively rare. It is, however, more common in some of the alternative institutional arrangements. Financial reserves are frequently required in private-sector pension plans in order to help assure that pension promises are met. Programs based on social insurance can be financed on a "pay-as-you-go" basis only because they are backed ultimately by the taxing power of the government (see Myers, chap. 13).

Some of the characteristics discussed in this list are necessarily linked. For example, if a social insurance program is to provide support to lower-income households, it must redistribute from higher-income participants to lower-income participants (characteristic f). But a program that redistributes explicitly and significantly must also be compulsory (characteristic a) or higher-income persons will choose not to participate. And a program that is compulsory must be sponsored by the government (characteristic b).

Other characteristics combine to give social insurance some of its key attributes. For example, advocates of the social insurance approach argue that it delivers benefits in a way that promotes a sense of individual worth and dignity among recipients. They argue that this result flows from the fact that social insurance is financed by explicit contributions (characteristic c) and that entitlement to benefits derives from the payment of these contributions (characteristic d). The underlying philosophy of the program, then, is that beneficiaries have earned the right to receive their benefits by paying their contributions. The linkage between contributions and benefits can also serve as an incentive for compliance with Social Security taxes, although the strength of this incentive will obviously depend on how closely benefit amounts are linked to prior contributions.

Some advocates of the social insurance approach also argue that it introduces fiscal discipline into the political process. Beneficiaries of social welfare programs (whether pensioners or health care providers) naturally favor raising the level of benefits paid under the program. Because of the combination of contributory finance (characteristic c) and the separate accounting of program receipts and benefits (characteristic g), however, program expansions are likely to require an increase in contribution rates. Thus, they argue, wage earners, who will have to pay higher contributions to finance program expansions, have an incentive to support restraints on the growth of social insurance benefits.

2. Employer Mandates

Another approach to providing social welfare benefits involves government mandates that all employers (or all large employers) provide or finance specific social welfare benefits to their employees. Examples of mandated employer benefits in the United States include workers' compensation in some states and health insurance in Hawaii.

Employer mandates and social insurance both are employment-based approaches, and they share many characteristics. In both cases, eligibility for benefits is connected to employment, participation is compulsory, benefits are financed primarily from employer and employee contributions, and benefits are financed according to an explicit plan. Employer mandates invariably involve specification in law of a minimum benefit package, although employers are usually free to offer a better package than the minimum. (Social Security programs also tend to offer a uniform package of benefits, with employers having the option of offering separate, supplemental programs.)

The two approaches differ first in that employer-mandated benefit programs are not likely to redistribute from higher to lower earners; contributions by (or on behalf of) each worker should pretty much accord with the expected costs of the benefits to be provided that worker. Second, employer-sponsored pension plans are more frequently (though not universally) advance funded; that is, financial reserves are accumulated in advance to pay claims.

3. Individual Mandates

Individual mandates have long been a part of the health insurance systems of several countries and have been used more recently—in Chile for example—as a means of providing pensions (World Bank, 1994). Individual-mandated programs are much like employer-mandated programs. They are sponsored and regulated by the government, eligibility for benefits is linked closely to the payment of contributions, and benefits are financed to a significant degree from contributions. Two differences between employer and individual mandates are worth noting. First, individual-mandated pensions must be advance funded, whereas employer-mandated programs can operate (where legal) on a pay-as-you-go basis. Second, in principle, a substantial amount of redistribution could be built into an individual-mandated program through the use of targeted government subsidies.[8] Designing an employer-mandated program with a substantial amount of redistribution would be more difficult, because it would be difficult to target the subsidy to particular participants.

4. Voluntary Approaches (Tax Expenditures)

Governments often encourage employers to sponsor (and/or individuals to make) private arrangements that either replace or supplement public-sector social welfare programs. This encouragement usually takes the form of a "tax expenditure," an arrangement whereby someone's (usually the individual's) tax liability is lower than it otherwise would be as a result of undertaking the activity. The largest tax expenditure in the United States, larger even than the deduction for home mortgages, is for employer-sponsored pensions. In fiscal year 1995, the estimated tax expenditure for exclusion of employer pension contributions and earnings was about $65 billion. This also includes preferential tax treatment for private retirement savings. For example, persons with modified adjusted gross incomes of $25,000 or less in certain circumstances may deduct contributions to Individual Retirement Accounts (IRAs). Higher-income persons may defer payment of taxes on interest earned on IRAs.

Voluntary approaches (tax expenditures) also subsidize health care costs and benefits in many countries. In the United States, employers may deduct their contributions to health insurance, and those with relatively high medical expenses may deduct some of these expenses, including their share of health insurance premiums, from their income for purposes of computing tax liability.[9] The total in forgone tax revenues in fiscal year 1995 is estimated to be $63 billion (U.S. Office of Management and Budget, 1993).

Voluntary programs by definition are not compulsory, but their shape frequently is influenced by the government because activity qualifying for the special tax treatment must meet certain minimum conditions. As with the employer and individual mandates, these programs rarely redistribute explicitly.[10] Voluntary programs targeted at individuals do not have to be connected in any way to particular employment patterns or situations, although they can be effective only for individuals who have a reasonable income from which to make the voluntary contributions.

5. Means-Tested Programs

Means-tested programs (discussed in chapter 3) pay benefits to (or on behalf of) claimants who first demonstrate limited economic resources.[11] Major examples include Aid to Families with Dependent Children (AFDC), Food Stamps, Medicaid, and Supplemental Security Income (SSI). Entitlement has nothing to do with prior earnings or payment of taxes. In one sense, a major advantage of means-tested programs, in contrast to social insurance, is that eligibility for benefits is not linked to prior economic behavior. As a result, benefits can be tailored to current individual circumstances and assistance can be concentrated on those with the fewest resources, those who need it most.

Means-tested programs are financed from government general revenues (income and corporate taxes) so that program costs are not easily identified (other than by budget analysts). While obvious thought is given to future spending, no specific funding plans are made for years beyond the current budget cycle. Public expenditures for this kind of program totaled $145.6 billion, or 14 percent of all public social welfare funding, in 1990.

6. Universal Programs

Some programs provide social welfare benefits to all legal residents. Examples include public education in the United States and health insurance and part of the old-age pension in Canada. Universal programs share several characteristics with social insurance: benefits are prescribed in law and participation is compulsory (to the extent that participation is a meaningful concept for these programs).

They differ in other important ways. Financing for universal programs usually comes from general revenues; eligibility is tied to residence rather than previous earnings or contributions; and financing for the program is not planned separately from the planning for other types of government expenditures. Since there is no separate financing arrangement, advanced funding through the accumulation of reserves is not feasible.

7. Combinations and Hybrids

Although the approaches are presented here as being separate and distinct from one another, the difference among them sometimes blurs in actual practice. Societies often construct social welfare systems that rely on a combination of the approaches. For instance, public pensions in Canada are provided through the combination of a flat rate, universal program and an earnings-related social insurance program. Occasionally, a new approach is developed by combining features of two or more of the traditional approaches. For instance, the United States retirement income system combines nearly universal Social Security with voluntary employer supplementation encouraged through tax expenditures (private pensions, employer-administered savings plans, and the like), and government-financed, means-tested programs for the low-income elderly (Supplemental Security Income and Food Stamps). The Supplementary Medical Insurance program (Medicare Part B) illustrates a hybrid approach. It has some characteristics similar to social insurance, in that eligibility is dependent on premium payments that also provide a substantial proportion of required receipts. And financing is separated in government accounting. It resembles universal programs, however, in that all eligible citizens (by reason of age or disability benefit receipt) are allowed to participate, and the vast bulk of the funding is derived from the general budget.

OBJECTIVES

Objectives of the social welfare system can be considered in two broad categories.[12] The first involves attributes related to providing effective social protection to the population:

- Treating people with dignity and respect.
- Assuring the most complete coverage possible for the system. A social welfare system cannot provide effective protection to people that it does not cover.
- Distributing equitably the costs and benefits of the system; in particular, assuring that those with more limited economic resources are adequately protected.
- Operating social welfare institutions efficiently so that, to the extent possible, the resources devoted to them go to the improvement of beneficiary welfare rather than administrative overhead.

The second cluster involves attributes that can help promote a healthy economic environment.[13] It recognizes that an effective social welfare system can rest only on the foundation of a healthy economy and includes

- Encouraging individual thrift and not intentionally discouraging individual work effort.[14]
- Fostering responsible government fiscal policies by discouraging the tendency to overpromise social welfare benefits and assuring that private saving is available to finance capital formation.

• Facilitating the smooth operation of markets, especially labor markets, particularly by constructing institutions that minimize the social costs of economic change.

INTERACTIONS OF APPROACHES AND OBJECTIVES

The following discussion compares the strengths and weaknesses of social insurance to the other approaches to providing for social welfare and evaluates the extent to which each achieves the differing social and economic objectives.

1. Individual Dignity

Social insurance, as well as employer mandates and voluntary approaches, scores well in maintaining individual dignity. Universal programs also score well, with one caveat. In most cases, means-tested programs fail. As noted earlier, social insurance promotes individual dignity and respect through the philosophy that those who make contributions have earned the right to the benefits. Other employer-provided benefits, as well as voluntary and individual-mandated approaches, are effective in promoting this objective. In contrast, those who receive means-tested benefits are often stigmatized.

Universal programs are as effective at promoting individual respect and dignity as are the employment-based programs, so long as they remain universally available. Some fear, however, that universal programs are politically unstable, that they will be vulnerable to the introduction of means-testing as a way of dealing with some future budget crisis.

Those who value highly the objective of assuring the dignity of recipients and fear that universal programs may eventually become means-tested usually advocate one of the employment-based approaches: social insurance or employer or individual mandates. They see the explicit contributions associated with social insurance as building a political bulwark against future means testing: those who have been paying the contributions will resist program change that would deprive them of the benefits they believe they have earned.

Developments in the Canadian pension system do, in fact, raise concerns about the stability of universal programs (and suggest that social insurance is somewhat more stable), but they fall short of confirming the worst-case scenario just outlined. The Canadian public pension consists of two separate programs: (1) a universal flat pension financed from general revenues, supplemented by (2) an earnings-related pension paid under a contributory social insurance program. In 1988, in response to budget difficulties, Canada amended its personal income tax law to "claw back" at least part of the universal pension payment from the higher-income elderly and to tax it away entirely from those whose income is above a certain higher level. Canada does not claw back social insurance benefits.[15]

2. Coverage

Social welfare programs cannot be effective if they do not reach the population in need. Broad coverage is achieved easily under universal programs for which, by definition, everyone is eligible. Broad coverage is more difficult under both social insurance and employer and individual mandates because eligibility usually requires attachment to employment. Some people simply do not have a sufficient attachment to gain eligibility; others are employed in informal and casual labor markets, in which many employees and employers do not comply with the law. Individual mandates are likely to be even harder to enforce than are employer mandates; voluntary programs are likely to have an even lower rate of participation. Finally, means-tested programs may fail to reach a substantial fraction of the population they are intended to serve, in part because not all of the target population knows the program is available and in part because some of them are discouraged by the barriers that commonly arise in applying for benefits or the stigma associated with accepting them (Menefee, Edwards, and Schieber, 1981, pp. 3–21).

The sizes of the differences in coverage depend on program structure. For example, gaps under social insurance and employer mandates are likely to be larger when eligibility is determined by current or recent activity (typical for health and unemployment coverage) than when it is based on lifetime credits (typical of pensions).

Voluntary employer-sponsored programs—those encouraged through tax provisions but not mandated—are unlikely ever to come close to universal coverage. In 1993, an estimated 61 percent of all public and private sector wage and salary workers were covered by employer-sponsored health insurance programs and 49 percent were covered by employer-sponsored retirement plans (U.S. Department of Labor, 1994). Since the mid 1980s, the number insured for health care has slowly but steadily declined. The proportion covered by retirement plans declined slightly in the early 1980s but has been relatively stable since then.

Gaps in social insurance coverage can be narrowed by loosening the linkage between eligibility and current contributions or by extending the basis for contributions and coverage beyond wages to alternative sources of income support such as welfare or unemployment benefits. For example, a social insurance approach could generate nearly universal health insurance coverage. An employer-mandate approach could provide nearly universal coverage only if it were combined with a substantial and separate backup program for those not covered through work.

Finally, the consequences of gaps in the current coverage of employer-sponsored benefits depend on the alternatives available to those not covered. For example, problems associated with the health insurance gap have become more serious; increasing numbers of people not covered through their employers have no other affordable and effective access to health insurance.

The pension gap is somewhat less serious. Essentially all workers are covered by Social Security, and those workers who get proportionately less from Social Security, that is, those with higher earnings, are most likely to be covered by private pensions. Gaps in the private pension system would become more serious, however, if Social Security benefits were scaled back across the board or if the benefit structure were made substantially less progressive.

3. Distribution of Benefits and Costs

The distribution of benefits and costs under a system of social insurance is likely to differ from that under a universal program only to the extent that the revenue bases of the two programs differ. Social insurance contributions in the United States tend to be proportional to wage income, except among the highest earners. Furthermore, earnings tend to be a larger fraction of total income for households in the middle of the income distribution and a smaller fraction for households at the lowest and highest income levels. As a result, wage-related financing is more regressive than personal income taxes, but is not necessarily more so than corporate taxes or sales, excise, and value-added taxes. A universal program financed by higher personal income taxes would probably be more progressive than social insurance; one financed by increases in value-added taxes may well be less progressive.

In general, social insurance approaches will be more redistributive than private sector arrangements, whether these arrangements are mandated or voluntary.[16] The financing of health insurance is more progressive because it comes from wage-related contributions, rather than flat-rate premiums. Health insurance benefits are not progressive; the expected value of benefits does not vary by income level. With pensions, progressivity tends to derive from the provisions that afford lower-wage workers proportionately higher benefits under social insurance programs. In principle, some greater redistribution can be built into private-sector programs through the use of targeted government subsidies. This would appear to be more feasible for government mandates and voluntary individual programs, where a subsidy can be based directly on the household income of the intended recipient, than it is for employer-based programs, where the subsidy cannot be targeted to apply only to particular participants.

Persons with relatively less taste for redistribution will be more likely to favor private sector approaches. Higher-income workers occasionally argue that they should not be required to participate in Social Security because they could get a higher return on the amount that they must contribute to the program if allowed to invest it privately.[17] Younger, higher-wage workers are probably correct. But the lower return they receive under Social Security is mainly the result of the redistribution built into the program (U.S. Congressional Budget Office, 1994b; U.S. General Accounting Office, 1991b). Whether an entire birth cohort can receive a higher return under private arrangements depends on the relationship between the rate of growth in productivity and in the population, on one hand, and the real interest rate on the other. Whatever the relationship may be, the gap between the two is not likely to be large and consistently in one direction or the other for long periods (Aaron, 1966, pp. 371–374).[18]

Means-tested programs assure a greater redistribution because other social welfare programs are less effective at targeting benefits to those who are most in need. Paradoxically, their more effective targeting does not mean that means-tested benefits are necessarily more effective in serving low-income beneficiaries. These beneficiaries are less apt to apply for benefits that carry the stigma associated with the means test than they are for benefits paid through a universal or social insurance system.

4. Administrative Cost

Administrative expenses increase the total cost of the social welfare system without increasing benefits the system can pay, and these expenses can vary dramatically from one system to another. Major administrative cost elements include the cost of revenue generation, money management, benefit eligibility determination, and ongoing benefit administration.

Of the alternatives discussed here, universal programs probably have potentially the lowest administrative cost. Revenues are raised as a part of general tax collection procedures. There are no money management costs, and eligibility usually depends on meeting a few relatively easily verified conditions. The administrative costs of social insurance are also potentially quite modest since eligibility tends to be based on information that can be collected and maintained relatively easily. On the other hand, means-tested programs can be rather expensive to operate because of the need to collect and verify extensive financial information in order to assure that individuals are (and remain) eligible for benefits.[19]

Generalizations are more difficult about the relative administrative costs of public- and private-sector programs. Public-sector programs usually enjoy greater economies of scale in their operations and avoid a substantial amount of the sales expenses of private sector institutions. At any given time and place, however, inefficiencies inherent in many public-sector enterprises, such as facilities or excess staff resulting from political pressures, may more than offset the potential advantages enjoyed by the public sector, especially if the private-sector firms are exposed to effective competition.[20]

5. Work and Saving Incentives

For several decades economists have explored the effects on individual behavior of various elements of the social welfare system (Aaron, 1982; Leonesio, 1993).[21] As Quadagno and Quinn discuss in chapter 8, their analyses suggest that work effort would be somewhat higher in the absence of cash benefits. The magnitudes are not overwhelming, however, and the studies do not address such crucial issues as whether, on balance, social welfare is increased by allowing the elderly to work less. These studies do suggest that restrictions on the amount that can be earned while still receiving retirement benefits will further reduce work effort among the elderly, at least somewhat. In general, studies have not attempted to analyze differences in the impact of the different approaches to constructing the social welfare system.

Studies of the effect of taxation on work effort have, in general, also shown only weak linkages. Higher tax rates may have as much of an impact on compliance as on actual work effort. In principle, tax payments that are linked to future benefit increases might introduce less of a work disincentive, but the effect, if any, appears to be slight.

As discussed by Gramlich (chapter 9), a number of economists have examined the effect of pay-as-you-go Social Security in the United States on individual savings. On balance, their results do not support the fear that such a system will seriously erode savings and capital formation. On the other hand, studies in this country also suggest that funded pension plans do have a positive effect on savings. National savings may increase by 30 to 40 percent of any increase in the aggregate amount of assets being held in pension and other retirement accounts.[22] Taken together, these two results suggest that, in the absence of offsetting changes in government fiscal operations, shifting from a pay-as-you-go social security system to an advance funded pension system would have a positive effect on national savings. The option is discussed by Bosworth in chapter 10.

6. Fiscal Discipline

Another objective is to counter the natural tendency for political decision makers to overpromise. Granting benefit increases is popular, but it entails the assumption of future liabilities. If these liabilities become too large, their costs can eventually have undesirable economic and social consequences such as

- Increased evasion of legislated responsibilities or the growth of the informal sector, either of which makes the social welfare program less effective at protecting citizens.
- Inflationary pressures, as governments seek to support a greater level of expenditures that can be financed through current tax receipts, which will eventually interfere with economic growth.
- Reduced benefits for current beneficiaries, who might have arranged their economic affairs differently had they known that promises were not going to be kept. (Benefit reductions can occur either directly through legislated reductions or indirectly through inadequate adjustments for inflation.)

Of the various approaches, social insurance and individual mandates are unique in mobilizing countervailing political pressures to constrain program costs. As discussed earlier, the possibility of an increase in social insurance contribution rates to balance revenues and expenditures helps to create a political constituency for restraining benefits (although in practice this appears to have been more effective in western Europe and North America than in Latin America). The linkage between current contribution rates and future benefit level is even more obvious under individual mandates.[23]

In contrast, under other approaches, the cost of social welfare programs is frequently less visible. Cost increases in programs financed out of general revenue generate pressure on politicians to devise ways to finance the additions to the total budget. But they do not translate directly into tax increases that voters will realize are directly linked to developments in social welfare programs. Fiscal discipline can be preserved if appropriate budget procedures can be adopted and enforced. But these procedures operate on total spending and do not prevent runaway costs in a social welfare program from crowding out expenditures on other governmental activities.

Similarly, sooner or later, increases in social welfare costs imposed on employers will show up as smaller increases in wages. In this way, workers will ultimately pay for the social welfare benefits that their employers are required to provide. But the linkage is far less direct and far less obvious to workers. Thus, workers cannot be counted on to form an effective constituency for restraining the costs of employer mandates.

Politicians are not the only members of society prone to overpromising. The same phenomenon can affect private-sector institutions. Left to themselves, employers may promise their workers that smaller wage increases today will allow for improved pensions in the future and then never actually set aside the resources necessary to assure payment of the pensions. Similarly, competition for business may cause investment companies to undertake risky investments in the hope that they can produce a better return than their competitors. In either case, the government may eventually find that it is required to fulfill inadvisable promises made by private sector institutions. The irony, then, is that where the government wishes to rely on private sector institutions, it may be forced to regulate these institutions closely to assure that they respect the fiscal discipline of the marketplace.

The status of the national government's budget can also influence both the structure of social welfare institutions and the economic effect of social welfare policies. For one thing, political choices may be influenced by a desire to minimize the costs that appear in the budget. A major disadvantage of universal programs is that they involve substantial budget outlays. Measured by budget outlays, social insurance programs are almost as expensive as universal programs; presumably, they would be equally expensive if coverage were as extensive. One potential advantage that social insurance has, however, is that by construction, it brings its own revenue stream with it. This doesn't change the total amount that government must raise or will spend, but it may make raising revenues easier. An advantage of means-tested programs is that they require far less public resources.

The great attraction of employer and individual mandates is that their cost does not appear directly in the government budget (though the cost of employer mandates may be reflected indirectly in lower business tax collections). Even when they must be supplemented by gap-filler programs, mandated programs are likely to appear cheaper.

Another important impact of government budget policy involves the linkage, if any, between retirement savings and national savings. History gives many examples of social insurance programs in which large surplus balances were diverted to other government uses, either directly through politically motivated investments or indirectly through government borrowing of the social insurance surplus to cover deficits elsewhere in the budget. In either event, government actions serve to offset the increased savings and capital formation that would otherwise have been supported by retirement program surpluses. It may be that governments are somewhat more likely to spend reserves in public sector programs than they are those in private sector programs. If this is the case, and if retirement program surpluses are to be used as a mechanism for increasing national saving, use of mandated private-sector programs would have a somewhat higher probability of actually producing the desired economic result.

7. Facilitating Market Adjustments

Though economic growth benefits society as a whole, frequently growth disrupts the lives of particular people and institutions. Less productive firms and industries must be allowed to shrink to make room for more productive firms and industries. Such changes cause jobs to move from one firm to another and, perhaps, from one geographic area to another. Minimizing the impact of such economic shifts on the social welfare of the population is worthwhile in itself, and it will increase the political acceptability of the economic growth and change process.

The approaches to constructing the social welfare system that are most vulnerable to disruption as a result of economic growth and change are those tied closely to particular employers—either the employer mandate or the voluntary tax expenditure approach. The other approaches break the link between social welfare benefits and any particular employer, thereby helping to insulate the system from the disruption of change.

SUMMARY

This chapter has shown that each approach to meeting social welfare objectives has its own strengths and weaknesses. For example, if the priority is on maximizing coverage while minimizing administrative expenses, then the choice is probably a universal program such as a demogrant. If target efficiency is the priority, a means-tested program is in order.

In this chapter, the strengths and weaknesses of the social insurance approach were reviewed, assessing the approach against the objectives of social welfare systems. Social insurance promotes individual dignity and respect through the philosophy that those who make contributions to the system have earned the right to benefits.

Totally comprehensive coverage can be achieved only in a program that is not employer or employment driven. Thus, coverage by social insurance programs, which depends upon employment, is not as wide as programs that are by definition universal. Nevertheless, these programs typically offer better coverage than means-tested programs, programs that are tied to particular employers, or programs that are voluntary.

In terms of equitable distribution of costs and benefits, social insurance again rates relatively high. Except for the highest earners, contributions tend to be proportional to earnings. In health insurance, the expected value of benefits varies little by income. In OASDI, benefits are proportionately higher for lower-wage earners than for higher-wage earners. Social insurance ranks high, next only to universal programs in terms of minimal administrative costs associated with collecting revenues and disbursing benefits.

The many efforts to evaluate the effect of social insurance cash payments on work suggest that work effort might be higher in the absence of cash benefits. But then, the objective of old-age pensions is to enable older workers to retire. Studies of the effect of OASDI on savings have, in general, shown only weak linkages.

One of the strengths of social insurance is its potential fiscal discipline, protection from the tendency to overpromise. As long as the system is financed entirely, or almost entirely, from payroll contributions, the need to increase contributions in order to finance more generous benefits helps to create a political constituency for constraining benefits.

Finally, economic expansion or recession can disrupt businesses, with the less productive shrinking or closing and the more productive growing. Jobs may move from one geographic area to another. Since social insurance benefits are fully portable, they are more isolated from economic disruption than are programs that are tied directly to one or another employer.

CONCLUSION

On all measures of the objectives we would like to see a social welfare system achieve the social insurance approach ranks high or very high. If one is attempting to design a new social welfare approach or to improve an existing one, it is important to consider the extent to which it achieves the objectives of preserving individual dignity and respect, assuring comprehensive coverage, distributing costs and benefits equitably, operating efficiently, encouraging personal saving and not unintentionally discouraging work, fostering fiscal responsibility, and being relatively impervious to labor market change.

ENDNOTES

1. Entitlements make payments to recipients who are eligible and apply for funds. Payments are governed by formulas set in law and are not constrained by annual appropriation bills.

2. A common fallacy is that Social Security cash benefits were intended only as a supplement and that the program has since grown beyond this original vision. Robert Myers has shown, however, that the level and structure of the replacement rates produced in 1980 by the law in effect in the late 1930s would have matched quite closely the level and structure actually experienced in 1980 (Myers, 1993b, pp. 361–365). See also Moon (chapter 4) on this point.

3. Whether the return is positive includes considerations of "high-risk" premiums (to cover the eventuality that the annuitant will live long), as well as high administrative loads or costs.

4. If we were speaking about social welfare policy more broadly, we would also have to consider a seventh approach: direct provision of social welfare services by the government. This is a common strategy for delivering health services, but it is not relevant to the discussion here, focusing on public pensions. It should be noted that this chapter disregards private transfers: individual or intrafamily and charitable organization.

5. This list is adapted from the definition of social insurance developed by the Committee on Social Insurance Terminology of the Commission on Insurance Terminology of the American Risk and Insurance Association. This group also specifies that social insurance coverage must extend beyond government employees (Myers, 1993b, p. 877).

6. But if they are covered, they cannot opt not to be covered.

7. In the United States, there is much controversy about the subsidy of benefits for nonworking wives by workers (see Holden, chapter 6).

8. As a practical matter, this may be more important for health insurance than pensions. A good case can be made for subsidizing health insurance costs for those with low current-period income. It is less clear whether one would want to subsidize pension contributions for those with low current-period income. Presumably, in pension programs, redistribution is more appropriately based on lifetime income than on current-period income.

9. Tax policy also can discourage employers from spending "too much" on social welfare. One source often suggested to provide potential revenue to finance universal health insurance is a tax on employer-provided medical benefits.

10. However, the form of a tax expenditure influences whether it helps higher- or lower-income persons. Tax credits are more valuable to lower-income tax filers, while tax deductions generally benefit higher-income filers more.

11. The term means testing is sometimes incorrectly used to describe the taxing of social welfare benefits at the same rate as (or a lower rate than) applied to other forms of income. Although the result is that higher income beneficiaries receive less after taxes, the same higher-income individuals also receive a lower fraction, after taxes, of wage, interest, and other private-sector incomes. The income test is being applied not to any particular income source, but rather to the contribution toward general government receipts that the individual is being asked to make.

12. Other categorizations are equally valid. For example, see Barr (1992, pp. 741–803), who developed the following objectives of the welfare state: macroeconomic efficiency, microeconomic efficiency, economic incentives, poverty relief, protection of accustomed living standards, income smoothing, vertical equity, horizontal equity, dignity, social solidarity, intelligibility, and absence of abuse. See also Steuerle and Bakija (1994, pp. 12–30). In a slightly different context, the authors cite four principles for judging reform: redistribution (progressivity), individual equity, horizontal equity, economic efficiency, and opportunity costs. In addition, they note four rationales for a broad public annuity program: the need for popular support, the correction for market failure, the avoidance of the inequities and inefficiencies associated with means-testing, and the problem of dissolving a pay-as-you-go-system.

13. Both objectives pertaining to social protection and to a healthy economy will be addressed in later sections of this book.

14. Since the major purpose of retirement programs is to allow people to retire, these programs necessarily will produce some reduction in work effort relative to the situation that would exist in their absence. If they did not produce any reduction in work effort, they would have failed. Other things being equal, however, one would want them to not discourage work effort prior to retirement or to prevent those who decide to retire from supplementing their retirement incomes, should they desire to do so.

15. Nor does that claw back policy apply to Canadian health insurance, which also follows the model of a universal program.

16. Steuerle (1994, pp. 106–115) notes that redistribution in the United States Social Security retirement program is different for cohorts who participated in the system before it was fully mature than for those who will be retiring in the future. For all cohorts, the ratio of the present value of expected benefits received to the present value of expected tax payments is higher for lower-wage workers than for higher-wage workers. For the cohorts that passed through the system before it was fully mature, however, the actual dollar gap between the present value of expected benefits and the present value of expected tax payments may well be larger for higher-wage earners. This phenomenon occurs only in those cohorts where all workers implicitly could expect above-market rates of return on expected tax payments.

Some have argued (World Bank, 1994, p. 12) that the old-age pension system's progressivity is offset by the shorter lifetimes and the tendency toward longer work lives of low-income workers. Steuerle (1994, pp. 115–119) found that because of the weighting in the Social Security benefit formula, any effect is fairly weak. The effect is even more weak if one considers the greater likelihood that low-wage workers will receive disability or survivors' benefits.

17. This and other related issues are discussed at length in chapter 3.

18. The Congressional Budget Office 1994 report (1994b) notes, moreover, that when individuals are allowed to choose how their retirement funds are invested they typically select low-risk, low-return options.

19. The old-age and survivors' portion of Social Security averages about 0.8 percent of annual benefit payments. In comparison, administrative costs of the means-tested Supplemental Security Income program, also administered by the Social Security Administration, average about 7.6 percent of benefit payments.

20. United States and Canadian experience with health insurance illustrates the potential gap between private- and public-sector institutions and among public-sector institutions employing different approaches. The Canadian national health insurance system follows the universal model and experiences administrative costs of just under 1 percent of total outlays. The administrative costs of private health insurance companies average 10 to 12 percent of outlays (U.S. General Accounting Office, 1991a, p. 31).

21. Economic incentive issues are discussed at greater depth in chapter 9.

22. Presumably, the rest of the increase in pension assets either is offset by larger liabilities elsewhere in the economy or replaces asset accumulation that would have occurred in the absence of private pensions (Munnell, 1982).

23. One can see the importance of this effect in recent reforms in German health-care financing. Germany uses contributory social insurance to help finance personal health-care services and, in recent years, has enacted a series of reforms that have reduced physician incomes and pharmaceutical company revenues. These reforms could be achieved even though important interest groups were being forced to absorb economic losses because they were advertised as necessary to keep worker contribution rates from rising. In other words, the political influence of those paying the contributions offsets the political influence of those benefiting from the program. The same effect was illustrated in the United States in 1983, when the Congress adopted limited taxation of Social Security benefits and a higher retirement age (after some two decades) as part of a package to restore fiscal balance to that program. Neither proposal would have been adopted had not the alternative been another increase in the Social Security contribution rate.

CHAPTER 2

The Historical Development of Social Security in the United States

EDWARD D. BERKOWITZ

This essay uses history to consider how policy debates in Social Security and the related Medicare program have unfolded over time. In this context, Social Security refers to the Old-Age Insurance program initiated by the Social Security Act in 1935 that has grown into today's Old-Age, Survivors, and Disability Insurance. Medicare refers to Hospital Insurance (HI) and Supplementary Medical Insurance (SMI). The objective is to examine the major issues in Social Security (and the related Medicare program) from the point of view of the policymakers who faced those issues as they arose. In this manner, the current Social Security program becomes the product of its past. Contemporary issues such as the stability of Social Security financing, the adequacy of benefits, and the control of disability expenditures acquire a new dimension when they are observed over time.

Historians rely on the concept of periodization to categorize change. In the case of Social Security, one might think of four distinct periods. Before 1935 the very concept of social insurance struggled to gain legitimacy in a political order that emphasized private and local initiative. Between 1935 and 1950, Social Security fought for its survival in the face of considerable competition from Old Age Assistance, a welfare program that was more easily implemented in most states than was Social Security. Between 1951 and 1972, the program entered into a period of incremental expansion combined with considerable political debate over extending its boundaries to include disability and health care and over the passage of health insurance for the elderly. In the period after 1972, Social Security faced challenges from critics who objected to growing cost, unstable financing patterns, and heavy reliance on a public approach to private savings.

THE SOCIAL SECURITY ACT OF 1935

Historians continue to debate the true origins of Social Security, with its reliance on the social insurance approach and on the federal government to collect payroll taxes. Some see it as a response to industrialism. Others regard the pressure exerted by the elderly themselves, acting through mass movements such as that spawned by Dr. Townsend, who promised every elderly citizen $200 a month, as the decisive factor in Social Security's passage. Still others regard Social Security as a reaction to the internal crises of American capitalism during the depression decade.

If the program was a response to industrialism, this response came far later in this country than in western Europe. The German government gave serious consideration to the passage of social insurance measures in 1878, and by 1884 that country had created a workers' compensation and a sickness insurance program. To cite another example, 11 countries adopted compulsory unemployment compensation laws between 1919 and 1930. Identifying the reasons for the arrival of social insurance in western Europe and the relative delay of similar measures in the United States has occupied the talents of a generation of social scientists.

The growth of an industrial economy facilitated the development of social insurance programs in all of the countries, even though each country created such programs from within a distinctive political culture. The development of an industrial economy does not explain why one country adopted social insurance before another; yet it does provide a broad explanation for the phenomenon. In particular, social insurance depends, as Thompson and Upp discuss in the previous chapter, on a pooling of risk, so that, for example, workers can set aside money to cover the contingencies of ill health, disability, and old age. It requires an economic surplus in order to accomplish this pooling of risk. By increasing the productivity of individual workers and widening the margin between actual and subsistence incomes, industrialism was the economic means by which western nations accomplished this surplus.

Industrialism also introduced new rhythms to working life. Although agricultural work was dangerous and insecure, workers experienced a continuous relationship to their work. On a farm, even under conditions of crop failure, the concept of unemployment made little sense: there was always work to do. Similarly, retirement was something alien to the agrarian experience, since people of all ages could contribute to farm work. In an industrial economy, however, workers often found their work interrupted by stoppages over which they had no control. Also, employers prized efficiency and tended to lay off those who could not match the pace of production. Hence, unemployment entered the modern lexicon. Social insurance, in this sense, marked a response to involuntary unemployment. It was a means of harnessing industrial productivity to cushion some of its shocks.

The appeal of social insurance was as great in America as in western Europe; yet we chose to handle the problems of industrial insecurity differently. Our first large system of social benefits aided veterans of the Civil War, not veterans of industry (Skocpol, 1992). Our second large system of social benefits, created around 1912, provided social insurance through workers' compensation, programs designed to protect against risks related to work-related injuries. Yet we relied heavily on state governments and private insurance companies to deliver the actual benefits. In the progressive era, we experimented with survivors' benefits in the form of means-tested widows' pensions; yet in this program, as in workers' compensation, the administrative burden fell on state, and even county, governments. In the 1920s, we offered a very fragmentary program of means-tested, old-age pensions that reached only a small portion of those in need. In the United States, therefore, we chose to deal with the problems of industrialism in ways that privileged veterans over civilians, local over national government, and private over public sector.

At the same time, a strong movement for social insurance existed in this country, beginning in the progressive era, gaining strength among workers' compensation administrators, and culminating in the work of academic economists and state administrators in such places as Wisconsin. The depression provided a sense of crisis and a change of political regime. Those conditions made it possible for a group of social insurance advocates to gain influence over the nation's political agenda and to create what became the Social Security Act of 1935.

In the most immediate sense, then, the Social Security Act was the product of a report from the Committee on Economic Security. Created by President Roosevelt in the early summer of 1934, the committee was chaired by Secretary of Labor Frances Perkins. Social insurance experts staffed the committee from top to bottom, practically guaranteeing that it would recommend creation of a social insurance program to cover the risks of old age and unemployment (Altmeyer, 1996; Witte, 1963).

In 1934, social insurance, to which the committee staff was intellectually predisposed, also met pragmatic political needs. It depended on the taxing power of the federal government, which was explicitly sanctioned by the Constitution. Indeed, the need to gain approval of the Supreme Court figured prominently in the committee's discussions. Social insurance relied on payroll taxes that supplied a source of revenue independent of income and other taxes. At the time, the income tax provided a very uncertain means of collecting money for social projects. As Mark Leff has noted (1984, p. 46), the "narrow base" of the income tax limited its expansion and made it an unreliable vehicle for covering Social Security's obligations; it was an era in which 95 percent of Americans paid no income taxes. The alternative was payroll taxes or some combination of general revenues and payroll taxes.

As matters turned out, the exact structure of the Social Security tax plan became an object of considerable controversy among the president's advisors. At issue was how to schedule the taxes over time and how to blend payroll taxes and general revenues. The staff working on the problem decided to recommend a gradually rising tax rate that would accommodate the growing number of people who would retire in the future. The tax would begin in 1937 at a rate of 2 percent, split evenly between the employer and the employee, and rise every two years until it reached 5 percent in 1957. According to the staff's calculations, which were subject to the vagaries of trying to predict population, wage levels, and unemployment rates into the future, the system would develop a deficit by about 1967. At that time, should such a deficit develop, the government could remedy it by adding general revenues.

President Roosevelt objected to this formulation and insisted that the tax rates be redrawn so as not to allow a deficit. Accordingly, the committee staff substituted a plan, which Treasury Secretary Morgenthau presented to Congress toward the end of the Ways and Means Committee's hearings on the bill, in which the combined employer and employee tax rate reached 6 percent by 1949. Employers and employees would pay taxes on the first $3,000 of the employee's income (Berkowitz, 1991).

Requesting only this reworking of the tax rates, Roosevelt passed the committee's recommendations along to Congress in the beginning of 1935. Congress reacted politely, as it might to any administration proposal that followed the election of 1934. At the same time, no ground swell developed in support of social insurance programs because they did not affect the major problems of relieving the victims of the depression. Old-age insurance and unemployment compensation, two social insurance programs proposed by the committee, bore little relationship to the urgent business of coping with the consequences of massive unemployment or the poverty of old age. To aid people in immediate distress, states would have to continue to depend on their old poor laws, supplemented by federal emergency public works programs (Berkowitz and McQuaid, 1991).

Despite this problem, President Roosevelt persevered. At several points, Congress threatened to drop old-age insurance from the omnibus economic security bill, which also included welfare (aid to the elderly, the blind, and dependent children), unemployment compensation, vocational rehabilitation, child welfare, and public health components. The president insisted that the various parts of the legislation be kept together. As a consequence, Congress passed a federally administered old-age insurance program for industrial and commercial workers, funded by payroll taxes that initially amounted to 2 percent of the employee's first $3,000 in wages. Then, as now, employers and employees split the tax. One percent was deducted from an employee's paycheck, and 1 percent was paid by the employer. The only issue concerning old-age insurance that animated Congress concerned the right of people who already had private pensions not to participate in the government's new program. After considerable debate, Congress rejected the notion of voluntary participation—what became known as the Clark plan, after its Senate sponsor Bennett Champ Clark (D-Missouri).

THE STRUGGLE FOR SURVIVAL, 1935–1950

The formulation of the legislation and its presentation to Congress had important implications for the future of Social Security policy. Because the bill rested on the government's power to tax, it went to the tax committees in Congress. By 1939, provisions were worked out in which the money collected for Social Security was automatically placed in a trust fund. That meant that the Social Security program bypassed the appropriations process and became the exclusive preserve of the House Ways and Means and Senate Finance committees in Congress. That, in turn, provided a source of continuity and support for the program that other social welfare programs, which had constantly to fight for appropriations, lacked (Derthick, 1979).

Despite this advantage, the Social Security program initially had far more liabilities than assets. In the years between 1935 and 1939, issues related to the long-term financing of the program dominated the policy agenda. Between 1939 and 1950, the chief issues concerned the competition between Social Security and welfare over which would become the dominant program in aiding the elderly. Legislation in 1939 settled the financing issue, and important amendments in 1950 ended much of the competition between Social Security and welfare. The entire period between 1935 and 1950 might be thought of as one of political peril for the Social Security program.

The problems had several dimensions. One concerned the relationship of contributions to benefits. Social insurance, by definition, depended on what I have described as the "pay to play rule" (1991, p. 21). Someone who contributed nothing received nothing from the program. That meant that someone already old in 1935 could not expect a pension, undermining the program's relevance as a vehicle for providing a floor of protection for the old. Those nearing retirement age who contributed only a little to the program could expect little back from the program. To bolster the pensions of those nearing retirement age, the program relied on the contributions of younger workers to supplement those of older workers, a feature that greatly complicated the financing plans.

Another dimension of the problem was that the program would show up as a payroll tax before it began to pay benefits. This situation created political vulnerabilities that faced any program that relied on a tax and raised questions related to the role that the tax would play in macroeconomic policy. A final dimension of the problem was inherent in the long-run financing of the program, if it were to be self-supporting from payroll taxes. At first, the costs of the program would be low. Over time, as more people who had contributed to the system retired, these costs would rise. The question arose as to whether the system might prefund its liabilities. If it were not to use general revenues, then payroll taxes would have to be set so as to yield early surpluses that could then be used to pay later expenses. The alternative was for early program participants to pay very low taxes and later program participants to pay much higher taxes.

Each of these problems posed early stumbling blocks to the expansion of the system that were not resolved until 1950. The fact that so few people initially benefitted from the program meant that welfare programs for the elderly became more popular than Social Security. State welfare programs for the elderly, known as public assistance programs, were subsidized by the federal government through general revenues. Under the terms of the Social Security Act, the federal government agreed to match the first $15 that the state contributed toward the pension of an elderly person. These state administered pensions were gratuities, not entitlements. The states awarded them only to people who could prove they were poor and reserved the right to rescind them for such things as immoral behavior. Still, old-age assistance (welfare) reached far more people and paid much higher benefits than did old-age insurance (social insurance or Social Security) in the period between 1935 and 1950. As Mark Leff (1988), Brian Gratton (C. Haber and Gratton, 1994), and other historians have noted, over a fifth of the elderly population received old-age assistance payments by the end of the 1940s; in a few states, such as Colorado and Louisiana, the percentage was over one-half. Not only did more of the elderly receive old-age assistance than old-age insurance, but also the welfare benefits were, on average, 70 percent higher than the Social Security benefits (Achenbaum, 1986).

In this situation, many people questioned the purpose of Social Security taxes. The program appeared to lack social relevance, and the taxes created macroeconomic difficulties. Congress reacted to this situation by simply abandoning plans to raise Social Security taxes every three years. In 1939, before the tax raise scheduled for 1940, Congress opted instead to maintain the current tax rate. Each time a scheduled benefit increase approached, in 1943, 1946, and 1949, Congress voted to freeze the tax rate at its 1937 level. In 1947, the Republican Congress seriously considered reducing *future* payroll tax raises, dropping future maximums from 3 percent to 2 percent. The tax rate did not rise until 1950; the "taxable wage base" did not increase until 1951 (Leff, 1988; Derthick, 1979).

Part of the reason for abandoning plans to raise taxes was a fear that, contrary to the president's desires in 1935, the program's liabilities could not be prefunded by building up a large reserve. The "reserve fund" became an object of ridicule from both the Left and the Right. Conservatives, such as presidential candidate Alfred Landon, branded the plans for a Social Security fund a "cruel hoax." Liberals, such as those associated with the CIO, could not see the point of building up a large reserve when current economic conditions were so bleak and the needs of the elderly so pressing (Berkowitz, 1983). In 1939, by expanding the range of benefits to include survivors' benefits, deciding that married couples should receive higher benefits than single workers, and lowering the size of the reserve fund, Congress helped to ease some of the pressure on the program, but Congress could not assure the program's long-term survival.

The program remained in precarious condition through the 1940s. The whipsawing of the economy from depression to prosperity failed, at least initially, to increase the popularity of what was then known as old-age and survivors insurance. The administrators tried to position themselves for a postwar recession. In 1941, for example, Arthur Altmeyer, the chairman of the Social Security Board, argued that the Social Security program could tax workers' wages in a time of prosperity and become a vehicle for social spending in a time of depression. His immediate proposal was for a greatly expanded federal social insurance program that would retain old-age and survivors' benefits and add disability, unemployment, and health insurance benefits to the system. He hoped that the new program would cover more of the labor force and pay substantially higher benefits than the existing Social Security program.

Congress rejected nearly all of Altmeyer's suggestions, but if it had acquiesced in the plan, the expanded Social Security program would have run a substantial normal surplus and made an estimated $1.7 billion available for the Treasury to spend on defense.[1] Then, after the war, if a depression of 1930s magnitude had developed, the new Social Security program would have supplied a sustained purchasing power of at least $6 billion per year. Such devices as the federal government paying 26 weeks of unemployment benefits would have pumped billions into the economy.[2]

Despite this appeal to the fear of a postwar depression, Social Security administrators failed to advance their plan. With a war to pursue and a conservative Congress with which to contend, President Roosevelt hesitated to put the Social Security proposals at the top of his agenda. When the postwar depression failed to materialize, the plans of the Social Security administrators were thrown into further disarray. Social Security appeared to have lost its urgency during the war and the immediate postwar eras. The welfare program appeared more than able to take up the slack. As Congress refused to countenance increases in the Social Security tax rate, it twice took the time to raise the level of federal contributions to the welfare program.

The work of an advisory council that met in 1947 and 1948 helped to rescue the Social Security program from its early dilemmas. This council, relying heavily upon data generated by the Social Security Administration and on staff director Robert Ball's ability to tutor the members on the fundamentals of social security without appearing to dictate to them, issued a series of reports between April and December of 1948. The key report on old-age and survivors insurance arrived in April. The council accepted the Social Security Administration's social policy formulation that equated preventing dependency and reducing the need for public assistance. The best way to lower the public assistance rate, according to the council, was to extend Social Security. In this manner, the council came to recommend a major expansion (report reprinted in W. Haber and Cohen, 1948).

On August 28, 1950, after considerable congressional scrutiny and debate, the recommendations of the advisory council became law. Through this law, the proponents of Social Security gained much of what they wanted: a greatly expanded social security program that paid substantially higher benefits. The increase in benefits was 77 percent. Further, the impasse over Social Security taxes was broken. Congress agreed to raise the tax level to 3 percent and to raise the taxable wage base from $3,000 to $3,600. Once again, Congress, reaffirming the principle that the system should never have to depend on general revenues, included a schedule of future tax increases in the measure, with a maximum rate of 6.5 percent to be reached in 1970. The 1950 law also added a new feature to the tax. A majority of self-employed persons received Social Security coverage, at a tax rate of 2.25 percent of taxable payroll. This change meant that the program no longer was limited to commercial and industrial employees. Instead, self-employed persons could pay Social Security taxes through their income tax returns. Arthur Altmeyer, who remained in charge of the program throughout the Roosevelt and Truman years, later termed the 1950 law "crucial" to Social Security's survival. It meant that Social Security had finally attained parity with welfare (Achenbaum, 1986; Altmeyer, 1966, p. 169).

What produced these amendments? One explanation began with the fact that unions, particularly those in the coal, steel, and automobile industries, had recently secured more adequate retirement pensions from employers. These collectively bargained agreements provided for pensions that took Social Security benefits into account. In agreeing to this provision, the unions gave the employers an incentive to favor higher social security benefits. Social Security, the argument went, was cheaper for employers than private pensions. Among other things, employees contributed to Social Security pensions, and the program contained special benefits for low-income workers. So, when the time came to testify on the 1950 Social Security amendments, the union leaders did so enthusiastically, and the business leaders did not oppose higher Social Security benefits. This coalition made higher benefits possible (Cohen, 1951; Quadagno, 1988).

For Social Security's supporters, the 1950 amendments became a source of almost instant satisfaction. In an article that appeared early in 1952, Wilbur Cohen, an important figure within the Social Security Administration, described 1951 as a milestone year. He noted that in February 1951, for the first time in the nation's history, more people received Old-Age Insurance than received Old-Age Assistance. In August 1951, also for the first time in the nation's history, the total amount of insurance payments exceeded the amount of Old-Age Assistance payments (Cohen, 1952).

INCREMENTAL EXPANSION AND DEBATES OVER DISABILITY AND HEALTH CARE, 1951–1972

In the period between 1950 and 1954, the issues in Social Security policy shifted from the program's survival to the program's expansion. In this period, policymakers learned how to harness postwar prosperity as a force to expand benefits. By 1954, support for the program had become truly bipartisan, with the Republican Eisenhower administration as invested in Social Security as the preceding Democratic administrations had been.

1. The Bipartisan Politics of Incremental Expansion

After 1950, the incremental engine of Social Security expansion kicked into high gear. If past experience served as a guide, the Korean War should have made the passage of Social Security legislation almost impossible. It had taken Congress 11 years to amend the Social Security program in a significant way. The 1940s passed without a single major development in the old-age insurance law. Since Congress had devoted so much time and energy to Social Security in 1949 and 1950, and since the country was fighting a war, one could expect another long hibernation period.

Although they recognized that many factors worked against an increase in benefits in 1952, the bureaucratic leaders of Social Security believed that Social Security benefits should nonetheless be increased for reasons related to the actuarial traditions of the Social Security Administration and the state of the economy. In making long-run estimates of the program's costs, the actuaries established a number of conventions. One crucial assumption was to base cost estimates on a level average annual wage. In the postwar era, this assumption flew in the face of reality. "No economist today would maintain that the trend in wages which has been so clearly upward will suddenly become level for the next 50 years," noted two exasperated economists in 1951. The actuaries, in their defense, argued that it would be inappropriate to show a rising wage rate in combination with a static benefit formula. That would seriously understate the costs of the program. Instead, the actuaries chose to overstate the costs by, in effect, consistently underestimating the increased revenues that would come from rising wage levels (Killingsworth and Schroeder, 1951, pp. 207–208).

That meant that the program was always receiving windfalls. In 1944, for example, the trust fund received $1.4 billion, and the program spent only $238 million on benefits, occasioning a large net growth in the trust fund (for these and other data see the various issues of *Social Security Bulletin: Annual Statistical Supplement*). In 1944, of course, the government needed the revenue collected for Social Security to finance the war effort. After the war, the Republican Congress halted any plans to expand Social Security. Social Security supporters hoped that the 1950s would be different and that part of the Social Security surplus created by rising wage rates would be spent on increased benefits. The fact that more people were insured by Social Security (the percentage of insured workers went up to 78 percent by 1960) because of the 1950 amendments provided one source of encouragement. More congressmen had a stake in Social Security benefit increases in the

1950s than in the 1940s. The 1950 increase in benefit levels also made Social Security more attractive in the 1950s than in the 1940s, as did the newfound union and management support for the program. So Social Security advocates hoped that rising wages after 1950 might occasion a benefit increase in 1952.

The irresistible thing was that, because of rising wages, benefits could be increased without raising the tax rates already specified in the 1950 law. At the time, Wilbur Cohen referred to this phenomenon as a "miracle" that made it possible to change the system "without changing the contributions of the program or impairing the actuarial soundness of the system" (quoted in Berkowitz, 1995). The members of the Ways and Means Committee, some of whom had acquired expertise in Social Security while working on the 1950 amendments, understood the opportunity they had in 1952 to raise benefits without any sort of tax increase.

Chairman Robert Doughton (D-North Carolina) decided to introduce a comprehensive Social Security bill. This bill moved quickly through the Ways and Means Committee. It took a year and a half for Congress to consider the 1950 amendments. In this instance, Ways and Means Committee decided to skip hearings altogether and reported the 1952 bill out in four days. Although this bill failed to pass for reasons related to the politics of disability insurance, Representative Daniel Reed (R-New York), the ranking Republican on the Committee, soon introduced another Social Security bill that included an increase in Social Security benefits. For the first time, the Republicans and the Democrats agreed on the political desirability of an increase in Social Security benefits, and both thought that such an increase would be helpful to them in an election year. Four weeks after the introduction of Reed's bill, the House voted to reconsider and pass Doughton's original bill. On June 26, 1952, the Senate passed its version of the bill by a voice vote. The bill, complete with a 15 percent raise in benefit levels, became law on July 18, 1952.

As Wilbur Cohen reported in his private correspondence, the legislation "gets us away from the idea that OASI is a depression phenomenon and that it will be another 10 years before benefits can be increased."[3] Cohen astutely grasped the fact that the 1952 amendments were different, that they were the first of what would be a steady stream of incremental expansions of Social Security, the first bipartisan endorsement of the program, the first real manifestation of Social Security's political popularity.

In 1952, with the program finally in high gear, the election of Republican Dwight D. Eisenhower posed another problem for the program's expansion. As matters turned out, even a change in political regime in both the presidency and the Congress failed to halt the growth of Social Security. When President Eisenhower delivered his State of the Union message on February 2, 1953, he recommended that the "old-age and survivors insurance law should promptly be extended to cover millions of citizens who have been left out of the Social Security system" (quoted in Cohen, Ball, and Myers, 1954, p. 16).

After a brief period in which the administration considered converting Social Security to a noncontributory old-age pension similar to the Townsend plan of the 1930s, things once again fell in place for the expansion of Social Security in the fall of 1953. The administration conducted an intensive internal review that fall to prepare a comprehensive Social Security bill that would be ready in January. In November Wilbur Cohen reported to Altmeyer, who had retired from the government, that, "After much travail I think the recommendations will be on the constructive side. We have shed a lot of blood in the process but we are eating lots of red blood to make up for our loss."[4] As these comments implied, the administration decided to follow the incremental path established by the 1952 amendments. It opted for a major extension of coverage to farm operators and other groups, for raising the average level of Social Security benefits by 13 percent, and for raising the tax base from $3,600 to $4,200. In addition, the administration acquiesced in the scheduled tax increase from 3 to 4 percent of covered payroll. As President Eisenhower expressed it in a letter to stockbroker E. F. Hutton, "it would appear logical to build upon the system that has been in effect for almost twenty years rather than embark upon the radical course of turning it completely upside down and running the very real danger that we would end up with no system at all."[5]

2. The Politics of Disability Insurance

Between 1954 and 1956, the issues in Social Security shifted from the expansion of benefits to the creation of disability insurance, a major new form of Social Security coverage. The issue of disability shadowed Social Security from its inception, and the control of disability expenditures has remained an issue from the beginning of the program to the present day. Two of President Roosevelt's advisors had prepared a report on the subject for the Committee on Economic Security. Both the president and Frances Perkins decided, however, that the report was too controversial to be released. They preferred to have old-age insurance established before turning to health and disability insurance. The first permanent disability insurance proposal did not get unveiled until October 1938 and then only at a private meeting of a Social Security advisory council. The members of this group reacted cautiously to the proposal. They agreed only that disability insurance was "socially desirable" but could not recommend that Congress start such a program in the near future (quoted in Berkowitz, 1987, p. 59). In part, the members of the advisory council feared that disability benefits, intended for those with physical impairments that led to permanent incapacity, would instead become a convenient means for people to drop out of the labor force before the age of 65.

Indeed, disability insurance became a real source of tension not only within the advisory council but also among the employees of the Social Security Board. The trouble was that the actuaries, taking their cues from actuaries who worked for private insurance companies, regarded disability insurance as extremely problematic: a difficult program in which to contain costs and predict future expenditures. As Jerry Mashaw discusses in chapter 7, disability was more difficult to define than old age, and the actuaries feared that it was an elastic concept that would respond to such factors as unemployment. Administering a disability program required federal administrators to decide just who was capable of working and who deserved a ticket out of the labor force. These problems created a sense of caution in the same actuaries who enthusiastically supported the old-age and survivors insurance program. When the matter was first discussed in 1938, W. Rulon Williamson, the agency's actuary, said that he could not possibly give one estimate of disability insurance's cost and "maintain his professional dignity."[6]

Despite these real concerns, the advisory council that met in 1947 and 1948 recommended that Congress pass a disability insurance program. In 1950, the House of Representatives went so far as to pass such a program, only to have the proposal die in the Senate. In 1952, Social Security administrators tried to get Congress to pass a modified proposal, known as a disability freeze, that preserved the benefit rights of a person with a disability. This meant that such a person could receive benefits at age 65, despite having dropped out of the labor force at the onset of the disability. Even this compromise measure encountered substantial opposition from insurance companies, particularly from the American Medical Association, which regarded disability as the "entering wedge" for national health insurance. The disability freeze failed to go into effect in 1952.

Beginning in 1954, Social Security advocates, buoyed by the success of Old-Age and Survivors Insurance, put disability insurance at the top of the legislative agenda. In that year, the Eisenhower administration agreed to sponsor the disability freeze, which passed Congress and became part of the 1954 Social Security Amendments. Administration officials regarded the freeze as a means of identifying candidates for vocational rehabilitation. Once a person applied to the Social Security Administration, he or she would be referred to state vocational rehabilitation programs and put on a regimen of counseling and other services that would enable that person to overcome a disability and get a job. Social Security advocates, by way of contrast, saw the disability freeze as an incremental step toward the passage of disability insurance.

In 1956, acting against the wishes of the Eisenhower administration, which favored the expansion of Social Security but not the creation of disability insurance, the Democratic Congress passed a disability insurance program. The incremental process that led to this result forced Social Security advocates to make a number of important concessions. As passed, disability insurance had its own trust fund, so that Congress could closely monitor program expenditures. Disability determinations became the responsibility of state offices acting under contract to the federal government. In most cases, states placed their disability determination services within the same bureaucratic structures as their vocational rehabilitation programs. In this manner, they hoped to forge a link between rehabilitation and disability benefits, and Congress hoped to send a signal to the American Medical Association that disability insurance would be administered in a cautious manner and not lead to federal influence over the practice of medicine. In another concession, Congress limited disability benefits to those 50 or over and did not extend benefits to the dependents of disability beneficiaries. Even with these concessions, the measure passed by the barest of margins in a dramatic vote on the floor of the Senate. In this manner, the program expanded to include benefits for a person who was "unable to engage in substantial gainful activity" by virtue of a medical impairment that was expected to result in death or be of long-continued or indefinite duration (Berkowitz, 1987).

3. The Politics of Health Insurance

Between 1956 and 1965, the leading issue in social insurance policy concerned the establishment of health insurance for Social Security beneficiaries. To be sure, the incremental expansion of Old-Age, Survivors, and Disability Insurance continued during these years. In 1958, acting under the leadership of newly appointed Ways and Means Committee chairman Wilbur Mills, Congress opted to raise OASDI benefits by 7 percent. In that same year, Congress extended benefits to the dependents of disabled beneficiaries and in 1960 broadened disability coverage to workers of all ages, eliminating the age 50 requirement. Even as these events occurred, however, Congress faced the question of whether to use the undisputed popularity of Social Security as a base from which to take on the American Medical Association and begin a program of national health insurance.

As with disability insurance, program administrators had modified their health insurance proposals over the years. As conceived in 1935, health insurance was to take the form of federal grants to the states. In the 1940s, social insurance advocates explored the possibility of funding health insurance through the same payroll tax mechanism as Social Security. Political pressure from the American Medical Association, the relative unpopularity of the Social Security program, and the rise of Blue Cross and other private forms of health insurance all combined to defeat the measure. President Roosevelt endorsed the concept of national health insurance but never submitted or actively supported a specific piece of legislation to implement the concept. President Truman's administration made proposals, but they never came close to passage.

In 1951, program administrators seized upon the idea of limiting health care benefits to retired people already on Social Security. From that time forward, this idea guided the debate over national health insurance. In 1957, a proposal incorporating the idea received attention from the Ways and Means Committee but failed to gain the committee's endorsement. In 1959, a subcommittee of the Senate Committee on Labor and Public Welfare publicized the issue of health insurance for the elderly in dramatic hearings at which elderly citizens spoke of their inability to secure adequate health care. The common citizens, delivering details that historian Sherri David (1985, p. 21) described as "heart-rending," generated enough publicity to make health insurance, in Wilbur Cohen's words, "the major issue in Social Security in Congress and in the nation in 1959."[7] During the following year, Senator John F. Kennedy (D-Massachusetts) chose to highlight health insurance for the elderly, which he called Medicare, as a campaign issue. After the Democratic convention, the Senate considered and rejected Kennedy's plan to use a social insurance approach to help pay hospital bills for elderly beneficiaries.

In this manner, Medicare developed into a legislative priority for the Kennedy administration. The measure first came to a vote on the floor of the Senate in the summer of 1962. The amendment (to a welfare bill) on which the Senate voted made provisions for intermediaries to handle billing arrangements with the hospitals and intercede between the federal government and the hospital. Under this scheme, the hospital would send its bills to the intermediary, rather than the federal government, and the intermediary would reimburse the hospital. This arrangement closely resembled what hospitals already did for their customers who subscribed to one of many regional Blue Cross plans. The measure also included a controversial provision that permitted the federal government to reimburse private insurers for those who preferred to continue their private health insurance at retirement. Despite these concessions, the administration lost the Senate vote by what proved to be a one-vote margin. If Senator Robert Kerr (D-Oklahoma) had not persuaded Senator

Jennings Randolph (D-West Virginia) to vote against the Medicare amendment, the Senate would have passed it in 1962.

It took until 1964 for Congress to reconsider Medicare. On September 2, 1964, the Senate approved a version of the legislation for the first time. Among other features, this iteration included a mechanism, proposed by Senator Jacob Javits (R-New York), to encourage the purchase of supplementary private insurance to cover doctors' bills and other expenses not handled by Medicare. Another idea that surfaced in the 1964 discussion but that was ultimately not included in the final measure was for beneficiaries to have a choice between receiving Medicare benefits and getting higher cash benefits. Although Wilbur Mills expressed some interest in this option, he could not bring himself to support Medicare in 1964. Because of Mills' opposition to Medicare, conferees in the Senate and the House agreed to disagree, and the measure once again died.

After Lyndon Johnson's landslide in the 1964 election, Medicare supporters hoped to use the measure passed by the Senate as a guide for a bill that would pass both houses in 1965. On New Year's eve in 1964, Wilbur Cohen, at the time an assistant secretary at the Department of Health, Education, and Welfare, distributed the administration's latest version of the "Hospital Insurance, Social Security, and Public Assistance Amendments of 1965." This version provided for inpatient hospital services for up to 60 days, with a deductible equal to the average cost of half a day of hospital care. Other covered services included physician services associated with hospital care, such as pathology and radiology; outpatient hospital diagnostic services; and posthospital extended care in a nursing home or similar recuperative facility. The bill also included a 7 percent across-the-board Social Security benefit increase. All in all, it amounted to a large, complicated, and expensive package.[8]

As matters turned out, Wilbur Mills substantially modified the administration's proposal. In particular, he jettisoned the Javits notion of complementary private insurance in favor of what was known as the Byrnes Bill, after John Byrnes (R-Wisconsin), its chief congressional sponsor. The Byrnes proposal was based on a plan available to employees of the federal government through the Aetna Insurance Company. It was a classic indemnity plan in which employees paid monthly premiums, deducted from their paychecks, and the federal government contributed a percentage of the premium as well. When an employee got sick, the plan paid the doctors' and hospitals' bills, minus a portion that the employee was expected to pay himself. Byrnes proposed to offer this sort of protection to the elderly. It would be voluntary, subsidized in part by the federal government through general revenues, and comprehensive in that it covered both doctor and hospital bills. It would also involve out-of-pocket payments by the elderly both for the premiums (analogous to the payroll deductions) and for the costs of medical care they were expected to share with the insurance plan. Social Security advocates, such as Wilbur Cohen and Robert Ball, objected to the voluntary nature of the plan, the costs to the general revenue, and the way that it would pay doctor and hospital bills based on "charges" rather than "costs" (it was an item of faith at the time that the elderly cost less to serve than did younger people). Above all, they thought it inadvisable to make a person pay for health insurance during his retirement "when his income is lowest." The administration plan, by way of contrast, required a person to pay for health insurance during his working lifetime and enabled him to earn a paid-up policy upon retirement.[9]

Wilbur Mills decided to ignore these arguments. Instead, he proposed and Congress accepted a plan based on the administration's Medicare proposals for the payment of hospital bills and on Congressman Byrnes's plan for the payment of doctors' bills. Mills arrived at this idea during a closed session of the Ways and Means Committee that took place on March 2, 1965. "Without any advance notice," according to Cohen, "Mills asked me why we could not put together a plan that included the Administration's Medicare hospital plan with a broader voluntary plan covering physician or other services?" (see Berkowitz, 1995). Cohen and many of the others in the room were stunned by this suggestion. Robert Ball and Arthur Hess of the Social Security Administration called the development "unexpected" (Ball and Hess, 1993, p. 2; Harris, 1996; Marmor, 1973).

In this apparently spontaneous manner, after years of congressional deliberation, Medicare was created. By July 21, 1965, the bill emerged from a conference committee, in Senator Clinton Anderson's words, "in generally good shape."[10] The scope of the legislation was amazing. In addition to starting Medicare Part A (Hospital Insurance), Medicare Part B (Supplementary Medical Insurance for doctors' bills), and Medicaid (health insurance for welfare beneficiaries), it also raised the earnings base on which Social Security taxes were paid, contained a substantial 7 percent increase in Social Security benefits, made it easier for Social Security beneficiaries to work without losing their benefits, liberalized the definition of disability, began a program of rehabilitation services for people on disability insurance, extended the scope of childhood disability benefits, and lowered the age at which widows could receive benefits. The bill also increased federal payments for welfare and expanded the maternal and child health and children's services programs. On July 28, 1965, the measure, the most far-reaching amendment to the Social Security Act since the act's passage in 1935, received final approval from Congress and reached the president's desk.

4. The Politics of Incremental Expansion Redux

In retrospect, the 1965 amendments marked the high tide of expansion of the social insurance approach to economic well-being. Although the entire debate centered on Medicare, the incremental engine that expanded Social Security continued to operate throughout the process. As in all Social Security legislative exercises, prosperity played a major role. The expanding economy permitted program administrators to recommend, and Congress to accept, a raise in benefit levels, combined with reduced tax rates. As the law was written before July 1965, the combined employer–employee Social Security tax rate was to have been 8.25 percent in 1966. In the new law, Congress reduced the rate to 7.7 percent, and even adding in the new hospital insurance program, the total 1966 rate was only 8.4 percent. As projected in 1965, the 1968 rates for hospital insurance and Social Security would actually be lower than the rates that had earlier been projected for Social Security alone. Prosperity enabled Social Security benefits to rise by $1.4 billion, the elderly to have most of their hospital bills paid for, and hospitals and doctors to receive generous subsidies without raising long-term tax rates on workers.[11]

Nor did the expansion of the program stop after 1965. The 1967 amendments, signed in 1968, involved considerable controversy over the growth of welfare programs. The Old-Age, Survivors, and Disability Insurance program, by way of contrast, continued to bask in the glow of congressional approval. Congress increased benefits by 13 percent. In 1969 Congress raised benefits by another 15 percent, and in 1972 it permitted a spectacular 20 percent increase in benefits. The 1972 legislation also contained provisions that allowed disability beneficiaries to receive Medicare after a two-year waiting period and that extended Medicare coverage to those with end-stage renal disease.

THE AGE OF RECONSIDERATION, 1972–1996

In retrospect, one could notice a change in the inevitability of social insurance expansion as early as 1965. The first subtle signs of a shift away from expansion and toward a consideration of cost containment became evident then, particularly in the Medicare program. The problem with Medicare concerned its role in increasing the costs of medical care. One historian, writing in 1984 went so far as to describe the program as "a ruinous accommodation between reformers and vested interests" that produced run-away inflation in health-care costs (Matusow, p. 228).

What had happened? For one thing, hospital insurance grew expensive quickly. The hospital insurance part of the program cost $1 billion in calendar year 1966, $3.4 billion in 1967, and $4.3 billion in 1968. In those same years, expenditures on Supplementary Medical Insurance increased from $200 million to $1.7 billion. In part, these increases followed from Medicare's mission, which was to ensure access to health care for the elderly population, not to control health-care cost inflation or to reform health-care delivery. If the government had attempted to change the health-care financing or delivery systems, as later critics such as Matusow implied it should have, Congress would certainly have objected and would probably have defeated the measure, as it did in 1957, 1960, 1962, and 1964. Medicare resembled the Blue Cross plans enjoyed by working Americans, and few people in 1965 regarded such plans as breeding inflation. Indeed, the preoccupation with inflation was largely a post-1965 phenomenon. Only in retrospect would Medicare appear to be flawed. In this manner, yesterday's solution became today's problem.

From the very beginning, however, rising Medicare costs attracted the attention of Wilbur Mills and Lyndon Johnson. In March of 1967, for example, the president complained to Wilbur Cohen that Wilbur Mills was "all over the ticket" on the increased costs of hospital care. Mills was genuinely worried that rising hospital costs would cut into the money that might otherwise have gone to raise basic Social Security benefits.[12]

Adding to the doubts about the future of social insurance programs, administrative problems surfaced in both the disability and Medicare programs. State administration of disability insurance led to inconsistent decisions from state to state. Private carriers who were to implement the Supplementary Medical Insurance program in the Medicare program often were inadequate to the task, not handling the claims swiftly or accurately enough. Adverse publicity attracted political attention. Nursing homes proved to be difficult institutions to regulate. In general, charges to patients increased in all of the health insurance programs. The first increases in co-payments and deductibles became effective in 1968.

Even more critical were the problems that developed in Social Security. In the 1970s, a combination of circumstances made the program vulnerable to a downturn in the economy. In part as a response to the criticisms of economists and in part for reasons of partisan politics, Congress had opted in 1972 to index future benefit increases to the rate of inflation, rather than continuing the system of ad hoc benefit increases of the sort that Wilbur Mills had done so much to negotiate. The large benefit increases in 1968 and 1969 encouraged the Republicans in their thinking on this matter. When prices rose faster than wages, as they did in the years of the Carter administration, a crisis developed. In 1977 Congress attempted to deal with the problem by passing remedial legislation that, among other things, increased tax rates and raised the amount of a person's wages that were subject to Social Security taxation.

The 1977 legislation failed to put the Social Security system on a firm financial footing, in part because the economy continued to worsen. In 1980, for example, the benefit increase, as determined by the automatic indexing formula, was 14.3 percent, but wages went up only 9 percent and employment remained sluggish (Kingson, 1984). The effect on Social Security was direct. From a high of $37.8 billion in 1974, the old-age and survivors trust fund declined to a low of $19.7 billion in 1983. At one point in 1983, there was the possibility that the program would not be able to meet its obligations and send out checks to beneficiaries.

A solution to the financing problem was worked out by an informal bipartisan group including members of the Greenspan Commission (which had been created by President Reagan to deal with the crisis), such as Robert Ball, and top Reagan administration officials, such as James Baker. With only minor modifications, Congress endorsed this solution in 1983. Key parts of the compromise involved treating up to one-half of benefits as taxable income, expansion of coverage to new federal employees, a six-month delay in the cost of living adjustment that amounted to permanent benefit reduction for Social Security beneficiaries, and slight payroll tax increases. Congress also chose to raise the normal retirement age to 67 over a 24-year period, beginning in 2003. Because of the provisions in the 1983 amendments and the small size of the depression age cohort that began to retire in the 1990s, the Social Security trust funds showed an impressive rate of recovery. The old-age and survivors trust fund, for example, stood at $267.8 billion in 1991 (Berkowitz, 1991). The politics of the situation began to shift toward old fears about the meaning of a large Social Security surplus at a time of substantial federal deficit.

CONCLUSIONS

By the 1990s, Social Security taxes were no longer invisible to the general public, nor was the link between contributions and benefits so direct as it had once been. A system that had once approached bankruptcy and once again faces a long-term financing problem had lost some of its political goodwill. People once again debated the advisability of maintaining such high Social Security taxes at a time when economic policymakers were trying to stimulate the economy and induce a greater rate of economic growth. Yet the fact remained that Social Security had weathered the stagflation era, the Reagan economic reforms, and the neoliberal experiments of Bill Clinton and managed to grow in the process. For all of the loss of the program's innocence, Social Security remained America's most important form of social policy. Little indicated that the situation would change soon.

Beyond that simple statement, it is not my intention to indulge in speculation about the future; I leave that to other contributors such as Robert Ball in chapter 18, Robert Myers in chapter 13, and Eugene Steuerle in chapter 17. Nor can the history of Social Security (and the related Medicare program) be encapsulated within such a short and such a diffuse essay. Nonetheless, I hope that readers come away with an understanding of the many issues faced by Social Security policymakers and of how these issues have shifted over time. The fluidity of the decision process can be seen in such matters as the last minute shifts in Social Security financing in 1935 and the content of the Medicare bill in 1965. Once these and many other decisions were made, however, they had fateful consequences for this country's most important social insurance programs, Social Security and Medicare. In this area of policy, as in so many others, we can best understand the present as the sum of what has happened in the past.[13]

ENDNOTES

1. 8/13/41, "An Expanded Social Security Program," and Cohen to Byron Mitchell, Chief Budget Examiner, June 6, 1941, both in Box 26, Wilbur Cohen Papers, Wisconsin State Historical Society, Madison, Wisconsin.

2. "An Expanded Social Security Program," Cohen Papers, Box 26.

3. Wilbur Cohen to Elizabeth Wickenden, August 1952, Elizabeth Wickenden Papers, Wisconsin State Historical Society.

4. Cohen to Altmeyer, November 3, 1953, Cohen Papers.

5. Eisenhower to Edward F. Hutton, October 7, 1953, Central Files, Box 848, File 156-C, Dwight D. Eisenhower Presidential Library, Abilene, Kansas.

6. See Wilbur J. Cohen to Arthur Altmeyer, 13 October 1938, Record Group 47, Records of the Social Security Administration, File 025, Box 10, National Archives, Washington, DC.

7. Wilbur J. Cohen, "Social Security Legislation, 1960: Issues and Proposals," March 12, 1960, mimeo, p. 2, Box 270, Cohen Papers.

8. "Brief Summary of `Hospital Insurance, Social Security, and Public Assistance Amendments of 1965'" RG 235, General Counsel Records, Accession 71A-3497, Box 1, File AW, December 31, 1964, Washington National Records Center.

9. Memorandum from Wilbur J. Cohen to the president, January 29, 1965, RG 235, Accession 69A-1793, File LL, Box 16, Washington National Records Center.

10. Anderson to the president, July 21, 1965, Box 1103, Clinton Anderson Papers, Library of Congress, Washington, DC.

11. On the tax rates, see Cohen to Lawrence O'Brien, July 21, 1965, Cohen Papers, Box 83.

12. Cohen to the Secretary, March 8, 1967, Cohen to the president, March 8, 1967, both Box 91, Cohen Papers.

13. The author wishes to thank the volume editors and Robert J. Myers for their helpful comments.

PART II

Social Security Issues

CHAPTER 3

Should Social Security be Means-Tested?

ERIC R. KINGSON AND JAMES H. SCHULZ

This chapter examines an evolving debate about whether receipt of Old-Age, Survivors, and Disability Insurance (OASDI) should be based on some measure of financial need or continue to be paid to all who make the required payroll tax "contributions" regardless of income levels. As we shall see, this is a long debate that has taken a new turn. In the past, the discussion focused on whether income and/or assets-testing should be used to restrict eligibility to low-income persons. Today, there is new controversy about whether some form of income test should be used within OASDI to exclude or sharply lower benefits to the well-off. Proponents of the new approach argue that it would direct federal spending away from those who do not need support, thereby helping to address current federal deficits and future OASDI financing needs. Advocates of a universal Social Security program argue that the new approach represents a radical transformation of OASDI that would seriously undermine its political support, ultimately placing low- and moderate-income Americans at great economic risk.

In reviewing the history, and the arguments for and against, means-testing, this chapter examines whether the old arguments against it remain relevant, given new proposals and a changed political and economic environment. First, traditional arguments for and against means-testing OASDI are examined in the context of Social Security's history and the nation's experience with means-tested programs. The emergence and appeal of the new genre of means-testing proposals is then discussed, and the relevance of the old arguments is assessed.

This is an important topic to address today. The idea of means-testing away all or part of the benefits of high-income elderly and other Social Security beneficiaries has found increasing appeal among some politicians and working-age persons (and even among some retirees). At first glance, proposals to limit publicly funded transfers to high-income retirees may appear reasonable, given other pressing social needs. Yet, as this chapter will discuss, excluding higher-income persons from benefit receipt looks better in theory than in practice and would create more problems than it would solve. While the evidence is not incontrovertible, on balance it is clear that support and public approval of Social Security is strongly linked to its continuance as a program where all citizens participate and receive benefits in return for work-related payroll tax contributions.

THE NATION REJECTS MEANS-TESTING

Social Security is currently the core institution in the American approach to social protection. Prior to the enactment of the Old-Age Insurance Program in 1935, economic security rested on the ability, discretion, and goodwill of families, charities, and government officials to supplement individuals' actions. The results were far from satisfactory, as documented by a large body of research (see, for example, Leiby, 1978; Lubove, 1961). The passage of the Social Security Act marked a major turning point for social provision in the United States. Provision shifted from a substantially haphazard and residual selective enterprise that was economically and socially inadequate to a more universal and more adequate model. With its passage and subsequent amending (e.g., 1939, 1950, 1956), the recurring means-testing debate was ultimately resolved in favor of using social insurance. Today, OASDI, along with other universal social insurance programs (e.g., Medicare and Unemployment Insurance), serves as the foundation of the social safety net, supplemented by public assistance ("welfare") programs such as Aid to Families with Dependent Children (AFDC), Medicaid, and Supplemental Security Income (SSI).

1. The Early Means-Testing Debate: 1900–1950

The early Social Security debate focused on whether the foundation for public welfare, especially for the elderly, should be based on a universal approach or a selective welfare approach. Early in the twentieth century, the nation rejected the approaches to social welfare that emerged from the poor-laws tradition. The county poorhouses, the orphanages, and the intrusive supervision of the poor by charity organizations were viewed as dehumanizing vestiges of a tradition dominated by programs designed, first and foremost, to minimize malingering and sloth. The basic idea of the old tradition was that the conditions of relief should be so harsh as to discourage only the most needy from seeking support. Thus, the poorhouse became the last refuge of the desperate and destitute old, serving also as a warning to workers and families of the consequences of having to become dependent on public programs (Skocpol, 1990). Orphanages separated poor widowed mothers from their children, with, for example, an estimated 2,716 New York State children taken in 1914 from their widowed mothers (Coll, 1973). Private charity organizations, intent on "uplifting" the poor, generally opposed public "outdoor relief" (i.e., relief to people living in their homes). Viewing such relief as dependency creating and a source of political corruption, charity workers called instead for the poor to be institutionalized or for the administration of public funds to the poor by voluntary agencies.

   In reaction to these unsatisfactory earlier approaches to social provision, a new approach was sought, ultimately resulting in what came to be known as social insurance. The new approach was based on the idea that certain common risks faced by almost everyone in industrial societies could and should be protected against through a collective mechanism; the right to benefits was to be based on some combination of prior financial contribution, work history, and precipitating condition (e.g., unemployment, work injury, or old age).[1] The industrial transformation of society, with an increasingly wage-dependent work force, created a need for social protection to insure social, political, and economic stability (Schulz and Myles, 1990). Also, employees and employers needed an effective means of addressing problems arising from workplace injuries and the declining ability of employees to work as they got old.

The New Deal reformers of the 1930s were faced with unprecedented economic dislocation and were suspicious of what President Franklin D. Roosevelt referred to as the "gimme" syndrome (what in today's jargon might be thought of as a sense of dependency-creating entitlement). In this context, "Roosevelt took as his major premise the corrosive effects of welfare on the human spirit" and "saw in social insurance an uplifting rather than soul-destroying program" (Berkowitz, 1991, p. 91). Social insurance, with its emphasis on entitlement as an earned right, was viewed as a superior mechanism to means-tested public assistance, though the latter was seen as necessary to respond to immediate need. Indeed, as Berkowitz (chapter 2) notes, the means-tested Old Age Assistance program was initially the most popular provision of the original Social Security Act, since it quickly distributed benefits to the states and to their needy older residents. In fact, the original Social Security program, called Old-Age Benefits, was not scheduled to provide benefits until 1942 and then to only a relatively small portion of retired workers. Even so, it was anticipated that as more workers earned benefits through social insurance and as new benefits categories were added (e.g., for widowed mothers), the need for means-tested benefits for the old and for dependent children would decline and eventually be obviated by social insurance (Berkowitz, 1991).

President Roosevelt also saw great advantage to making Social Security an *explicitly earned right* and gradually extending coverage to all Americans (i.e., promoting *universality*). Given the long tradition of self-reliance and the great stigma (often deliberately created) that was attached to the early social protection provisions, Americans were overwhelmingly hostile to "welfare programs" and participation in them. Promoting an earned right through a broadly participatory scheme was vitally important in building public support. Moreover, a highly visible and earmarked payroll tax was seen as a necessary vehicle for both maintaining *fiscal discipline* and strengthening *political support* for the system. The designers of Social Security believed that both politicians and workers would be cautious about raising benefits beyond what could be borne through reasonable payroll taxation. Workers and beneficiaries, it was thought, could also be counted upon to oppose efforts to radically reduce social insurance commitments, since they would have paid into the system over the course of their lives (Berkowitz, 1991).

The universality principle did not go unchallenged in 1935. As Berkowitz (chapter 2) mentions, Senator Bennet Champ Clark (D-Missouri) proposed to allow employers and employees who were already covered by private pensions to opt out of the Old-Age Insurance Program. Allowing workers who were the "better risks" to opt out, many thought, would seriously undermine Social Security. Unlike a private insurance plan, the public program could not exclude anyone deemed a "poor risk." The fear was that the private sector would leave the most expensive risks for the public sector to insure and those least likely to pay for Social Security.

Opting out would also undermine the program's ability to spread the cost of retirement pensions among all groups of workers and to redistribute some of the program's income to persons with the lowest incomes. Those out of the program were not likely to support program liberalization or higher levels of taxation to fund liberalizations.

The initial old-age pension program was highly restrictive and carefully designed not to depart too radically from contemporary private pension models based on individual equity. As Berkowitz (chapter 2) discusses, pressures arose immediately for changes. As indicated, the political focus was more on assisting those people needing immediate help, than on building up credits and rights to pensions for future cohorts of retirees through payroll tax contributions. Moreover, Social Security was generating financial surpluses, and the popular Townsend Movement was still calling for a universal flat payment to everyone age 60 and over. Pressure mounted on Congress to refocus the program away from individual equity and toward greater targeting and improved adequacy. Influential Republicans, including Senate minority leader Arthur H. Vandenberg (R-Michigan), seized on this opportunity to forge a Townsend-Republican coalition for the 1938 elections. Large Republican gains were made in the elections, in part a result of Republican support for additional pension legislation. "To conciliate the national demand for increased old age security, to head off the demands of the radical pension lobbyists, and to cut the ground from under the Republicans, the Democratic leadership undertook to liberalize its Social Security Act" (Holtzman, 1963). The 1939 legislation improved the adequacy of benefits, especially for low- and moderate-income workers. Also, auxiliary benefits were added for the widowed mothers and children of deceased workers and for the wives and dependent children of retired workers (see chapter 2 for more details).

Liberalization of OASI in 1950 increased benefits above the state Old-Age Assistance benefit levels and extended coverage to new classes of workers. As Berkowitz (chapter 2) points out, with these amendments the question of whether social insurance or welfare would be the dominant source of income support for elderly Americans seemed to be finally settled. By February 1951, for the first time, more elderly Americans received benefits from Social Security than from Old-Age Assistance.

2. Persistence of the Issue

Clearly, the social insurance approach to retirement income was firmly established by 1951. However, periodically the question of the relative merits of means-tested, versus social insurance, programs was raised, generally outside the context of Social Security. That is, the means-testing issue was still alive during the 1950s and 1960s, even though it was not central to OASDI policy discussions after 1956.

In the early 1950s, conservative legislators successfully opposed expanding Social Security (OASI) to include disability protections. Instead, a means-tested program was legislated for disabled low-income persons.[2] During the 1950s, social insurance advocates proposed (unsuccessfully) a social insurance approach to health-care financing for the elderly population (Medicare). Again, conservative members of

Congress pushed a means-tested alternative—the Kerr-Mills health assistance program for the elderly, passed in 1960.

With John F. Kennedy's election, Medicare became a legislative priority, though it was successfully blocked by conservatives opposing a social insurance approach (see Marmor, 1973). In the next presidential campaign (1964), Senator Barry Goldwater (R-Arizona) called for state, local, and private solutions to social problems including health care for the elderly. Echoing the sentiments behind the 1935 Clark amendment, he advocated a voluntary Social Security program. Conservatives argued that hospital insurance for the old would be too costly and would not differentiate between the rich and poor elderly

Goldwater's landslide loss to Lyndon Johnson muted advocates of the voluntary approach and helped to assure passage of health care legislation for the elderly (Marmor, 1973). The Medicare Hospital Insurance program (Part A) was passed in 1965, along with supplemental physician insurance (Part B) and an expanded means-tested health program (Medicaid).

Except for a few advocates on the extreme political Right and Left, the voices in favor of means-testing Social Security were silent until the early 1990s. Even during the Social Security financing crises of the mid-1970s and the early 1980s, proposals to introduce means-testing in Social Security were not seriously entertained. For example, a bipartisan Social Security commission chaired by Alan Greenspan in 1982 unanimously agreed that Congress "should not alter the fundamental principles of the Social Security Program" and rejected "proposals to make the Social Security program a voluntary one, or to transform it into . . . a program under which benefits are conditioned on the showing of financial need" (National Commission on Social Security Reform, 1983). While welfare programs, especially AFDC, came under increasing criticism and were often subject to explicit cuts or inflation-based erosion in the value of benefits, Social Security remained relatively immune to substantial cuts or to proposals to move away from its universal base.

3. The Experience with Means-Tested Cash Programs

There were many historical reasons for not considering a means-test in Social Security. Not only does the program seem to work and have broad political support, but the American experience with means-tested programs has been almost totally negative. Those opposed to social insurance often view means-tested programs as a last resort, and hence a necessary evil, to assist truly needy groups and, in any case, clearly preferable to social insurance programs; they are considered less costly, less destructive of employment and savings incentives, and a less intrusive governmental intervention than widespread social insurance initiatives. Supporters of social insurance see an important role for means-tested programs (despite their flaws); they are potentially compassionate and, in any case, a necessary protection for groups who "fall through" the public and private group insurance layers of social protection.

As noted earlier, the welfare provisions of the Social Security Act did not fade away as social insurance provisions expanded. The survivors insurance provisions of OASDI substantially replaced the need for AFDC for widows and their children, but the AFDC rolls continued to grow, in part a result of increased divorce and out-of-wedlock births. Today, political support for the AFDC program (often perceived as giving benefits to many people "able to work") is at an all-time low, and the erosion of benefit levels is testimony to the hostility. Since 1970, the inflation-adjusted value of the average monthly AFDC benefit per family has dropped by more than 40 percent, from $676 to $373 in 1993 dollars (U.S. Congress, 1994). Some conservatives seek the program's elimination for parents under age 21.[3] Some have called instead for an expansion of orphanages, work requirements for all able-bodied parents over age 21, and adoption for children whose parents are unable to provide support through work, family, or private charity (Flint, 1994). A less radical strategy involves "ending welfare as we know it" by more reliance on the Earned Income Tax Credit, limiting welfare benefits to two years, expanding work requirements, and providing more day care and training opportunities. But, as initially developed, the moderate alternative assumed movement towards a universal health program which would reduce the work disincentives from the loss of Medicaid benefits when welfare beneficiaries returned to work.

The Supplemental Security Income program for very poor persons who are old, blind, or disabled is the other large federally funded cash benefits welfare program that is means-tested. Since legislated in 1974, it has been less controversial.[4] However, SSI has also fallen short of its goals. As a means-tested federal income guarantee (with state option to supplement) for aged, blind, or disabled persons, SSI replaced state Old-Age Assistance, Aid to the Blind and Aid to the Permanently and Totally Disabled. When SSI was legislated, its supporters argued that it would be administratively more efficient, reduce stigma to recipients, and provide more adequate benefits (using a national standard). Right from the beginning, the SSI program was plagued with major administrative problems and evolved into a complex federal/state partnership (Derthick, 1990; Schulz, 1984). Today, the major administrative problems are (1) complex application procedures, together with minimal assistance from officials; (2) staff cutbacks and backlogs in both SSI disability determinations and review of current beneficiaries (SSI Modernization Project Experts [SSI], 1992);[5] and (3) controversies surrounding determination of disability benefits for some children.

While SSI has succeeded in providing a level of protection that is higher than that provided to AFDC families, the relatively low participation rates of aged persons eligible for SSI has been a continuing concern. About 40 percent of the eligible aged do not participate in the program (Leavitt and Schulz, 1988), mainly because of perceived stigma, lack of knowledge about the program, and a hostile administrative structure (Drazaga, Upp, and Reno, 1982; Families USA, 1992). Moreover, many of those who are *ineligible* are kept off because of an excessively stringent, clearly punitive, asset-test level (SSI, 1992). The assets-test is so stringent that small amounts of savings or other resources can prevent the truly needy from receiving benefits. In 1984, one-third of those eligible for SSI based on income were ineligible because they had assets exceeding SSI eligibility maximums, with one-half having income-producing assets of less than $5,000, hardly enough to produce interest in excess of $40 a month (Leavitt and Schulz).

Clearly there has been (and still is) widespread dissatisfaction with the functioning of means-tested programs for low-income individuals. Other major problems that have been documented repeatedly are the high administrative costs, the imprecise targeting (i.e., including or excluding the wrong people because of the typical complexities of rules and procedures), the stigma related to receiving benefits, the abuse of power by those determining eligibility, and the consequent low participation rates of those who are eligible (Danziger, Haveman, and Plotnick, 1981; Garfinkel, 1982; Schulz, 1984; Thompson, 1994). The result has been widespread hostility to this approach by large numbers of citizens and policymakers alike. This hostility has been heightened further by both the resulting disincentives to participation and the incentives for cheating that typically arise (e.g., assets transfer by middle-income elderly persons to meet eligibility requirements for Medicaid's nursing home benefits).

Many people also point to the economic disincentive issues associated with public assistance programs. Benefits must be kept inadequate; otherwise there will be a strong incentive for people not to work or to work less (Feldstein, 1987; Garfinkel, 1982). Even when benefits are very low, evidence exists that welfare programs sometimes "trap people in poverty" as a result of the work disincentive created by the implicit high marginal tax rates resulting from the various rules related to program eligibility. Moreover, these programs typically negate any incentive to save, since program eligibility is usually dependent on participants keeping savings below some minimal amount.

EMERGENCE OF THE NEW MEANS-TESTING APPROACH

Notwithstanding the nation's bad experience with means-tested programs, the idea of means-testing Social Security is finding more fertile ground in the mid-1990s than at any other period during the program's history. New and creative proposals for means-testing have emerged that differ from earlier proposals along two important dimensions: the income classes subject to benefit reductions and the bureaucratic instrument for administering the test of income or assets. The old approach sought to restrict public benefits to the poor or near-poor; financial eligibility tests were administered by a public agency. In contrast, the new approach seeks to reduce benefits to higher-income persons by an income-test applied through the tax system.

Mickey Kaus (1994) wants the United States to consider a means-tested approach with very high income and assets-tests. This would be similar to the approach used in Australia to determine eligibility for their "Old Age Pension," a benefit that has been received, in part or whole, by as many as four-fifths of Australians who meet age eligibility requirements.[6] Peter Peterson has advanced a proposal for a comprehensive entitlement means-test, an approach that some refer to as an "affluence-test." Under this proposal, (a) income from OASDI; (b) unemployment insurance payments; (c) selected veterans benefits, farm payments, and welfare programs; and (d) the insurance value of Medicare would be subject to a graduated income-test, ranging from 10 to 85 percent, for all tax payers with incomes from all sources that exceeded $40,000. The highest income beneficiaries—for example those with over $150,000—would generally lose 85 percent of the benefits targeted by the test (Concord Coalition, 1993).

In contrast with the past, those advancing these proposals can be found across the entire political spectrum. Deficit politics has created strange bedfellows. The

Concord Coalition—whose board of directors includes such figures as John Gardner; William Gray, III; the late Barbara Jordan; Peter Peterson; Warren Rudman; Paul Tsongas; and Paul Volcker—recommends the Peterson approach and sees its proposal as a moral imperative to preserve the American dream for the nation's young. Relatively few nationally elected officials have publicly supported proposals to means-test or "affluence-test" Social Security. Senator Bob Kerrey (D-Nebraska), the Democratic chair of the 1994 Bipartisan Commission on Entitlement and Tax Reform, and former Senator John Danforth (R-Missouri), the Republican vice chair, proposed extending the Concord Coalition means-test proposal to Medicare and Unemployment Insurance.

Political and economic change explains why this new means-testing approach is receiving increased attention and support. The public is clearly frustrated over the inability of government to deal effectively with many domestic and international problems and the intrusion and cost of government attempts to find appropriate solutions. Debates have been influenced by the relatively slow economic growth of the past 20 years, declines in national savings, large federal deficits, growing health care costs, and the impending retirement of the baby-boom cohorts. Projected deficits in the Social Security and Medicare Hospital Insurance programs add to the economic uncertainty. As Myers (chapter 13) and Steuerle (chapter 17) note, these projections indicate that Medicare expenditures are expected to outpace revenues in the near future but that OASDI financing is generally adequate for the next 30 years, after which big deficits loom. Thus, there is recognition of the need to deal quickly with health-care costs and to think about ways to deal with Social Security's long-term financing.

Changes in the relative economic status of various age groups have also increased interest in means-testing Social Security. As Moon (chapter 4) points out, statistics show a remarkable improvement in the economic well-being of older persons since 1960 (also see Schulz, 1995), in large part due to economic growth during the 1950s and 1960s and to liberalization of Social Security benefits. Today, the general economic circumstances of the elderly resemble those of other adult groups, and the living standards of most middle-aged and young adult workers are roughly comparable to those of their parents at similar stages of life. But living standards have grown very slowly for most working Americans, and the consequent reality falls short of expectations (Levy, 1987), leading to much anxiety about future economic prospects.

These changes have coincided with the emergence of a new stereotype for the old. Price-indexing of Social Security protected the elderly from the double-digit inflation of the early 1980s, and wage-indexing of the benefit formula has maintained the wage replacement rates of benefits for new beneficiaries. Paradoxically, this new ability to "keep up" with the working population has been characterized as a big problem (e.g., "greedy geezers") by some commentators (Chakravarty and Weisman, 1988). The elderly are increasingly portrayed as a group who realize exceptionally large returns from Social Security to the disadvantage of other age groups (Binstock, 1983). As Marmor, Cook, and Scher discuss (chapter 12), the new stereotype is drawn upon in much contemporary discussion about equity between working-age and retired Americans and facilitates the efforts of those seeking to make means-testing a viable policy option.

ARGUMENTS FOR THE NEW MEANS-TESTING APPROACH

The argument for the new means-testing approach rests on five propositions: The first proposition is that the nation cannot afford existing Social Security, Medicare, and other entitlement commitments, especially in light of pressures that will result as the baby boom cohorts age. Economic pressures in the United States and elsewhere have created pressures on the welfare state, making means-testing more appealing as a strategy to control the growth of social spending (Kaus, 1994; D. Mitchell and Gruen, 1995). In the United States, it is argued that without means-testing and other substantial reductions in program commitments, Social Security will be unable to meet its commitments to baby boomers and those who follow them into old age (Concord Coalition, 1993; Howe and Longman, 1992; G. Peterson, 1994). Thus, it is argued that means-testing deserves careful consideration because it is "a way to save a lot of money," bringing anticipated Social Security revenues in line with promised benefits and reducing the federal deficit (Kaus, 1994, p. 118).

Second, the new means-testing approach is presented as not harming low- and middle-income OASDI beneficiaries, now or in the future. The Concord Coalition's "affluence-test" would not affect beneficiaries with household incomes less than $40,000, and this threshold would be inflation adjusted according to G. Peterson (Bipartisan Commission on Entitlement and Tax Reform, 1995).

Third, it is said that a means-tested program would do a better job of targeting resources to those in greatest need. Many argue that the current OASDI program provides large benefits to high-income persons "who do not need them." This is consistent with the view, expressed by some advocates of means-testing, that the purpose of Social Security should be only to insure against poverty (Phillips, 1996), not to provide widespread protection against lost wages. From one analytical perspective, today's elderly cohorts are, as Chen and Goss (chapter 5) and Steuerle (chapter 17) discuss, already receiving large returns relative to their payroll tax contributions, a subsidy that is particularly beneficial for those who are well-off.

Fourth, proponents of the new means-testing suggest that it represents the fairest way to impose fiscal sacrifice, by placing the burden on those who can best afford it. Given the need to reduce OASDI and federal deficits, many say that it is unfair for low- and moderate-income workers to pay for upper-middle- and high-income beneficiaries.

Fifth, it is suggested that the new means-testing proposals avoid many of the pitfalls pointed to by the critics of traditional means-testing. Since the new proposals would be administered through the tax system, administrative costs would be much lower than are typically associated with "welfare bureaucracies." Nor, argue its proponents, is an affluence-test likely to undermine the dignity of beneficiaries through intrusive investigation and public disapproval of persons who receive benefits. As a program that would still provide benefits to the vast majority of Americans at some point in their lives, there is little likelihood of stigma being attached to benefit receipt, especially since the right to a benefit would still arise from work-related contributions (Kaus, 1994). Moreover, as pointed out by some who oppose means-testing of Social Security, all means-tested programs are not necessarily undermining of the dignity of those who receive benefits (Greenstein, 1994). For example, the "earned income tax credit" (available only to low-income people meeting certain requirements) does not undermine dignity, because this cash payment is administered through the tax system and is work-related.

One more point needs to be made. Some advocates of the new means-testing hold views not unlike those who opposed Social Security from its inception. They simply do not believe in large-scale social interventions. Historically, those favoring means-tested eligibility criteria to limit benefits to the poor or near-poor have always sought a residual and limited public approach to social welfare. From this perspective, individuals, not government, should have primary responsibility for retirement preparation and disability protection; government intervention should be restricted to situations of extreme hardship. The new means-testing debate presents individuals and groups with those value preferences with an important opportunity to advocate for a substantially smaller public welfare commitment. The introduction of a means-test, even a seemingly "liberal" means-test, is seen as a potentially important step towards redefining the role of government.

ARGUMENTS AGAINST THE NEW MEANS-TESTING

As Wilbur Cohen (1958) cautioned, programs for poor people are likely to be poor programs. History indicates that adequate benefit levels are politically difficult to maintain for a program that is explicitly targeted to the poor. A means-tested social insurance program may be perceived to be a welfare program; the result is that its political support is likely to unravel. According to Cohen and other supporters of universal programs, the result will be that low- and middle-income Americans will suffer from the consequent major loss of income protection.

But times have changed and so have the proposals. The new proposals, in theory, will not be particularly expensive to administer, nor are they as likely to stigmatize the high-income beneficiaries affected. Might the traditional arguments against means-testing no longer apply? We think the answer to this question is no.

The main argument against the new approach to means-testing OASDI is that it would initiate a process that is likely to seriously undermine what is considered America's most successful social program, and, in the long-run, be particularly deleterious to low- and moderate-income households. Other concerns are the savings and work disincentives that will be created and interactions that will necessitate increased welfare and private pension expenditures. Finally, means-testing Social Security is likely to intensify differences between social classes, with those who would no longer receive benefits resenting those who did. These arguments lack the 30 second "sound bite" quality that makes the idea of "affluence-testing away the benefits of the rich" seemingly attractive to many, and so they bear further elaboration.

We begin by reviewing what OASDI has accomplished, particularly the income protection it provides to low- and moderate-income elderly households. We then examine problems with the new approach to means-testing Social Security. Finally, we discuss how some goals that the new means-testing strategies seek to achieve can be better addressed through other policy mechanisms.

1. Benefits of the Current Program

In chapter 1, Thompson and Upp set forth the rationale for social insurance and explain why "Social Security ranks high or very high" with respect to widely accepted goals of a well-functioning social welfare system. Universal protection against income losses resulting from old age, severe disability, or survivorship is the basis for the program, combining widespread protection across income classes with redistribution provisions particularly beneficial to lower-income groups. Earmarked payroll taxes and wide-coverage universality enhance the public's interest in the program's financial stability and continuity. In exchange for making payments over a long period of time, workers earn the right to public retirement and disability and life insurance protection for themselves and their families (Kingson and Berkowitz, 1993).

Private insurance provides protection to those who can afford and choose to protect themselves. Means-tested programs provide limited protection to the poor. However, as Thompson and Upp point out in chapter 1, only social insurance does very well in meeting all the major objectives nations would like social welfare systems to achieve. Above all, social adequacy—the principle that benefits should be sufficient to provide a floor of protection for all the population—is the driving principle and primary rationale for Social Security. Absent the concern to protect widely, there would be no need to require that nearly all workers make payroll tax contributions and earn a right to benefits (Myers, 1993b). Without this concern, the rationale would disappear for the weighting in the benefit formula that provides proportionately larger benefits to low-income workers, effectively cross-subsidizing such workers from the payroll tax contributions of higher-income workers and their employers.

In the United States, concern for *adequacy* (and the implementing of redistribution provisions) has been combined with the principle of individual *equity* in structuring OASDI. Thus, high-income contributors get higher monthly benefits, although they receive a rate of return on their payroll tax contributions that is roughly one-half of what low-income workers receive. If someone is forced to contribute to social insurance primarily for the benefit of persons of more limited means, then the distinction between social insurance and welfare diminishes, and the two concepts begin to merge. Absent some return on their payroll tax contributions, the interests of higher-income people, the program's best risks, become alienated from the program and the rationale for earmarked taxes becomes difficult to sustain.[7]

As the heart of the nation's retirement income system, Social Security provides the essential building block for the savings and private pension income of middle- and even higher income households. As Moon discusses (chapter 4), most of the roughly two-fifths of elder households with private or public employee pension income still count on Social Security to provide a substantial portion of their retirement income, and private pension plans are almost always structured with this in mind. In 1991, Social Security provided about two-fifths of the aggregate income going to households headed by persons aged 65 and over, with most of the rest coming from asset income (21 percent), other pension income (20 percent), and earnings (17 percent). As a source of income, Social Security is substantially more important for low- and moderate-income households. This can be seen in data showing that Social Security provided 74 percent of the aggregate income of elderly house-holds with less than $10,000 in 1991, compared with 31 percent of households with $30,000 to $49,999.

As Ball (chapter 18) and Steuerle (chapter 17) also note, major programmatic fea-tures assure that Social Security targets benefits (e.g., a benefit formula "weighted" to help the poor, "minimum pensions," survivors and disability benefits, and the taxation of benefits going to pensioners with high incomes). The program's main benefit formula provides for proportionately larger monthly benefits for persons who worked for many years at low- or moderate-earnings levels.[8] For example, the weighted formula replaces about 59 percent of preretirement earnings for a hypo-thetical worker who worked consistently at one-half of average wages and first re-ceived retirement benefits at age 65 in 1993; it provides about 26 percent for a re-tiree with earnings consistently at the maximum taxable level.

By itself, Social Security does more to reduce poverty and inequality than either welfare programs or the American tax system (U.S. Bureau of the Census, 1988). In 1992, it decreased the elderly poverty rate from 56 to 15 percent,[9] and their "poverty gap" from $50 billion to $7 billion (U.S. Congress, 1994).[10] In other words, although it is not means-tested or identified as being a program for low-income peo-ple, Social Security acts as a major antipoverty program.

2. Flaws in the New Means-Testing Approach

Thompson and Upp (chapter 1) conclude that the onus is on those who want radical alterations in Social Security to show how they would measurably improve an ap-proach that is working well. They observe that the OASDI program, as structured, goes a long way toward preserving individual dignity, operating efficiently, avoiding negative side effects (e.g., savings and substantial work disincentives), assuring com-prehensive coverage, distributing costs and benefits equitably, and fostering fiscal re-sponsibility. Moreover, it can be argued that OASDI has passed the test of political sustainability, a not inconsequential accomplishment given the nation's ambivalence towards many existing social programs. It also seems to have passed the test of eco-nomic sustainability, although this is a more controversial conclusion. As Myers (chap-ter 13) and Ball (chapter 18) point out, yearly actuarial cost projections provide early warning of financial problems that lie ahead, thereby allowing adequate time for ad-justments to respond to anticipated economic and demographic changes.

Stigma.   Assessing the new approach against the criteria outlined by Thompson and Upp, it would seem that a means-test that uses the tax system to exclude the well-off from receiving benefits will almost certainly be less stigmatizing and eas-ier to administer than a traditional means-test and may only marginally increase the cost of administration. While Americans prefer to receive benefits that are clearly defined as earned, we are persuaded that the new approach goes a long way toward answering the charges of the critics regarding administrative costs and maintaining the dignity of beneficiaries.[11]

Saving Disincentive.   However, like the old approach, the new approach is likely to introduce serious disincentives for savings (Ball, 1994; Bernstein, 1990; Myers,

1994b; Steuerle, 1994; Walker, 1994). The new approach to means-testing (unlike the old) discourages savings by the very people who currently save the most, high-income households.[12] Certainly, the millionaires and the billionaires frequently cited to support the change will never miss Social Security benefits (if means-tested away) and will not alter their savings behavior; however, upper-middle class households (by far more numerous) would face a very real choice between saving more and losing benefits. Each dollar of income from personal savings (or earnings) might be substantially offset by losses of Social Security income.

Consider two neighbors with the same earnings history and the same life-long financial responsibilities. One was a saver during his working years, accumulating large amounts of income-generating assets. The other was a spender, who purchased a large home, bought expensive cars, and traveled widely. Ironically, if an income-test were introduced, it would be the prudent person who would be penalized, not the spender. "Means-testing Social Security benefits offers . . . comparatively affluent workers a clear message: If you increase your private saving for retirement [or work in retirement], the state will sharply reduce your Social Security pension" (Burtless, 1995, p.12).

In this regard, Australia's experience is instructive. Many people point to Australia as an example of a country with a well-functioning means-tested program that provides the bulk of public retirement income. Yet the potential economic disincentives of this program have been the basis of major debates throughout its entire history.[13] For example, it was the Australian government's desire not to penalize savers that was the main reason the asset-test component of the means-test was abandoned in 1976 (Carey and Hanks, 1986). The asset-test that Australians faced encouraged them to manipulate their financial investment behavior in order to achieve eligibility. The test was reintroduced in 1985 primarily because of budgetary problems and the need to cut government expenditures (Schulz, Borowski, and Crown, 1991). However, once again, "it was the incentive for . . . manipulation provided by the new income-only test that served as an important rationale for the reintroduction of an asset test" (p. 230). Some people achieved eligibility by investing either in assets that appreciated in value but produced no income or in low- or no-interest deposit accounts.

In the United States, we recently had an example of this same phenomenon. The Medicare Catastrophic Coverage Act of 1988 (later repealed) generated similar behavior. Special taxes on persons aged 65 or more with high incomes were imposed to help finance this new health coverage. The new tax triggered a major advertising appeal by financial investment companies urging people to put their money in tax-free mutual funds and other types of financial investments. The response, according to industry spokesmen at the time, was significant (Gilman, 1988).

Integration Issues. The introduction of an affluence-test would also have negative consequences on other parts of the nation's retirement and disability income system. It would place pressures on the nation's private and public-employee pension systems to provide more adequate protection for middle- and upper-income workers and retirees—programs that continue to have major problems in coverage, equity, financing, and perverse labor force incentives (see Turner and Beller, 1989; Woods, 1989). At the same time, it would encourage some workers to turn away from employee-sponsored pensions and other types of retirement income mechanisms, causing greater interest in higher take-home pay and immediate consumption. And if a means-test resulted in declining progressivity within Social Security or, conceivably, Social Security's collapse, then SSI and other welfare programs would need to be radically expanded (Ball and Aaron, 1993; Bernstein, 1990).

Equity. The new means-testing would clearly compromise the protection of the existing Social Security program and destroy any earnings-based standard of individual equity (Meyer and Wolff, 1993; Thompson, 1983). Arguably, the program could still be defined as providing coverage against the risk of not being well-off in retirement, disability, or survivorship, but no longer could everyone reasonably expect more than a minimal return from their contribution.

Of great concern is the strong possibility that a means-test directed at the well-off would be the first step down the slippery slope of full means-testing. If testing begins at the $40,000 level (as proposed by the Concord Coalition), the way is open for reducing the exemption level at any future time, pushing further down into the income distribution. This introduces a whole new level of unpredictability and insecurity into individuals' retirement planning, making it very difficult for middle class households to plan for retirement. Moreover, as Howard Young (1995) noted, "the widespread objection to the current Social Security earnings test—which primarily affects Social Security beneficiaries with substantial earnings—provides an "indication of the dissatisfaction that would result from means-testing (even as newly defined)."

Indeed, some people who call for the new means-test falsely assume that a large proportion of elders have relatively high incomes. They assume that large savings would accrue from taking Social Security benefits away from the "very rich." Analyzing a proposal that would reduce all entitlement benefits by 50¢ for each dollar in excess of $100,000 for individuals and in excess of $120,000 for couples, a recent U.S. Congressional Budget Office study (1994) showed that this simply is not the case. Such a proposal would only reduce OASDI spending by less than 2 percent in 1996. In other words, given the small portion of elders with income over $100,000—about 1 percent of recipient households according to the same Congressional Budget Office study—means-testing would need to begin well below the $100,000 level to reap significant savings, probably dipping to levels that most people consider middle-income.

The issue of fairness in the distribution of costs and benefits is complex. On the one hand, it certainly seems appropriate to place a larger share of the burden of addressing the Social Security and federal deficits on those who are most well-off. The new means-testing approach would certainly do so. *But there are other ways of achieving such results, and the argument for affluence-testing the rich tends to ignore the reality that Social Security serves multiple ends.* By design, and over its history, individual equity, while not dominant over social adequacy, has been, nonetheless, an important part of social insurance in America. The goal is that even the well-off should have a reasonable return on their Social Security "investment."

What a *reasonable* return is, however, is certainly an open question. As Chen and Goss (chapter 5) indicate, there is a long history of debate over whether people get their "money's worth" from Social Security. Some, already perceive violations of individual equity because the future rates of concern will be relatively low for some people. This occurs in a mature pension system with significant redistributive elements. The tilt in the benefit formula, for example, works to the advantage of low- and moderate-income workers. Currently, up to 85 percent of benefits are reportable by high-income beneficiaries as taxable income. Others would push the principle of social adequacy yet further by shaving the return of higher-income persons. But few would defend the means-testing away of up to 85 percent of benefits and the subjecting of most of the remaining benefit to income taxation as fair to persons who have made lifelong contributions into the program.

Weakened Political Support and Financial Viability. Perhaps the most important fact to consider is that the new proposals to means-test Social Security fail to pass the test of assuring the continuity of the program and, in particular, of assuring that low- and middle-income workers will be afforded adequate protection in the future. While it is impossible to be certain, there is good reason to believe that the introduction of such a means-test would, in the long run, undermine the political support, the legitimacy, and, ultimately, the financial viability of Social Security. As indicated earlier, even without means-testing, Social Security is often criticized by higher-income workers as not giving them their money's worth. While the balance that is struck between the principles of adequacy and individual equity is somewhat arbitrary and open to debate, there is likely to be a point of no return, where changes that move too far from the principle of individual equity so undermine its economic and political support that they risk its destruction. If rates of return on Social Security investments are reduced to the point that they become inconsequential for upper-income groups, it is almost inevitable that large numbers of the nation's opinion leaders and other elite will become increasingly hostile to the program and "generate massive pressures to permit higher paid people to opt out of social security" (Ball and Aaron, 1993, C4). Were this to happen, low-income beneficiaries are likely to be the greatest losers because the redistribution of income, which mostly benefits low-income persons, would be difficult to sustain without the inclusion of higher-income people.

In other words, absent inclusion of the entire cross section of the work force, a program such as Social Security that emphasizes social adequacy through redistribution (e.g., using a weighted benefit formula) is, in the long run, likely to collapse—for both mathematical and political reasons. As many chapters in this book emphasize, OASDI's financing problems are not so great as to justify radical changes within it.[14] Nor are the problems posed by federal budget deficits in the absence of sharp cuts in OASDI.

Generational Solidarity. Although arguably highly speculative, there is yet one more problem of means-testing that deserves mention. Means-testing Social Security could create schisms between those who benefit and those who do not, doing damage to the ties that bind a diverse nation. Senator Bill Bradley (D-New Jersey) referred to Social Security as the nation's best expression of community. Social Security represents a commitment to share risks and assure basic economic security, a commitment of growing importance to Americans concerned about their own and their children's future. Moreover, the program is one of the few institutions in which virtually all Americans—young and old, rich and poor—participate and benefit.[15] In an increasingly diverse and rapidly changing society, it is important to encourage common commitments to a national community while simultaneously allowing for differences among communities, regions, and groups. As Baldwin pointed out, social insurance programs do not "first and foremost safeguard the interests of the poor as poor. Within social insurance, redistribution does not primarily take place vertically between classes or income strata . . . but horizontally over the lifespan of the individual and, in cross-section at any given moment, between risk categories (from healthy to sick, young to old, ambulatory to disabled, working to unemployed) that only secondarily and partially overlap with social groups as defined in other terms" (1990, p. 9).

3. Better Ways

The new means-testing is often advanced by its advocates as a fair and necessary way to address large federal deficits and the financing pressures that are anticipated as the baby-boom cohorts move into their retirement years. There is no question that a means-test could be structured to place the greatest burden on those among the beneficiary population most able to bear it. But to the extent that one judges means-testing as politically undermining OASDI, then the cost to the integrity of the program may be viewed as being too high. Moreover, there are better ways of achieving a similar distribution of burden.

Changing Marginal Tax Rates. General income tax rates could be raised at higher-income levels without the risk of pulling apart support for Social Security. Why "tax" benefits at extraordinarily high rates (at marginal tax rates up to 85 percent!), as proposed by the Concord Coalition and do nothing to increase levels of taxation on earnings, rental income, and income from other assets of the "rich"? By imposing an excessive "tax" on Social Security income, a Social Security means test would violate "a principle of horizontal equity, that households with equal income should be taxed at the same level" (Myles and Quadagno, 1995, p. 14).

Deficit reduction is certainly an important concern, but again there is no reason to risk destroying a central American institution to reduce the deficit, especially when Social Security is projected to run large annual surpluses until roughly 2015 and when the major cause of projected future increases in long-term federal deficits are decisions made in the 1980s to cut taxes and increase defense spending and the rising cost of health care, not OASDI. If one chooses (quite erroneously and misleadingly) to count Social Security revenues and expenditures for deficit-calculating purposes, this program is already reducing the deficit (by $72 billion dollars in 1996 alone) because of the large annual surpluses it is running and is expected to continue to run, as noted, until about 2015.[16]

Incremental Changes in Social Security. Clearly, the projected long-term deficit in OASDI needs to be addressed. But, as a number of authors in this volume suggest, the projected OASDI financing problem is not so large that it cannot be addressed through incremental change by selecting among many possible policy options: extension of coverage to all state and local public employees, further taxation of Social Security benefits, crediting OASDI with all the receipts from taxation of benefits, a payroll tax rate increase in 2020, improved measurement of inflation, an increase in the age of eligibility for full benefits, partial investment of trust fund assets in broad equity funds, and changes in the benefit formula that create modest reductions in benefit levels (to name only a few of the options).

There is a world of difference between proposals to means-test Social Security and these other proposals, some of which push at the boundaries of a universal social insurance program without undermining the program. For example, treating benefits as taxable income and increasing the age of eligibility for full benefits have been justified as needed adjustments in light of changing social, demographic, and economic circumstances. They are variously viewed by their proponents and opponents as properly or improperly either enhancing or compromising one or more of the program's multiple goals (e.g., stable financing, social adequacy, individual equity, surety of benefits), but they do not require a radical change in the nation's public retirement income policy, neither in its basic principles nor its programmatic rules.

Treating the portion of benefits that is not a return on after-tax employee contributions as taxable income comes closest in our view to challenging the social insurance foundation of OASDI. The current policy of treating up to 85 percent of Social Security benefits as taxable income is usually viewed as progressive and sound tax policy, conforming to the view that all income should be taxed at some point in the life course. This approach improves the financing of Social Security (and Medicare's Hospital Insurance program) while simultaneously maintaining the universal eligibility provisions of the program and placing greater responsibility on middle- and higher-income beneficiaries (Kingson and Berkowitz, 1993). Others view these changes as well-targeted benefit reductions and, in some cases, define the tax treatment of benefits as a type of means-test.

Certainly, treating OASDI income as taxable lowers the rate of return for higher income people and alters (as would means-testing) the relationship between adequacy and individual equity. Not surprisingly, it has angered some relatively well-off beneficiaries who have called for changes. For example, in 1995 Republicans in the House of Representatives proposed, as part of their Senior Citizens' Equity Act, that the tax be reduced from 85 to 50 percent on the maximum portion of benefit income subject to taxation.

Even so, we would argue that there is a qualitative difference between taxing Social Security income and means-testing the program, even if means-testing only affects the well-off. The confiscatory marginal tax rates that follow from all current proposals to means-test Social Security are inappropriate because they alter the understanding and views of the population with regard to the program. They also violate a major principle of the program from its inception (i.e., an implicit understanding of the citizenry) that *workers at all income levels will receive some reasonable return in exchange for making payroll tax contributions during their working lives.* The result is that means-testing destroys this "contract with America," undermines the integrity of government, and provides strong economic and political incentive for high income persons to withdraw their support from the program. Moreover, as previously discussed, it would introduce disincentives for encouraging savings, both for retirement and economic growth.

In contrast, the current taxation of benefits is consistent with widely-accepted tax principles and does not devastate rates of return. Equally important, the taxation of benefits is not widely-perceived as breaking the Social Security "contract" or as turning Social Security into a welfare program. Thus, it is less likely to pose significant threats to political support for the program.

Raising the Retirement Age. The scheduled gradual increase from 2003 through 2027 by two years in the age of eligibility (to 67) for full Social Security benefits[17] (and proposals to further increase that age or increase it more quickly) can be understood as reasoned accommodation to improvements in mortality and to financing pressures accompanying demographic change. Retirement age changes adjust the terms of eligibility and carry important implications for the adequacy of Social Security. Much of the cost of the retirement age change probably will fall on *lower-income* early retirees as opposed to the large number of early retirees who are relatively healthy, leave work by choice, and have higher retirement incomes (see Sammartino, 1987). For the most part, however, such changes do not represent a threat to the universality and continuity of the program, except in one respect. If retirement age changes are perceived of as unfairly reducing the benefits of future cohorts of retirees and as making Social Security benefits less reliable (i.e., subject to constant renegotiation), then such changes may serve to reduce support for the program.[18]

Changes in Existing Means-Tested Programs. Better targeting of resources to low-income persons has also been identified as a reason for the new and old means-tests. To the extent that increased targeting is desired, it can be done in ways that do not undermine broad support for the program. The SSI Modernization Project Experts (1992) recommended increasing SSI benefits to at least 100 percent of the poverty line, liberalizing the SSI assets-tests to make it easier for persons with limited assets to qualify, increasing the program's staffing levels to allow for more personalized service delivery and more outreach, and allowing SSI beneficiaries to live in the homes of family members or friends without being penalized with a one-third benefits reduction. Smeeding (1994) also pointed out possibilities for better targeting within a program like SSI, which is already highly targeted. He called for taking a careful look at the subgroups within SSI (the blind, the disabled, and the elderly) and assessing whether the current general rules and regulations should be different for each subgroup.

Targeting Within Social Security. On the OASDI benefits side, the special minimum benefit formula[19] could be liberalized, and this benefit could be changed in a manner that recognizes the cost in lost Social Security coverage for low-income workers who left the labor force at various times to care for children or other relatives. Consideration could be given to incorporating "earnings sharing" provisions in the event of divorce and to reducing spouse benefits in exchange for increases in benefits for surviving aged widow(er)s—the groups at greatest risk of poverty in old age. Also, "progressive" deliberalizations (i.e., benefit reductions falling disproportionately on higher-income groups) could increase targeting. For example, one congressional package (H.R. 4245) that has been proposed to strengthen OASDI long-run financing includes a provision to alter the program's benefit formula to "gradually reduce benefits for new groups of beneficiaries" over 50 years (Rostenkowski, 1994, p. 2). Low-income earners would not be affected, but the benefits of average-income earners would, relative to current law, be reduced by roughly 8 percent and high-income earners by about 20 percent after the phase-in period. On the financing side, consideration could be given to provisions that would lead to greater progressivity in the payroll tax (FICA), without undermining the contributory principle. For example, the maximum tax ceiling could be lifted on the employer's portion of the payroll tax.

CONCLUSION

In sum, means-testing Social Security (both the old and new versions) is a poor idea. If affluent people do not receive any return on their payroll tax contributions, they will view Social Security as unfair, and the program will lose their important political support.

There is a viable option. Social Security's long-term financing problems can be addressed without compromising or radically altering its basic goals and achievements. Moreover, further targeting in Social Security and improvements in selective programs such as SSI do not contradict, and may enhance, a public retirement income strategy built upon social insurance principles. Also, there are many alternatives to means-testing. Some, such as the taxation of benefits, may push the boundaries of universality, but, unless taken to extremes, they do not risk seriously undermining a program that has withstood the test of time. Thus, we conclude that universal eligibility for Social Security remains sound policy and an essential feature of a public pension program designed to provide widespread protection, especially to low- and moderate-income populations.

ENDNOTES

1. A different group of reformers called for cash pensions for the "blameless" worthy poor (mainly widowed mothers, their children, and the poor old) to be administered outside the context of the poor laws. These pensions were intended as compensation to the poor for family services provided, such as caring for their children (Leiby, 1978). As implemented in various states, however, the Mothers' Pensions and Old-Age Pension programs contained many of the elements that the reformers had sought to avoid: intrusive eligibility investigations, supervision of beneficiaries, and so on.

2. By 1956, however, a disability program without a means-test was added to Social Security.

3. Also, there is considerable support for eliminating AFDC as an entitlement program with benefits funded as a matter of right to low-income families within broad federal guidelines. Instead, some would substitute a system based on block grants, which would give states great authority over the conditions of eligibility and the structure of benefits.

4. The structure and administration of the SSI disability provisions are becoming increasingly controversial.

5. These two problems are also problems for the disability program under OASDI.

6. Professor Allan Borowski, of the University of New South Wales, reported that in "June 1993 there were 1,515,682 age pensioners and they represented 62.31 percent of the population of age pension age."

If benefits paid to service pensioners (veterans) are included, then 76.3 percent of the age-eligible population received one of these pensions. "Of the age pensioners (only), 67.2 percent were not affected by either the income or assets test and, thus, received a full pension," the rest receiving reduced pensions (personal communication, 1995; Departments of Social Security and Veterans' Affairs, 1994).

7. Given the dual goals of adequacy and individual equity, the program is open to criticism as being unfair when different balances are sought, either implicitly or explicitly, between these two principles. Rates of return on the Social Security "investments" in various types of workers provide a case in point. As is typically the case when companies begin new, defined-benefit, private pension plans, Social Security eligibility rules have been favorable to the first cohorts of older workers to receive monthly benefits (and benefit improvements). The first, and even today's, beneficiaries have generally received large "rates of return" on their "investments." To do otherwise would have seriously compromised the adequacy goal of the program, resulting in much lower standards of living in retirement for today's and yesterday's elderly. But doing so also assured what some consider unfair returns measured in total dollars received in excess of contributions (as opposed to proportions of preretirement income replaced), especially to high-income elders (Steuerle and Bakija, 1994). In the future, the return to cohorts as a whole will generally be more closely comparable to their combined employee and employer contributions. (When measured in absolute dollars received relative to tax payments, the pattern of redistribution will be less favorable to single and two-earner high-income families.)

8. A few analysts, including Steuerle (chapter 17), suggest that this feature serves essentially as a means-test on lifetime earnings.

9. This is a legitimate means of measuring the poverty-reduction effect of Social Security, but it does not show what would happen in the real world if Social Security did not exist. Rather, it provides a measure of the magnitude of the adjusting compensation that would need to be made to offset the loss of Social Security benefits.

10. The poverty gap means that all elderly persons could be removed from poverty by spending $7 billion, if these expenditures were "perfectly targeted" to persons below the poverty line.

11. While we believe the new means-testing approach substantially addresses these concerns, Merton Bernstein has pointed out that a number of problems could arise in its implementation. Given the incentives it would introduce for beneficiaries to shelter or otherwise hide earned and unearned income, there might be a need for ongoing review of income reports. Also, eligibility procedures are likely to become more complex, thus introducing new barriers to receipt of benefits (Bernstein, personal communication, 1995).

12. Years of economic statistics on savings rates document that lower-income households save virtually nothing during working years, except a growing equity if they have purchased a home. The result is that only higher-income older households have significant *financial* assets (see, for example, Radner, 1993a; Schulz, 1995; U.S. Bureau of the Census, 1990).

13. A detailed description and discussion of the issues are provided in Schulz, Borowski, and Crown, 1991.

14. Under the intermediate assumptions, there is a roughly 14 percent shortfall over the 75-year period for which estimates are made. As discussed elsewhere in this chapter and later in the book, this problem could be addressed by a set of moderate changes.

15. We are apt to forget that Social Security provides more than a worker retirement benefit. For example, about one-fifth of OASDI benefits are paid to survivors of various ages—totaling over 7 million persons in 1992.

16. Robert Myers, the former chief actuary of the Social Security Administration, has pointed out that there is a contradiction in the position of those arguing that means-testing Social Security would reduce the federal deficit *and* address projected shortfalls in the combined OASDI trust funds. If revenues from means-testing Social Security were transferred to the General Fund, this would reduce the general budget deficit and, thus, the national debt. But it would do nothing at all to improve the financing of OASDI. Conversely, if the money were left in the trust funds, OASDI financing would be strengthened and the projected 75-year deficit reduced. But this would not reduce the general budget deficit or the national debt. It only means that the trust funds would own more of the national debt and the general public would own less of it. (Robert J. Myers, personal communication, 1995). As he observed, "you can't have it both ways, 'Eat your cake and have it too.' "

17. The 1983 amendments to the Social Security Act legislated a gradual increase, from 65 to 67, in the age of eligibility for full retirement benefits over a 24-year period beginning in 2003. A related reduction in the value of benefits for persons accepting early retirement benefits and for spouses of retired workers will be phased in beginning in 2000. Thus, for those first accepting early retirement benefits at the earliest possible age (62), their value will ultimately drop from 80 to 70 percent of a full benefit. Spouses subject to the new retirement ages will experience similar benefit reductions. Widow and widowers first claiming benefits after age 60 will also have larger benefit reductions beginning in 2000 as their age for full benefits begins to rise to 67.

18. Benefit reductions such as further increases in the age of eligibility for benefits or an across the board reduction in future benefit amounts would compromise the adequacy of the program. On the other hand, payroll tax increases would place a greater burden on workers and their employers. But neither approach threatens to pull apart the political consensus for an institution that has served the nation so well. Moreover, while benefit cut and tax increase proposals will unquestionably be controversial, they are less likely to result in strong political opposition of senior groups, labor, and other traditional supporters of Social Security.

19. The special minimum benefit provides an alternative way of computing OASDI benefits. It is designed to benefit those who have worked consistently, but at low wages, in jobs covered by OASDI.

CHAPTER 4

Are Social Security Benefits too High or too Low?

MARILYN MOON

Judgements about the adequacy of Social Security benefits play a critical role in the debate over the future of the program. But there is not a simple, straightforward answer to the question of whether benefits are too high or too low. While a myriad of statistics, such as the fact that benefits for a retired worker averaged $674 per month in 1993 (U.S. Congress 1994), can be offered to support various perspectives, it is difficult to make an abstract argument that this figure is too high or too low. The most honest response is "it depends," because there are many possible interpretations of both the intent of the question and the facts that one would use to answer it.

Thus, a first step in providing an answer is to understand the context in which the question is posed. The issue might be, for example, whether benefits are too high to be sustained over time as the population ages. Or, the question might focus on whether benefits are too high in comparison to earnings of the younger population that helps to pay for the program. Finally, we might ask whether benefits are too low for those beneficiaries who remain poor or near-poor even though they qualify for a program called Social Security.

For purposes of this chapter, the question represents a useful rhetorical device to help understand the various ways that people look at Social Security and why they may see a program that is too generous, too limited, or just right. The question of the adequacy of Social Security will be posed in several contexts:

- Does Social Security meet its major goals as outlined in the original legislation and later modifications?
- Does Social Security meet the needs of its beneficiaries (both on the whole and for various subgroups of the beneficiary population)?
- Has Social Security struck a reasonable balance between the workers who contribute and those who currently benefit from the program?

- Have we overpromised benefits for the future relative to our ability to pay for them? Are there other complicating issues that color our attitudes toward the level of benefits?

Like so many issues, there are a wide range of alternative measures and statistics that can be brought to bear on these questions. Consequently, a second task needed to provide a reasonable answer is to choose the most relevant measures for presentation. While reasonable people can disagree on which are the most relevant indicators, that is not the same as saying that all measures are valid or equally useful. But, ultimately, a conclusion about whether Social Security is too high or too low requires subjective interpretation. Issues such as fairness and affordability require value judgements. And those judgements will reflect individual interpretations; what this chapter strives to do is establish a framework for basing such judgements on sound information.

THE HISTORICAL CONTEXT

One way to position arguments concerning the present and future of Social Security relies on an appeal to the past. What was the intent of the program? What were the original goals and limits of the legislation? Such an effort can be instructive, but both critics and supporters of the system can find solace in historical lessons. As with any piece of major social legislation, Social Security's passage mixed the motives and goals of many different lawmakers. Some viewed the legislation as activity that would be helpful during economic downturns such as the economy was experiencing in 1935. In fact, early in the process, much of the attention of the work of the Committee on Economic Security focused on unemployment compensation, rather than on retirement (Achenbaum, 1986). Other supporters of public pensions proclaimed Social Security to be the beginning of a new handling of old age in America that would forever change our treatment of retirees. In contrast, some critics of Social Security look back on its genesis as a unique period in history that we have outgrown, and with it our need for the Social Security program as we know it (Peterson and Howe, 1988).

One aspect of Social Security made quite clear at passage was that the program was to be a combination of assistance and insurance, a characteristic that remains today. That is, Social Security was designed to establish a floor of security to protect those with the lowest lifetime earnings and above that to allow the benefits to rise for those who made greater contributions. The formula that was generated essentially returns higher payments as a share of contributions to persons with the lowest average earnings, while still paying more to those who contributed more into the system. This formula has been altered over time, but the basic premise of its "progressive" structure has not changed.[1] This characteristic of the program makes simple judgements about fairness and adequacy more difficult, however, since, by design, benefits are not the same for all participants.

In addition, Social Security was not intended to be a full wage replacement program. The assumption has always been that other forms of retirement income would be necessary to maintain a reasonable standard of living. Moreover, those with higher incomes were expected to supplement an even greater share of their incomes from other sources. Consequently, the formula used to determine benefits replaces only a portion of earlier wages, and as wages rise, the formula becomes less generous.

Both of these concepts are captured in the "replacement rate," one measure used to illustrate the generosity of Social Security benefits. This figure is presented as a percentage that indicates how retirement benefits (taken at the normal retirement age) compare to preretirement earnings. While it is generally agreed that benefits should amount to a portion of preretirement earnings, the exact share is subject to debate. It is also interesting to note that the replacement rate is higher for low-wage workers and lower for high-wage earners, reflecting the deliberate use of a formula that is more generous to those who have lower earnings over their lifetimes, thus showing the program's progressivity.

As shown in Table 4.1, an average worker retiring in 1940 could have expected only a 26.2 percent replacement rate (U.S. Congress, 1994).[2] After the early expansions in the program, in which the rate grew in an ad hoc fashion, the 1972 amendments sought to stabilize the replacement rate by adjusting for wage and price increases. But because of an error in the formula adopted in 1972, the replacement rate grew at an unprecedented clip for persons born between 1911 and 1916. This error was corrected in the 1977 amendments.[3] The replacement ratio for average workers now hovers just over 40 percent. Thus, Social Security's generosity has risen over time, but the replacement rates have now been stabilized for persons born, roughly, after 1920. For example, the replacement rate that a person born in 1975 (with average earnings) can expect is quite similar to what someone born in 1920 would have received. Rates of high- and low-wage workers have also changed in a similar pattern over time, except that there is a continued slow rise for high-wage workers into the future. After the early years of the program, a historical perspective indicates that the level of generosity has not changed very much over time.

Another early characteristic of Social Security that may affect our analysis of adequacy was the limited nature of the initial benefits established in 1935. The original legislation covered only workers. Moreover, the legislation precluded any payments under the retirement system until 1942 at the earliest. But Social Security remained on the political agenda, with numerous calls for expansions of various sorts and some concern about the drag on the economy that would come from building a large reserve (while tax contributions were made but no benefits were paid out). Consequently, the program was expanded in the 1939 amendments (Achenbaum, 1986), extending coverage to dependents and survivors, and accelerating the payout of benefits. No longer was Social Security limited to workers and no longer were benefits to be tied so closely to contributions. This marked a major liberalization of the program.

As Berkowitz (chapter 2) notes, major expansions in Social Security occurred again in 1950 and continued intermittently into the 1970s, with ad hoc increases in benefits and coverage. These benefit increases more than compensated workers for inflation, which otherwise would have cut the value of benefits over time (Schulz et al., 1974). These changes reflect a society sharing its economic growth with its retired citizens. Moreover, the impact of this generosity can be seen in the sharp declines in poverty among the elderly that occurred in the 1960s and 1970s (Moon and Mulvey, 1995). Legislation continued to indicate support for generous benefits

TABLE 4.1. Social Security Replacement Rates, 1940–2040.

Year of Birth	Year of Attaining Normal Retirement Age	Replacement Rates (in percent)		
		Low Earner[a]	Average Earner[b]	Maximum Earner[c]
1875	1940	39.4	26.2	16.5
1885	1950	33.2	19.7	21.2
1895	1960	49.1	33.3	29.8
1900	1965	45.6	31.4	32.9
1905	1970	48.5	34.3	29.2
1910	1975	59.9	42.3	30.1
1911	1976	60.1	43.7	32.1
1912	1977	61.0	44.8	33.5
1913	1978	63.4	46.7	34.7
1914	1979	64.4	48.1	36.1
1915	1980	68.1	51.1	32.5
1916	1981	72.5	54.4	33.4
1917	1982	65.8	48.7	28.6
1918	1983	63.5	45.8	26.3
1919	1984	62.6	42.8	23.7
1920	1985	61.1	40.9	22.8
1921	1986	60.3	41.1	23.1
1922	1987	59.5	41.2	22.6
1923	1988	58.4	40.9	23.0
1924	1989	57.9	41.6	24.1
1925	1990	58.2	43.2	24.5
1935	1991	57.1	42.4	25.6
1944	2010	56.0	41.7	27.1
1954	2020	56.0	41.7	27.8
1963	2030	55.7	41.5	27.6
1973	2040	55.7	41.5	27.5

[a]Earnings equal to 45 percent of the SSA average wage index.
[b]Earnings equal to SSA average wage index.
[c]Earnings equal to the maximum wage taxable for Social Security purposes.
Source: U.S. Congress, House Committee on Ways and Means. (1993), Table 8.

to an ever-broader portion of the population, achieving nearly universal coverage of workers by 1965 (Ball, 1978). Most of this legislation passed with little objection or criticism.

What then should we conclude about the intended generosity or stability of the program? If we focus only on the original legislation, then Social Security as we know it today is much more generous and expansive than intended. But if we look at the pattern of amendments over time—which speaks to the intent of several generations of legislators—there is a long history of sharing economic growth with retirees. That is, as the economic well-being of workers increased in the 1950s and 1960s, benefits for retirees were increased substantially. In that way, retirees were able to benefit from economic growth.

SOCIAL SECURITY AND THE NEEDS OF ITS BENEFICIARIES

Alternatively, rather than looking at the historical record, the question of adequacy of benefits could focus only on whether the needs of America's elderly citizens are being met by Social Security. To do this we need to look at a number of measures.

1. Income

The ultimate test of adequacy is the standard of living enjoyed by Social Security's beneficiaries—dominated by persons aged 65 and older.[4] The major measure of how Social Security affects well-being is its impact on the income of older persons. Social Security payments constitute the largest source of income for Americans over the age of 65, accounting for about 39 percent of the total.[5] But for those who are out of the labor force and have more moderate incomes, Social Security plays a more critical role (Grad, 1994). For example, the two-fifths of elderly families with the lowest resources rely on Social Security for more than 75 percent of their incomes (see Table 4.2). These individuals and couples have very low incomes, due in large measure to their lack of pensions and income from savings. For these families, Social Security, even if quite low, is their main safety net.

By any measure of economic well-being, the circumstances of older Americans have improved substantially since the mid 1950s. Average incomes and assets for persons over 65 have risen dramatically. For example, per capita incomes for those 65 and older have grown steadily, from a median of $3,408 in 1975 to $10,808 in 1993 (Cleveland, 1995; Henson, 1990). After controlling for inflation, this represents a 24 percent gain in the purchasing power of this age group.

But while it is perfectly correct to say that the elderly as a group have shown impressive gains, that is not the same as arguing that each elderly individual experienced such gains. Older Americans vary greatly in their well-being, depending on their age, ethnic origin, and marital status. For example, in 1992, black men had per capita median incomes of $7,539, or less than two-thirds the level of their white

TABLE 4.2. Shares of Aggregate Income of the Elderly, by Total Income Quintiles, 1992.

		Quintiles[a]				
Unit Source of Income	Total	1st	2nd	3rd	4th	5th
Percentage of income from:						
Social Security	39.5%	81.0%	77.3%	61.8%	46.2%	20.0%
Any pension	19.6	2.6	7.8	16.7	23.9	21.9
Public pensions	9.4	1.2	3.6	7.2	10.6	11.2
Private pensions or annuities	10.2	1.4	4.2	9.5	13.3	10.7
Earnings	17.1	0.1	2.8	6.5	10.6	27.1
Income from assets	20.6	3.3	6.4	11.6	16.4	29.0
Public assistance	0.9	11.4	3.0	0.5	0.1	0.0
Other	2.3	1.6	2.6	2.8	2.7	2.0
Total Percentage	100.0	100.0	100.0	100.0	100.0	100.0

Source: Susan Grad (1994), Table VI.B.5.

[a]Couples and unmarried persons age 65 and over for quintile limits of $6,939, $11,226, $17,645, and $29,052.

TABLE 4.3. Median Incomes for Various Groups of Older Americans, 1992.

	All Elderly	Single	Married
Age			
65–69	$12,551	$11,500	$12,884
70–74	11,294	10,651	11,658
75–79	10,426	10,262	10,678
80–84	9,600	9,591	9,609
85+	9,100	9,152	8,910
Male			
White	$12,118	$12,893	$12,007
Black	7,539	7,833	7,408
Other	9,585	11,984	8,963
Female			
White	$11,000	$10,043	$11,901
Black	6,442	6,290	7,308
Other	9,333	7,849	8,458

Source: Calculated by author using data from the Current Population Survey, March 1993.

counterparts. Black single women have the lowest median incomes in Table 4.3, averaging just 57 percent of that for all elderly persons (Moon and Mulvey, 1995). Moreover, median incomes decline steadily with age, leaving the oldest old with lower incomes and less flexibility to adjust their incomes over time for needs such as health care expenses. These differences reflect both cohort effects (the fact that each new age grouping tends to be better off than the last) and an aging effect (i.e., the decline of income as individuals age).[6]

2. Poverty

Another way to look at the economic status of older Americans is through measures of poverty. Since one of Social Security's explicit goals was to alleviate poverty, this is a particularly relevant measure. The long-term trend in the poverty rate, which focuses attention on those at the bottom of the income distribution, has declined dramatically for the elderly, again implying that well-being in general has improved (see Figure 4.1). The share of the elderly in poverty dropped from 28.5 percent in 1966 to a low of 11.4 percent in 1989. The largest declines in poverty rates for the elderly occurred before 1975, however, and the rates have remained relatively flat since 1984 (U.S. Bureau of Census, 1969 through 1993b). By 1992, the poverty rate had again risen to 12.9 percent—above its 1985 level. In 1993, it fell back to 12.2 percent (U.S. Congress, 1994).

Moreover, within the elderly population, poverty rates, like income levels, vary substantially. The most important distinctions are by race and by living arrangements. Women living alone show particularly high rates of poverty; three out of 10 women living alone over the age of 80 are poor (Table 4.4). Black women between the ages of 80 and 84 have poverty rates approaching 50 percent.

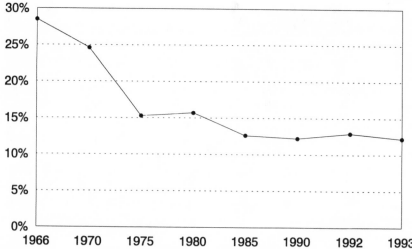

Figure 4.1. Official poverty rates for persons age 65 and over. *Source:* Based on data from Current Population Reports, Consume Income Series, P-60, U.S. Bureau of the Census.

These statistics are based on the standard poverty definitions used by the Bureau of the Census, and thus are important for purposes of comparison and consistency with commonly reported data. But measurement issues surrounding these statistics have led to claims of both higher and lower rates of poverty than the official numbers. For example, reporting problems are thought to result in an understatement of income for the elderly on the most commonly used survey.[7]

In addition, poverty numbers have been questioned by researchers who would add the value of noncash benefits, particularly for the Medicare and Medicaid health care programs, to income for purposes of calculating poverty (Hurd, 1989; Smeeding, 1982). Such an approach yields much lower poverty rates, particu-

TABLE 4.4. Poverty Rates by Selected Groups, (as a percentage) 1992.

	All	White	Black	Other	Living Alone
Men					
65–69	9.08	7.25	25.77	26.79	19.69
70–74	6.97	5.59	20.45	3.80	15.91
75–79	8.92	6.76	36.09	33.90	16.07
80–84	10.96	8.74	35.28	23.12	19.11
85+	13.18	10.89	31.35	15.63	18.66
Women					
65–69	11.47	8.85	32.81	30.44	22.08
70–74	14.06	12.0	36.66	24.33	25.31
75–79	17.02	14.53	44.59	20.67	25.65
80–84	21.70	19.46	47.56	46.67	31.26
85+	22.67	21.85	32.41	48.32	30.16

Source: Current Population Survey, March 1993.

larly among the elderly, for whom medical benefits are very large. But although these programs have certainly helped many low-income older Americans, estimating poverty in this way yields the peculiar result that the sicker the demographic group, the better off it will be when medical benefits are counted as income. Since persons over age 65 have expenditures about three times as high as younger persons, medical benefits covered for the elderly will always have a greater impact on reducing poverty if the insurance value is simply added in as part of income.

And as health care costs have risen since the early-1980s the problems of using such a measure have become more apparent. For example, spending for the same benefit package has far outstripped income growth, so that if nothing else changed, it would appear that fewer elderly persons are in poverty each year. Using those methods, a very elderly homeless person with no cash income, but who was eligible for Medicare, still would not be counted as poor—certainly a nonsensical result. In practice, incorporating the value of these benefits in reducing poverty is a difficult task and one likely to need to be undertaken only in conjunction with other changes in the poverty threshold measure itself.[8]

In recent years criticism of poverty measures has led to other actual and proposed modifications that raise the numbers of elderly persons defined as poor. For example, even with Medicare coverage, many seniors have substantial out-of-pocket liabilities for health care that should be taken into account. Recent work by Weinberg and Lamas (1993) indicated that just adjusting for medical care costs could raise the aged poverty rate to as high as 20.1 percent.

Another analysis of poverty measurement suggests other reasons why the rates may be understated overall (Ruggles, 1990). Ruggles argued that these problems are particularly important for measuring poverty among the elderly. First, the official estimates use lower poverty lines for one- and two-person households with heads over age 65, even though those distinctions now make little sense in terms of the consumption patterns and needs of the elderly. Further, the measures of poverty we use for all persons have lagged behind the growth in our living standards in general. Updating these measures would result in even more persons being classified as poor. Poverty rates for the elderly are particularly sensitive to the level of the poverty thresholds used, because a very large number of older persons have incomes just above or below the official poverty lines.

The 1992 poverty rates for all elderly persons would rise from 12.9 percent, if the traditional measure were used, to 23.7 percent if poverty were measured by an alternative standard, that is 1.25 times the nonelderly threshold (Moon and Mulvey, 1995).[9] Various subgroups of the elderly show similar dramatic differences in reported poverty rates (Figure 4.2). Over one-third of those age 85 and above would be poor by this alternative measure, and more than two-fifths of women living alone would be classified as poor.

Poverty statistics thus indicate that gains made by seniors may have been overstated. Poverty has not been eliminated; indeed, it is in actuality likely to be substantially higher than reported in the official statistics, perhaps approaching one-fourth of all persons aged 65 and above, although these are rather imperfect measures. Social Security benefits, which are very important to the lowest income groups, have still not been able to eliminate poverty.

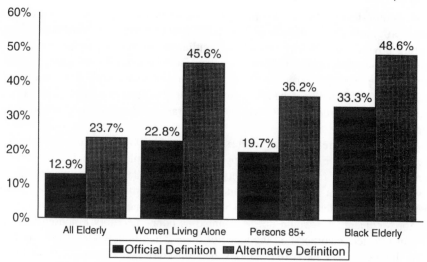

Figure 4.2. Impact of alternative poverty definitions on rate of elderly poverty. *Source:* Based on M. Moon and J. Mulvey. *Entitlements and the Elderly.* Washington, D.C.: Urban Institute Press, 1996. Table 2.5.

3. Assets

Another element of economic well-being, wealth, is generally reflected in the asset incomes of the elderly. But before drawing conclusions concerning the economic status of older Americans using only income, it is important to consider their assets as well. Assets have advantages in addition to the income they generate; control over a stock of resources and the implicit advantages of, for example, owning one's own home also enhance well-being. Persons can deplete their assets to supplement their incomes, either formally by purchasing annuities or informally by dipping into these reserves to meet their needs. Even when assets are not drawn down in this way, they represent a type of insurance available to older persons against the need to meet unusual expenses. And older families do have higher assets than younger families. For example, median net worth for all households was $41,472 in 1991, but $85,226 for those whose head householder was over age 65 (Eller, 1994).

One response by casual observers to the modest incomes of the elderly is that they may be income poor but asset rich. This claim is considerably exaggerated, however. Most of the elderly who have substantial assets, particularly financial (liquid) assets, also have substantial incomes. Older persons with modest means are likely to hold much of their wealth in housing, an asset that is difficult to liquidate to meet short-term needs and that may carry substantial burdens in the form of high taxes or maintenance costs as well. For example, median net worth falls from $85,226, to $27,673 if home equity is excluded from the overall net worth numbers. Financial assets, which can be readily used to meet short-term needs, are very unequally distributed across the elderly population. Elderly households with incomes in the bottom quintile of the population (which captures about 35 percent of elderly households with the lowest incomes) have median net worth excluding home equity of $3,577.[10] Elderly families who rank in the top 20 percent of all households in the United States have net worth excluding home equity of $299,679. Thus, while the elderly hold more assets, on average, than other families with low and moderate incomes, even if these assets are taken into account, relatively few of today's low-income elderly would be counted as well-off.

The overall picture of the well-being of older Americans is mixed. They have experienced considerable improvement over time, but certain subgroups of the elderly remain financially vulnerable. Moreover, it is difficult to conclude whether Social Security benefits are *too* high or *too* low without further comparisons to other people or across time. Thus, another issue is how well off Social Security beneficiaries are as compared to others.

INTERGENERATIONAL COMPARISONS

One benchmark for making judgements about Social Security is whether these benefits are reasonable in comparison to the standard of living of younger families who are currently paying taxes to support these benefit levels. Since Social Security operates on a pay-as-you-go basis, it is quite natural to compare whether those who fund the beneficiaries are as well off as the recipients of these payments. This is a natural question to ask as well because incomes for many Americans did not grow very rapidly in the 1970s, 1980s, and early 1990s. Is the generosity of legislation passed in the early 1970s to expand Social Security (reflecting earlier economic growth) putting the economic status of retirees ahead of that of workers? If so, this would be one potential reason to conclude that Social Security benefits are too high.

There are a number of alternative ways to measure these intergenerational comparisons. The most straightforward is to compare income between the young and the old. For example, in 1992 the median income of households headed by persons under the age of 65 was $35,639. For households headed by persons aged 65 or older the median income stood at $17,160. This may be somewhat misleading, however, since younger households are larger than older ones.[11] If we examine instead per capita incomes, the figures would be closer, for example, $22,013 for men under age 65 and $14,548 for men aged 65 and older (U.S. Bureau of the Census, 1993a). And if after-tax incomes were examined, the amounts would be closer still.

Between 1962 and 1984, the elderly's income growth outstripped increases in income for the population under age 65. For example, Radner (1995) has found that the ratio of aged to nonaged median incomes (adjusted for size of unit) rose from .526 to .727 over that period (see Table 4.5). While average before-tax incomes for elderly families still lagged behind those of younger families, after adjusting for differences in family size and tax liabilities, the disposable (posttax) incomes of older Americans began to compare favorably with those of the young. In fact, some researchers have claimed that the overall well-being of the elderly now is on a par with or even exceeds that of younger families (Danziger et al., 1984; Smeeding, 1986). Even this optimistic view would not suggest that all the elderly are rich, but rather that their economic status is now more on a par with the young.

Between 1984 and 1989, the status of elderly families declined relative to the young, with the ratio of aged to nonaged adjusted income falling to .693 (Table 4.5). It then bounced up again to .725 during the recession year of 1990 and back to .710

TABLE 4.5. Ratio of Aged to Nonaged Family Unit Median Incomes, Adjusted for Size of Unit and Age, Selected Years, 1967–1990.

Year	Ratio
1967	0.526
1972	.572
1977	.603
1979	.604
1980	.631
1981	.668
1982	.699
1983	.710
1984	.727
1985	.712
1986	.706
1987	.697
1988	.693
1989	.693
1990	.725
1991	.720
1992	.710

Source: Radner (1995), p. 31.

by 1992. It is inevitable that in some years one group will gain relative to the other. For instance, the early 1980s were a period of decelerating inflation, and lags in Social Security payments are likely to have helped the elderly "catch up" relative to the young. Further, older Americans are less sensitive to upturns in unemployment, so, as expected, that ratio rose again in 1990.

Poverty statistics tell a parallel story. In 1982, for the first time, the official rate of poverty among the elderly was lower than that for the rest of the population, and the gap has widened since then. The discrepancies are particularly large between children and persons over age 65. If the comparison, instead, is among adults, rates of poverty are still higher for the elderly. And, as indicated, because of the large numbers of elderly persons with incomes just above the poverty level, if an alternative, and somewhat more generous measure, of poverty is used, the elderly look even worse relative to younger families and individuals. For example, at 1.25 times the poverty level, 19.2 percent of the nonelderly and 37.2 percent of children are listed as poor, but 23.7 percent of the elderly and 45.6 percent of elderly women living alone would fall under 1.25 times the poverty level (if held the same as for the under 65 population) (Moon and Mulvey, 1995).

OTHER COMPLICATING FACTORS

As discussed earlier, a final judgement on whether Social Security benefits are too high or too low must be answered subjectively by each questioner. In addition to the issues just laid out, which provide statistics for that debate, are a number of additional, more subjective, factors. These do not directly relate to the question of whether benefits are too high or too low, but likely color the attitudes of anyone analyzing Social Security.

One of these is the issue of *windfall gains*. Over the history of Social Security, many beneficiaries have drawn out of the system much more than they paid in. This occurs for many reasons. Some of the windfalls went to very early retirees who benefitted from the rules that paid benefits before they had contributed for very long into the system. This phenomenon is probably best viewed as an artifact of the Great Depression. It was viewed as essential to provide relief to older Americans at a period when they were desperately poor.

A second source of windfall has occurred in part because of the "success" of programs aimed at older persons. Today Americans live much longer than they did when Social Security was first instituted, probably due in part to the benefits that Social Security brought in terms of higher income and better medical benefits (under Medicare). Moreover, growth in the economy in the 1960s and 1970s was shared via ad hoc increases in the benefit formula, impacts that have carried over into this era of lower wage growth. Another reason for these windfalls was the Social Security "notch" issue that provided higher benefits to a group of retirees born between 1911 and 1916 (and corrected for anyone born after that date).[12] Whatever the reason, however, some Americans look at current beneficiaries' payment levels and conclude that they are higher than they "deserve" to be.

Another way to look at the issue of the adequacy of benefits is in terms of what is affordable in the future as the population ages and more people become eligible for benefits. Essentially, there are two issues that need to be considered. The first is the practical question of meeting the promises that are made for benefit levels into the future. Benefits might be considered too high merely because it will be difficult to raise the funds necessary to meet the obligations. For example, maintaining a stable replacement rate over time may create problems when other factors are changing, particularly those that affect our ability to finance future benefits. Just as earlier periods sought an orderly rise in the replacement rate, should we consider a slow decline? If the answer is yes, we might view the current benefit formula as too generous.

And related to that is the issue of intergenerational equity: how much burden should be placed on future workers to pay for the retirees of the future? While the issue of the future health of Social Security is addressed explicitly elsewhere in this volume, it colors any discussion of the adequacy and reasonableness of the promises made. The long lead time necessary for a stable transition to any changes in retirement benefits implies that change needs to begin before a crisis is at hand. For purposes of equity, lower benefits might be appropriate, even if not essential, to bring the system into actuarial balance. Moreover, future cuts in benefits will affect the working population, who might view cuts on current retirees as important for the symbolic purpose of demonstrating shared sacrifice.

But it is also important to recognize that we do not know what the future will hold. Demography is not destiny; while the future balance between working and retiree populations will certainly make it more difficult to afford benefits, other factors will also influence future burdens. Projecting the rise of wages over time, which is essential to determine future burdens, is fraught with uncertainty. Imagine, for example, estimating in 1935 the economic circumstances of workers in the 1970s.

CONCLUSIONS

Social Security has been very successful in helping to raise the standard of living of older Americans and persons with disabilities. It now accounts for a higher share of income for persons over age 65 than in 1962 (Grad, 1994). The buying power of seniors has improved and rates of poverty have declined.

Are benefits too low because poverty remains? A good case can likely be made that survivors' benefits are too low to provide an adequate floor of protection (Burkhauser 1994). But in other areas, it may be very difficult to use Social Security to solve the remaining problems of income, particularly for persons who have been poor all their lives. The introduction of Supplemental Security Income in 1974 was intended to bolster the incomes of low income persons, and many advocates of eliminating poverty stress the importance of improving SSI rather than Social Security if that is our principal goal (Munnell, 1977).

What about the other side of the question, that is, is Social Security too high? Even if further protections are offered for low income persons, should the overall average come down? The main reasons for arguing this side of the question would likely center on the future affordability of sustaining such benefits, in which case this answer is more relevant for some point in the future, particularly since there are practical reasons why it is difficult to fund future benefits with cuts on today's beneficiaries.

Alternatively, the progress of the elderly relative to the young in our society has created somewhat of a backlash. It is the very success of the Social Security system that has led to some calls for reducing its generosity even for current beneficiaries. The evidence does seem to indicate that, as a society, we have done a reasonably comprehensive job of sharing economic growth with elderly and disabled persons outside the mainstream of the economic system. But there is considerable room for debate about exactly where older Americans stand relative to the young. And, it would be a mistake either to attribute all of the narrowing of economic well-being between the two to the burdens that Social Security places on the young or to use that as the major reason for cutting benefits.

Finally, it is likely to be more realistic to consider changes for the future to gradually alter Social Security rather than proposals that lead to rapid reductions in benefits in the near term. Older Americans in their 50s and 60s have already made a lot of decisions about retirement, savings, and other activities, based on expected benefits. Adjusting to change takes time, and so, even if benefits seem too generous, proposals for change need to be balanced against these constraints.

ENDNOTES

1. The term "progressivity" is more often applied to taxation—and then in the opposite direction—requiring higher tax contributions as a share of income from those with higher incomes.

2. See also the discussion of historical replacement rates in Reno and Friedland (chapter 11).

3. The indexing error from the 1972 amendments became apparent when rates of inflation exceeded wage growth in the mid-1970s. Efforts to correct this problem led to the 1977 amendments. But the correction has also proven to be controversial, leading to the so-called notch problem. A vocal group of retirees born after 1916 who were subject to the correction noted that their benefits were lower than benefits for similar persons born in 1915 or 1916. Essentially, they want to have the same error in their favor that the earlier retirees received. A good discussion of this issue can be found in a study by the National Academy of Social Insurance (1988).

4. In actuality, only 73 percent of Social Security beneficiaries are over the age of 65, but it is difficult to obtain information on the other beneficiary groups' income. And by retiring between age 62 and 65, workers accept lower lifetime monthly benefits.

5. In practice Social Security operates as it was intended: as a partial replacement program in which individuals and families are expected to supplement these benefits with other income sources.

6. For example, after adjusting for inflation, median incomes of persons aged 65 to 69 in 1987 were higher than for the same cohort in 1992 (when they were aged 70 to 74).

7. An alternative, The Survey of Income and Program Participation, seems to have better reporting of income and thus finds lower rates of poverty as well. But the census has not reconciled these differences, so the official poverty numbers are reported in this paper.

8. If changes are made to both resources and the standard against which those resources are judged, the problems of bias from health benefits disappears.

9. For nonelderly persons, the formal poverty rate is 14.7 percent, and 19.2 percent are below 1.25 times the threshold (U.S. Bureau of the Census, 1993b).

10. The census study (Eller, 1994) divided the entire population into fifths (or quintiles) of households based on levels of income. When the income limits that divide the groups are applied to elderly households, a larger proportion are in the bottom quintile and a smaller proportion are in the top income group.

11. Making broad comparisons of this sort requires a number of assumptions about equivalence that are subject to considerable debate. For example, most analysts agree that we ought to adjust incomes for differences in family size in comparing across different demographic groups, but there is no consensus about what the exact adjustment should be. Showing income per family tends to understate well-being for the old (since family sizes are smaller for those over age 65), but per capita numbers are biased in exactly the opposite direction. Thus, there can be disagreement about exactly how the elderly compare to the younger population, but it would be very difficult to argue that the elderly are substantially better off than their younger counterparts, as some have claimed.

12. In fact, these benefits were so high that the group of retirees born just after 1916 have termed themselves notch babies and sought to share in this windfall.

CHAPTER 5

Are Returns on Payroll Taxes Fair?

YUNG-PING CHEN AND STEPHEN C. GOSS

INTRODUCTION

Attempts to answer the question of what return on taxes Social Security benefits provide are generally referred to as "money's worth" studies.[1] The concept of money's worth has come to include a wide range of questions and several analytical approaches to answering these questions. In essence, the central question is whether an individual or a group of persons can expect to get a "fair" return in the form of benefits for the tax contributions made to the Social Security program, defined as Old-Age, Survivors, and Disability Insurance (OASDI).

Unlike an annuity purchased from a private insurance company, Social Security benefits are not intended solely to provide fair or equitable rates of return to all groups of workers. The program was, and still is, designed to strike a compromise between the desire to provide a minimally adequate "floor of protection" for even those workers with very low earnings and the desire to provide a reasonably equitable return for even the highest-paid workers. Providing a floor of protection requires that some groups receive more than a financially equitable return, while others receive less than an equitable return. For this reason, we should expect to find divergent rates of return for different groups of workers.

Moreover, the success and value of the program cannot be determined through individual money's worth calculations alone. For example, the monetary and social value of the program to higher-paid workers transcends the amount of benefits that they may personally expect to receive. Absent Social Security, many lower-paid workers could not save enough to provide a minimally adequate retirement income and would thus require some form of public assistance in their old age. The mandatory withholding of Social Security payroll taxes from the lower-paid workers assures that they will make some reasonable contribution toward the cost of their retirement income. The resulting cost to the higher-paid of subsidizing the retirement income needs of the lower-paid is thus almost certainly less when financed through the Social Security program than if, for example, it were financed with income taxes through public assistance.

While the analysis of rates of return in the form of benefits for Social Security taxes paid for different groups must be viewed in this broader context, the analysis is still of interest. It provides a measure that may be used to describe the effects of the program in balancing the goals of social adequacy and individual equity.

In a broad financial sense, the return on tax contributions made to Social Security is remarkably fair and efficient. Because of the scope of coverage (virtually the entire work force) and the mandatory nature of Social Security (no need for a sales force), administrative expenses amount to less than 1 percent of benefit costs. Thus, over 99 percent of all income into the system will be paid out in the form of benefits. No private insurer approaches this level of administrative efficiency. This straightforward observation, however, gives little assistance in answering questions related to the fairness of return for specific groups of workers.

Questions about the fairness of return may relate to any specific group of taxpayers identified by age, year of birth (or cohort), race, sex, marital status, or earnings level. The method of assessing fairness of return generally involves comparing tax contributions made to Social Security by a group to the actual or expected benefits received by the group.

Because benefits for individuals are usually received many years after their contributions are paid, the amounts of benefits and contributions are generally accumulated forward or discounted backward, with interest, to a common date, in order to adjust for the time value of money. So adjusted, the amounts are said to be expressed in their present value as of the common date. Comparisons using present value thus effectively determine whether expected or actual Social Security benefits are less than, equal to, or greater than the amount that could have been paid to the group had their contributions all been invested in an account and accumulated with interest until they retired, died, or became disabled.

For the very large majority of workers, payroll taxes are paid in equal shares by the employee and the employer. Whether rates of return from the workers' perspective should compare the value of benefits to taxes paid by the employee only, or to taxes paid by both the employee and the employer, has been the subject of extensive debate. The answer depends on whether and to what extent the burden of taxes paid by the employer is shifted to the employee.[2]

In fact, rates of return for various groups differ considerably for a number of reasons, including the following:

1. The "weighted" benefit formula tends to provide a greater rate of return for lower-paid earners.
2. Parameters such as retirement age and reduction for early retirement are gender neutral and race neutral. Thus, for example, groups of workers with relatively longer life expectancy (such as females) may expect to receive a greater than average return in the form of primary retired-worker benefits due to the common retirement age. Because the common reduction and increment factors for early and delayed retirement are too large for groups with longer life expectancy, their higher return is greatest when retirement is delayed and least when it is early.

3. In addition to primary worker benefits, Social Security also pays benefits to spouses and children of workers under certain circumstances. As a result, the return on taxes should be expected to be higher, on average, for married than for nonmarried workers.

4. The Social Security program is a redistributive group insurance program, not an individual savings vehicle like the Individual Retirement Account. Thus, like any insurance, Social Security will tend to benefit some individuals more than others, depending upon the chance occurrence of early death, disability before reaching retirement age, or longer-than-average life after retirement.

5. The Social Security program is financed on a "temporary partially advance funded" basis, not far from a pay-as-you-go basis. As a result, the cost to each successive generation of workers will depend upon the average number of children earlier generations had, and the extent to which earlier generations experienced increases in average life span. For example, workers born in periods when birth rates were relatively low will need to pay relatively higher taxes if benefit levels are to be maintained for the relatively large cohorts of retirees collecting during their working careers.

The intent of this chapter is to summarize some of the recent research that explores the answers to the many questions related to money's worth. We hope that this summary will provide a guide for the interested reader to explore the wealth of literature in this area.

TYPES OF MONEY'S WORTH ANALYSIS

There are two basic types of money's worth analysis, empirical and hypothetical. Empirical analysis is based on the availability of actual earnings and benefit records for individuals who have retired. In the pure form, empirical analysis would be limited to cases where benefits were exhausted due to death. In practice, however, this approach would be impractical because analysis would be restricted to cohorts where all, or the vast majority, have died. Therefore, this approach is generally applied to samples of recent retirees where benefits for the remainder of life are estimated, based on projected life expectancy. True case-to-case variation in money's worth is thus lost, but average money's worth relationships for differing groups by age (birth year), sex, race, and income level are possible. It is this kind of distributional analysis for workers who survive to retirement age that is best supported by empirical money's worth analysis.

In contrast, hypothetical money's worth analysis involves the constructing of one or more hypothetical-worker or hypothetical-family cases. The hypothetical earnings records are generally assumed to be at constant levels relative to the average wage level (most often average wage, low earner at approximately minimum wage, and high earner at maximum wage subject to payroll taxes) for each year of working age. In a limited form, survival to retirement age may be assumed to be certain, thus restricting the analysis in the same way as occurs for empirical studies. Some studies, however, consider more fully the range of risks covered by the OASDI program by modeling the probability of death or disability starting immediately after entry into the work force. In this comprehensive form, hypothetical studies can assess money's worth, including the total OASDI tax rate because all benefits payable on the basis of such taxes are included. Limited hypothetical studies and empirical studies must make some adjustment in the amount of the OASDI taxes included because benefits for disability and for some or all survivor situations are excluded. The hypothetical money's worth approach is not as readily applicable to analyzing differences among certain groups, especially racial groups adjusted by income level, because the life tables necessary for hypothetical studies are not available by race and income level. However, hypothetical analysis permits estimating money's worth for persons retiring in the future, thus allowing effective analysis of intergenerational variations over long periods of time.

Another dimension in types of money's worth analysis involves the way in which the relationship between the present value of tax contributions and the present value of benefits is presented. Approaches are: (1) rate of return—the implied interest rate on accumulated contributions that equates the present value of contributions and the present value of benefits, (2) money's worth ratio—the ratio of the present value of benefits to the present value of tax contributions, (3) tax-benefit ratio (the inverse of the money's worth ratio)—the ratio of the present value of tax contributions to the present value of benefits, (4) repayment time—the number of months that benefits must be received in order to get back in benefits the present value of contributions, and (5) net subsidy—the difference between the present value of benefits and the present value of contributions.

Assessing money's worth for each of these approaches is accomplished differently. Rate-of-return analysis involves comparing the implied rate of return to the rate of return that might have been realized under other circumstances; for example, if contributions had been invested at some market interest rate and withdrawn at retirement for the purchase of an annuity. Money's worth ratio and tax-benefit ratio provide direct measures of money's worth at the assumed interest rate used for computing present value. Repayment time provides a rough basis for comparing relative money's worth for different groups or generations, but requires comparison with life expectancy for each group if the level of money's worth is to be fully understood. Net subsidy analysis provides a different and interesting approach to money's worth analysis. However, because net subsidies are presented in dollar-level form, care must be taken in presenting net subsidies for different generations; whether the net-subsidy dollar amounts for generations with different years of retirement are made "comparable" by indexing with price changes, wage changes, or interest rates makes a substantial difference.

DATA SOURCES AND METHODOLOGY

1. Data Sources

Empirical Studies. The data most often used by researchers for empirical money's worth analysis are derived from several large random sample datasets:

- 1973 Exact Match File—combines relevant information about individuals from the Bureau of the Census, the Internal Revenue Service, and the Social Security Administration.
- Social Security Administration (SSA) 1988 Continuous Work History Survey— preserves the complete work histories from 1937 to 1988 of approximately 1 percent of all covered workers who retired before 1988.
- SSA Retirement History Survey—tracks a random sample of workers from 1969 through 1979 who were between ages 58 and 64 in 1969.
- 1967 Survey of Economic Opportunity—records earnings data for a large cross-sectional sample of the population for 1966.

Hypothetical Studies. Hypothetical studies require life tables (specifically death or survival rates), or life expectancies, for the group(s) to be studied. Life tables for such analysis are available from a number of sources including tables by year (past and projected) and by sex produced by the Social Security Administration for the annual Trustees Reports; tables by year (past and projected), by sex and by race, produced periodically by the Bureau of the Census; and the Decennial United States Life Tables (most recently available for 1979–81), by sex and by race, produced by the National Centers for Health Statistics.

Life table functions may be used to simulate the likelihood of surviving to retirement age and beyond, for single workers, as well as for married couples and survivors. With the addition of disability rates based on data from the Social Security Disability Insurance program, the full range of potential benefits payable under the OASDI program can be modeled with the hypothetical approach.

2. Methodology

Each researcher must develop a methodology for making money's worth comparisons. How is money's worth to be computed? And what groups of workers and recipients are being compared? The most common groups used to illustrate differences in money's worth are those distinguished by earnings level, taxable-earnings level, income level, age at entry into labor force, marital status, race, sex, education, cohort during one or several consecutive years, wealth (value of total assets), age at retirement from work, and age at initial entitlement to a Social Security benefit.

Money's worth compares the value of a worker's benefits to the "cost" of those benefits, that is, his or her taxes. The costs are incurred over the worker's career, and the benefits are received monthly until the worker and spouse, if any, are deceased. To fairly compare taxes and benefits, one must recognize (1) the principle of the time value of money and (2) the principle of the uncertainty of survival. The first of these principles tells us that the only dollar that is worth exactly one dollar *today* is the dollar that I possess, receive, or spend *today*. The dollar that I earned or spent 10 years ago should be worth much *more* than a dollar today because, had I invested it in the bank, I would today have the dollar plus the compound interest accumulated on the investment for the past 10 years.

Correspondingly, the dollar that I will receive or spend 10 years from now is worth *less* than a dollar today because I would need to invest much less than one dollar in the bank today in order to have an accumulated balance of one dollar 10 years from now. I could have put a smaller amount in the bank at compound interest and used the original deposit plus the interest to cover the dollar due in the future. This valuation process for recognizing the time value of money is called "discounting to present value" or simply "present value." Every money's worth researcher uses it.

To compute the present value of a tax or benefit payment, one must select an interest rate to use (e.g., the assumed interest rate the bank would pay if I left the money to accumulate at compound interest). Within limits, selection of the interest rate is within the researcher's discretion. The "riskless" rate of return on long-term United States government bonds is often used. Often a discrepancy in results between researchers can be explained by differences in the interest rates used.

The second principle tells us that the value of taxes we plan to pay or the value of benefits we plan to receive in future years is progressively less for more and more distant years, because of the progressively increasing uncertainty of surviving to ever more distant years. For hypothetical studies (and for empirical studies after the closing date for data), discounting for the "expected value" of future amounts based on the uncertainty of survival is accomplished by applying estimated death rates in order to compute the likelihood of surviving to each successive age until the probability of survival reaches zero. For some studies, survival up to retirement is taken to be certain, thus excluding the implications of the uncertainty of survival through the working years.

Using discounting principles for both present value (interest) and expected value (survival) in the method of valuation, researchers have divided Social Security benefits into two basic components: The "actuarially fair" component and the "redistributional" or "transfer" component.

The *actuarially fair* component is the amount of benefits that could be provided to a group or an individual based on the payroll taxes paid. A social insurance system is actuarially fair for a group or an individual if the present value of the taxes paid (or expected to be paid) equals the present value of the benefits received (or expected to be received). Stated another way, if paying the same amounts at the same time as I paid in payroll taxes to purchase a private annuity from a reputable insurance company operating in a perfectly competitive market would get me the same benefits at the same time as I received them from Social Security, then my Social Security benefits are actuarially fair.

In computing whether expected benefits are actuarially fair, it is necessary to decide whether only employee taxes or both employee and employer taxes will be considered (for wage and salary earners, payroll taxes are paid half by employees and half directly by employers). Most money's worth analyses permit making this assessment either way.

A *redistributional* or *transfer element* is the difference between the actual level of Social Security benefits and the actuarially fair level of benefits associated with taxes paid. This element may be analyzed from two different points of view: "intragenerational" and "intergenerational" transfers.

Intragenerational transfers result from differences in the characteristics of individuals within a generation. For example, lower-earning workers receive monthly benefits that are proportionately greater, relative to their contributions, than higher-earning workers'. If worker A makes exactly twice as much as worker B, and pays twice the payroll taxes, he or she will generally receive a monthly benefit higher than A, but not twice as high. In this way some of the taxes paid by high earners are "transferred" to the lower earners. For another example, workers with spouses and children who may receive benefits based on the earnings record of the worker effectively receive transfers from other workers with the same earnings and taxes who have no spouses or children.

Intergenerational transfers may occur between generations because Social Security is financed on essentially a temporary, partially advance funded basis, not far from a pay-as-you-go basis. Younger workers' taxes are used, to a considerable extent, to pay benefits to current retirees. Whenever changing birthrates and life expectancies result in a changing ratio of current beneficiaries to current workers, workers paying taxes at the time this ratio is high tend to have higher tax rates, thus making transfers to members of the generation that is currently receiving benefits. In the discussion of research findings for the "cohort" variable, the magnitude of the intergenerational transfer is discussed further.

RESULTS

All researchers agree that, until a short time ago, almost all workers who reached retirement age could expect to receive at least their money's worth (for their employee taxes) in the form of Social Security retirement benefits; in other words, the Social Security retirement annuity was at least actuarially fair. They have, however, also found very large redistribution components, both intragenerational and intergenerational. Results of analysis of money's worth issues differ somewhat depending upon whether the analysis was empirical or hypothetical.

1. Empirical Studies

As mentioned earlier, empirical data allow analysis of a number of issues that are difficult to deal with in hypothetical studies. Empirical studies are particularly good for analyzing the extent to which two or more characteristics of workers may be associated or correlated, and thus may tend to offset or compound their expected effects.

Earnings Level. The Social Security benefit formula is designed to provide higher rates of return for lower-paid workers when all else is equal. Most researchers working with empirical data have found the *progressivity* relationship between earnings level and rate of return (Duggan, Gillingham, and Greenlees, 1993; Freiden, Leimer, and Hoffman, 1977; Hurd and Shoven, 1985; Meyer and Wolff, 1987b). Two factors have been found that tend to strengthen the progressivity intended in the benefit formula: interrupted work histories and periods of work outside covered employment, both of which are more common for lower-paid workers. These operate to enhance progressivity by increasing the difference in "career average" earnings, or AIME (Average Indexed Monthly Earnings), between higher- and lower-paid workers.

However, two factors have tended to reduce the strength of this relationship between earnings level and rate of return. First, lower-paid workers tend to have higher mortality rates than higher-paid workers, so they and their survivors receive benefits for a shorter period of time (Duggan, Gillingham, and Greenlees, 1993). Second, lower-paid workers tend to enter the labor force earlier than higher-paid workers, who often complete their schooling only in their mid to late 20s though they usually work while in school or during summers. Earlier entry into the labor force makes lower-paid workers likely to have more years of nonzero earnings, lessening the effect of the progressivity in the benefit formula. Thus, the difference between the average levels of career average earnings or AIME (and thus benefit levels) is smaller for higher-paid workers, versus lower-paid workers, than might be expected.

Because of these effects, some researchers have even found some *regressivity* among certain classes of workers. One study by Burkhauser and Warlick (1981) found that the very highest income groups ($10,000 + income in 1972) get better rates of return than the next highest group ($6,000 to $10,000), resulting in regressivity at the top earnings levels. Another study (Duggan, Gillingham, and Greenlees, 1993) found that among workers retiring between 1960 and 1968, the highest-paid third received higher rates of return than the lowest-paid third. Still another study (Meyer and Wolff, 1987a), which focused specifically on progressivity, found that the effects of shorter longevity and early work-force entry *diluted,* but did not eliminate, the progressivity of the benefit structure. But Aaron (1977) found that these two factors reversed progressivity and made the system slightly regressive for whites. It should be noted, however, that Aaron used life tables based on education, not on income, in measuring progressivity, and it may be that, for whites and blacks respectively, the correlations between education and earnings are not the same. It should also be noted that most of these results were based on the benefit formula in effect before the 1977 amendments. These amendments, along with increases in the maximum taxable amount, increase progressivity for future retirees.

Cohort. All researchers have found that earlier cohorts (workers born in more distant past years) have higher average rates of return. For example, one study (Duggan, Gillingham, and Greenlees, 1993) found that individuals retiring between 1960 and 1968 received an astounding 12.5 percent real rate of return on the taxes paid by and for them, while workers retiring from 1982 through 1987 received a much lower 5.9 percent real rate of return. All studies projecting future trends (see hypothetical studies, hereafter) have shown much lower real rates of return for future cohorts. The reasons for such high real rates of return to the original group of retirees are that (1) tax rates, which have always been set on a roughly pay-as-you-go basis, were initially very low because of the small numbers of persons who qualified for benefits at that time, and (2) the number of years after 1936 for which early beneficiaries needed to have paid taxes in order to qualify was relatively small. As the Social Security system has matured, (1) the number of beneficiaries has increased relative to the number of workers, thus necessitating higher tax rates; and (2) the number of years in which taxes are paid by the average beneficiary has increased. This phenomenon, however, has just about run its course, as maturation of the Social Security system is now essentially complete. Taxes would need to be raised dramatically, in an ever increasing spiral, if we desired to continue paying the high rates of return obtained by early cohorts of retirees.

Marital Status. In general, married couples get higher rates of return than do single workers, due to the availability of spousal and child benefits, which are provided for the married worker at no higher tax rate than for a single person earning the same wage. However, two-earner couples do much worse than one-earner couples (Leimer, 1978; Meyer and Wolff, 1987a) because in this case the taxes paid by the lower-earning spouse may result in little or no additional benefits for the couple; the benefits that can be received may be no greater than had the spouse not worked at all and merely claimed benefits on the other's earnings records. Of course, a two-earner couple will always receive at least as good a return as they would if they were not married.

Race. In general, nonwhites have been found to do better than whites (Duggan, Gillingham, and Greenlees, 1993; Freiden, Leimer and Hoffman, 1977; Meyer and Wolffa, 1987), largely because their average earnings are lower than whites, and they thus enjoy the benefits of progressivity. But other factors associated with low earnings (discussed previously) attenuate progressivity. Some studies have found that highly paid nonwhites have lower rates of return than highly-paid whites (Aaron, 1977; Leimer, 1978).

Sex. Single women have been found to have much higher rates of return in the form of the worker benefit than do single men, because their earnings are generally lower (letting them benefit more from progressivity), and they generally live longer (letting them receive benefits for a longer period of time). Rates of return for married men and women depend greatly upon whether the benefits that are compared to the individual's taxes are selected as benefits paid on the worker's account (including benefits paid to a spouse or children) or as benefits payable to the individual worker (including spouse benefits that are payable on the basis of the partner's account). The empirical analysis for married persons has been hampered because of the inability to match contributions and survivor benefits, most of which are paid to women.

Retirement Age. The early-retirement adjustment, whereby workers who retire before the normal retirement age (currently 65) receive a reduced monthly benefit, is approximately actuarially fair; in contrast, the delayed-retirement credit, under which workers who delay retirement until as late as age 70 receive increased monthly benefits, has been less than actuarially fair (Myers and Schobel 1992; Meyer and Wolff 1987b). The 1983 Social Security amendments, however, will eventually correct this "inequity" by gradually increasing the delayed-retirement credit over the next 15 years. Freidan, Leimer, and Hoffman (1977) reported finding considerable variability in the actuarial fairness of the early- and delayed-retirement adjustments over different worker types. Money's worth also varies by retirement age for another reason. Those who retire later tend to have more years of nonzero earnings and thus obtain less of the progressivity in the benefit formula.

2. Hypothetical Studies

As mentioned, hypothetical studies are useful for analyzing the effect of a single characteristic on money's worth, with all other characteristics kept constant. This is particularly the case for comparing money's worth across several birth cohorts. While cross-cohort analysis is difficult for empirical studies because the necessary longitudinal data for successive cohorts are generally not available on a consistent basis, simulating successive hypothetical cohorts is relatively easy. As a result, cross-cohort comparison has been a primary focus of hypothetical analyses.

Chen and Chu (1974) calculated tax-benefit ratios and rates of return for men retiring in 1974 and for men entering the work force at ages 18 and 22 in 1974.[3] Computing benefits for 1974 retirees on a life annuity approach (calculations were also made for certain survival up to the life expectancy of the retiree), they found that the present value of expected benefits was more than double the present value of employee plus employer taxes in every case (the tax-benefit ratio was less than one half). For new workers in 1974 (at either age 18 or age 22), the present value of expected benefits was found to be more than the present value of employee taxes (tax-benefit ratio less than one) but less than the present value of employee plus employer taxes (tax-benefit ratio greater than one) in every case.[4]

Restricting contributions to *employee* OASI taxes, Myers and Schobel found very high money's worth ratios (expected benefits were more than four times the value of employee contributions) for those retiring through 1980.[5] For those retiring after the year 2000, through 2027, money's worth ratios were much lower, but benefits were still greater than or about equal to the value of employee contributions for all but maximum earner males retiring in 2027 with benefits discounted at 3 percent. Money's worth ratios were, of course, found to be consistently higher for females (due to their longer life expectancy at retirement) than for males, and consistently lower for maximum workers than for average workers (due to the progressive benefit formula). Mortality assumptions varied by sex, age, and cohort, but not by earnings level. Thus, as with most hypothetical analyses, the effect of longer life expectancy for higher earners, which is indicated in empirical data, was not included.

Kollmann (1993) also considered single retirees across a range of cohorts (retirees at age 65 in years 1940 through 2030. Avoiding the use of mortality rates altogether, he computed the number of years for which benefits would need to be received in order to "recover" the present value of tax contributions. He considered steady minimum (federal minimum wage), average, and maximum earners and used the intermediate assumptions from the 1993 Trustees Report, including an ultimate real interest rate of 2.3 percent.

Kollmann considered tax contributions on two different bases, both excluding Disability Insurance (DI) taxes, because disability benefits were also excluded from consideration. The first approach included all employee OASI taxes, like Myers and Schobel's. For the second approach, Kollmann estimated "retirement" contributions by excluding a proportionate share of OASI taxes equal to the proportionate share of OASI payments used to pay survivor benefits (single workers generally have no survivors). He found that the numbers of years of benefits needed to recover employee contributions was very low (under 5) for workers retiring through the year 1980, whether OASI or retirement-only contributions were used. The number of years increased steadily for retirements thereafter, reaching 18.1 years for recovery of employee OASI taxes and 13.5 years for employee retirement taxes for maximum earner retirees in 2030. For the purpose of evaluating the absolute level of these values, he also provided life expectancies at age 65 from the 1993 Trustees Report, which were 16.7 years for men and 20.6 for women.

Kollmann also showed that the number of years needed to recover tax contributions from both the employee and the employer are more than double the number of years needed for employee contributions only, even though the present value of contributions at age 65 is precisely double. This results from the fact that the assumed discount rate (for interest) after retirement is greater than the rate of price inflation. Because Social Security benefits are increased at the rate of price inflation for each beneficiary after retirement, the present value of benefits for successive years decreases.

Goss and Nichols (1993) presented money's worth ratios for single workers and for married couples with one worker and two children. Unlike Myers and Schobel, or Kollmann, they started with workers entering the work force and included the probabilities of disability and death at each age, thus including the full range of disability, survivor, and dependents' benefits. Intermediate assumptions from the 1992 Trustees Report were used, including an ultimate real discount rate of 2.3 percent. Ratios were calculated assuming steady work with low, average, or maximum earnings until becoming disabled, dying, or reaching either age 62 or Normal Retirement Age (NRA), for cohorts that would reach age 62 in years 1982 through 2062.

Goss and Nichols found little difference in money's worth ratios between groups retiring at 62 or NRA. They found that the value of expected benefits exceeded the value of expected employee and employer contributions for all single men and women who would reach age 62 in 1982, for single low earners of any generation, and for one-earner married couples of any generation. While the value of benefits was found to exceed the value of employee taxes for all generations (even for single maximum earners), the authors noted that currently scheduled OASDI tax rates are insufficient to pay for scheduled benefits past about 2030. Thus, assuming some future increase in taxes or reductions in benefits, actual money's worth ratios will be somewhat lower than those based on present law.

Nichols (1994) updated the foregoing analysis on the basis of the intermediate assumptions of the 1994 Trustees Report and went further by assuming tax-rate increases beginning in 2020 that would be needed to continue financing the OASDI program on a pay-as-you-go basis. He found that, for the generation that would reach age 62 in 2056, the present value of benefits for the one-earner couple would generally exceed the value of the employee and employer taxes (equal to 99 percent of contributions for maximum earners), as too for single low earners (equal to 97 percent for men and 113 percent for women). The value of benefits for even single maximum earners was found to be about as high as the value of employee taxes (equal to 96 percent for men and 111 percent for women).

Steuerle and Bakija (1994) focused their analysis on present-value dollar amounts of benefits and contributions, as well as the difference between these amounts. The difference (benefits minus taxes) is referred to as the amount of transfer made to the particular type of beneficiary. They considered steady low, average, and maximum earners reaching age 65 in the years the 1965 through 2030. All cases were assumed to survive to retirement at NRA without disability, and OASI tax rates for both employees and employers were used. Cases included single men and women, one-earner couples, and two-earner couples. Although transfers were computed on a present value basis for each generation, amounts were expressed in 1993 dollars (indexed for price inflation) for comparing the transfer values across generations.

Steuerle and Bakija found positive transfers for all retirees through 1980, with the largest transfers in absolute dollar amount going to the *highest earners*. By 2010, transfers for retirees were found to be negative for single workers with average or higher earnings, and for two-earner couples with one high and one average earner. Positive transfers continued for low-earner single workers, all one-earner couples, and two-earner couples with one average and one low earner.

The results of these and other hypothetical studies confirm our expectations and the results of empirical studies: money's worth is greater for female than for male single workers, for one-earner couples than for two-earner couples or single workers, for low earners than for high earners, and for retirees through 1980 than for those retiring after the year 2000. Moreover, these studies point out the different perspectives on money's worth that may be gained by considering the years of benefits needed to recover taxes, the ratio of benefits to taxes, or the net transfer (benefits minus taxes). Even though all of these studies were based on essentially the same assumptions, the results obtained vary somewhat due to the approach taken to measure money's worth.

While money's worth ratios utilizing both employee and employer taxes are exactly half as large as ratios using only employee taxes, recovery times are somewhat more than twice as long, and net transfers worsen in a variety of ways with both employee and employer taxes included. While hypothetical money's worth ratios and recovery times are always less favorable for higher earners, net transfers are highest for maximum workers retiring through 1980. All approaches are consistent, however, on the fact that money's worth was higher for past retirees than it will be for future cohorts of retirees. This consistent conclusion results, of course, primarily from the fact that tax rates were set at very low levels in the early years of the Social Security program, when only a small percentage of the elderly population qualified for benefits. With the maturing of the OASDI program, virtually all members of more recent retiree cohorts have qualified for Social Security benefits. The higher payroll taxes that have resulted over the years have eliminated the highly favorable money's worth relationships experienced by the earliest retirees in the history of the program.

Future changes in the money's worth of the program for future retiree cohorts will depend on the level of birthrates, interest rates, and life expectancies for future cohorts of retirees. High birthrates result in a growing population with a high ratio of working-age to retirement-age persons. High birthrates thus allow lower tax rates and higher money's worth value. High interest rates relative to rates of growth in wage and price levels result in more discounting of the future value of benefits, thus making money's worth values lower. Increasing life expectancies necessitate either increasing tax rates or increasing NRA for successive cohorts. For each individual cohort, however, increasing life expectancy makes money's worth higher than if its life expectancy were no greater than that of prior cohorts.

CONCLUSIONS

On the whole, there is no doubt that the Social Security program provides exceptional money's worth. Program administrative expenses absorb less than one cent out of every dollar collected, with over 99 cents paid out in the form of benefits. However, due to the program's progressive benefit formula, provision for dependent benefits, sex- and race-blind provisions, and financing on an approximately pay-as-you-go basis, money's worth does, by design, vary considerably by several characteristics of tax-paying workers, including income level, family status, and year of birth.

The two basic approaches to money's worth analysis, empirical and hypothetical, have been utilized by a number of researchers who have contributed greatly to our understanding of this issue. Hypothetical studies, with their ability to focus clearly on variation in one characteristic at a time, have precisely quantified the program's tendency to provide greater returns per tax dollar for workers with lower earnings levels, for workers with nonworking spouses and children, and for those who have already begun to receive benefits. The greatest contribution of hypothetical studies, so far, has been to demonstrate the level of variation in money's worth by year of birth (cohort). Low tax rates in the early years of the history of the program, made possible by the approximate pay-as-you-go financing approach and the fact that few of the nation's elderly were eligible for benefits in 1940 and several years thereafter, resulted in very favorable money's worth for all types of workers in the early years, including those who have retired recently. Due to the maturation of the program to the point where now virtually all of the nation's elderly are eligible for some Social Security benefit, money's worth for current and future workers will be less favorable, providing only a reasonable rate of return, on the average.

Empirical studies have made a considerable, and growing, contribution to our understanding of money's worth differences for *real* groups of workers, reflecting the complex mix of characteristics that occur within subgroups of our population. For example, while hypothetical analyses illustrate the *tendency* of the program to provide greater money's worth to workers with lower earnings levels, empirical studies have shown that this tendency is sometimes more than offset by the effects of variation in other characteristics between high- and low-paid workers. Among these characteristics are life expectancy, which tends to be greater for higher earners, and starting age of employment, which tends to be later for higher earners. Both of these characteristics, as shown in empirical studies, work to offset the money's worth disadvantage provided for the high earners in the progressive benefit formula.

Although the Social Security program is intended to provide the same benefits and the same money's worth for workers of different sex or race, variation occurs because of differences in characteristics such as life expectancy and earnings level. Single females receive greater money's worth than single males due to their longer life expectancy. Variation in money's worth for married couples varies greatly depending upon whether one or both spouses work and pay payroll taxes. Money's worth for husbands and that for wives is further complicated by the question of whether to consider benefits paid to each spouse (which favors wives), or benefits paid on the basis of earnings of each spouse (which favors husbands).

Variation in money's worth by race, like that by sex, is not intended in the program design and thus depends on the variation in other characteristics among the races. Empirical studies have suggested that the tendency for nonwhites to have lower earnings levels and shorter life expectancies than whites tends to have offsetting effects on money's worth. More study will be needed to clarify variation in money's worth by race. For example, do shorter life expectancies result from differences in education or in income or in other factors?

We therefore find general agreement among researchers that the highest rates of return go to those who are members of an early cohort, are female, are members of a single-earner married household, and enter the labor force late. Researchers using empirical data disagree, however, upon the degree of progressivity and the extent of exceptions to it, due to the effects of increased mortality and lower earnings of those who are given the more progressive (or higher marginal) returns. The effect of a worker's race on progressivity is also in dispute, but there is agreement that race (like sex) per se is not a factor—it is race's strong association with earnings and mortality that make it a factor.

Research on money's worth has contributed to our understanding of how the Social Security program actually works and how well it accomplishes the variety of social objectives that have been set out for it. The financing currently scheduled in the law for the program will be insufficient to permit timely payment of benefits past the first 30 years of the next century, based on the intermediate assumptions used in the 1995 Trustees Report. Thus, further changes will be made to the tax and/or benefit structure of the program into the 2010s. Further work in the money's worth area will, undoubtedly, continue to contribute to the evolution and the shaping of the program as it changes to meet future challenges.

ENDNOTES

1. The authors acknowledge the valuable assistance of Richard W. McConaghy.

2. It is a reasonable assumption that an employer will attempt to shift his taxes onto someone else, either forward to the consumer by means of higher prices, or backward to the worker in the form of reduced compensation, or backward to the providers of other production factors. Otherwise, the employers' rate of return on capital investment will fall, reducing the profitability and viability of the business. In the process of shifting, however, the employer encounters much resistance, which takes time to overcome. Ultimately, workers will bear part of the employer taxes both as employees with reduced compensation (in backward shifting) and as consumers with higher prices (in forward shifting). In the long run, therefore, labor as a group would most likely bear a substantial part of the taxes formally paid by the employers. Even though it is impossible to ascertain the precise amount of the employer tax that falls upon the worker, it seems unreasonable to assume that no such shifting takes place. On the other hand, the assumption that the entire amount of the employer taxes is automatically borne by the worker, too, appears stringent. In the "Results" section in this chapter cited studies reflect a range of views on employer-tax shifting. In general, it is easy to translate results among the perspectives of considering only employee taxes, considering both employee and employer taxes, and considering something in between. For a discussion of this subject, see Chen (1967).

3. For years after 1974 they assumed average wage increases at 5 percent per year, price inflation at 3.125 percent per year, and real interest at 3 percent per year, along with mortality consistent with that used for the 1973 Trustees Report. Because workers were assumed to work and survive up to retirement at age 65, disability benefits were not reflected, nor were possible survivor benefits for early death. Payroll taxes were used in calculations, which were made for steady average and steady maximum earners, who received either a worker benefit only (single), a worker and a spouse benefit (married), or a family maximum benefit (married with eligible children). Calculations were made reflecting employee taxes only, employee plus employer taxes, and employee plus half of employer taxes.

4. The fact that the results for the new workers in 1974 are comparable to the results of later analyses by others is due to the fact that Chen and Chu did not estimate future benefit levels based on the flawed benefit formula in effect at the time (this formula tended to "double index" benefit levels from one generation to the next, reflecting increases in both wage and price levels), but rather indexed benefit levels between generations by wage increases alone, thus anticipating corrective legislation that would not be enacted until 1977.

5. Myers and Schobel (1992) estimated the present value of contributions and expected benefits for workers retiring at their normal retirement age (NRA), that is, the age at which unreduced benefits are first available, in the years 1960 through 2027. They simulated retirees who had steady average and steady maximum earnings, were single, and were never disabled. Mortality after reaching retirement and other assumptions were taken from the 1991 Trustees Report. Contributions were restricted to employee OASI taxes. The complications of disability and death before retirement were excluded from the analysis. Present value was computed using actual trust fund interest rates for accumulating contributions, but benefits were computed with real discount rates of 0, 1, 2, and 3 percent (the ultimate intermediate 1991 Trustees Report assumption is 2.3 percent).

CHAPTER 6

Social Security and the Economic Security of Women
Is It Fair?

KAREN C. HOLDEN

INTRODUCTION

Social Security is a major source of economic security for workers and their families, both for workers when retired and for surviving family members. For female workers, who historically have been less likely to qualify for employer-provided pension coverage, Social Security may be the sole source of retirement benefits derived from their years of employment.[1] For wives of retired workers, Social Security's survivor benefits provide an income that guards them against even sharper falls in income when their husbands die (Burkhauser, Butler, and Holden, 1991).

Studies have documented both the fall in income and the consequent rise in poverty among women when husbands die, as well as the importance of Social Security for poor elderly women (Holden and Smeeding, 1991; Hurd and Wise, 1989). In 1990, 27 percent of women 65 or older and living alone had incomes below the poverty threshold ($6,268). Among the elderly poor, Social Security accounted for almost 80 percent of their income (U.S. Social Security Administration, 1993). While Social Security continues to be recognized as an important source of economic security for women against the income consequences of their own retirement and disability and of their husbands' disability, retirement, or death, there is growing controversy over whether the current structure of benefits is "fair to women."

The fairness controversy is rooted in disagreement over what is a "fair" distribution of benefits in a system that insures against earnings loss upon retirement, disability, or death while also redistributing benefits in favor of certain beneficiary groups. A strict insurance system would provide equal retirement benefits to workers with identical earnings without regard to family structure. Increased earnings would lead to greater benefits when that individual retired.[2] Though Social Security retired and disabled worker benefits are based strictly on lifetime average covered earnings, a progressive benefit formula replaces a higher percentage of earnings for low-income workers, and noncontributory benefits to children, spouses, and survivors increase the replacement rate for certain families. These benefits shift benefit outcomes away from those obtained under a strict earnings-related insurance system. The progressive benefit formula favors workers with lower earnings and, as shown later, relative to unmarried workers with identical earnings, it favors couples who are able to share earnings efforts. Spouse benefits favor married, single-earner couples, but without these benefits, married, single-earner couples would receive substantially lower benefits than would two-earner couples with identical combined earnings. Survivor benefits protect only workers with a spouse or dependent child, but two-earner couples receive substantially lower survivor protection than do one-earner couples.

Different notions of a fair social insurance system lead to quite different conclusions about the fairness of the distribution of benefits across families and individuals. Even a strict earnings-related system that distributes benefits equally across individuals with identical earnings may be judged unfair to workers with lower earnings and families with greater consumption needs. This chapter discusses the different approaches to judging fairness in a social security system: gender bias in benefit determination, benefit inequality in favor of individuals and families with the greatest income needs, benefit inequality across individuals with identical earnings, and benefit inequality across family units with identical total earnings.

The social adequacy provisions of the Social Security system were intended to favor families and individuals with assumed greater consumption needs. Changes over time in the work roles of women and men have substantially changed the relative sizes of certain beneficiary groups and the characteristics of the individuals and families targeted by the social adequacy provisions in ways that may now be inconsistent with original assumptions about family income needs. To illustrate the effect of changes in the work roles of women and men, this chapter compares benefit outcomes across hypothetical earning units. The progressive benefit formula and spouse and survivor benefits are described, and current benefit outcomes are contrasted with original benefit intent. While arguing that adequacy goals of the program remain valuable, the chapter concludes that policy changes are required, principally to provide greater insurance protection to the most vulnerable of beneficiary groups: survivors in couples in which the sharing of earnings efforts have over time reduced the social security protection provided to them.

DEFINING FAIRNESS

How does one judge a program or policy to be fair or unfair? The American Heritage Dictionary defines "fair" as *"Free of all favoritism or bias; ... Just to all parties; equitable; ... Consistent with rules, logic, or ethics."* By this dictionary standard, an evaluation of the fairness of a system requires both (1) determination of the groups ("parties") whose treatment is to be compared, and (2) identification of the underlying logic of the system with which the outcomes must be judged consistent. Bias, defined in this same dictionary as a *"Preference or inclination that inhibits impartial judgment; prejudice,"* may be easily identified in public programs that are expected to provide benefits to women and men without regard to their gender. The next section asks whether Social Security is fair to women in this sense.

The second part of the definition presents a more formidable challenge. While program rules may be easy to identify, it is more difficult to reach consensus on the relevant logic and ethics that determine whether the outcomes of those rules are fair. In a multifaceted program there may be a multitude of goals that allow conflicting fairness criteria. A system may be judged as fair on adequacy or strict equity grounds; because the conclusions drawn from these two approaches often conflict, reaching a consensus on the fairness of the Social Security system has always been difficult.

Even if this conflict had been resolved and program rules had been developed that were based on a widely accepted logic and social ethic, this resolution may have since been fundamentally altered by subsequent social change. Program rules and logic may have become inconsistent with wider social and legal changes out of which have arisen new standards governing the social and economic relationships among individuals.

At the heart of the current debate over the fairness of Social Security towards women are changes in work and family roles that have altered the patterns of economic dependency among family members in ways that may no longer be in accord with the family and work relationships upon which Social Security rules and concepts of fairness were originally based. Later sections discuss how the original logic underlying provision of benefits to wives and widows provides insight into a benefit structure that has been questioned for its fairness to women. The final sections discuss reforms in the benefit structure and their consistency with the original and prevailing logic of this social insurance program.

JUDGING FAIRNESS BY THE LEGAL TREATMENT OF WOMEN IN SOCIAL SECURITY

In contrast to gender neutrality in calculating retired-worker benefits over most of the program's history, until the mid-1970s spouse and survivor benefits were provided with gender-based distinctions.[3] Gender distinctions in these benefits, which have been popularly termed "dependent benefits," reflected a system bias against married women as potential providers of economic support to other family members.

In 1939 the Social Security Advisory Council recommended the payment of an annuity to widows of insured workers. The council argued that

A haunting fear in the minds of many older *men* is the possibility, and frequently the probability, that their *widow* will be in need after their death. The day of large families and of the farm economy, when aged parents were thereby assured comfort in their declining years, has passed for a large proportion of our population. This change has had particularly devastating effect on the sense of security of the aged *women* of our country. (quoted in Brown, 1977, p. 27, emphasis added)

Upon the council's recommendation, the 1939 Social Security Amendments provided for a benefit to aged wives and widows (then limited to those 65 and older)

of fully insured workers. These benefits were extended to husbands in 1950, but until a 1975 Supreme Court decision ruled otherwise, men were eligible only if economic dependency on their wives prior to the wives' retirement or death could be established. On the one hand, this provision was interpreted by some as showing favorable treatment to women; as wives and widows they merely had to document marriage at the time of their husbands' retirement or death. The 1975 Supreme Court, in *Weinberger* v. *Weisenfeld* (respectively, the Secretary of the U.S. Department of Health, Education, and Welfare [HEW] and the plaintiff), ruled that it was discriminatory against women since it reduced the income protection provided to their families only on account of their sex.[4] Weisenfeld was a recently widowed young father who, as the higher earner when his employed wife was alive, was ineligible to receive survivor benefits, although his wife could have done so had she lived and he died.[5]

Weinberger v. *Weisenfeld* set in motion the gradual elimination of all sex-based distinctions in benefit calculations. Two years later, *Oliver* v. *Califano* (respectively, plaintiff and Secretary of HEW), brought in the District Court of Northern California, successfully contested the benefits paid since 1965 to divorced elderly wives but not to divorced elderly husbands. A 1978 decision in *Cooper* v. *Califano* granted benefits to husbands of retired workers caring for an eligible child (a benefit that had been paid to wives since 1950). In 1979 *Yates* v. *Califano* granted to surviving divorced fathers (caring for the deceased workers' minor children) the benefits that had been paid to surviving divorced mothers since 1950. In 1980 *Ambrose* v. *Harris* struck down the distinction made in 1965 between surviving divorced elderly wives and husbands. All remaining gender distinctions were statutorily eliminated in 1983. If a fair system is one that shows no preference or bias based on sex alone, the Social Security system must be given excellent marks. The system has, for most of its history, provided identical retired-worker benefits to male and female workers with identical average covered earnings, and since 1983 dependent benefits have been paid without regard to the sex of the worker or of the dependent.

JUDGING FAIRNESS BY THE OUTCOMES FOR WOMEN UNDER SOCIAL SECURITY

If the standard of fairness and equity in a program were only that identically positioned women and men experienced identical outcomes, this chapter would end here. However, the discussion of fair treatment by the Social Security system is more often of the fairness of outcomes experienced by differently positioned individuals.

Table 6.1 illustrates the differences in average outcomes for male and female Social Security beneficiaries that have sparked debate over the fairness of the system towards women. At the end of 1993 female retired-worker beneficiaries were paid a lower average monthly retired-worker benefit than were males ($581 versus $759), though benefits were calculated in precisely the same manner for females as for males.

Women (and men) eligible for a retired-worker benefit may also be eligible for a larger spouse benefit (which is equal approximately to 50 percent of their spouse's benefit) or, if widowed, a larger survivor benefit (which is equal approximately to

TABLE 6.1. Social Security Beneficiaries and Benefits.

Benefit Type	Beneficiaries (1000s)[a]		Average Benefits	
	Females	**Males**	**Females**	**Males**
Retired workers	12,447	13,649	$581	$759
Dually entitled[b]	2,258	25	$406	$365
spouse surviving spouse	2,864	83	$754	$701
Disabled workers	1,371	2,358	$516	$714
Dependents[c]				
Spouse[d]	2,988	29	$352	$214
Surviving spouse	4,800	37	$632	$460

Source: Reprinted from *Social Security Statistical Supplement,* 1994, Table 5.A1, Table 5.G3.
[a]Data are for beneficiaries in current pay status at the end of 1993.
[b]Defined as receiving spouse or surviving spouse benefit that is higher than their own retired-worker benefit. Total benefit is given.
[c]Spouse and surviving spouse beneficiaries are those who are not eligible for their own retired-worker benefit.
[d]Spouses of retired workers, entitled based on age.

100 percent of their deceased spouse's benefit).[6] Such a "dually entitled" benefi-ciary will receive only an amount equal to the highest benefit amount. This dual en-titlement provision applies to all benefits and to both men and women.[6]

During the early years of the program, when fewer married women worked and were more likely, if they did, to work in noncovered employment, women eligible for their own retired worker benefits and those eligible for benefits as a spouse or survivor of a retired-worker were distinct groups. In 1952 only 6 percent of all re-tired-worker female beneficiaries were eligible for a larger spouse or survivor ben-efit. As shown in Table 6.1, there is now considerable overlap. Over 40 percent of retired-worker female beneficiaries are currently dually entitled, and this number is expected to grow as successive cohorts of women reach age 62 with at least 10 years of covered work.

The lower average retired-worker benefits paid to women are consistent with, and help explain, the far larger fraction of dually entitled female than male beneficia-ries (41 percent versus .8 percent). Since, by the definition of dual entitlement used in this table, the spouse benefit paid women labelled dually entitled must be the larger benefit for which the individual is eligible, total benefits paid to dually enti-tled wives and survivors are not far different from those paid to fully dependent fe-male beneficiaries; these women appear not to have gained in terms of increased retirement benefits from their own covered work.[8]

A simple comparison of average benefits paid to women and men, however, is not sufficient to assess the fairness of the benefit structure. The receipt of different benefit amounts is not in itself problematic unless some individuals or groups are thereby provided less protection and economic security in a manner that is incon-sistent with either the goals of the program or the currently accepted ethics about a fair system of income protection. Such an assessment of the Social Security bene-fit structure requires an understanding of the logic behind the benefit rules of three key provisions: the progressive benefit structure, the payment of dependent bene-fits, and the dual entitlement provisions.

The progressive benefit formula awards to each individual worker a benefit that is absolutely larger than, but a smaller percentage of, earnings as average covered earnings rise. Table 6.2 presents illustrative retired-worker benefit amounts for workers at various earnings levels.[9] Because the three highest earners have earnings above the taxable maximum, retired-worker benefits are not different for them. For a single (unmarried) earner (column 3) the replacement rate steadily decreases as earnings rise. If the worker were married to a nonworking spouse, total benefits paid to the couple would be 50 percent larger and the replacement rate raised accordingly at all earnings levels (column 4). Column 5 presents the replacement rate that would be obtained if the hypothetical earnings (in column 1), rather than being earned solely by one spouse, were evenly split between spouses (e.g., in row 2 each spouse earns $12,000, for a combined total of $24,000). The replacement rate for the two-earner couple is lower than for the one-earner couple at all earnings below the taxable maximum but higher than the replacement rate for the single earner. Above the taxable earnings maximum, couples' benefits are larger when earnings are equally shared between spouses.[10]

Table 6.2 illustrates the complex equity dilemma presented by the current benefit formula, which includes provisions intended to provide greater security to families with presumed greater consumption needs. Column 3 represents a strict individual-worker system: individual benefits are based on covered earnings and the replacement rate falls as income rises (and the presumed need for additional retirement income diminishes). Spouse benefits, intended to provide for the additional consumption needs of couples, substantially raise replacement rates for couples at all earnings levels (column 4). For most couples (currently 94 percent of all earnings are below the taxable maximum), the spouse benefit raises the replacement rate above that obtained by couples who choose to divide earnings efforts equally. For all three types of beneficiaries the fall in replacement rate as earnings rise is main-

TABLE 6.2. Estimated Benefits from Social Security

Current Earnings[a] (1)	Monthly Benefit[b] (2)	Earnings Replacement Rate[c]		
		Single Earner (3)	One-earner Couple[d] (4)	Equal Two-Earner Couple[e] (5)
$ 15,000.00	$ 540.00	43.2%	64.8%	60.1%
24,000.00	738.00	36.9	55.4	47.4
27,000.00	804.00	35.7	53.6	45.1
30,000.00	869.00	34.8	52.2	43.2
34,000.00	926.00	32.7	49.0	41.2
48,000.00	1020.00	25.5	38.2	36.9
60,000.00	1063.00	21.3	31.9	34.8
68,000.00	1063.00	18.8	28.2	32.7
120,000.00	1063.00	10.6	15.9	21.3

Estimated using Life Cycle Savings (see endnote 9).
[a]Assuming constant real earnings over lifetime of worker now age 64 and retiring at age 65.
[b]Of retired worker with earnings amount in col. 1.
[c]Benefits divided by pre-retirement earnings.
[d]Col. 2 plus spouse benefit.
[e]Earnings in col. 1 equally divided between spouses.

tained. But even if adequacy concerns would argue for the payment of additional benefits to couples, spouse benefits clearly overcompensate for the consumption needs implicitly presumed by the system to be adequately met by the combined retired-worker benefits of two-earner couples (column 3 versus column 4). Sharing of earnings between spouses leaves some couples worse off than they would have been had only one spouse worked, even though total earnings—and presumed consumption needs—remain the same.

Table 6.3 illustrates how different earnings-sharing ratios affect benefits; it compares Social Security benefits when married and when only one spouse survives of couples who divide identical total earnings ($48,000) differently. The retired-worker benefits for which each spouse is eligible and the *full* spouse benefit are given in columns 2 and 3, respectively. The amount actually paid is the combined amount of the *higher* benefit for which each spouse is eligible when married (column 4) and when only one spouse survives (column 5). The last two columns show the replacement rate obtained during the two life stages. As already suggested in Table 6.2, the 50 percent spouse benefit gives the advantage to the one-earner couple I over all two-earner couples, when both spouses are alive. While the differences are rather small at this earnings level, it is the couple in which the wife is the more modest earner that loses most (couple II receives benefits lower by 8 percent). In this case the couple is no better off in terms of Social Security income than a one-earner couple with average real covered earnings of $36,000. Column 7, however, shows that two-earner couples are at a distinct economic disadvantage when only one spouse survives; despite identical combined covered earnings and Social Security benefits when married that are only 4 percent lower than couple I's, cou-

TABLE 6.3. Monthly Benefits Paid to Four Hypothetical Couples.

	Annual Real Covered Earnings (1)	Retired-worker Benefit (2)	Spouse Benefit[a] (3)	When Married Benefit[b] (4)	Survivor Benefit[b] (5)	Earnings Replacement	
						Couple Benefit (6)	Survivor Benefit (7)
Couple I							
Spouse 1	$48000.00	$1020.00	.00	$1530.00	$1020.00	38.2%	25.5%
Spouse 2	.00	.00	$510.00				
Couple II							
Spouse 1	$36000.00	$942.00	$237.00	$1416.00	$942.00	35.4%	23.4%
Spouse 2	$12000.00	$474.00	$471.00				
Couple III							
Spouse 1	$30000.00	$869.00	$303.00	$1475.00	$869.00	36.9%	21.7%
Spouse 2	$18000.00	$606.00	$434.50				
Couple IV							
Spouse 1	$24000.00	$738.00	$369.00	$1476.00	$738.00	36.9%	18.5%
Spouse 2	$24000.00	$738.00	$369.00				

[a]For which each person is eligible.
[b]For each spouse, the higher of retired-worker or spouse benefit.

ple IV receives a survivor benefit that is 38 percent smaller. What is starkly evident is that, as couples share earnings more equally, protection against the death of one spouse declines.

Tables 6.2 and 6.3 illustrate how the payment of spouse benefits alters the relative benefits received by couples with identical total earnings. Taking adequacy arguments into account, it appears that spouse benefits do increase equality among couples in total Social Security payments received (i.e., Table 6.3, column 6 versus a 25.5 percent rate without spouse benefits), although one-earner couples are favored in this distribution. This result, however, comes at an explicit cost: it reduces the observed gain to a dually entitled spouse's work effort (e.g., Couple II in Table 6.3). Large differences among couples, however, arise when only one survives. Relative to one-earner couples, more equal sharing of earnings efforts between spouses substantially reduces the security provided to their family should one spouse die.

Note that the differences between one- and two-earner couples are gender neutral. These inequalities in benefits among spouses with identical aggregate earnings result regardless of the gender of the lower- and higher-earning spouse. While it is the growing proportion of dually entitled women that has been responsible for much of the fairness debate, it does not matter whether the wife or husband is the lower earner.

As couples increasingly share earnings efforts, replacement rates among couples are likely to fall at lower earnings levels and rise at higher levels. These changes are unlikely to alter substantially the percentage of couples who are poor in retirement, since only a small percentage are now just above the poverty level (Holden and Smeeding, 1991). But the substantial decline in the implicit value of the survivor's insurance policy protecting workers and their families (Table 6.3, columns 6 and 7) is more likely to plunge into poverty the far larger percentage of elderly widows who hover above poverty. Ironically, increased sharing of earning roles between spouses, assumed to increase women's access to protective wage-based insurance, substantially lowers the economic protection provided to them as widows (compared with one-earner couples with identical earnings). Over time more couples will look like Couple IV, with somewhat lower benefits as a couple but substantially lower benefits when one alone survives.

ASSESSING REFORMS AGAINST PROGRAM GOALS AND ETHICS

Rawls argues that a society's definition of justice requires a shared view of the principles under which the population wishes to live and which it wants to shape their lives. When a society selects a just distribution of scarce resources, it must be "(a) to the greatest expected benefit of the least advantaged ... ; and (b) attached to offices and position open to all under conditions of fair equality of opportunity" (Rawls, 1983, p. 154).

Reading the history of the provisions that moved away from a strict, proportional earnings-related benefit structure makes it clear that each proposed departure from a strict earnings-related formula reflected the centrality of adequacy goals to the framers of the Social Security system: the progressive benefit formula (targeting low-income workers); even the earlier retirement age for women (advocated as a means of providing for the additional consumption needs of a couple when husbands, typically older than their wives, reached aged 65); and—"one of the most important departures from the proportionality principle"—the provision of benefits to wives and widows (Burns, 1949, p. 95). While it was recognized that these departures meant that "the higher paid worker, or one who has neither an aged wife nor eligible dependents at death, [would] pay relatively more for what he (sic) gets out of the program," they were supported as a means to achieve the more central goal of assuring "a *uniform* minimum sum which would on average and in the vast majority of cases meet *minimum living needs*" (p. 415, emphasis added). These benefits were intended to supplement the incomes of individuals, to "enable them to tide themselves over the period of income stoppage for which social insurance benefits are payable without the necessity of recourse to public assistance" (p. 413). One-earner couples were assumed to be most at risk without these additional benefits from Social Security. It seemed reasonable to provide for these couples, reducing this payment when a second earner could provide for these higher consumption needs.

In a 1977 essay, J. Douglas Brown, Chair of the 1937–38 Social Security Advisory Council and member of four succeeding councils, reaffirmed the centrality of adequacy goals to members of the earlier council:

The greatest contribution of the Social Security Advisory Council of 1937–38 was its unanimous affirmation that protection against hardship should be the fundamental guide in the establishment of the benefit structure of a national system of social security. (Brown, 1977 p. 4).

As sharing of earnings effort by spouses becomes a more prevalent earnings pattern, efforts by the Social Security system to adjust its benefits to that reality are appropriate. Table 6.2 has shown that couples are differently treated depending on the way in which earnings efforts are shared between spouses. Spouse benefits increase replacement rates *uniformly* for one-earner couples, raising the incomes of high earning couples well above a "minimum sum" (Burns, 1949, p. 415). The consequence is that while progressivity in replacement rates is maintained, it is one-earner couples with higher earnings who receive absolutely more spouse benefit dollars (Holden, 1982). For these couples, spouse benefits are hardly necessary as "protection against hardship," nor can they be judged to distribute dollars preferentially to the "most disadvantaged."

On the other hand, Table 6.2 shows that spouse benefits do in effect move towards more equal benefit outcomes for one- and two-earner couples with identical total covered earnings. This greater equality between couples comes at a cost to the equal treatment of individual workers with identical covered earnings. A single earner with average earnings of $48,000 has 25.5 percent of earnings replaced by Social Security. Without a spouse benefit this would be the replacement rate for one-earner couples as well, while a married couple equally sharing earnings effort would have 36.9 percent of covered earnings replaced.

A difference of greater concern arises upon widowhood. Sharing of earnings between spouses makes an enormous difference in the replacement of prior earnings upon which a survivor may have depended when the marriage was intact. Unmarried earners leave no spouse survivor, so the difference between them and married couples does not present the same replacement inequity as occurs upon retirement. However, a spouse in a two-earner marriage receives less protection from the loss of the couple's earnings than does the spouse of a one-earner couple with identical total earnings. As shared earnings efforts become universal among couples, differences in benefits when only one survives will be closely linked to who earned what share of the couple's total earnings.

CAREGIVING AND BENEFIT OUTCOMES

This discussion has only briefly mentioned what is in fact a major contributor to lower retired-worker benefits of women and what is often described as a major gender inequity in social security law: the disregard in the benefit calculation for unpaid but socially productive caregiving efforts, which, because they are performed primarily by women, reduces the chances that their families will benefit from the program's protective insurance. It has been shown that while benefits may be identically computed for women and men, the consequent reduction in retired-worker benefits from years out of the work force for caregiving is substantial for parents, women in particular (Kingson and O'Grady-LeShane, 1993). Adjustments for years of caregiving through an explicit wage credit for those years when absence from the work force was due to caregiving or through a reduction in the number of years over which covered earnings are averaged would increase retired-worker benefits for women in particular, but would reverse the current system's neutrality towards reasons for work absence or low wages. Currently voluntary and involuntary absences from the work force, part-time work by high-wage earners, and full-time work by low-wage earners are treated identically in calculating Social Security retired-worker benefits. Years with highest covered (indexed) earnings are averaged over a fixed period (now 35 years for persons born after 1939), with all zero years of earnings treated the same. Periods out of the work force due to personal illness, factory closing, and planned childbirth, which may evoke social sympathy, and those due to voluntary quits, firing for nonperformance, incarceration, or pregnancy for a teenage high school dropout are treated alike in calculating the Social Security benefit. Ironically, early in the history of the Social Security program the pattern of lifetime earnings was taken into account, although in a way quite the opposite of current proposals for caregiver credits. Prior to the 1950 Social Security Amendments the average earnings calculated were incrementally raised for additional years of creditable wages with the purpose of rewarding retirees for the persistence of (not just income from) their work effort (Burns, 1949).[11] The 1950 amendments made the system indifferent to the earnings patterns underlying any particular average monthly wage. To accord special treatment now to caregiving requires that the Social Security system again implicitly assign greater merit and social worth to certain patterns of work.

It must be noted that because the different treatment of men and women under Social Security is prohibited, adjustments to benefits for periods of caregiving would be available to either spouse. A requirement to document an earnings reduction or period out of the work force linked to caregiving would not be unlike the earlier and since rejected dependency requirements imposed on husbands and widowers.[12] If adjustments were allowed for either parent without direct linkage to the caregiving period (e.g., by reducing the averaging period), a couple would wisely choose this option for the parent whose consequent increase in benefits would raise the couples combined benefit—and the wife's potential survivor benefit—by the greatest absolute amount. For couples with sharply different earnings and in which both spouses have some zero earning years, the greatest gain in lifetime benefits would be obtained by granting the adjustment to the higher earner, for example, by eliminating from consideration years in the long training period of a highly paid professional.[13] Such a choice by couples would increase, rather than reduce, the gap in retired-worker benefits paid to women and men.

SYSTEM REFORM

The sharing of earnings between spouses has substantially changed the survivor insurance package offered to different types of couples and has thereby handicapped the achievement of equitably protecting families against the loss of income when one worker dies. One-earner couples are given the greater survivor protection, while two-earner couples with identical combined earnings receive less survivorship protection. The continuing high poverty levels among widows (Holden & Smock, 1991) suggest that achieving adequacy and equity standards for this group remains one of the unmet social goals set by the framers of the Social Security system.

The explicit rationale for spouse and widow benefits was to provide income to the most needy. Without survivor benefits, widows of one-earner couples would have no share in the Social Security benefits acquired during marriage. However, couples in which the spouse have equal earnings have no protection against the loss of the deceased spouse's benefits; the dual entitlement provisions leave the survivor with only her retired-worker benefits. During the early years of the program, widows were the relatively economically disadvantaged and it seemed evident, given their "normal dependence on income from [their husband's] earnings," that a continuation to them of some share of their husband's benefit was justified (Burns, 1949, p. 49). Though the additional benefit paid to married couples was concurrently and similarly motivated by income adequacy concerns, spouse and survivor benefits must now be distinguished in discussions of the fairness of Social Security towards women. These benefits perform different functions and need not be directly linked in reform proposals. Spouse benefits, originally argued on the basis of the greater income needs of one-earner couples, overcompensate one-earner couples for differences in the consumption needs of a couple, compared with an individual with identical earnings.[14] An explicit "earning sharing" proposal in which each spouse's benefit would be based on one-half of the combined covered earnings of married couples would provide equal benefits to one- and two-earner couples. Treating each spouse upon retirement as if lifetime covered earnings had been equally shared would also reflect the growing consensus that spouses' earnings are marital property, and, more important, it would eliminate the effect on total benefits of the pattern of shared earnings effort between spouses. Unfortunately, this reform has had little support from the Social Security Administration or Congress, in part because its implementation would be administratively costly and because some couples would be worse off under earnings sharing (including low-income, one-earner couples). Those whose benefits would fall would be expected to resist benefit reform unless compensated at additional costs to the program.

If covered earnings were equally divided between spouses at retirement and each spouse treated as an independent retired worker, survivors of one-earner couples would be worse off than under the current system. That is, a survivor of a one-earner couple would be treated as is a two-earner couple with equal earnings (Table 6.3). Thus, unless an argument can be made in favor of the lower benefits now paid to survivors of a two-earner couple, reform of the widows' benefit is called for. Burkhauser and Smeeding (1994) propose a survivor benefit equal to some fixed fraction of the couple's combined benefit; this would result in more equal protection for two- and one-earner couples, although couple I in Table 6.3 would remain advantaged, especially in comparison with couple II, since identical total earnings would still produce different combined benefits when married. In contrast, basing widows' benefits on the average of the couple's combined covered earnings would provide equal survivor benefits to two- and one-earner couples with identical total earnings. Under this scenario all couples in Table 6.3 would receive a benefit equal to that of couple I.

Reform that focused on the equal treatment of widows without regard to shared earnings decisions when both were alive would also improve the economic position of another economically disadvantaged group: surviving divorced spouses who now are eligible for benefits on the same basis as is a current spouse. Paying a legislated fraction of the sum of their own and their deceased ex-spouse's average covered earnings benefit would implicitly encode into the Social Security system one of the most significant social changes since the mid-1970s: the recognition that some share of income and benefits acquired during marriage remain the property of the divorced spouse, regardless of the ability of the spouse to earn after that marriage ends.

CONCLUSIONS

It is not that society's basic concepts of a just social security system have changed, but rather that increases in earnings, more generous benefits paid on covered earnings, and patterns of behavior underlying that system have substantially altered its ability to achieve its original equity and adequacy goals. Increased work effort by wives has not changed the intended progressive relationship between a couple's earnings and benefits. Spouse benefits are now far less likely to be the sole benefit paid to any married female beneficiary. While this may lead to their quiet demise through legislative action, it is also the case that, for the few remaining one-earner couples, Social Security benefits would be substantially lower without spouse benefits than those of two-earner couples with identical total earnings (compare columns 3 and 6 of Table 6.2). The current 50 percent spouse benefit, however, overcompensates one-earner couples relative to similarly positioned two-earner couples (Table 6.2, columns 4 and 5, and Table 6.3, column 6). A lower (or progressive) spouse percentage would reduce this difference, though probably at small savings over time as more women accumulate longer-covered work histories.

In contrast, how earnings are shared between spouses will continue to matter enormously to the size of survivor benefits paid. This result is obtained because survivor benefits are based solely on the benefits paid to the higher-earning spouse. Reform in survivor benefit amounts should be explicitly unlinked to spouse benefits.

A. Heaworth Robertson, former chief actuary of the Social Security system, argued that "Social Security is structured to reward life patterns... that are becoming much less representative of modern life. The net result is that Social Security is not meeting the income security needs of women in today's world as well as it did some forty years ago. The need for some kind of change is irrefutable" (1981, 152). The lower protection against death that two-earner couples receive argues for a different accounting for survivor benefits. Reforms linked to the combined final average earnings of both spouses would cause the gender-neutral program to be work-role neutral as well. A system that has explicitly rejected rewarding particular patterns of individual earnings should also be neutral with regard to the patterns of earnings sharing between spouses.

ENDNOTES

1. The lower receipt of pension income by retired female workers has several causes. Women are more often employed in sectors for which pension coverage is not provided to any worker (e.g., household labor, clerical work in the private sector, retail jobs). They more often work part time and, hence, may not meet minimum annual hours of work requirements for pension coverage. They are more likely to work part-year or have breaks in service that serve to disqualify short periods of full-time work as counting towards vesting requirements.

2. Social Security pays benefits in the case of the death, retirement, or disability of an insured worker. For ease, we refer only to retirement when discussing general Social Security provisions even though the provisions may apply across all three risks.

3. The 1935 Social Security Act provided that benefits be paid to fully insured workers who were at least 65 years of age, using the same benefit formula for women and men. The uniformly equal treatment of male and female retired workers was temporarily violated in 1956 when female retired workers were permitted to receive reduced benefits at age 62. In 1961 these early benefits were granted to males on identical terms.

4. J. Douglas Brown, Chair of the 1937–39 Advisory Council and of four subsequent Councils, criticized this decision since "The Court ignored the fact that . . . both level and coverage of benefits have . . . been based upon the considered judgement of Congress in establishing priorities in the wise use of dedicated tax funds in providing protection against hardship according to a predetermination of imputed need" (1977, p. 18). This couple, in fact, typified the dilemma faced by a system that had structured benefits when two-earner couples were the atypical group of beneficiaries.

5. At the time of this case, children of female workers were eligible for child benefits. In 1939 child benefits were granted to children of male workers who were fully insured. In 1950 benefits were extended to children of female workers who were fully and currently insured. The "currently insured" requirement imposed a recent work requirement on females alone.

6. A person may be eligible for multiple benefits. For example, an individual may be eligible for a retired-worker benefit; as the widow of a deceased worker, for a survivor benefit; and as a spouse in a second marriage, for a spouse benefit.

7. The Social Security Administration defines as "dually entitled" only those whose spouse or survivor benefit is larger than the individual's own retired-worker benefit. A person who is eligible for a spouse benefit that is smaller than their retired-worker benefit is not so defined by the Social Security Administration. Including among the dually entitled any individual eligible for both a spouse or survivor benefit and a retired-worker benefit would result in virtually all husbands and wives in two-earner couples being deemed dually entitled.

8. Although a woman's Social Security benefit may be not be raised by her covered work, protection prior to her own retirement is afforded to her and her family through the disability provisions (a young disabled nonworker receives no protection), her ability to retire independently of her husband's retirement behavior, and the survivorship benefits payable to her children and spouse should she die.

9. Benefits are estimated using the Life Cycle Savings program, a retirement planning program produced by Expert Systems Laboratory in the Department of Family Resource Management, The Ohio State University. For the simulations in Table 2, workers are assumed to have constant real earnings (shown in 1994 dollars) in each year between age 29 and age 65, when they retire. These estimates may not be identical to those estimated by the Social Security Administration for a person born in a particular year.

10. Earnings above the taxable maximum are not included in determining Social Security benefit amounts. Sharing earnings include a larger proportion of the earnings of high-earning couples in the benefit formula. Thus, couples with total earnings above the maximum will have higher benefits if earnings are shared.

11. This was done by raising the Average Monthly Wage (unindexed in those years) by 1 percent for each additional year of creditable wages.

12. When equal treatment by sex was required, policymakers chose to eliminate the dependency requirement rather than demand proof of dependency by all eligible beneficiaries.

13. Consider a couple with one spouse earning (indexed) earnings of $20,000 in each of 15 years and the other with (indexed) earnings of $40,000 in each of 30 years. In determining Social Security retired-worker benefits, covered earnings will be first averaged over a fixed period of 35 years. Thus, both will have this average reduced by some years of zero earnings. Using the benefit formula applicable to workers reaching age 62 in 1994, the full benefit (unreduced for receipt prior to age 65) paid the wife and husband would be $562 and $1,195, respectively. Reducing the averaging period by five years (to 30) for whichever spouse claimed absence for caregiving would increase the monthly benefit by a higher percentage for the lower earner (7 versus 6 percent) but by a greater absolute amount for the higher earner ($71 versus $38). The couple would maximize their joint retirement income and that of the survivor by reducing the averaging period for the higher-wage earner. Sandell and Iams (1994) have shown that women who are most likely to be eligible for a reduction in the averaging period on account of caregiving are more likely to remain out of the work force because of marriage to a relatively high earner.

14. The increase in needs implied by the spouse benefit is 50 percent. The poverty threshold implies that a couple requires 26 percent more income than does a single elderly person.

CHAPTER 7

Disability
Why Does the Search for Good Programs Continue?

JERRY L. MASHAW

INTRODUCTION

Programs in aid of persons with disabilities are some of the most common and durable social policies in modern societies. Indeed contemporary policies can trace their roots to pre-industrial legislation. Under the Elizabethan Poor Laws, for example, invalids were one of the few categories for whom begging was not a criminal offense. And, when Chancellor Bismarck decided to throw the weight of the German state behind social policies that would mollify an increasingly restive industrial working class, sickness funds and workers' compensation headed the list of his social welfare innovations. Most contemporary nations, like the United States, have multiple programs in aid of those with physical and mental limitations (Stone, 1984).

The long history and commonplace nature of disability policies, however, mask a startling heterogeneity among the approaches taken to assistance for persons with disabilities and the recurrent battles over their appropriate functions in welfare state provision (Berkowitz, 1987). Both heterogeneity and, as Berkowitz's discussion (chapter 2) highlights, controversy are a function of the multiple sources of social concern that motivate disability policies and a series of unavoidable anxieties about the appropriate structure of disability programs (Mashaw, 1983). The results in the United States, and elsewhere, are a set of disability initiatives that are complex, compromised, and the source of almost continuous concern and reform.

The multiple normative underpinning for our attempts to ameliorate the plight of persons with disabilities are not difficult to appreciate. At an intuitive level the desire to help those with functional limitations springs from a deep-seated moral sense that they are among the least advantaged in modern societies. Simple altruism calls upon us to help our neighbors who are in need because of disabling physical or mental conditions. This fellow feeling doubtless has roots in our own sense of vulnerability to the risk of invalidity. To be born helpless and to spend some portion of our adult lives coping with physical and mental limitations is perhaps our common fate. But we would like somehow to insure against the risk that these limitations will be visited upon us in our middle years, when we are expected to be economically productive. Some form of cash benefit to cushion loss of market income is often the logical answer to this demand for insurance against the risk of disability (Committee on Economic Security, 1935).

We have other concerns related to disability as well. We want not only to help our neighbors and ourselves by establishing various income substitutes when productive capacity is impaired, but also to promote improvement. Disability policies should assist people to become functionally more capable and perhaps, ultimately, to return to a condition of self-support and independent living (Berkowitz, 1987). Nor do income support and rehabilitation exhaust our interests in disability policy. We are concerned for families who must bear the burdens of rearing developmentally disabled children, and equally concerned that those children be given the greatest possible chance to develop the capacities that they have. We know, further, that disability is highly correlated with impoverishment, and we are, therefore, prepared to make special efforts to ameliorate the poverty of those whose lack of success in the competitive economy is attributable to their functional incapacity.

We also recognize a darker side of our reaction to those with severe mental or physical limitations. While they bring out our charitable instincts, they may also provoke aversion, prejudice, and discrimination. Whether this aversion is aesthetic, a desire not to be reminded of our own vulnerability, or born of ignorance and callousness, as a society we are concerned to regulate these baser human instincts by prohibiting discrimination against those with physical and mental limitations (West, 1991).

Our recognition of the multifaceted needs of persons with disabilities and our multiple social goals lead almost necessarily to a complex set of social interventions. They include income replacement, monetary compensation, medical care, rehabilitation services, special education, and other social and personal supports, as well as attempts to break down architectural and transportation barriers and to eliminate discrimination against persons with disabilities in employment, housing access, and elsewhere. In short, multiple purposes beget multiple programs (National Academy of Social Insurance [NASI], 1994, App. C). Here, as elsewhere in social provision, there is a patchwork quilt that has its own moral and historical logic, that responds to multiple needs and multiple goals, but that also may fail to fit together in a fashion that provides a warm and secure covering for those whom disability policy seeks to protect or empower.

Inevitable questions about the coherence of the design of disability policy lead directly to the principal focus of this chapter. For disability policy is not only ubiquitous, durable, and multifaceted, but also a source of continuous anxiety for policy planners, legislators, and most particularly, those who must rely on disability policies for essential supports in their daily lives. In the domain of disability policy we find ourselves in all too familiar territory. We have a set of policies for which there is strong conceptual justification and political support; yet, with apologies to Mel Brooks, these policies are also a source of high anxiety in virtually every society (Derthick, 1990; Stone, 1984).

ANXIETIES OF CAUTIOUS BENEVOLENCE

Although any number of categorizations are plausible, I will discuss the major sources of anxiety about disability policy under six headings. *Actuarial Uncertainty* discusses the difficulty of predicting the costs of disability policies, even over fairly short time periods. *The Problem of Perverse Incentives* deals with the concern that entitlements to income, goods, and services on the basis of disablement reinforce a social role that we should like to ameliorate, if not avoid entirely. *The Problem of Entitlement Security* demonstrates the difficulty of defining with clarity who is entitled to what, over what periods of time, and under what conditions. *Administrative Legitimacy* denotes the problem of coping administratively with the highly contestable and judgmental nature of determinations of disability entitlement. *Unmet Needs* highlights a concern not only that we fail to understand clearly what needs should be met, but also that attending to our multiple anxieties about disability policy may create gaps and uncertainties that exacerbate the difficulties of those we seek to assist. Finally there is *The Issue of Crosscutting Goals,* the concern that our patchwork quilt is not just potentially full of holes, but may also be misshapen or distorted in ways that make it fit our purposes badly.

This last concern introduces an idea that will be a recurrent theme in the pages that follow: dealing with one source of anxiety about disability policy may well make other concerns worse, just as acting on one impulse to assist the disabled may be at cross purposes with assisting others in this highly heterogenous population. In short, our multiple purposes in constructing disability policies and our multiple concerns about avoiding doing bad while doing good generate a dense complexity that renders policy coherence an elusive goal.

We constantly search for that optimal policy, or set of policies, that will meet all our goals and avoid all the pitfalls that can render programs dysfunctional. But this is necessarily a frustrating search. As we focus first on one purpose and one problem and then on another, we seem to find much to criticize and little to praise. That this should be the fate of disability policy is unfortunate. For, as I will argue in these pages, overall disability policy can only hope to achieve some degree of balance among its necessarily competing goals, rather than fully realizing any of them. Moreover, many of the problems *for* disability policy-making are not necessarily problems *with* disability policies. Properly understood, their solutions lie elsewhere—in other forms of social provision, labor market policies, and the like—notwithstanding their profound impact on the structures and the issues that surround programs for persons with disabilities (PWDs).

1. Actuarial Uncertainty

The Committee on Economic Security formed by President Roosevelt in the early 1930s recognized that insurance against the risk of disability was one of the important problems to be addressed in a comprehensive set of social insurance programs. But, as Berkowitz (chapter 2) notes, concern about the national government's capacity to contain the expansive dynamic of such a program (combined with American Medical Association opposition) contributed to a 25-year delay between the formal recognition of disability insurance as an integral part of economic security and the enactment of amendments to the Social Security Act providing income support to persons with severe disabilities.

Somewhat ironically, anxiety about actuarial uncertainty was rooted in the same depression era events that made the need for social insurance against disablement acute. Unemployment puts significant stress on disability programs, as those who are long out of work begin, perhaps quite properly, to rationalize their lack of success in finding new employment in terms of functional limitations stemming from medical impairments. Moreover, adjudicators faced with claimants exhibiting chronic ailments, and no alternative source of income, are loathe to turn them away empty-handed. Hence, they tend to reinterpret the disability standard in ways that allow them to meet severe needs.

It was this dynamic that drove virtually all private disability insurers into bankruptcy during the Great Depression. A massive and unpredicted increase in claims, combined with the courts' tendencies to construe disability insurance contracts in favor of coverage, confounded the insurers' prior projections concerning the likely incidence of awards to the covered population. And while economic collapse, combined with the collapse of the private market for disability insurance, clearly signalled a need for publicly provided disability insurance, the experience of other countries with disability programs was upsetting. Indeed, the tendency of awards to exceed actuarial projections has appeared so uniform across cultures and time periods that Deborah Stone has argued that disability programs are inherently expansionary, perhaps ultimately uncontrollable (Stone, 1984).

Nevertheless, the need for social insurance against disablement would not go away. The United States, therefore, belatedly "backed into" disability insurance as an ancillary to the Social Security retirement program that it had adopted in 1935. The initial step was "disability freeze" legislation, passed in 1954, which protected the eligibility for social Security retirement benefits of persons who became disabled prior to age 65 even though, because of their disability, they failed to make further contributions to Social Security.

It was but a short logical step to conclude that, if a person was unable to contribute to Social Security because of complete inability to work, that person might well be considered eligible for early (disability) retirement. By 1956 (after considerable political struggle) politics had followed logic, and persons who had disabling conditions (1) that made them unable to work at any job in the national economy and (2) that could expect the situation to be permanent or to result in death were made eligible for early retirement benefits. Initially disability retirement benefits were made available only to persons over age 50, but the age limit was later removed.

From these beginnings the expansionary logic of disability income support programs seemed to establish itself as a defining characteristic of America's disability insurance experience. In 1965 the definition of disability was liberalized from "long-continued and indefinite duration" to "expected to last at least one year, or to result in death." Minor, liberalizing adjustments were also made in 1967, 1969, 1971, and 1972, and, as Berkowitz (chapter 2) notes, legislation increased the real value of Social Security Disability Insurance (DI) benefits during this period.

Other, more dramatic, expansionary policies followed. In 1972 Medicare coverage was for the first time extended to persons who had received cash disability benefits for 24 months. And, in the same year, the federal government passed legislation that "federalized" the older state grant-in-aid program of Aid to the Totally and Permanently Disabled (APTD), creating a new Supplemental Security Income (SSI) program. SSI employed the same definition of disability as the Social Security Disability Insurance program, but it conditioned eligibility on lack of income and resources rather than on prior contributions to the insurance fund. The federal SSI program not only put a national floor under means-tested disability benefits, but also extended federal administration into states that had historically been reluctant to make awards under the ATPD program. Moreover, the SSI program provided benefits to the families of disabled children, a category not covered under ATPD.

During this same period the Congress enacted the Black Lung program, which first took effect in 1970. In one sense this program simply recognized the special health risks of coal mining and the special responsibility of those employing mine workers to help compensate for those risks. But from another perspective the Black Lung program was a liberalization of disability payments designed to preserve the integrity of the DI and SSI programs. For, as the soft coal industry fell on hard times and miners by the thousands were thrown out of work, the disability system in the most severely affected states responded by increasingly liberal treatment of miners who applied for disability benefits.

As might be expected, all of this incrementally expansionary legislation led to significant increases in the disability rolls, both in the Social Security Disability program and in the means tested SSI program. Additional pressure was put on both programs by the major economic shocks of the early 1970s and the high unemployment that accompanied the stagflation of the post-1973 era. By the mid-1970s Congress was increasingly concerned with the rapid growth of the rolls and the cost of disability cash benefits programs. The DI program, for example, had gone from making 350,000 new awards in 1970 to 600,000 new awards in 1974.

Confounding the claim that expansion was the only plausible direction for the development of Social Security and SSI disability income supports, congressional and administrative attempts at controlling the expansion of these programs characterized the period from 1975 through the early 1980s. In 1977, for example, Congress passed amendments reducing the income replacement rates in DI, particularly for younger beneficiaries. Moreover, the Congress required that the Social Security Administration (SSA) tighten adjudication of disability programs by reviewing all state agency allowances of disability benefits before their payment. It further demanded that the SSA conduct continuing disability reviews (CDRs) every three years for Social Security and SSI disability recipients whose impairments had not been found to be permanent and ordered the SSA's Appeals Counsel to reinstate its "own motion review" of a substantial percentage of awards by administrative law judges.

Meanwhile the Social Security Administration, under congressional pressure, had initiated its own series of implementing changes to attempt to control growth. New regulations and directives from the secretary emphasized the use of "objective criteria" when making disability awards; modified the SSA criteria for conducting CDRs, making them into *de novo* redeterminations of eligibility, rather than mere determinations of whether there had been "medical improvement in the case; and, in general, through quality assurance activities and elsewhere, altered the "climate of adjudication" in the direction of cautiousness rather than benevolence. In 1980 Congress further limited benefits available under the DI program by enacting replacement rate caps and, for the first time, added work incentives that it hoped would begin to remove persons from the rolls who could work but who were afraid to try because of the way that work attempts endangered their entitlements.

This combination of activity, both legislative and administrative, produced dramatic results. Whereas 53 percent of applicants had been awarded benefits in 1975, by 1982 the award rate had dropped to 27 percent. Even more important from the perspective of subsequent events, a vastly increased CDR program, operating under new and more stringent rules, completely transformed existing beneficiaries' prospects for removal from the rolls. Whereas prior to 1980 this risk had been trivial, in the early 1980s hundreds of thousands of beneficiaries were declared no longer eligible for benefits.

The overall effect of stricter adjudicatory standards and an aggressive removal policy shifted the incidence of payments from 7.3 per 1,000 insured workers in 1975 to 3.0 per 1,000 insured workers in 1982. But retrenchment was ill-timed (these activities had their major effects during the deep recession of the early 1980s) and poorly administered. (CDRs in particular were carried out with a sense of urgency that produced a very substantial number of erroneous denials and terminations.) The result was a major political reaction.

Class-action suits forced the reinstatement of large numbers of terminated beneficiaries and reinterpreted various provisions of the Social Security Act to expand eligibility. Eventually, over 20 states, either under court order or on their own initiative, were refusing to carry out the continuing disability reviews that were terminating the benefits of many of their severely disabled citizens. Abruptly reversing course, Congress, by legislation adopted in 1982 and 1984, undid a number of the policies that had produced the retrenchment of the late 1970s and early 1980s. Nevertheless, an inclination toward caution has prevailed. While DI awards thereafter rose as a percentage of applications and as a function of the number of insured workers, they have not again approached the levels seen in the mid-1970s.

These events suggest that while there is an expansionary logic to disability income support policy, politics *can* produce retrenchment as well as expansion. Moreover, while the history that has been recounted may tend to suggest that policy change is the major determinant of expansion or contraction in the disability program, this is not necessarily the case. Although disability policy was relatively stable in the period from 1985 through 1990, there has been a very substantial increase both in claims and in awards in the 1990s (see Figure 7.1).

The precise reasons for recent expansion are puzzling both to the Social Security Administration and to outside observers. And puzzlement about the exact causes of recent growth reinforces the notion that cash income supports for persons with disabilities have an inherent level of uncertainty attached to the actuarial projection of program costs. Nevertheless, the general reasons for actuarial variability are now well understood. The demand for and availability of disability benefits are susceptible to alteration because of *both* changes in the broader environment of disability policy and fluctuating political and administrative emphasis on the competing goals of benevolence and caution that are the twin pillars of disability income support

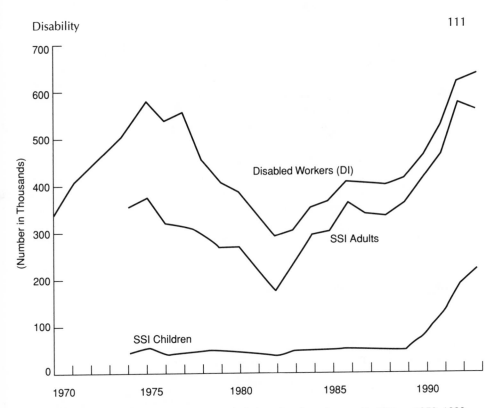

Figure 7.1. Number of persons awarded benefits based on disability, 1970–1993. *Source:* Office of Research and Statistics, U.S. Social Security Administration.

policy. Moreover, these two general classes of change agents may interact to reinforce or cancel each other's effects.

Within these categories investigators recently have offered a range of explanations for the upsurge in disability claims and awards during the early 1990s. Some believe the major explanation lies in structural changes in the economy that have negatively affected opportunities for workers in general and have had a particularly severe adverse impact on persons with disabilities (Yelin, 1992). Others emphasize the paucity of other income supports for persons who both lack employment and have reasonably severe impairments. They would put the explanation for increases in the DI rolls at the doorstep of relatively underdeveloped social welfare supports in other areas of American social welfare policy and the secular decline in the real value of cash benefits under alternative programs (Burkhauser, Havman, and Wolfe, 1993).

Yet another explanation involves changes in the availability of health insurance coverage and its role in influencing choices about work and benefits acceptance. As private health insurance has unravelled for the chronically ill, they have been forced to turn to public programs to meet their medical expenses (Employee Benefit Research Institute, 1993). Others emphasize changes in the recognition and treatment of disabling conditions, particularly mental illnesses. SSA's mental illness categories have been updated to cover more conditions. Simultaneously, many persons who would previously have been institutionalized, and therefore been ineligible for disability payments, are now treated in the community and are eligible for such assistance (Mechanic and Rockefort, 1990) (see Figure 7.2). There has also been a growth in the number and sophistication of claimants' representatives, as well as a growing interest on the part of state and local governments, employers, and insurers to qualify persons for disability benefits who would otherwise have to be supported by alternative state or private programs (NASI, 1994).

This is, indeed, but a partial list of the causes that have been put forward for recent growth in the disability rolls (Lewin-VHI, Inc., 1994). While all seem plausible, no one has a very good explanation of exactly how much of a contribution each of these changes might be making to the demand for and provision of disability income benefits (U.S. General Accounting Office [GAO], 1994), or to what degree they represent waves or trends. Actuarial uncertainty thus remains an inevitable source of anxiety in disability policy planning.

2. The Problem of Perverse Incentives

It is a truism that any social program that provides a benefit for persons who meet established criteria of entitlement encourages persons to qualify for the benefit by meeting those criteria. The language of insurance analysis and economic analysis labels this a problem of "moral hazard" and "perverse incentives" respectively, suggesting, sometimes erroneously, that such difficulties might be avoided. But alas perverse incentives are ubiquitous. Thus, for example, providing benefits only to

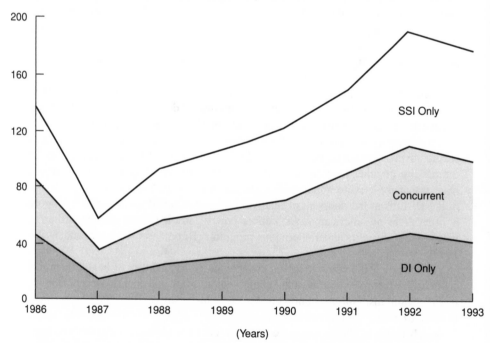

Figure 7.2. Number of DI and SSI allowances based on mental illness, 1986–1993, state agency initial decisions. *Source:* Office of Disability, U.S. Social Security Administration.

those who demonstrate a continuous and extended inability to work may be thought of as a perverse incentive. For the very stringency of the disability standard can be seen as encouraging people to emphasize their incapacities in order to qualify for benefits rather than developing their capacities in order to engage in productive work. On the other hand, this same definitional stringency can be viewed as avoiding work disincentives for those with lesser or more temporary impairments. However you define the benefit, perverse incentives (or moral hazards) will arise.

All income support programs employ complex strategies for managing or ameliorating the perverse incentives problem. The triad of conventional techniques involves making the benefits standard stringent, making benefits criteria objective, and making payment levels relatively low. As we have noted, definitional stringency is clearly a hallmark of the DI and SSI programs, and even then it is possible to view these programs as providing unfortunate incentives to take up the "disabled role." The other techniques for avoiding perverse incentives are even less available or attractive in disability programs. Very low payment levels seem an unsatisfactory response. If people really cannot work, as the stringent definition of disability seeks to assure, then it is important to provide them an adequate income replacement. Indeed, the general acceptance of disability cash benefits policies is premised in part on the belief that recipients are not abandoning the work force in pursuit of benefits but because of their severe impairments.

The problem, of course, is that the perverse incentives problem would disappear completely only if we assumed that we could determine with absolute accuracy who can and who cannot work. Such an assumption is heroic to say the least (Mashaw, 1983). On the other hand, once we recognize that disability entitlement determinations are necessarily uncertain or ambiguous, that is, inherently nonobjective (a topic to which we shall shortly return), then the perverse incentives problem reemerges. Indeed, by responding to concerns about perverse incentives, our current disability programs arguably provide severely inadequate levels of income support. As these words were written, DI cash benefits for individuals averaged $641 per month, while federal SSI monthly payments were $446 for an individual and $669 for a couple (states may supplement these payments). Both programs deny initial eligibility to those who engage in "substantial gainful employment" at the modest level of $500 of gross earnings per month. In short, disability benefits alone leave recipients in poverty, and earnings below the poverty level may disqualify a claimant from receipt of any cash benefits.

Entirely justifiable attempts to make disability programs meet more of the real needs of the disabled population may create further perverse incentives. For example, one of the greatest needs of the population of persons with disabilities is secure access to medical treatment, including pharmaceuticals; personal assistance; and durable medical equipment. In order to meet at least some of these needs, those entitled to DI and SSI cash benefits are also provided entitlements, respectively, to the Medicare and Medicaid programs. Indeed, given the uninsurability of many persons with disabilities in private insurance markets, not to provide eligibility for public medical insurance programs would be grotesque.

Nevertheless, as Quadagno and Quinn (chapter 8) also observe, for many persons with disabilities, once they are on the DI cash benefit rolls and, after a waiting period of two years, eligible for Medicare, the continuation of health benefits may be the major element of the program that keeps them from attempting to return to work. People with chronic and expensive medical conditions, who are uninsurable in the private insurance market, simply cannot take the risk that their attempts to return to work may be sufficiently successful to disqualify them for DI and medical benefits but sufficiently unsuccessful to produce enough income to support themselves and meet their unusually high medical expenses. (Similar problems confront some persons who receive SSI disability benefits.) These so-called notch effects occur in any system that connects lumpy in-kind benefits to a cash benefits entitlement. The two-year waiting period for Medicare (itself a somewhat objectionable feature of current arrangements, given the needs of the disabled population) may prevent people from going on DI to gain medical benefits, thus avoiding the perverse incentives on the intake side. But, once on the rolls and qualified for Medicare, this entitlement could discourage an attempt to return to the competitive work force.

Finally, as we mentioned earlier, the existence of social programs of income support and medical benefits for persons with disabilities may provide perverse incentives to other actors in the environment of disability policy. In particular, the primary role in the rehabilitation of persons with disabilities falls to states and private insurance companies. But the ability to qualify recipients for federal DI and SSI payments, and ultimately for Medicare and Medicaid, shifts the cost-benefit calculation of states and private insurers as they consider whether to attempt rehabilitation and reemployment of impaired workers. In the absence of disability payments from the federal government, both states and private insurers (including self-insuring employers) would have much greater incentives to rehabilitate and place disabled workers because their costs for continuing income support for those workers would rise steeply.

Recognizing these multiple-incentive problems, the Congress has enacted a host of measures that attempt to ameliorate them. As previously mentioned, it has attached work incentives to both the DI and the SSI programs. In the latter program it also has created a sliding scale withdrawal of benefits, continued eligibility for Medicaid after cash income assistance has been removed because of increased earnings, and enacted a special program (the Plan to Achieve Self-Support, PASS) that allows earnings above the usual $500 per month limit during a period of training and rehabilitation designed to lead to self-support. Congress also has provided a "buy-in" opportunity to preserve Medicare coverage for those leaving the DI rolls and has attempted to upgrade state vocational rehabilitation efforts and target them toward producing long-term employment for those who would otherwise be disability income recipients. These efforts have, however, had very modest effects. A vanishingly small number of recipients return to work. No one knows whether this is the result of perverse incentives in the system of income and in-kind supports or simply because persons sufficiently disabled to receive a DI or SSI award are necessarily very disadvantaged in the labor market.

The history of the development of the DI and SSI programs nevertheless suggests three central lessons about dealing with perverse incentives in those or, indeed, in all income support programs. First, standard techniques for reducing perverse incentives have major impacts on the adequacy of the support available for those who need it. Relatively low support levels and very long waiting periods for medical coverage are major examples of these aspects of DI/SSI program design. Second, attempts at fine-tuning through work incentives, special set-asides, and the like enormously increase program complexity and administrative costs, but they may have modest effects on return to work by program beneficiaries. Third, attempts to avoid work disincentives by stringent requirements for qualification may tend to assure program integrity, but simultaneously reduce incentives or possibilities for exit by those who clear those stringent eligibility hurdles. Maintaining work incentives at the point of entry may have the opposite effect on incentives for exit.

The basic message bears repeating: some level of perverse incentives is a given in any program of social provision. Attempts to correct or ameliorate these problems in disability policy-making create critical trade-offs between promoting independence and self-support and maintaining the adequacy and administrative simplicity of income supports. Moreover, the same programmatic feature may create desirable incentives for some and perverse incentives for those who are differently situated. Finally, incentives are not behaviors. As continuing legislative attempts to provide new work incentives have demonstrated, even multiple inducements may have extremely modest affects. Any critique of disability policies based on the simple claim that they create perverse incentives should therefore be viewed as seriously unhelpful. The important policy issue is whether we can somehow do better in balancing our desire to preserve work incentives against other purposes such as adequacy, security, and administrative simplicity.

3. The Problem of Entitlement Security

The horrible personal costs, including a number of suicides, that were associated with the aggressive terminations of the late 1970s and early 1980s illustrate just how crucial entitlement security is for persons with disabilities (Derthick, 1990). Indeed, from the viewpoint of those who look at these programs from the bottom up, that is, from the claimant or beneficiary's perspective, entitlement security, the establishment of a comprehensible and stable criterion for determining eligibility, is perhaps *the* critical issue in disability policy-making.

For many claimants the experience of entitlement *in*security in the DI or SSI program begins as they come to understand the stringency of the disability standard that those programs employ. Few workers, or indeed few citizens, seem to comprehend that the requirement is an incapacity to do *any* job in the national economy that is available in substantial numbers *whether or not the person would be hired for such a job.* Under the current DI/SSI definition of disability, one can stand too far back in the labor queue ever to be hired and yet not be disabled for purposes of receiving cash income assistance. The poignancy of the uncertainty induced by this stringent definition is heightened by the realization that the decision is all or nothing. Either a person is "disabled," and entitled to income benefits and other services such as Medicare; or they are "not disabled," and entitled to nothing.

Once on the rolls, there is continuing uncertainty concerning the ability to maintain eligibility. Many persons with severe chronic conditions have major oscillations in their capacities over time. This is characteristic, for example, of persons with mental illness or with arthritis, both major categories of diagnoses for disability recipients. If these persons work during periods of remission they risk losing their disability benefits, and attached medical benefits, only to find that they need them again because of a shift in their medical conditions. Moreover, reexamination through the continuing disability review system may produce a disqualification if it occurs during a remission period, whereas it would have produced continued qualification were the examination done at another time. Congress has attempted to ameliorate some of these difficulties by creating smoother transitions off of and back onto the benefits rolls. But one need only talk to a small cross section of people who receive Social Security or SSI disability benefits to recognize the enormous anxiety they have about finding themselves suddenly bereft of either income or medical supports when they are sorely needed. This insecurity, of course, reinforces the incentive to emphasize incapacity rather than capacity, a behavior that is both understandable and individually and socially dysfunctional.

For those who take a broader historical view of social security policy, but still from a perspective of claimant entitlement security, other anxieties come into focus. In particular it is clear that over time both the Congress and the Social Security Administration have oscillated in their emphases on benevolence and caution in making eligibility determinations under the SSI and DI programs. This has led to significant litigation attempting, often successfully, to shore up the security of DI and SSI entitlements. But because these attempts at legal entrenchment affect only a part of the program, they may generate retrenchments elsewhere, if the effects on overall expenditures are significant. Hence, if legally constrained to treat claims from children, the mentally ill, and chronic pain sufferers more generously, a fiscally pressured administration may attempt to recoup by tightening up on other categories of claims at the margins. And, of course, Congress may also step in to "correct" the courts' interpretation of the Social Security Act (Mashaw, 1983). Congress and the administration and claimants and their representatives thus seem locked in a continuous sparring match that clearly *shifts* policy. But it is less clear that these activities increase entitlement security for the disabled population as a whole.

Finally there is the insecurity that arises from the propensity of legislative policymakers to engage in "policy by anecdote." In particular, if infrequent but arresting instances of error or abuse are reported to exist in a social welfare program, there is a reflexive political need to assert control, in the interests of "program integrity." Recent legislation to sharply limit the availability of disability benefits to alcoholics or substance abusers is a case in point, as is the campaign in some quarters to clamp down on SSI grants to children with attention deficit hyperactivity disorder. Although the two situations are substantially different, in both there seems to be an underlying fear, premised on some salient but not necessarily representative examples, that DI and SSI payments may simply be rewarding "bad behavior."

This sort of "program insecurity" has two unhappy consequences. First, real needs may not be met because of a fear of erroneous, but nevertheless tenacious, public perceptions of widespread abuse. Second, those active in disability advocacy can be pushed into rigidly defensive postures that then transform any attempt at needed programmatic adjustments into the political equivalent of trench warfare. Both the official reaction to anecdotal evidence of fraud or abuse and advocates' reflexive defenses to those reactions are understandable. But together they enormously complicate the task of maintaining the balanced approach to disability policy-making that is needed to reassure both the general public and those who are most in need or at risk in the absence of secure and predictable entitlements.

4. Administrative Legitimacy

Entitlement security is obviously closely related to the integrity or legitimacy of administration. The difficulty with legitimating SSI or DI determinations begins with the bipolar nature of decision making in both programs. Applicants are determined to be disabled or not disabled. Yet, a moment's reflection reveals that this statutorily bipolar world is not ours. In terms of our physical and mental capacities, age, education, and work experience, we, as a population, array ourselves across a broad spectrum with greater or lesser opportunities in the competitive job market. Whether claimants lie just to one side or the other of a statutory line that divides those fit for work from those who are unfit is an infinitely disputable decision.

Moreover, as we have learned more about persons with impairments and how they fare in labor markets, it seems increasingly plausible to believe that the differences between those who are successful at maintaining or achieving self-support and those who are not has much to do with factors that, strictly speaking, are not attributes of applicants or recipients themselves. The availability of social and familial supports, the willingness of employers to accommodate various physical and mental restrictions, the availability of transportation options and training opportunities, the general structure of labor markets, business cycles, and a host of other factors help determine whether an impairment or limitation results in a work disability. This is not, of course, to say that those with impairments are, or are likely ever to be, as well off in labor markets as those who are conventionally able bodied. Seventy percent of persons with severe disabilities in the United States are estimated to be not working. Fewer than 50 percent of those who make a claim for disability benefits, but are denied, ever return to substantial gainful activity (NASI, 1994). And, those provided with benefits leave the disability rolls very rarely indeed, save by death or transfer to the retirement program at age 65 (U.S. General Accounting Office, 1994).

While these findings may reassure us that there is a real problem with employment for persons having impairments and that the disability system, in gross terms, is tending to make awards to the more, rather than the less, impaired, there remain huge areas of contestable, judgmental decision making. To put the matter more concretely, workers who have a severe chronic illness, who have been told by their medical advisors that they cannot do their former jobs (and often that they should not work at all), and who perhaps have been told by vocational counselors that they have nothing to offer them by way of rehabilitation or job placement are unlikely to find a determination that they are not disabled very convincing. Yet, tens of thousands of applicants have this experience every year in a system processing approximately 2.5 million claims.

It is hardly surprising, therefore, that the disability determination process in the United States has become complex, multilayered, torpid, and increasingly adversarial. Accurate adjudication means the collection of substantial amounts of information about each claimant. And, while regulations that make certain conditions per se disabling attempt to provide speedy awards for the most severely impaired, claimants on average must now wait nearly nine months to receive an initial decision from a state disability determination service (DDS). Dissatisfied applicants may obtain reconsideration of their decision (which seldom results in a change in the outcome) and, if still dissatisfied, may appeal to an independent Administrative Law Judge (ALJ), where the case is completely redetermined after a hearing. Obtaining a hearing and decision at the ALJ level is likely to take an additional 15 to 18 months.

Although these delays are hardly shocking by comparison with the Dickensian civil adjudication processes of American courts, they are extremely distressing to persons with serious ailments and no income. Nor is it surprising that a substantial number of denied claimants remain sufficiently convinced of the erroneousness of the determination in their case to seek reversal of the ALJ decision by a federal district judge.

It would be nice to be able to assure denied claimants, notwithstanding their distress and their understandable confusion, that the Social Security Administration was nevertheless getting the cases right. The problem, of course, is that there is no external standard against which to measure the accuracy of these disability determinations. SSA and the state agencies may strive hard to bring the relevant expertise to bear on claims, to give claimants a full opportunity to explain their circumstances, and to treat like cases alike, but variations in adjudicatory outcomes both at any particular point in time and across time reveal that accuracy and consistency are elusive goals in the DI/SSI adjudicatory process. Investigations of award rates at any particular time have revealed considerable horizontal inconsistency from one disability determination service unit and one ALJ to another (Mashaw et al., 1978). And, there are striking dissimilarities between the award rates of DDS units and administrative law judges, a disparity that seems to be mounting over time (see Table 7.1). Moreover, as was suggested in our prior discussion of the periods of expansion and contraction in the DI program, illustrated in Table 7.1, there is very substantial inconsistency in overall award rates across time periods. Award rates in the early 1970s were nearly twice as high as in the early 1980s, while the early 1990s have seen a movement back toward, but not to, 1970s levels.

While knowledgeable observers often explain these variations in terms of what they call the "adjudicative climate" of the disability programs, this explanation is in many ways little more than a label. It says that the interpretive discretion exercised in the DI and SSI programs varies by location, decider, and time period. And it explains these variations in terms of a "policy climate" that cannot quite be quantified or captured in a way that would make particular policies have predictable results on acceptance or denial rates. In short we are faced with substantial unexplained variation in programs that are entitlements based and, supposedly, nationally uniform.

The result is a constant struggle to do better through training, quality assurance measures, restructuring of the adjudicatory process, reform of the "medical listings," and a host of other measures (Derthick, 1990; Mashaw, 1983). The data reveal these measures to be partially successful at best. Moreover, improving adjudicatory performance has been extraordinary difficult in the 1980s and 1990s when budget cuts have shrunk available personnel by nearly 20 percent. Accurate, timely, and acceptable adjudication of DI and SSI claims is a Herculean task under the best of circumstances. It is a virtual impossibility in the real world of episodic political, economic, and fiscal shocks to the system. In short, the integrity and legitimacy of Social Security DI and SSI adjudication is a source of continuing concern.

TABLE 7.1. Trends in Disability Application and Allowance Rates, 1970–1993.

Calendar Year	Incidence Rate[a]	Application Rate[b]	Allowance Rate[c]		
			Initial	Recon[d]	Hearing[d]
1970	4.9	12.2	54	35	42
1971	5.7	12.7	51	*	*
1972	6.1	12.7	55	*	*
1973	6.5	14.0	57	*	46
1974	6.8	17.0	54	31	41
1975	7.3	15.9	53	33	42
1976	6.7	14.9	47	*	43
1977	6.7	14.6	43	23	47
1978	5.4	13.7	40	19	50
1979	4.6	13.1	36	17	54
1980	4.2	13.3	32	15	56
1981	3.6	11.9[e]	27	13	55
1982	3.0	10.2[e]	27	11	53
1983	3.1	10.0	31	14	53
1984	3.6	10.1	33	16	52
1985	3.7	10.2	36	14	51
1986	4.0	10.5	36	17	48
1987	3.9	10.2	35	15	54
1988	3.8	9.2	34	14	56
1989	3.8	8.7	36	15	59
1990	4.1	9.2	37	17	63
1991	4.6	10.3	39	17	66
1992	5.4	11.2	39	17	69
1993	5.3	11.8	35	14	68

Source: From U.S. Department of Health and Human Services (1992), Table 2 and updated information from the U.S. Social Security Administration.

[a]Number of disabled-worker benefit awards per 1,000 insured workers not already receiving benefits.

[b]Number of applications for disabled-worker benefits per 1,000 insured workers not already receiving benefits.

[c]Ratio of disability awards to total disability decisions at initial determination, reconsideration, or hearing level of appeals.

[d]Fiscal year rates. Reconsideration allowance rates are combined experience for DI and SSI. Hearing allowance rates include all hearings (including SSI and Medicare), the vast majority of which involve disability issues.

[e]The abrupt decline in applications in 1981 and 1982 is due, in part, to improvements in SSA's computer systems implemented in October 1981. With the new system, local district office staff were able to check immediately whether an applicant met the insured status requirements for disabled-worker benefits, and, if that requirement was not met, a formal application was not filed. Before then, more applications were filed and then denied for lack of insured status.

Lest these comments be misunderstood, I hasten to add that variations in adjudicatory results are not necessarily all detrimental to claimants, if receiving an award is considered the best outcome for someone who applies. Deciders can be, and are, too lenient as well as too stringent. And many have criticized SSA for a failure to update its medical listings and other policies to recognize that advances in medical science and rehabilitation have made many who were functionally unemployable in the past employable today. The policy concern is therefore best understood as one of maintaining administrative legitimacy in a treacherous programmatic environment. For neither relentless stringency nor consistent profligacy have characterized SSA's history of attempting to adjudicate claims in a program designed to pursue the elusive goal of cautious benevolence.

5. Unmet Needs

The contested and contestable nature of disability adjudication results in substantial degree from the failure of overall American social welfare provision to supply supports for those who are seriously impaired but not necessarily totally disabled. Concerns about the unmet needs of denied applicants are particularly acute. We know that less than half of those denied ever return to anything like full-time employment. They are often without medical benefits of any sort because eligibility is attached to the DI and SSI programs or to employment-based insurance plans. They may also need many forms of personal assistance that are difficult to arrange, to say the least, when ill, impecunious, and left to negotiate the maze of chronically underfunded and uncoordinated social service programs that may, or may not, exist in particular localities.

Although many who are denied DI or SSI income benefits have been referred for vocational rehabilitation, VR's efforts to assist those with severe impairments to reenter the work force have been relatively unsuccessful. Many who are denied DI or SSI are rejected by vocational rehabilitation agencies as being too impaired to benefit from vocational rehabilitation efforts. And studies of vocational rehabilitation's "successes" find it extremely difficult to credit the VR programs themselves with being the sole, or even the major, cause of return to work by their clients (GAO, 1993).

If denied income and medical benefits, and unsuccessful at reentering the work force, prior to age 62, the impaired worker or potential worker often has little in the way of public or private supports to fall back upon. (At age 62, many are eligible for actuarially reduced early retirement benefits.) Private disability insurance and worker's compensation provide some palliatives, but coverage by private disability insurance is not common and the vast majority of disabling conditions are not "work connected" in the sense that is required for a worker's compensation award (NASI, 1994).

These unmet needs for income support, medical assistance, and other forms of social assistance have led many to suggest that the American disability system should attempt to compensate partial disabilities and/or temporary disabilities. But both of these approaches have such serious dangers that they seem unlikely additions to the existing set of supports for persons with disabilities. Permanent partial disability has been a major battleground, for example, in worker's compensation programs. This is the arena in which workers' compensation programs' actuarial experience is worst and its legal contests are most prevalent. Other nations, such as Holland, that have tried public partial disability programs have had very unhappy experiences. The availability of partial awards allows adjudicators to "give everyone something" in circumstances in which most cases certainly seem deserving of some form of assistance. Hence, partial disability awards tend to bloom like algae in the summertime. They can be squared with fiscal prudence only in programs, such as the veteran's programs in the United States, where the total number of potential beneficiaries is capped by a categorical qualification such as prior military service or work-connected injury or illness.

Temporary disability awards have also seemed attractive, particularly for those with serious conditions that are nevertheless expected to improve, or those with chronic conditions that are temporarily and recurrently, but not permanently, disabling. Temporary disability insurance is available, however, for a substantial number of workers through private "sickness" benefits attached to employment. This is also the largest category of worker's compensation claims, and temporary disability benefits have been mandated by several states. The prospect of an enormous caseload involving huge expense, combined with the historic allocation of the temporary disability issue to private and state programs, seems to have convinced most persons that temporary disability, at least as currently conceived, should not be part of the disability security provided by the Social Security Act.

The problem of unmet needs of persons with disabilities is not necessarily a problem that should prompt new targeted programs for persons with disabilities. Put another way, the problem of unmet needs may not be so much a function of the inadequacy of the DI and SSI programs as it is of the inadequacy of more general social supports that are needed by DI and SSI beneficiaries, denied applicants for those programs, and by many others with no severe impairments. For example, a strong system of transition-to-work and return to work programs, including medical benefits and vocational assistance, is a need of inner city youth and displaced workers, not just those with severe impairments. Nevertheless, strong universal programs of this sort might be particularly enabling for persons with disabilities.

Similarly, universal and secure medical insurance has very high salience in meeting the needs of a substantial portion of the population. Yet, again it is crucial to those with chronic diseases or disabling injuries. And, as an added bonus, universalization of medical insurance coverage would eliminate some of the work disincentives and notch effects that currently bedevil DI and SSI program design.

Finally, as a society we are just beginning to work on the problem of expanding opportunities for persons with disabilities by reshaping the work environment. We now have little idea what effect the Americans with Disabilities Act (ADA) will have on providing additional opportunities for those with severe disabilities. Nevertheless, it is surely sensible to think that programs like the ADA, that work on the demand side rather than only on the supply side of the labor market, should benefit persons with severe impairments. Moreover, work subsidies of some type represent another genre of program that has promise in aiding the return to work or transition to work for a broad range of persons both with and without severe impairments. Yet, to date we have done little to pursue subsidized employment beyond the earned income tax credit, which focuses most of its benefits on families with children (Burkhauser and Glenn, 1994).

6. The Issue of Crosscutting Goals

As the prior discussion will surely have made transparent, one of the major challenges for disability policy is the equilibration of its multiple and sometimes contrary aims. Judged by our programmatic efforts, as a nation we believe in providing income security at some level for those who are severely impaired and unable to work. At the same time we know that determining just who such people are is far from an exact science. And we believe that to the extent possible, both individuals and society are better off if persons with disabilities are rehabilitated and returned to competitive employment. We thus employ stringent eligibility standards and provide modest levels of income support. We are concerned about those with temporary or partial disabilities, but we have balked at instituting nationwide programs for fear that income support for such populations would invite dependency and court fiscal disaster.

We continue to believe that those with severe impairments are highly deserving of special treatment and support; yet, at the same time, we increasingly believe in mainstreaming persons with disabilities. This latter instinct suggests a policy focus, not only on the individual, but on the total environment, including discrimination, architectural barriers, transportation difficulties, and needs for special personal assistance. Indeed, effective programs of environmental change might eliminate some considerable portion of the need for individual income support for persons with disabilities. Thus our long-term commitment to policies that feature secure entitlements for individuals might be thought to be in tension with more recent efforts to operate on the environment rather than the individual, and to deemphasize, if not eliminate, the salience of disablement as a social classification.

In short, in conceiving disability policies, we want to support, rehabilitate, motivate, and mainstream persons with disabilities. We want to do these things all at the same time using modest program resources, operating with low administrative costs and limited personnel, while maintaining high levels of perceived program integrity and legitimacy and low levels of perverse incentives and actuarial uncertainty. In addition, of course, we want policies designed to eliminate all the unhappy tradeoffs among achieving our various goals and avoiding our various fears. "Mission Impossible" captures the flavor of this task, so long as we remember that this mission really *is* impossible.

WHITHER DISABILITY POLICY?

1. The Uncertain Future

As if disability policy did not have enough troubles, many see others approaching in the not too distant future. For one thing, the great American jobs machine seems to be in a sorry state of repair (Yelin, 1992). We now accept as "full employment" an unemployment rate twice that that was thought to be the full employment level 30 years ago. Moreover, while the economy is still creating jobs, it is not clear that it is creating enough good ones. There is an increasing bifurcation between the work opportunities for the highly skilled and educated minority and those available to everyone else. These developments have a particularly devastating impact on the "doubly disadvantaged," that is, those who have low skill and education levels combined with severe impairments. Thus, it is argued, the combination of corporate restructuring and downsizing and underdeveloped personal support and job policies is leaving large numbers of workers in their middle years stranded. They have no good job opportunities, chronic conditions that impair their marketability, and problematic eligibility for any form of income support, rehabilitation, or even medical assistance.

The demographics of the population are also moving in a direction that suggests increased pressure on disability programs. It is no secret that we become less healthy as we age, and we acquire more and more chronic conditions that impair our functioning. The famous baby-boom generation is now reaching middle age and will predictably make more and more demands on income support programs as they encounter increasing difficulties with their health and the opportunities available to them in the labor market.

The trend lines in retirement policy are not moving in directions that will meet the needs that are suggested by these demographic and economic shifts. Eligibility for retirement pensions, in particular retirement benefits under the Social Security Act, seems to be moving in the opposite direction from the desired age of retirement of most of the population. As jobs become less plentiful for older, unskilled workers; their health deteriorates; and eligibility for social security retirement recedes, we can expect significant pressure on disability income supports as the only alternative for many individuals. In short, one would expect the actuarial experience of the DI and SSI program, already a source of considerable political concern, to get worse before it gets better.

2. Aspirations and Possibilities

Although much of the preceding has been about the persistent difficulties in constructing disability policies with which we are completely satisfied, there are some hopeful aspects to our current situation that help to counterbalance the signs of future troubles. One of the most positive developments for disability policy would be a strengthening of universal supports such as universal medical insurance. The severe work disincentive effects of attaching medical benefis to disability income payments have produced both inadequate coverage and significant interference with the opportunity to return to work. A two-year waiting period for medical benefits in DI, after a determination of total disability from a medical condition, seems inhumane. Yet, in a polity without universal medical coverage and the significant prospect of denial of coverage for those with chronic conditions, this procrustean condition seems necessary to protect the fiscal integrity of the DI, SSI, Medicare, and Medicaid programs.

While programmatic changes have been made to attempt to reduce the work disincentive of loss of medical coverage, the implementation of these provisions is sufficiently complex and uncertain that few recipients seem to be reassured by them. If, as I fervently hope, the United States is moving, however haltingly, toward universal health insurance coverage—and if that coverage is reasonably comprehensive for persons with long-term chronic conditions, rather than merely meeting acute care needs for hospitals and physician services—then a major design issue in disability income policies will have been solved.

A second hopeful trend is the shift, both ideologically and practically, toward thinking about ways in which persons with disabilities can be enabled rather than disabled. This involves working both on the demand side for disabled workers, as does the ADA, and on the supply side through more vigorous efforts at return-to-work programs and a reenergizing of our approaches to vocational rehabilitation. Many experiments and demonstration projects are currently underway that might conceivably bear fruit.

Whatever these enablement initiatives' practical impact on the work status of persons with disabilities, or the numbers in "payment status" under the DI and SSI programs, this is a shift in focus that is justifiable in its own terms. To the extent possible, people should not be defined by their disabilities but by their abilities. As far as we are able, we should be concerned with maximizing the autonomy and social functioning of all our citizens, including persons with disabilities, not just with securing their economic survival.

Hopefully these symbolic shifts will ultimately have practical significance. The more we are able to focus on abilities, rather than disabilities, the more we are likely to emphasize those sorts of habilitation, rehabilitation, return-to-work and personal assistance activities that maximize the employment possibilities for persons with disabilities. The more we see autonomy, independent living, and inclusion in the community as the real aspiration of persons with disabilities, the easier it will be for us to work harder on the environmental barriers, both attitudinal and physical, that currently limit the participation of persons with disabilities in a broad range of social and economic functions.

Perhaps such a vision is Panglossian, but one can see these positive trends having salutary effects on the DI/SSI income support programs over time. If medical and other supportive services become more available outside of the ambit of the income support programs, then, not only might there be less pressure on the pool of resources for income support, but also the decision about whether to provide it becomes less an all-or-nothing proposition. Failure to achieve income support eligibility would leave applicants not with nothing, but with a preexisting set of both universal (e.g., medical insurance) and particular (rehabilitation, work subsidy, and so on) supports to fall back on.

As these developments progress, others become more feasible. Disability administration, for example, can move further from its current detached and legalistic posture toward claimants. It can and should become more social service oriented, engaging individuals *as* individuals with widely differing needs. Alternatively, administration could move toward the greater use of vouchers or tax subsidies that would empower individuals to pursue their own enablement through the purchase of services and supports as and when they determine them to be needed.

In some ways this visionary new world might look rather like an older one. For, it might well be that, under these new circumstances, disability income support could return to its early-retirement roots. It might become a permanent entitlement only for that subset of persons with disabilities who are nearing retirement age and for whom significant investments in rehabilitation, personal assistance, and other vocationally oriented expenditures would be both individually and socially unproductive. For others, disability income replacement would be a way station or a transitional support that looked toward reintegration of the individual both into productive economic functioning and those standard forms of social interdependence that we, somewhat paradoxically, label "independence."

CONCLUSIONS

Note that the title of the immediately preceding subsection: "Aspirations and Possibilities," is a view of the future of disability policy from the stratospheric heights of the space shuttle. Realizing that vision at ground level will reveal the poignant trade-offs, uncertainties, and political constraints that the body of this chapter has been at pains to recount. Progress on return to work, enablement, and mainstreaming will be a major benefit for some portion of the population of persons with disabilities. Such developments hold out little real promise to others, for their dependencies are too profound. Emphasizing new goals such as independent living, while protecting the economic and health security of those who remain highly dependent, will again challenge our ability to maintain appropriate programmatic balance where goals are multiple and populations heterogenous.

Nor will this struggle always play itself out in the bland rhetoric of the armchair policy analyst. In a legislative environment often long on aspiration and short on appropriations, services are likely to be promised that administrative cost cutting renders incompetent. When attempting to shift policies in new directions, experiments inevitably will fail. And the fallout from those failures may weigh most heavily on the most vulnerable. "Politics as usual" will continue and in that politics anecdotes may be more powerful than carefully collected data. "Waste" will be discovered in new initiatives and "fraud" will not be unknown. There will remain a capacious arena within which those whose major concern is meeting the needs of persons with disabilities, and those whose major concerns are "program integrity" and the public purse, can both find reforms to be "total failures."

Progress toward the brave new world that I have sketched will, should it occur at all, be incremental and contested. This is the unhappy truth about disability policy reform—a domain characterized by multiple and shifting ends that must be implemented through fallible means in an uncertain environment. If we are to be both reformers and realists, we must understand that success lies in the maintenance of a balanced pursuit of our multiple goals, not in the convincing and complete realization of any one of them.

Lest readers find the maintenance of balance too uninspiring a goal for reforming disability policy, I will conclude with a reminder about the past and a question about the future that might dissuade them from that view. First remember the early 1980s CDR disaster. A relentless focus on cost containment led to a political backlash that has probably pushed the program too far in the opposite direction. SSA now does virtually no CDRs, even though there are many conditions for which medical improvement can be expected. This failure to pursue the changing conditions of beneficiaries may undermine the perceived integrity of the program and may also not be in the best interests of those who should expect to be reexamined periodically.

Meanwhile the growth of the rolls has again become a riveting issue. Given the experience of the 1980s, we are unlikely to purge the rolls by reinventing the CDR fiasco. But how will we respond to other quick fixes like "entitlement caps" that would make cost predictions perfect and costs controllable, but at the expense of both the adequacy and predictability of benefit amounts? Will we forget about entitlement security in the pursuit of actuarial certainty? Reformers whose aim was maintaining balance, rather than responding definitively to the problem or enthusiasm du jour, would not.

CHAPTER 8

Does Social Security Discourage Work?

JILL QUADAGNO AND JOSEPH QUINN

One of the most remarkable demographic changes in the United States and the rest of the industrialized world during the postwar period has been the trend toward earlier retirement. Older workers, especially men, are leaving the labor force much earlier than they used to. In the United States, both Social Security and the private pension system have grown at the same time. An important question is whether these phenomena are linked, whether Social Security and private pension plans are discouraging work and influencing the retirement decisions of older Americans. The evidence suggests that they are.

A closely related issue is the long-term fiscal stability of the Social Security system. Currently legislated future Social Security taxes are insufficient to pay for promised future benefits, and some combination of increased taxes and reduced or delayed benefits will be necessary to restore fiscal balance. An important question is how changes in Social Security rules will affect the labor supply decisions of future workers.

In this chapter, we first outline recent retirement trends in the United States and abroad, and discuss the determinants of the individual retirement decision, focusing on financial factors. We argue that there are strong incentives to retire (disincentives to continuing work) built into Social Security and many private pensions, that the size of these incentives can be large, and that individuals respond to them as expected. We then ask why these incentives were created; were they intentional or an unintended consequence of policies with other goals? By reviewing the historical development of the United States system, we will argue that they very much were intentional—a primary goal was to move older workers out of the labor force. Finally, we discuss the future of retirement and suggest that the current incentives, even if they made sense in the past, may be inappropriate for the labor markets of tomorrow.

POSTWAR RETIREMENT TRENDS

1. United States

Labor Force Participation. A remarkable demographic development has oc-curred in the United States and in other developed nations during the last several decades. Older workers, especially men, have been leaving career jobs, and often the labor force as well, at younger and younger ages. In 1950, for example, nearly half of all American men aged 65 and over were in the labor force; today, fewer than 1 in 6 are.

The early retirement trend can be seen in detail in Figure 8.1, which shows labor force participation rates (that is, the proportion of the population either working or actively looking for work) for 5-year cohorts of older American men since the mid-1960s. The long-term pattern is clear. The percentage declines since 1964 are about 30, 40 and nearly 50 percent for men aged 60–64, 65–69, and 70+ respectively. For the younger two groups, men aged 50–54 and 55–59, the declines are unmis-takable though less dramatic—decreases of 7 and 14 percent.

Figure 8.1 also suggests that these long term trends may have come to a halt. For all the male cohorts shown, participation rates have changed very little since the mid-1980s. There are several possible reasons for this. During the second half of the 1980s, the American economy was recovering from a severe recession; the na-tion's unemployment rate declined from almost 10 percent in 1982 to near 5 per-cent in 1989, and it has remained in the 5 to 7 percent range since. Workers, in-cluding older workers, have seen improved job opportunities. Second, people are living longer and are often healthier at any given age. Finally, work disincentives built into our public and private pensions systems may be declining, a point that is the focus of upcoming discussion.

For women (Figure 8.2), the trends are very different because two offsetting phe-nomena are at work. People are retiring earlier, but women, especially married women, are more likely to work than before. For the oldest two female cohorts (aged 65 and older), the resultant trends are flat; for the younger two groups, the latter trend dominates, and participation rates are on the rise. For the middle group, women 60–64, the long term trend is flat, but there has been a noticeable rise since the late 1980s.

More detailed data for older men illustrate another interesting point. Figure 8.3 shows participation rates since 1968 for men aged 60–65, by individual age. The long-run trend and its recent demise are seen again, as is the increasing importance of retirement at age 62, the earliest age of eligibility for Social Security retirement benefits. In 1968, the largest behavioral change (the largest gap at the left of Figure 3) appeared between ages 64 and 65. Now, the biggest jump occurs between ages 61 and 62. A large gap at 65 still remains, but much of the labor force withdrawal has already occurred by then. Single-age data for women are similar: the behavioral change at age 62 is slightly greater than at 65.

Part-time Employment. Not only do Americans retire earlier than they used to, but also those who do keep working often work part-time. As seen in Figure 8.4, the prevalence of part-time work rises dramatically with age. Although fewer than

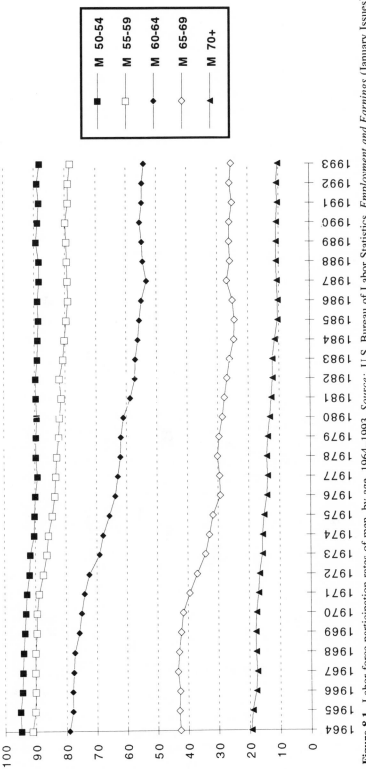

Figure 8.1. Labor force participation rates of men, by age, 1964–1993. *Source:* U.S. Bureau of Labor Statistics. *Employment and Earnings* (January Issues).

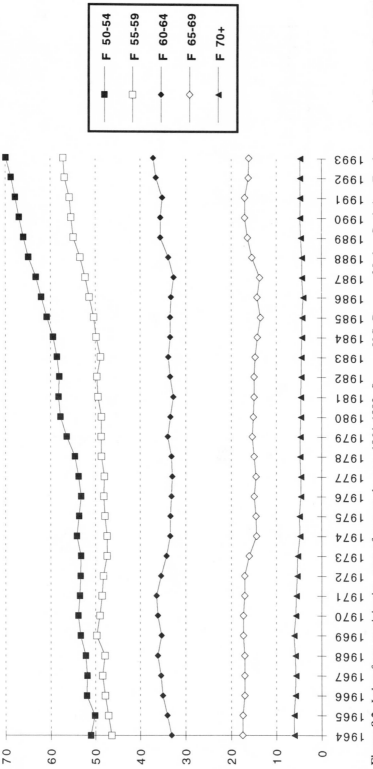

Figure 8.2. Labor force participation rates of women, by age, 1964–1993. *Source:* U.S. Bureau of Labor Statistics. *Employment and Earnings* (January Issues).

130

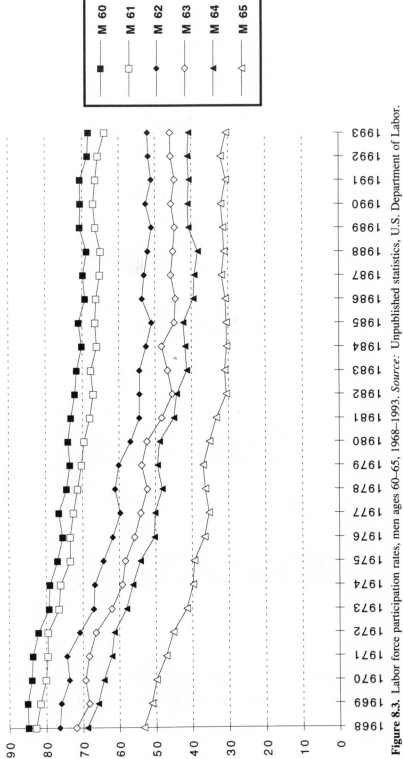

Figure 8.3. Labor force participation rates, men ages 60–65, 1968–1993. *Source:* Unpublished statistics, U.S. Department of Labor.

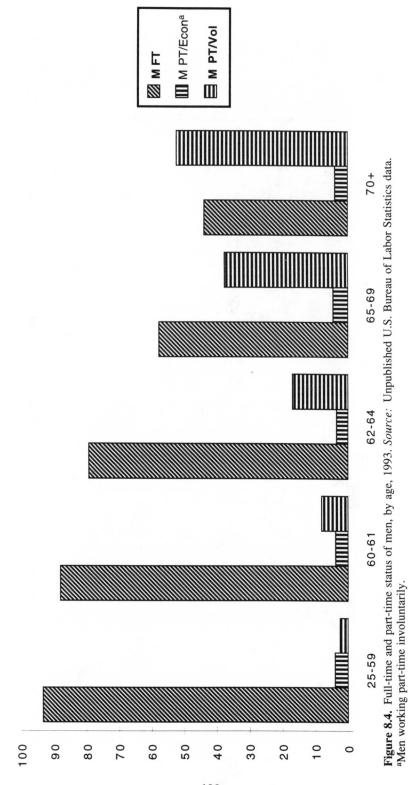

Figure 8.4. Full-time and part-time status of men, by age, 1993. *Source:* Unpublished U.S. Bureau of Labor Statistics data.
[a]Men working part-time involuntarily.

7 percent of men aged 25–59 in the nonagricultural sector work fewer than 35 hours per week, 16 percent of those aged 60–64, 42 percent of those 65–69 and well over half of the men aged 70 and over do. There is a noticeable increase from those aged 60 and 61 (12 percent part-time) to those 62–64, who are eligible for early Social Security retirement benefits (21 percent part-time).

For women, part-time work is more prevalent at all ages; about 20 percent of employed women aged 25–59 work part-time. But a third of women aged 60–64, 57 percent of those aged 65–69 and two thirds of the women aged 70 and over work part-time. The increase at age 62 is even more pronounced: the proportion working part-time jumps from 28 percent at ages 60 and 61 to over 40 percent among those 62–64. The vast majority of older Americans who work part-time say they are doing so voluntarily.

Since the beginning of the 1970s, the importance of part-time work in America has increased slightly. Among older workers, however, the increases in the proportion working part-time have been significant, from 38 (in 1970) to 48 percent for men aged 65 and over and from 50 to 60 percent for women this age. In this sense, the long-term early retirement trends may be continuing still, not through labor force departure, but rather through the reduced hours of those still employed.

The Retirement Transition in America.   Considerable recent research has focused on the nature of the retirement transition in America. Using the Social Security Administration's Retirement History Study (RHS), which followed a sample of over 11,000 older Americans from 1969 until 1979, researchers have shown that a substantial number of older Americans did not follow the stereotypical retirement route even back in the 1970s; that is, they did not leave the labor force completely when they left full-time status on their career jobs (see Quinn, Burkhauser, and Myers, 1990). Gradual or partial retirement is an important phenomenon in America. Among wage and salary workers, for example, more than a quarter did not retire completely in one move. A few of them dropped to part-time status on their career jobs, but most found new jobs. Among the self-employed, who have more control over the amount and kind of work they do, only half went directly from full-time career work to complete retirement. Of those who kept working, half moved to part-time hours on the same job, and the other half found a new job.

Most of those who changed jobs moved to a new occupation and industry, and the majority moved down the socioeconomic ladder, from skilled to unskilled and from white collar to blue collar. There was some weak evidence that those at the ends of the economic spectrum—the rich and the poor—were the most likely to stay in the labor force after leaving their full-time career jobs. One reasonable hypothesis is that the poor do so because they have to, lacking pension coverage and personal savings and often eligible for only modest Social Security benefits, while the rich do so because they want to, enjoying interesting jobs with important nonpecuniary benefits (Quinn, Burkhauser, and Myers, 1990).

Christopher Ruhm (1995) has updated our knowledge of the retirement transition using data from a Harris poll of older Americans. Comparing men aged 58–63 in 1969 (from the RHS) with men the same age in 1989 (from the Harris survey), he found that employment rates at each age had dropped over these two decades. This is consistent with the aggregate data discussed earlier. He also confirmed that there are now much larger labor force participation declines at ages 60 and 62 than there used to be. In 1969, the employment rate dropped by only 2 percentage points between ages 59 and 60, and by 5 points between ages 61 and 62. In 1989, however, the analogous declines were 13 and 18 points. These abrupt changes at these particular ages suggest that pension and Social Security eligibility are influential retirement determinants; 60 is a popular age for employer pension eligibility, and age 62 is the earliest that one can claim Social Security retirement benefits.

Ruhm also found that partial or gradual retirement is widespread. Between 30 and 40 percent (depending on age) of those aged 58–63 who were employed in 1989 were working on a postcareer "bridge" job, and these proportions were higher than they were in 1969.

Research has shown that retirement routes in America are many and varied. The stereotypical transition—directly from full-time work to full-time leisure—is only part of the story. Many Americans keep working after they leave their career jobs. This transition often involves part-time employment, usually on a new job and in a new line of work. One explanation for this phenomenon is that Social Security and pension incentives encourage it.

As we will see, America is aging. Retirement issues will become more and more important over time, especially as the baby boomers approach retirement age. When and how older Americans decide to leave the labor force will have profound effects on future labor markets and on our massive Social Security system.

2. Other Developed Nations

Labor Force Participation.   With regard to labor force participation trends, the United States is not alone. The trend toward early retirement has occurred in all industrialized nations, although the magnitude and timing of the declines have differed from country to country.

The Organization for Economic Co-operation and Development (the OECD) recently completed a major study of retirement in the developed world. Researchers calculated the proportion of men and women aged 55 and over who were working, from the late 1960s through 1990. In the United States, for example, this employment rate for men dropped from 53 to 37 percent, a decline of nearly a third (OECD, 1992, table 5.2). The male decline was near 40 percent in Australia, (West) Germany, Ireland, Italy, Spain, and the United Kingdom, and near or over 50 percent in Finland, France, and the Netherlands. In Canada and Japan, where the declines were only about 15 percent, the same phenomenon occurred, though in more modest proportions.

The evidence is more mixed for women aged 55 and over. In Canada and Sweden, female employment rates increased by 20 percent (OECD, 1992). They changed little in Australia, Italy, Japan, and the United States. In the other countries, they declined noticeably, although almost always by less than they did for men in the same country.

In summary, employment among men aged 55 and over in the industrialized world has declined significantly in a relatively short period of time. Among those 65 and over, work is now the rare exception, not the rule. In Japan, the one outlier here, more than a third of these older men still work. In Sweden and the United States, about 1 in 6 do (in the United States, nearly half did in 1950). But in most indus-trialized countries, fewer than 10 percent of men aged 65 and over are working, and in many, such as France, Germany, and the Netherlands, it is closer to 5 percent.

WHY AMERICANS RETIRE WHEN THEY DO

Decisions about when and how to retire are complex. Many factors are important, including individuals' physical and mental health, attitudes toward work and leisure, job opportunities and characteristics, and finances. Researchers have investigated the importance of these and other factors in two ways: by direct inquiry (asking people why they retired when they did), and by using complex behavioral models to predict statistically who retires and who does not. Health factors tend to be promi-nent when people are asked directly, although some researchers fear that the im-portance of health may be overstated here, since some respondents may use it as a socially acceptable reason for retirement. In the more complicated behavioral work, the role of financial incentives plays a dominant role.

We concentrate here on these financial factors, particularly on the impact of Social Security and employer pensions on individual retirement decisions. These retire-ment programs have two types of economic effects. They sometimes increase the wealth of individuals, by paying out benefits that exceed the value of the contribu-tions made. If wealthier people tend to retire earlier, because they can afford to, then this windfall gain would encourage the early retirement we have seen. In ad-dition, however, Social Security and pensions can alter a worker's compensation in subtle ways. As we will see, they can impose surreptitious pay cuts on older work-ers. If compensation influences work decisions, then this is likely to affect when people choose to retire.

1. Social Security Wealth

The simplest economic explanation for the postwar early retirement trend is that we have grown wealthier over time. Therefore, we can afford to start work later, work fewer hours per year, and retire earlier than we once did. Recent cohorts of retirees have enjoyed a generally robust economy and dramatic increases in the value of their real estate holdings. In addition, their wealth has been further augmented by the Social Security system, because the benefits they are receiving, in aggregate, vastly exceed a fair return on the contributions made by them and their employers (Burkhauser and Warlick, 1981; Moffitt, 1984; Steuerle and Bakija, 1994; U.S. House, 1991). Up to now, Social Security has been like a very successful manda-tory chain letter, with a large number of workers generously supporting a relatively small number of recipients.

Although common sense suggests that there should be a link between wealth gains and earlier retirement, it is difficult to prove empirically. It is true that the largest declines in the labor force participation rates of American men aged 60–64 occurred after the age of earliest Social Security eligibility was reduced from age 65 to age 62 (in 1961), and after very large increases in real benefits were legislated (1969–1972). Some researchers (e.g., Hurd and Boskin, 1984) have attributed most of the decline in elderly labor force participation to increased Social Security generosity. On the other hand, aggregate Social Security wealth rose dramatically in the 1950s, when coverage was increased significantly, and there was no dramatic early retirement trend then (Moffitt, 1984). Recent research suggests that the Social Security wealth impact, though important, has been modest. Jerry Hausman and David Wise (1985) and Richard Ippolito (1990) estimated that Social Security may account for about one-third of the participation decrease over time.

2. Retirement Incentives

But Social Security is very important in another way. It alters the pattern of compensation with age, and eventually results in pay cuts for older workers. Many employer pension plans do the same thing, and the combined effect can be substantial.

Both Social Security and employer pensions promise a stream of benefits once certain age, service and/or retirement conditions are met. Social Security retirement recipients must be at least 62 years old, have 40 quarters of covered employment, and earn less than a certain amount. Pension rules are many and varied, but most plans require departure from the firm (and sometimes from the industry) before benefits are paid.

What is the economic value of one's retirement income rights? Since they promise a stream of future income, with dollars coming at different times, they are best summarized by the present discounted value of the expected benefits. This is nothing more than the stock of wealth today which, if invested, could provide the promised benefit stream. For example, with a 5 percent annual interest rate, $100,000 in wealth can provide an income flow of $5,000 per year, forever. Even less could provide $5,000 per year for a limited expected life-span, because the capital can be dispersed too. Any stream of future income can be described by its present discounted value (its asset or wealth equivalent) today. A major advantage of this concept is that alternative streams, with different amounts coming at different times, are easy to compare once they are summarized in today's dollars—the bigger pile is worth more.

When one delays receipt of retirement benefits by staying on the job after the age of eligibility, two things happen. The bad news is that the worker forgoes current pension income; the good news is that, given Social Security and most pension rules, future annual benefits will be higher because of the delay in receipt. The choice is not between claiming a pension and not claiming one. Rather, it is between two different pension streams, one starting sooner, with smaller annual amounts, and another beginning later (say, after another year of work) but with higher benefits per year. Which stream is worth more? It depends on whether the future increments (the *increases* in future benefits caused by the additional year of work) are enough to compensate for the year of pension benefits forgone. If they just compensate, then the present discounted values are the same, and the pension is called actuarially fair. From a pension perspective, it does not matter whether the benefits are first claimed now or a year from now, since the total values over the expected lifetime are the same. If the future increments exceed the benefits forgone, then one gains twice by working another year, from the paycheck and from the increase in pension or Social Security wealth (called pension accrual). But if the future increments are worth less than the benefits initially forgone, then pension accrual is negative (the present discounted value declines) and one loses expected lifetime retirement income by continuing to work. In this case, one's true compensation for the year of work is less than it appears to be; it is less than the paycheck by the amount of the wealth loss incurred.

Considerable research has shown that this last scenario describes many American retirement plans. At some age, workers who stay on the job begin to lose retirement wealth and thereby suffer a subtle pay cut. For Social Security, this occurs at age 65, when the delayed retirement credit (the percentage increase in future checks for each year's delay of benefit receipt) falls from about 7 percent to only 5 percent (in 1996), which is less than actuarially fair. It is more difficult to generalize about pensions, since they are so many and varied, but research suggests that the lifetime value of defined-benefit pension streams (those pensions whose rules promise a specific benefit at retirement) often peak at the earliest age of eligibility. After that, pension wealth often declines for those who stay on the job, encouraging workers to leave the firm and claim benefits before that happens.

Lawrence Kotlikoff and David Wise studied the accrual patterns of over 1,000 defined-benefit private pension plans, and found that "for a large proportion of the plans, the accrual rate after this age (the age of early retirement) is a sizeable negative number. Thus it would not be unusual for the reduction in pension benefit accrual after the age of early retirement to be equivalent to a 30 percent reduction in wage earnings" (1989, p. 54). More recently, Olivia Mitchell (1992) reported that in 1989 two-thirds of those workers whose benefits were reduced for early retirement faced reduction factors that were less than actuarially fair, encouraging workers to claim them as soon as they were eligible. Viewed from the other end, the rewards for working beyond early retirement age (which is the same as the annual penalty for retiring early) were insufficient to compensate for the benefits forgone. Retirement incentives and work disincentives are two sides of the same coin.

The Social Security earning restrictions (at age 65) apply to any earnings; the pension regulations (at various ages) nearly always apply just to earnings on a particular job. This may help explain the phenomenon of "bridge jobs" between career work and complete labor force withdrawal. When a pension penalizes continuation on one job (say, at age 60), a reasonable strategy is to leave that job and claim the pension at the optimal time (before the pension wealth declines), then work for several more years, often part-time, at a new job. Many Americans do just this, and, given Social Security changes underway (see later), there is reason to believe that this phenomenon may be even more important in the future.

Financial incentives imbedded in pension programs, then, can penalize workers who stay on the job too long. We are not arguing that workers must pay to work (that is, that their net compensation is negative), but only that their net pay is less than it used to be, because the paycheck is partially offset by pension and/or Social Security wealth losses. Empirical evidence suggests that workers behave as though they understand these incentives (see Quinn, Burkhauser, and Myers, 1990, chap. 3). The larger the potential pension wealth losses from continued employment, the more likely workers are to leave their career jobs, and often the labor force as well.

This can be seen in simple frequency distributions for retirement ages, which show large spikes at ages 62 and 65, important ages for Social Security and many employer pensions (see Figure 8.3; Hurd 1990; Leonesio 1990), and in distributions of the actual earnings of those receiving Social Security benefits, which tend to cluster just below the amounts at which benefits start being reduced (Burtless and Moffitt, 1984; Leonesio, 1991). It also appears in a great deal of sophisticated econometric work in which measures of these incentives consistently show up as statistically significant determinants of the timing of individual retirement decisions.

3. Mandatory Retirement

Mandatory retirement once covered nearly half of American workers, and many chose to retire at that age, usually 65. Federal legislation first delayed the earliest allowable age of mandatory retirement from 65 to 70 (in 1978), and then eliminated it altogether for nearly all American workers (in 1986), primarily on age equity grounds. Because of the popularity of retirement at age 65 when it was the most common mandatory retirement age, many thought that this legislation would induce a significant change in retirement behavior. This did not happen, and the financial incentives described earlier are a primary reason why. Mandatory retirement without pension coverage was rare, and the pension (and Social Security) financial incentives tended to go into effect at the same age as mandatory retirement. The carrots and the stick all worked together to induce the desired behavior: departure from the career job at a specific age. The stick was then outlawed, but the carrots remained and continued to do the job. Research suggests that at least half of what looked like a mandatory retirement effect was in fact due to the simultaneous financial incentives (Burkhauser and Quinn, 1983).

4. Voluntary or Involuntary Retirement?

Workers today appear to have much more choice about when to retire than they once did. Older Americans today are richer than prior cohorts, more are eligible for pensions, and mandatory retirement is no longer a factor.

In questionnaires in the 1940s and 1950s, nearly all retirees said that they had retired because of poor health, a layoff, or a mandatory retirement age (Quinn, 1991). Very few claimed to have retired voluntarily, in good health, and with a job opportunity at hand. By the 1960s and early 1970s, 20 to 30 percent said they retired because they wanted to, and the proportion who did was correlated with the size of their potential retirement benefits. By the early 1980s, more new Social Security beneficiaries appeared to be retiring voluntarily than involuntarily. In 1982, a third said that they wanted to retire, compared to a quarter who named health as the primary reason. The proportion voluntary rose with age (up to 65), and was much higher for those eligible for a pension.

An understanding of the financial incentives and other factors that many older workers face, however, blurs the distinction between voluntary and involuntary. Many Americans confront increasingly unattractive labor market options as they age. As we have seen, for many, net compensation on career jobs eventually declines as Social Security and/or employer pension wealth diminishes with additional work. In addition, continued employment at the career job may not be guaranteed, not because of mandatory retirement, but because of the threat of corporate downsizing and layoffs. Work on a new job, if available, usually pays much less than the career employment did. Faced with these options and uncertainties, many workers leave their career employers when their pension plans suggest they do, and many then leave the labor force as well. Is this voluntary? Yes, in that they chose to accept the pension and leave the firm, given the terms, conditions, and likelihood of continued employment that they faced. But no, in that more preferable options (continued employment at prior rates of compensation) may have disappeared as they aged.

WHY RETIREMENT INCENTIVES EXIST

Research indicates that Social Security and many employer pensions discourage work at some point, and that these financial incentives do influence retirement behavior. While public officials and private employers have had many objectives in establishing these programs, one goal has been to encourage older workers to leave the labor force. These labor supply effects have been intentional.

1. The Pre–Social Security Era

Prior to the Social Security Act of 1935, few workers were covered by pensions. As a result, more than 60 percent of men over age 65 were employed in 1930, and many more moved in and out of the labor force. Only the "wealthiest, the sickest, or the few guaranteed income" retired permanently (C. Haber and Gratton, 1994, p. 105).

Although private pension coverage had increased during the 1920s, being covered by a pension plan was no guarantee that a worker would receive a pension, for most plans included disclaimers stating that workers had no pension rights (Quadagno, 1988). Even employers who intended to meet their pension obligations found that the aging of the labor force and the increase in average wages, which determined pension benefits, seriously depleted company pension funds. Further, the financial success of the companies underwriting these plans fluctuated with the state of the economy (Schulz and Myles, 1990). As early as 1929, many firms abandoned their pensions as too costly. The Great Depression further drained the trust funds established to pay pensions, and the rise in bankruptcies eliminated pensions for thousands of workers (Latimer, 1929).

Before 1935, then, pensions did little to discourage labor force participation among older workers. Few workers were covered by private pensions, and many of those who were covered never received benefits. Even fewer received pensions from state pension programs, which were meagerly funded and granted only to the most destitute.

2. The Social Security Act of 1935

In 1934 President Roosevelt appointed a Committee on Economic Security (CES) to prepare an economic security bill covering both old age and unemployment (Kingson and Berkowitz, 1993). In planning an old-age insurance (OAI) program, the CES members chronicled the unfavorable position of older workers. Because mechanization favored younger workers, they noted, it had become increasingly difficult for workers over age 45 to maintain their skills and stay employed. Especially in heavy manufacturing industries, older workers were often unable to keep pace with the demands of machines. Not only were older workers at greater risk of becoming unemployed than younger workers, but also their spells of unemployment were longer. The Great Depression only exacerbated their problems (CES, 1935).

The CES relied on three arguments to justify the intrusion of the federal government into the labor market. First, after long years of productive labor, workers had earned the right to retire. Second, advanced age made older workers incapable of performing productive labor. Third, an older man who continued working prevented "a younger man from filling his place and gaining occupational skill, experience and promotion" (p. 137). As Senator Robert Wagner explained during the debates prior to the Social Security Act, "The incentive to the retirement of superannuated workers will improve efficiency standards, will make a new place for the strong and eager, and will increase the productivity of the young by removing from their shoulders the uneven burden of caring for the old" (Graebner, 1980, p. 185). Thus, justification for a national program of old-age insurance was based on the ideas that older workers should be able to retire with some base of economic security and that encouraging retirement would enhance employment opportunities for younger workers.

The original Social Security Act subjected covered workers to a very strict earnings test: a person lost all Social Security benefits during any month he or she earned $15 or more (a 100 percent benefit reduction rate after the exempt amount). The purpose of this earnings test was to encourage retirement and open the job market for younger workers. As one CES member explained, "the interest of Mr. Roosevelt was with the younger man.... That's why that little ridiculous amount of $15 was put in.... Let him earn some pin money but it had to be on retirement" (Graebner, 1980, p. 186).

3. Expanding Social Security Coverage

Initially, old-age insurance benefits were so low and coverage was so limited that few workers could retire. Gradually, however, Congress improved benefits and added new categories of workers, increasing the inducements to retirement (see Berkowitz, chapter 2). The extended coverage meant that more workers would be eligible for Social Security, and as more covered workers reached 65, more were drawn out of the labor force.

Enactment of disability insurance in 1956 initially did little to encourage retirement, however, because the rigid eligibility rules made it difficult for disabled people to qualify for benefits (see Mashaw, chapter 7). This is less true today. Recent literature suggests that the decision to apply for disability benefits is not just a function of health conditions but is influenced by the generosity of benefits and the ease of access (Quinn and Burkhauser, 1994). Some older workers with health conditions can work, if they have to, but would prefer to be on disability benefits. In such cases, the existence of disability programs can discourage work, and may have contributed to the dramatic declines in older labor force participation rates.

Amendments to the Social Security Act in 1956 allowed women to retire at age 62 with reduced benefits (80 percent of the age-65 benefits). In 1961, in the midst of a recession, this early retirement option was extended to men. According to a proposal from the Kennedy administration, the early retirement provision would help primarily that group of men who because of ill health, technological unemployment, or other reasons find it impossible to continue working until they reach 65. As Congressman Charles Vanik (D-Ohio) stated, "If two million male workers eventually retire under this program, two million job opportunities will be created, and unemployment will be reduced" (quoted in Kingson and Berkowitz, 1993, p. 48). Others viewed this proposal as a means of reducing high unemployment by redefining some of it as early retirement.

Beginning in 1968, real Social Security benefits were increased in four of the next five years, with the 1972 increase building in regular cost-of-living adjustments (Derthick, 1979; Myles, 1988). From 1975 to 1979, benefits were erroneously indexed to both wages and prices, resulting in a "double" upward adjustment of benefits, a mistake that was later corrected (see Myers, chapter 13). In total, these policy changes, coupled with general increases in the level of earnings on which benefits were calculated, led to a 51 percent increase in real average Social Security benefits during the 1968–1977 period (Hurd, 1990).

Until 1983, the Social Security system expanded in ways that encouraged retirement at age 65 and early retirement at 62. Then the direction of incentives began to shift. In 1983, in response to improvements in longevity and rising costs, Congress legislated an increase in the normal retirement age from 65 to 67 (to be phased in gradually early next century) and an increase in the penalty for early retirement at 62 (eventually, from 20 to 30 percent of the amount one would receive at the normal retire age). The amendments also increased the delayed retirement credit for those who first claim benefits after age 65. These measures will gradually reduce the Social Security work disincentives, by increasing both the penalty for early retirement and the reward for delayed retirement. In addition, the earnings test has been continually liberalized. In 1996, the earnings test reduces Social Security benefits by 50¢ for every dollar earned over $8,280 for recipients aged 62–64, and 33¢ for every dollar earned above $11,520 for those aged 65–69. Recent legislation will gradually increase the exempt amount to $30,000 for those who have reached the normal retirement age. At age 70, the earnings test no longer applies.

An interesting question is whether the liberalized Social Security earnings test, the elimination of mandatory retirement, and the increases in early retirement penalties and delayed retirement rewards are sufficient to counter the long-term retirement trend noted. Simulations based primarily on the retirement behavior of older workers in the 1970s (those in the Retirement History Study) suggested that these changes would delay retirement, as expected, but that the magnitudes of the delay would be modest, on the order of months, not years (Quinn, Burkhauser, and Myers, 1990). One reason is that early retirement is also encouraged by the incentives in private pensions, and these are not directly affected by the Social Security changes discussed earlier. On the other hand, aggregate data suggest that the long-term early retirement trend among men has tapered off and perhaps has ended, and these policy changes may be partially responsible.

4. Early Retirement and Private Pensions

Social Security was never designed to stand alone as an income source for retired workers. Rather, it is supposed to serve as a first tier, to be supplemented by employer pension benefits and personal savings. As Social Security developed, it became integrated in complex ways with the merging private pension system.

During the Great Depression, most employers opposed the idea of a national old-age pension. To encourage business support for the Social Security Áct of 1935, employers were allowed to deduct their Old Age Insurance contributions as a nontaxable business expense and to reduce their pension costs by integrating Social Security benefits with existing firm plans (Jacoby, 1993). Instead of increasing the total income of pensioners by adding Social Security to their benefits package, however, many companies reduced the firm's contribution to the total retirement benefit (Dyer, 1977). For workers with private pension coverage, Social Security was one part of a benefit package. Because few workers were covered by private pension agreements, most had only Social Security for retirement income.

The connection between Social Security and private pensions was strengthened in 1948 when the National Labor Relations Board ruled that pensions were a negotiable item in collective bargaining agreements. Immediately, the large industrial unions began demanding private pensions as part of the wage package. In 1949 the Ford Motor Company agreed to provide company-financed pensions of $100 per month to workers retiring at age 65 with 30 years of service. The $100 was only partly financed by the auto company, since the pension was integrated with Social Security. This program set a pattern for the industry, and soon the Big Three auto companies had similar pensions for their workers (Quadagno, 1988). The concept spread to other industries, and by the late 1950s over half of all unionized employees were covered by integrated pension plans. These private pensions provided a significant income supplement for workers, increased their retirement income benefits, and facilitated their departure from the labor force.

Shortly after early retirement benefits were added to Social Security, the private sector followed suit. In 1964 the first early retirement provisions appeared in the auto industry, allowing auto workers to retire with reduced benefits at age 60 if they had at least 10 years of service and at age 55 with at least 30 years of service. The key to early retirement provisions was the availability of "supplemental" benefits, an additional benefit paid until the worker was eligible for Social Security at age 62. To qualify for the supplemental benefit, the worker had to agree to limit earnings in retirement. The early retirement program outlined in the UAW contract was therefore aimed not only at early retirement from the auto industry itself, but early retirement from the labor force as well (Barfield and Morgan, 1969). Early retirement benefits stabilized retirement income by providing workers who retired before 62 with income equal to what they would receive once they reached the Social Security eligibility age (Schulz, 1991).

During the 1973–74 and 1981–82 recessions and periodically since then, many companies have added "sweeteners" to the usual early retirement benefits. These early retirement incentive programs (ERIPs) extend retirement opportunities to otherwise ineligible workers to increase the rate of retirement when a company needs to downsize its work force. For example, when oil prices were declining in 1986, Exxon Corporation offered immediate retirement to its employees aged 50 and over who had more than 15 years of service. The offer was open for about a month, and granted credit for an extra three years of service in calculating retirement benefits (Meier, 1986). Because these benefits are available for a short defined "window" of time and restricted to a portion of the firm's labor force, the cost to the employer is limited (Meier). Sweeteners, like supplemental early retirement benefits, have encouraged the trend toward early retirement.

5. International Patterns

In other developed countries as well, early retirement has been encouraged through a variety of government programs, including social security, unemployment insurance, and disability insurance. Much of the stimulus to encourage early retirement has been driven by efforts to alleviate high unemployment during the post-OPEC period of slow economic growth (Guillemard, 1991a).

France represents an extreme example of the international trend toward early retirement. The decline in labor force participation among those aged 55–64 has occurred mainly since 1970, largely the result of changes in the French pension system and the expansion of unemployment benefits.

Unlike the American Social Security system, the French public pension system was designed to keep older workers in the labor force to offset the labor shortages following World War II. The legal age for full retirement benefits was 65, although a worker could retire at age 60 with a half pension. Those who continued working past 65 received a pension increment of 5 percent a year. Later, as the labor shortages disappeared and unemployment rose, the age of eligibility for full pensions was reduced from 65 to 60. However, there remained a large pool of unemployed workers aged 55–59. The decline in their participation rate was facilitated by the unemployment program.

In 1972 France established a guaranteed income plan that provided compensation for workers over age 60 who had been dismissed from their jobs. The regular program of unemployment benefits covered workers until they reached age 60. Since the unemployment benefits exceeded those provided by the national pension program, they encouraged retirement (Guillemard, 1991b). During the late 1970s a dramatic increase in unemployment further reduced job opportunities for older men. By the 1980s an unemployment program that was originally designed to compensate wage earners for short periods of joblessness had assumed responsibility for covering jobless aging workers for as long as five years or more. It became a *de facto* old-age fund (Guillemard). Then in 1983 the unemployment compensation program was expanded to include workers who had resigned from their jobs. As a result, labor force participation among men aged 55–59 dropped from 83 percent in 1970 to only 67 percent by 1988 (Guillemard).

In the Netherlands high unemployment during the 1970s and 1980s was managed by expanding disability programs. By 1985, 42 percent of those age 60–64 and 33 percent of those 55–59 participated in a disability scheme (DeVroom and Blomsa, 1991). A similar though less extreme use of disability pensions to facilitate early retirement for workers aged 55–59 has occurred in Germany (Jacobs, Kohli, and Rein, 1991). Initially, disability was defined in strictly medical terms. Any individual who was capable of working even part-time was ineligible for a disability pension. Because part-time work was scarce for older workers, however, two court decisions in 1969 and 1976 allowed part-time workers to receive a full disability pension. These decisions encouraged early retirement among men and women 55–59 who are ineligible for other forms of support. In 1985, an important legislative change made it more difficult for older workers to retire through the disability system, and participation rates among men and women began to increase.

Germany has also provided an opportunity for the long-term unemployed to receive retirement benefits. Any 60-year-old man with a work history of at least 15 years who has been unemployed for at least 52 weeks within the past year and a half is eligible for this benefit. This provision has no effect on women, however, because women are allowed to retire at age 60 anyway (Jacobs, Kohli, and Rein, 1991).

In Great Britain, the main vehicle for encouraging early retirement was the Job Release Scheme (JRS). Implemented between 1977 and 1988, a period of increasing unemployment, the JRS allowed specific categories of older workers to retire early if the vacancies could be filled by unemployed persons (Laczko and Phillipson, 1991). Workers who were ineligible for the JRS had to rely on social assistance or unemployment benefits if they became unemployed before they became eligible for state pensions (age 65 for men and age 60 for women).

Unlike in Germany, labor market options are not considered when awarding a disability benefit in the United Kingdom. The benefit is based solely on health, and a physician determines whether a worker is capable of working. Disability benefits are higher than those received by the unemployed and are paid until age 70, whereas unemployment benefits are only paid for one year. Not surprisingly, the growth of unemployment in Britain has been accompanied by an increase in older workers claiming disability benefits (Laczko and Phillipson, 1991).

Although rates of labor force participation among older workers vary across nations, most developed countries have used some form of welfare or social insurance program to encourage retirement. These include straightforward pension programs, as well as disability and unemployment benefits. Regardless of the specific programs and incentives employed, the general result has been a decline in labor force participation, even among workers younger than traditional retirement age.

RETIREMENT IN THE FUTURE

In this chapter we have argued that government programs such as social security, disability, and unemployment insurance, whose primary function is to cushion earnings losses following these events, can also influence labor supply decisions. Older workers respond to the financial incentives inherent in unemployment and retirement income programs, and the generosity of disability programs can induce some workers to stop work and apply for disability benefits. In addition, we have argued that these labor market effects are generally not unintended or unexpected consequences, but rather are usually intentional. It is not surprising that, in the depths of the Great Depression, United States policymakers hoped that the new programs being contemplated would remove some of the vast numbers of unemployed from the labor force. In more recent years, Europeans have been active in redesigning their programs' eligibility criteria and generosity in response to changes in unemployment. Workers respond to the incentives they face, and policymakers have used this fact to influence labor force participation decisions of specific groups.

In anticipation of the significant demographic changes ahead, societies must ask whether their current programs remain appropriate. In the United States, because of rising Social Security costs and the potential of future labor market shortages, many think that postwar retirement trends should be reversed and that older workers should be encouraged to stay in the labor force longer than they now do. Given increases in longevity, this could be done without decreasing the proportion of life spent in retirement.

A major impetus for these concerns is that the industrialized world is aging. For example, the number of Americans aged 65 and over will double by 2030, while the number aged 55–64 will increase by two-thirds. This is the aging of the baby-boom generation. In stark contrast, the number of Americans under age 18 will decline slightly over the same period, while the population under 55 will increase by only 1 percent (U.S. Bureau of the Census, 1989, table F, middle series; U.S. Senate, 1991, chapter 1). As a result, the percentage of Americans aged 65 and over will increase from under 13 percent today to about 22 percent by 2030 (U.S. Bureau of the Census, table G). A third of all Americans will be 55 and older, and the median age will rise from 33–42.

The combination of fewer younger Americans entering the labor market and fewer older Americans staying in it could create labor shortages in the future. If this happens, one response is to encourage Americans to work longer, utilizing their labor market experience for a few more years. The same types of incentives that have induced older workers to leave in the past could be used to encourage them to stay in the future. Employers could structure wages, pensions, and other forms of compensation and provide flexible hours to induce older workers to stay on board. As we have seen, there are several changes already underway that move in this direction.

Mandatory retirement has virtually been eliminated, and Social Security work disincentives are being diminished. The exempt amount under the Social Security earnings has been increased significantly, and there is frequent discussion about eliminating it altogether. In addition, the age of normal retirement is scheduled to increase from age 65 to 66 by the year 2005 and eventually to 67 by 2022, and there is talk of accelerating this transition. To receive any given retirement benefit from Social Security, one will have to work longer. This can also be viewed as a benefit decrease, which it is—at any given age, one will receive less than one would have previously. Finally, the delayed retirement credit, currently 5 percent per year of benefit delay after the age of normal retirement, will slowly increase to 8 percent early next century. When it does, the average worker who continues to work beyond the normal retirement age will no longer lose Social Security wealth by doing so. The net result of all this is a lower benefit schedule and one that is closer to being age-neutral. Compared to the present system, this will encourage workers to stay on the job longer than they do now.

Among employer pensions in the United States, there is a trend away from defined benefit to defined contribution plans. The former, as explained, frequently encourage early retirement by decreasing the pension wealth of those who stay on the job too long. Defined contribution plans, in contrast, are really just saving accounts with significant tax advantages. They contain none of the work disincentives described. This trend should also encourage longer work lives.

Some argue that these changes do not go far enough, and that we should contemplate further delays in the normal retirement age (for example, to age 68 or 70) or delays in the earliest age of Social Security eligibility, currently 62. The latter, we think, would have dramatic effects on retirement trends, since many Americans now retire at age 62 voluntarily, in good health and with good job opportunities, and could easily work longer. Of course, for some, with poor health, poor job prospects, and little retirement income, this is not true, and a delay in the age of earliest eligibility would impose a serious hardship. An important question is whether this problem is best handled with the early retirement age for all workers or with more targeted programs such as Disability Insurance or Supplemental Security Income.

In summary, recent research on retirement has made several things clear. Many public and private policies, here and abroad, discourage work by the elderly. Older workers seem to understand and respond to the incentives they face. In the past, these incentives have induced older workers out of career jobs and often out of the labor market as well. There is no reason why they cannot be equally successful at the reverse: encouraging workers to stay active in the labor market longer than they currently do. Given the demographic changes on the horizon, this may be just what we need.

CHAPTER 9

How Does Social Security Affect the Economy?

EDWARD M. GRAMLICH

The rise in spending for social security systems throughout much of the world has led to a number of economic fears. Beginning with those at the most microeconomic level, every social security system has a number of rules defining benefits and tax payments. These rules, or provisions determining who gets what level of benefits, can distort the natural behavior of individuals and firms regarding when individuals retire, how much they earn in their retirement years, and how much they save in their working and retirement years.

At a more macroeconomic level, there is the question of economic competitiveness. As social security spending expands and/or as a country's population ages, benefits rise and taxes (on either present or future generations) must rise to finance these costs. These taxes, normally assessed on worker payrolls, lead to rising wage costs and perhaps to a loss of economic competitiveness. Whether wage costs rise depends in the first instance upon whether payroll taxes are shifted back onto workers. Even if not, whether a country loses economic competitiveness depends on how that country manages its international exchange rates—whether its currency parities are fixed or floating.

Then at the most macroeconomic level, expanding spending and taxes for social security could affect a nation's saving-investment balance. Economists are increasingly coming to the view that whether the economy is closed or open to international trade and capital flows, its long-run living standards are significantly determined by its national saving ratio: the sum of its private saving, social security saving, and other government current account saving, all divided by its total output. There are a number of interactions of each type of saving with one another, so it is not straightforward to determine what any set of policies, social security or any other, does to overall national saving. But it is clear that social security systems are now big enough to affect overall national saving, in a positive or a negative direction. This, then, becomes another potential way in which social security spending affects the economy, this time operating over a very long period.

This chapter examines these three types of economic impact of the United States Social Security system on the United States economy in the early 1990s. It focuses on the United States Old-Age, Survivors, and Disability Insurance (OASDI) system, excluding Medicare and other health insurance programs that introduce a number of separate complications. To make a long story short, the chapter argues that the economic dislocations currently resulting from Social Security are not major. There are some observable microeconomic distortions, but the costs of these distortions seem minor. Economic competitiveness seems basically a nonissue, given the apparent insensitivity of overall labor supply to wages and the freely fluctuating United States dollar. The impact of social security on overall United States national saving could be either negative or positive right now. (This is a highly controversial issue among economists.) But whatever the impact, even if Social Security spending begins expanding more rapidly, the impact could be made more positive for the foreseeable future with certain policy changes. With these changes, social security could actually be made into an institution that promotes national saving in the United States and higher living standards.

MICROECONOMIC DISTORTIONS

United States Social Security (OASDI) payroll tax rates have risen slowly, from 6 percent in 1960 to 8.4 percent in 1970, to 10.16 percent in 1980, to 12.4 percent in 1995. There is another 2.9 percent payroll tax to pay for medicare. The payroll tax for OASDI was assessed on all wages up to $62,700 in 1996, an amount that is indexed by average wages and covers about 87 percent of all wages paid.[1] This tax is assessed equally on employers and employees and, according to assumptions usually made by economists and further explained later on, most likely shifted entirely back onto workers. Self-employed workers pay a similar 12.4 percent.

There are a number of potential distortions implicit in this structure, some not very important and some possibly important. For one thing, historically, coverage has been incomplete, and Social Security could have been responsible for a shift from covered to uncovered employment. But gradually coverage has expanded so that Social Security now includes about 96 percent of the work force, with the only major excluded group of workers being state and local employees in some states. These employees do have their own pension programs, however, and it is difficult to imagine states and localities hiring workers fleeing from the Social Security system because they do not want pension coverage. Hence, while coverage could have been a problem historically, today's distortions from this source seem minor.

A second possible microeconomic inefficiency regards private saving. Any tax on current income can act as a disincentive to save. By taxing wage income, the most important component of current income, Social Security taxes may act as a moderate disincentive to save. Perhaps a bigger disincentive comes in the the form of crowding out—the fact that any time the public sector does something, such as provide old-age pensions to individuals, there could be less incentive for these same individuals to save to provide pensions on their own. But, as mentioned, there could also be some positive impact of Social Security on overall national saving working through the operation of the trust fund. Since this question is so closely integrated with the overall saving-investment balance issue, it is left for later discussion.

A third possible microeconomic inefficiency involves work effort in and around retirement years. The United Social Security system now pays benefits on the basis of a worker's payroll tax contributions over a 35-year period. These benefits are keyed to a normal retirement age, now 65 and slated to rise gradually to 67 in the next century. Workers have the option of retiring at age 62 and getting reduced benefits, or of retiring after 65 and gaining a delayed retirement credit. An earnings test then reduces benefits paid to nondisabled retirees between the ages of 65 and 69 by 33 percent for all earnings above $11,500; by 50 percent for all earnings above $8,300 between the ages of 62 and 65. There are separate provisions determining spouse benefits, survivors' benefits, and payments to husbands and wives of different ages. Also, to gain eligibility for disability insurance, one must claim a disability that keeps one from working, implying that disabled workers by definition must drop out of the labor force.

As discussed in the previous chapter, it is clear that Social Security benefits affect work behavior in and around the retirement years. There is a high density of retirement at age 62 and a lower density of retirement at age 65. This implies that Social Security does influence retirement behavior, though it is not clear how large the distortionary impact would be, because workers might well retire at similar ages even in the absence of a Social Security system. The work test could discourage work in retirement years, and the presence of the disability insurance program could do likewise, though disability insurance still covers only a tiny share of the work force. Many of these types of distortions are inevitable in a broad program such as Social Security. The work test is one distortionary policy that may not be necessary, though any evaluation of that must obviously weigh all the benefits and costs. But even with all these potential distortions, a large number of empirical examinations of these provisions have found the labor supply distortions to be minor (Chater, 1994; Honig and Reimers, 1989; O. Mitchell, 1991; Moffitt, 1987).

Saying that the labor market distortions of Social Security as now constituted seem to be minor does not mean that they will be minor under all circumstances. As Kingson and Schulz (chapter 3) discuss, one idea being floated now, as a way to reduce both current budget deficits and the long-term actuarial deficit of the Social Security system, is to means-test Social Security benefits. By this is meant to lower benefits depending on the current taxable income of retirees.[2] Were this to be done, there could be a much sharper disincentive for retirees to work in their retirement years and to save in their working years (Burtless, 1996).

ECONOMIC COMPETITIVENESS

Since it is funded by a payroll tax, Social Security is alleged to harm the economic competitiveness of the United States. As in the continuing United States debate about national health insurance, the payroll tax is said to raise business costs and prices, and to make it harder for United States firms to compete internationally.

The argument may sound good to politicians, but it is full of holes. One problem is that the Social Security payroll tax rate has not actually increased that much, recently from 10.16 percent in 1980 to 12.4 percent in 1995. While this could be viewed as a 22 percent rise in tax rates (2.24/10.16), a better standard is to compute what the rise in payroll tax rates does to unit labor costs. By this approach, the rise in unit labor costs has been only 2 percent (.0224/1.1016) over a 15-year period, an annual rate of increase of only 0.1 percent. Increases of this magnitude are tiny compared to all of the other influences on unit labor costs.

But even this calculation overstates the rise in unit labor costs. A realistic assumption seems to be that, for the whole economy, labor is supplied inelastically to firms; that is, there is very little sensitivity of overall labor supply to changes in wage rates. This means that the entire payroll tax, employer and employee component alike, is likely to be shifted back onto labor in the form of lower wage rates than would be earned without the payroll tax. This in turn means that at first approximation the rise in payroll taxes is unlikely to have any effect on unit labor costs.

In this sense, the argument about payroll costs is somewhat different from the one about health care. With health care, the policy question was whether to extend health insurance coverage to small firms, many of which could have been paying wages close to the minimum and have been unable to shift increased labor costs back onto workers by lowering wages. The degree to which this was true for health insurance is still unclear, but for the whole Social Security system, most wages are well above the legal minimum and there should be no reason why payroll costs would not already have been shifted back onto labor, hence implying little impact on economic competitiveness.[3]

Of course, if the aggregate labor supply were not inelastic, there could be some payroll tax impact on unit labor costs. But even then it is not clear that there would be an impact on the international competitiveness of the United States, because for more than a decade the United States has been under a regime of freely floating exchange rates. This means that any rise in labor costs and prices from whatever source should ultimately be reflected in a lower international value of the dollar, and again no impact on United States competitiveness.

SAVING AND INVESTMENT

In the end the most profound impact of Social Security on the economy, for good or ill, is its impact on national saving and investment. In the long run the most important policy-controlled determinant of a country's living standards is its national saving ratio, according to neoclassical growth models of the sort that were developed by Robert Solow (1956). In a closed economy, greater national saving adds to the capital stock that determines living standards in the long run. In an open economy, things become more complicated because increased national saving could also increase net lending to the rest of the world, but it is still true that national saving leads to higher national net worth and to higher living standards in the long run. According to many economists, the United States can now be thought of as a hybrid closed-open economy. It is clearly open to trade and capital flows, as would be a standard open economy. At the same time, the United States capital market is large enough that United States saving and investment quantities can perhaps influence world interest rates, as in a closed economy.

National saving, the key policy variable in determining long run living standards, can be expressed as

$$NS = PS + SS + FS$$

where NS is the overall national saving ratio, the sum of private and state and local saving (PS), Social Security saving (SS), and all other federal saving (FS), all divided by total gross domestic product (GDP). A comparison of how each of these components has changed since 1960, using mostly five-year periods to average out cyclical wiggles, is shown in Table 9.1.

As can be seen, this national saving ratio has dropped sharply, from 8.6 percent of the GDP in the early 1960s to 2.0 percent of GDP in the early 1990s. This sharp drop, if maintained, presages a period in which real wages and living standards are likely to grow even more sluggishly than they are now doing.

The table also decomposes movements in national saving, to illustrate further the sharp drop in national saving. Through the mid-1980s the main factor was non–Social Security federal deficits. Private saving remained as high as 9 percent of GDP into the mid-1980s, before dropping almost to 6 percent now. The Social Security system was generally operated on a pay-as-you-go basis until the mid-1980s, with the consequence that its direct contribution to national saving was essentially zero. In the mid-1980s, however, there was a political compromise to prefund some of the large anticipated future costs by running surpluses, now at the level of 0.8 percent of GDP. The deficit for the rest of the federal government, on the other hand, rose steadily from less than 1 percent of GDP in the early 1960s to more than 5 percent now.

The numbers in Table 9.1 show the direct contributions of the various components of national saving and are reasonably noncontroversial. But the struggle of economists to discern the full impact of the Social Security system on national saving, direct plus indirect effects, has been anything but noncontroversial. Originally, Martin Feldstein (1974) argued that the Social Security system would depress national saving by providing retirement income security on a pay-as-you-go basis through the government that might reduce the amount private individuals would oth-

TABLE 9.1. Saving Ratios as a Percentage of the Gross National Product, 1962–1994.

Years	Private	Social Security	Other Federal	National
1962–1965	9.4	−0.1	−0.7	8.6
1966–1970	8.7	0.4	−1.3	7.8
1971–1975	9.1	0.2	−2.1	7.2
1976–1980	9.8	−0.2	−2.7	6.9
1981–1985	9.0	−0.1	−4.6	4.3
1986–1990	6.5	0.7	−4.5	2.7
1991–1994	6.3	0.8	−5.1	2.0

[a]Private and national saving are measured by calendar years; federal and Social Security saving, by the overlapping fiscal year.

Source: Calculated by author based on U.S. National Income and Product Accounts.

erwise accumulate on their own behalf. This effect, known as the wealth substitution effect, could be offset by the impact of changes in retirement work behavior and by changes in bequests, in effect to compensate one's children for supporting their elders through the pay-as-you-go system. Theoretically, these effects are hard to disentangle. Empirically, Feldstein found a sizable saving reduction, while others such as Danziger, Haveman, and Plotnick (1981), Leimer and Lesnoy (1982), and Munnell (1977), found small or even positive impacts on overall national saving.

Looking into the future, the most recent trustees' report (Board of Trustees, 1995) for Social Security predicts that under present laws there will be continued small Social Security surpluses until 2018, at which point the baby-boom generation begins to retire, benefit payments rise, and the surplus disappears.[4] After 2018 these Social Security deficits rise fairly steadily, and the direct contribution of Social Security to overall national saving turns from positive to negative. The U.S. Congressional Budget Office (1994a) predicts that non–Social Security federal deficits will drop for a time before rising by the end of the century. It is not clear what will happen to private saving, but unless it rises fairly sharply, the direct federal components alone will depress national saving ratios even further.

But that all assumes no change in policies, for either Social Security or the rest of the federal government. Given the actuarial deficits facing the social security system in the long run, and assuming no change in macroeconomic policies, austerity changes in the Social Security system are clearly necessary. These could be made on either the tax side—by raising payroll tax rates—or on the benefits side—by cutting benefits or, perhaps, delaying the normal retirement age. These actuarial changes should eliminate the looming social security deficits, and at least arrest this source of decline in future national saving rates. Whether they would be large enough to arrest the drop in overall national saving ratios is another question.

PROMOTING HIGHER LIVING STANDARDS

Perhaps there is a way that Social Security could be made into an institution that actually promotes higher living standards. As Table 9.1 shows, the United States now saves an extraordinarily low share of its national output. The disappointing aspect of this low national saving is that as long as it persists, living standards are not likely to rise very rapidly in the future. The encouraging aspect is that if there were some way to raise overall national saving, the funds could be invested at very attractive rates of return and national living standards would rise. And if this rise could in some way be captured by the Social Security pension system, the difficult choice between Social Security tax increases and benefit cuts could be made much more agreeable.

There are two ways of capturing the gains from added national saving, one primarily a public approach and one primarily a private approach. The public approach has been proposed by Aaron, Bosworth, and Burtless (1989). They argue for prefunding the rise in benefit payments by raising taxes now and investing the proceeds in government bonds, as Social Security now does.

An even more extreme variant of this approach is presented by Bosworth in the next chapter. Under this new approach, payroll taxes would be raised now. But, instead of investing the proceeds in government bonds, Bosworth would split Social Security from the government budget and then permit the Social Security trust fund to invest a portion of its assets in private equities, hence permitting the Social Security system to capture more of the benefits of the high rates of return on new national saving. This approach permits the Social Security system to take advantage of what economists call the "equity premium puzzle," the fact that, over long periods of time, equities pay substantially more than bonds, even adjusting for risk (U.S. Congressional Budget Office, 1994b). Bosworth calculates that, under realistic assumptions, these changes alone would eliminate actuarial deficits for the foreseeable future, with only a 2 percentage point rise in payroll tax rates (from the present 12.4 percent to 14.4 percent).

Under either the Aaron, Bosworth, and Burtless or the new Bosworth approach, it would probably be necessary to remove Social Security from the federal budget.[5] As long as Social Security stays in the budget, and deficit targets are imposed on the overall unified budget, it can almost be guaranteed that any added Social Security surpluses will be offset by added deficits elsewhere in the unified budget. This means that any added Social Security saving will not even raise federal government saving, let alone overall national saving, and that there will be no added national income to be used to solve the long term difficulties of the Social Security system.

Under the new Bosworth approach it would also be important to control the investments of the Social Security fund. One obvious reason is the dictates of financial prudence. But there is another reason as well. Right now the size of the Social Security trust fund is more than 10 times as large as the next largest private corporate pension plans in the United States. Were payroll taxes raised even further to increase overall national saving, the size of the Social Security trust fund would increase that much more. Given the size of the fund, and the possibility its investments could be used in a political way, it would be very important to neutralize the political impact of Social Security investment, either by letting a number of competing funds managers do the investing or by having Social Security invest in broadly based index funds (Weaver, 1994b).

The private approach features a variant of the dual pillar system that the World Bank, among others, has been advocating (Weaver, 1994a; World Bank, 1994). In a gradualist version of the dual pillar proposal, future Social Security benefits for young, high-income people would be scaled back, but then supplemented by a mandatory universal pension system (MUPS). The MUPS would be invested in a market basket of stocks and bonds, presumably by certified investment funds. Again overall pension saving is supplemented by new national saving, again invested at going market rates of interest. This time, since the investment is by individualized MUPS accounts, there would be no particular fear of government political control of the investment of large funds balances. Particular firms or individuals would choose their own fund managers, and these management decisions would presumably be diversified enough to eliminate the political-control problem.

But there could be some other fears. One is the need to insure the safety of these MUPS funds; both the investment and annuity policies of MUPS accounts would need some regulation, and this would be unpopular. Another is the fear that as more high-income people rely more on their MUPS funds and less on Social Security proper, Social Security becomes more of a redistributive program and less of a communitarian program. This could threaten the unique political popularity of the Social Security system.

It is also possible to imagine an intermediate reform that still raises national saving. Instead of simply raising payroll tax rates, it might be possible to designate some of these added contributions as made on behalf of the individual, and to fold these contributions into the normal indexed annuity payment on retirement. Senator J. Robert Kerrey (D-Nebraska) and former Senator John C. Danforth (R-Missouri), the chair and co-chair of the Bipartisan Commission on Entitlement and Tax Reform (1995), recently proposed a measure along these lines.

However these policy issues play out, the underlying macroeconomic proposition is that, with an undersaving economy, there are profitable opportunities to invest at attractive rates of return.[6] These returns can be used to raise national saving and living standards, and simultaneously to supplement pension income and ward off the looming financial difficulties amply documented in the Trustee's Report. This saving could be done within social security, as in the Aaron, Bosworth, and Burtless; the Bosworth; or the Kerrey/Danforth plan, or outside of the system, as with a MUPS approach. These various approaches all have their advantages and disadvantages. But the key point is that there does have to be added national saving. Without this, society's living standards are no higher, and any greater returns from equity investment are only a form of higher Social Security tax on the rest of the economy (U.S. Congressional Budget Office, 1994b).

IMPLICATIONS

While fears about large and rising Social Security systems harming national economies may be well-grounded elsewhere, for the most part these fears seem misplaced in the United States. The rules determining benefits and taxes do make for minor perturbations in private behavior, bunching retirement ages around 62 and 65 and impeding work among younger and disabled retirees. But most empirical studies find these distortions to be minor.

As for economic competitiveness, the fears of economic harm seem quite misplaced. Under most reasonable assumptions, payroll costs are shifted back onto workers and do not affect unit labor costs at all. Even if there were some slight impact, any rise in national unit labor costs would likely be offset by a lower value of the dollar.

The one area where Social Security does have a major impact, and it could be positive as well as negative, is on national saving. Right now, the direct impact of Social Security on overall national saving is slightly positive; the indirect effect is difficult to discern but probably fairly small. Without further policy changes, the direct impact could become negative in the future when the baby-boom generation begins retiring. But the direct impact could also be made more positive by measures to increase national saving now and invest this added saving at attractive rates of return, in either bonds or stocks. In such a scenario, whether the saving is invested within or in tandem with the Social Security system, the United States Social Security system could even provide a convenient way to mobilize new national saving and provide for higher future living standards.

ENDNOTES

1. The recent budget bill removed the earnings ceiling for Medicare.

2. There is an important difference between means-testing, as described here, and the taxation of Social Security benefits within the personal income tax. Suppose all private pension saving were done under consumption tax treatment, where the initial income was not taxed but the ultimate distributions were. To establish neutrality, it would then be necessary to tax the part of Social Security benefits paid from the heretofore untaxed employer contribution, that is, to tax half of Social Security benefits at retirement. If private pension saving were taxed under deferred income tax rules, tax neutrality would be established by taxing more than half of Social Security benefits at retirement. Either way, the logic is entirely different from the logic for means-testing, and entirely in keeping with the logic of the rest of the income tax system.

3. Given this shifting, it also does not matter whether workers and employers view the payroll tax as a tax or as an installment payment on a defined contribution pension plan.

4. A more common way of looking at the balance of the Social Security trust fund is by what is known as the trust fund ratio: the assets of the fund as a share of annual expenditures. This ratio hits a peak in 2012 and declines to 0 by 2030.

5. Even though the 1990 Budget Enforcement Act removed OASDI from the budget and from estimates of the federal budget deficit, OASDI still continues to be presented and discussed as part of a unified budget.

6. Munnell and Ernsberger (1989) found that reserve accumulation contributed to added capital formation in both Sweden and Japan.

CHAPTER 10

What Economic Role for the Trust Funds?

BARRY BOSWORTH

An increasing number of Americans have become concerned about the long term financial viability of the Social Security system, and many younger Americans profess a belief that they will never collect any benefits. This concern is highlighted in a simple summary, shown in Figure 10.1, of the financial projections of the Old-Age, Survivors, and Disability Insurance (OASDI) funds provided by the 1994 Trustees' Report. As discussed by Gramlich (chapter 9), the contributions of the baby-boom generation (individuals born between 1945 and 1965) can lead to the buildup of a significant reserve during their working years; but they will begin to retire in the years after 2010, leading to a sharp rise in benefit payments. In the actuaries' intermediate projection, outlays will begin to exceed tax revenues in 2013. Interest income will cover the shortfall for another six years; but, starting in 2020, the fund will have to draw upon its assets, which will be exhausted by 2030.

These projections reflect a rather dramatic change compared with those of the mid-1980s. In the early 1980s, the system was faced with a short-run liquidity crisis, as the recession threatened to reduce income below the level of immediate benefit payments, by an amount that exceeded the system's reserves. The Social Security amendments of 1983, which were directed primarily toward resolving the short-run problem, also helped reduce some of the long-term solvency problems by speeding up previously enacted tax increases, raising the retirement age after 2002, and imposing an income tax on beneficiaries, with the proceeds to be returned to the OASDI trust funds. Having weathered the short-term crisis and benefitted from the legislated changes, the 1984 Trustees' Report showed the system to be in close actuarial balance over the 75-year horizon, and there was a projected buildup of reserves to about $3 trillion in mid-1990s prices by 2015.[2]

FUNDING PROBLEMS

In contrast, the 1994 report showed a large actuarial deficit equal to 14 percent of future discounted costs. Furthermore, the reserve was now projected to reach a peak

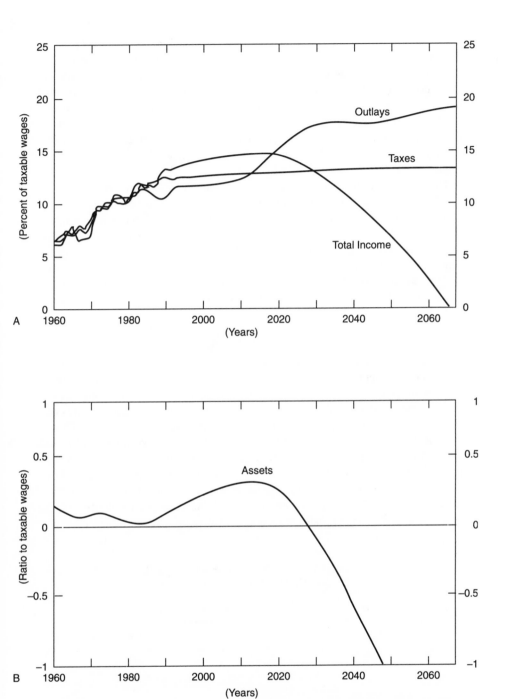

Figure 10.1. A, Income and outlay of the Social Security funds, intermediate case (in percent of taxable wages); **B,** Assets of the Social Security trust funds, intermediate case (ratio to taxable wages). *Source:* Board of Trustees. *1994 Annual Report.* Washington, D.C.: U.S. Government Printing Office.

of only a little more than \$1 trillion and to be dissipated at a much faster pace. The deterioration of the projected financial position over the past decade reflects a wide range of changes in the underlying economic and demographic assumptions and methodology used by the Social Security Administration's actuaries (see Table 10.1), but the result is a steadily more pessimistic assessment of the system's finances. In particular, costs were projected to rise at a much faster pace. For example, the cost rate, outlays as a percentage of taxable payroll, estimated for 2060, were dramatically increased from 15.45 percent in the 1984 report to 18.5 percent in the 1994 report.

These more current projections, of course, remain highly uncertain as forecasts of what will actually happen over the next 75 years, and the trustees' report includes both high- and low-cost alternatives to the commonly used intermediate estimates. The projected cost rate is shown in Figure 10.2 for all three alternatives. The variance of outcomes is between a situation of continuing surpluses for the indefinite future (low cost) and a liquidity crisis that emerges as early as 2015 (high cost).[3]

The sources of the cost increase, as well as the range of uncertainty, can be better understood by separating the cost rate into two components: the dependency rate (DR) and the benefit rate (BR)

$$CR = DR - BR.$$

The dependency rate, the ratio of beneficiaries to covered workers, reflects largely the role of demographic factors and retirement patterns.[4] The benefit rate, the ratio of the average benefit to the average wage, is reflective more of the changes in economic factors and legislated rules determining benefits.[5] The initial benefit is based on a worker's wage history, indexed to the average economy-wide wage. Thus, the ratio of the average benefit at time of retirement to the average wage can be treated as fixed by legislation. However, in subsequent years the benefit is adjusted only for price inflation. Thus, high rates of real-wage growth lower the benefit rate.

In the long run, however, changes in the system's costs are driven by demographic factors: birthrates, immigration, and mortality.[6] For example, the dependency rate is forecast in the intermediate projection to rise by 80 percent between 1995 and

TABLE 10.1. Changes in Estimates of the 75-Year OASDI Actual Balance, by Reason for Change, 1984–1994.
(Percentage of taxable earnings)

Actuarial Balance, 1984	−0.06
Change in the period of valuation	−0.45
Economic Assumptions	−0.80
Demographic Assumption	0.67
Disability Assumptions	−0.54
Methods	−1.07
Legislative	0.10
Other	0.01
Actuarial Balance, 1994	−2.13

Source: Data from Board of Trustees' Reports, various years, as compiled by John Hambor, U.S. Treasury Department.

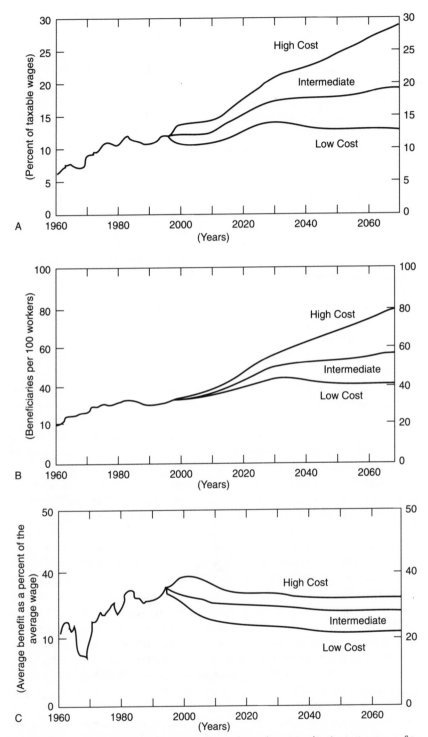

Figure 10.2. A, The OASDI cost rate under three alternative scenarios (as percentage of taxable wages); **B,** The OASDI dependency rate under three alternative scenarios (beneficiaries per 100 workers); **C,** The OASDI benefit rate under three alternative scenarios. (average benefit as a percent of the average wage). *Source:* See Figure 10.1.

159

2070, while the benefit rate declines by 10 percent. Furthermore, the dependency rate at the end of the projection period varies by 100 percent, depending on whether the optimistic or the pessimistic projections are used, (compared with 17 percent for the benefit rate).[7]

It is all too common to point to the discontinuity in the age distribution of the population induced by the baby-boom generation as the primary factor behind the escalating future costs. But the existence of that cohort only distorts the timing. Their entry into the labor force since the mid-1960s has swelled its ranks and held down the cost rate. They will continue to do so until 2010 (when they will begin to retire). Costs will then rise at a very rapid rate.

The fundamental force behind the rise in the dependency rate is the slowing of growth in the working-age population. Since 1970, the dependency rate has increased only marginally—from 27 retirees per 100 workers in 1970 to 31 in 1995—because a rapid expansion of the work force offset nearly all the growth in the number of retirees. As we look ahead, the growth in the number of retirees will actually slow, falling from an annual rate of 2.2 percent in the 1970–95 period, to 1.8 percent until 2030, to roughly 0.4 percent between 2030 and 2070. This will occur despite the retirement of the baby-boom generation. On the other hand, the growth of the population of workers needed to support the system will fall dramatically, from an annual rate of 1.6 percent in 1970–95, to 0.45 percent in 1995–2030, to only 0.1 percent in 2030–70. As a result, the dependency rate will continue to rise even after the baby boomers are gone.

Despite the uncertainties, it is hard to escape the conclusion that the Social Security system faces serious future funding problems (see Myers, chapter 13). The magnitude of current tax increases or benefit reductions required to bring the system back to actuarial balance over the 75-year horizon exceeds 2 percent of taxable payroll. That would only be the tip of the iceberg, however, because the simple passage of time would require further increases as the valuation period extends farther into the high-cost years of the twenty-first century. The tax rate would have to rise between 0.5 and 1 percentage points every 10 years just to maintain the standard. A 2 percent increase in the tax would cover outlays until 2020.

If the system operates on a pay-as-you-go basis, the intermediate projection suggests that the payroll tax rate would need to increase to about 16.5 percent in 2030 (when all of the baby-boom generation would be of retirement age), and it would have to rise further to about 18 percent in 2070.[8] Furthermore, once we include the hospital insurance portion of Medicare (Part A), the increases become much larger. In the intermediate projections, the cost rate rises from 15 percent of payroll in 1995 to 25 percent in 2030 and 30 percent in 2070. Overall, the magnitude of transfers from workers to retirees raises some serious concerns about the sustainability of the program. Despite the system's strong short-term financial conditions, today's workers should prefer that decisions be made soon to resolve the long-term problems, leaving them with a sufficient working period over which they could adjust their saving and retirement plans.

To date, most suggestions for reform of Social Security have focused on methods of reducing future benefits, or expanding the tax base.[9] By themselves, however, these actions do not provide a solution, in that the size of the future retiree population and their retirement needs will remain the same. The debate has accepted the view of a fixed pie of future resources, and the issue has become how to divide it between the young and the old, an inherently divisive issue (see Marmor, Cook, and Scher, chapter 12). In what follows, I wish to focus on a third option: increased saving as a means of meeting the higher costs of future retirement, that is, expanding the fund of future resources out of which the needs of both the young and the old will be met. This includes the possibility of advance or partial funding for future benefits, as well as some suggestions for changing the approach and responsibility for managing the buildup of a retirement fund.

Proposals for reductions in benefits seem particularly limited because the program in the United States is already quite modest by international standards. For the worker earning half the average wage, the couple benefit is at the poverty threshold, and for a single person it is below. Since these retirees have very little in additional assets, an across-the-board cut in benefits would result in either offsetting increases in Supplementary Social Insurance (SSI) payments or higher poverty rates. Yet, the existing system is already so redistributional that efforts to concentrate the benefit reductions among high-wage workers risk widespread disaffection and demands to opt out of the system.[10] Alternatively, means testing of the benefits on the basis of other retirement income, as proposed by some recent commissions, would go even further toward destroying incentives to save for retirement through private means.[11] Workers would be encouraged to consume during their work life, since any saving for retirement would be offset by reduced Social Security benefits.

Yet, current workers must also recognize that an ever-lengthening period of retirement cannot be supported without some rise in the tax rate that they pay during their working years. There has been a continual increase in average life-spans. Americans have taken this increased time, and more, in the form of a longer period of retirement. While the Social Security "normal age of retirement"[12] has remained fixed at age 65 since the program's inception, life expectancy at age 65 for men has increased by 25 percent (from 12 in 1940 to 15 years in 1995) and for women by 45 percent (from 13 to 19 years). Life expectancy, moreover, is expected to rise by an additional 10 to 20 percent by 2025. If the increase in life expectancy were entirely offset by a later retirement age, the normal retirement age of 65 in 1940 would be 72 today and 74 in the year 2030 (see Bartlett, chapter 15). Yet most Americans are retiring at an earlier age. The average age for receiving benefits was age 69 in 1950 and age 64 in 1990, and the labor force participation rate of older workers is expected to continue to fall in the future.[13] By the year 2030, the retirement period of an average worker will be nearly half that of his work life. These trends, which increase the population of retirees, could be moderated by raising the retirement age, but we would still be left with the contracting contribution base caused by the slowing of growth in the population of workers.

Too great a focus on means of moderating the growth in the cost rate, however, can limit a consideration of other options for resolving the financing system. It is not very useful as a means of measuring the burden the system places on future generations of workers. It represents the share of wage earnings that must be set aside to finance the retired, but it says nothing about the level of real wages out of which those benefits will be paid. For example, a one-shot increase in the level of labor productivity would raise the real wages on which future benefits are based and add to the future outlays of the Social Security system. Yet, the burden of the system on future workers would be less, because the wages out of which the benefits must be paid would have increased far more than the added retirement costs. From this perspective, *a focus on the cost rate understates the importance of changes in the growth of productivity and real wages in measuring the future burden.* If the current generation could provide a means of sharply raising the incomes of future generations, its retirement would not represent an increased burden, even though the cost rate might rise very sharply. On the other hand, if the growth in real wages continues to deteriorate at the pace of the decade 1985–1995, a rebellion by future workers seems increasingly likely.

PAY-AS-YOU-GO VERSUS FUNDED PROGRAMS

To date, nearly all industrial countries have financed their social insurance programs by some variant of a pay-as-you-go system in which each generation pays for the retirement costs of the currently retired, in return for a commitment for the same treatment during their retirement. Such a system has a obvious appeal to the first generation, but at its inception it also appeared attractive to subsequent generations.[14] Workers who spend their entire work life and retirement years within a pay-as-you-go system with constant tax rates will earn a return on their contributions equal to the growth in population plus the growth in the real wage.[15] In effect, the formula defines the growth in the pool of resources available to support retirees between the time of contribution as workers and retirement.

In the decades after World War II, the rate of return within a pay-as-you-go system was very high (see Chen and Goss, chapter 5). The population of covered workers grew at an annual rate of 2.4 percent between 1950 and 1995; and until the early 1970s, average real wages were rising in excess of 2 percent per year. In contrast, the common view of a funded program involved investing contributions in government securities with a real return of about 1 percent. Thus, quite apart from the benefits to the first generation, the choice of pay-as-you-go could be argued to be the right choice for subsequent generations.

In comparison, the current outlook is much different. The *intermediate actuarial projection* assumes an average annual growth in covered employment of less than 0.3 percent until 2070. Furthermore, the projected growth in real wages has been cut to only 1 percent annually (still above the average of the 1975–95 years). As a result of this wage assumption, the projected return of a pay-as-you-go system is now well below even the interest rate on government bonds. There has also been a significant change in the perspective on the alternative option of a funded program because of the emergence and success of private pension funds, which invest their assets in a combination of bonds and equities and earn a real rate of return in the range of 4 to 5 percent. Thus, it is not surprising that the current cohort of young workers might wish that the originators had opted for a funded program. Not only are they stuck with paying the retirement cost of a large baby-boom generation, but the economics of the system does not look very good even if all age cohorts were of equal size.

A clearer recognition of the benefits of a funded system may not have been enough to change the original decision. A funded program when Social Security was initiated would have required each cohort of workers to receive benefits equal to the present value of its past contributions. Few politicians would be willing to support a proposal in which the benefits of a new tax would not begin to flow for several decades. Moreover, funding would have delayed for many years the nation's effort to respond to poverty among the elderly. Furthermore, expectations about wage growth and the need for additional capital were much different then.

THE BENEFITS OF INCREASED SAVING

Much of the discussion of funded, versus pay-as-you-go, has been skewed by an excessive focus on the government bond rate as the relevant measure of the rate of return on a funded system. While that rate is appropriate for evaluating the financial condition of a Social Security fund that limits it investments to government securities, it is not at all appropriate for measuring the benefits to the nation or future generations. The Social Security fund earns 2 percent return because it opts to invest in risk-free government securities. But in buying government securities, it frees up resources that pass through capital markets and can be used by others who are willing to invest in riskier forms of capital earning a higher rate of return. In particular, if the saving of Social Security (the excess of its tax and interest income above outlays) ends up adding to national saving, it can finance an increase in physical capital. For example, if the funds were ultimately utilized by corporations to finance their investments, they might earn much higher rates (an average real return before tax of 7.8 percent over the 1960–93 period).

The before-tax return in the corporate sector probably overstates the average return on capital in the total economy, since corporate capital is more heavily taxed than investments in homes and noncorporate business. There is no reason to assume that all of any increment going to national saving would go to the corporate sector. An estimate of the economy-wide, before-tax return to capital can be computed from the prior estimates for the corporate sector if investments in the different sectors are assumed to yield an equal after-tax return. Existing studies of effective tax rates can be used to calculate equivalent before tax rates of return for housing and the noncorporate business sector. The result is an estimate of 6.2 percent for the real return on capital employed in the domestic economy.[16]

How are those benefits distributed? The answer to that question depends on whether we view the United States as a closed economy, in which all saving must be invested in domestic capital, or we recognize the recent opening of international capital markets and the free flow of resources across national borders.

First, in a closed economy the added physical capital will raise output; and the income derived from that output, under the assumption of fixed full employment, will accrue to the owners of the new capital. After allowing for depreciation, the increase in aggregate income is measured by the previous estimate of the net return to capital. Thus, multiplication of the net return by the increment to capital yields the increase in net income to the nation. The increase in the capital stock, however, will have secondary implications for the distribution of income between workers and the owners of existing capital. The additional increase in capital per worker will raise the productivity of workers, and they will benefit through an increase in their real wage. This gain to workers is paid for by a loss of income to holders of old capital. As measured by the rise in the capital-output ratio, labor has become more scarce relative to capital, and its return rises, while that of capital falls. In effect, entrepreneurs with ideas for new investments and workers gain from the increase in saving, while owners of old capital lose. The direct benefits to the Social Security funds are the interest earnings on their investment in government bonds and a higher future level of receipts equal to the tax rate times the rise in the real wage. These benefits are, of course, substantially less than the gain in national income.

In an open economy the process is somewhat different because the increment to national saving can now flow abroad. No American is going to invest in a foreign asset that provides a return below that available from domestic investments. Moreover, in a completely open capital market, it would be most reasonable to assume that the risk-adjusted return of foreign and domestic investment are equal. In fact, rough estimates of the value of American corporate investments overseas suggest that they earn a rate of return equal or above that on domestic capital.[17] If the global market is assumed to be so large that marginal changes in saving within the United States have no effect on the return, the increment to United States saving will spill over into the global market, where it will earn the same return and generate the same increase in American national income as occurred with the rise in the stock of domestic capital. Because there is no increase in the amount of domestic capital per worker, however, there is no significant effect on wage rates in the United States, and no corresponding loss to old capital. This has some implications for Social Security. While the Social Security funds receive a similar interest return on investment, they do not benefit from any increase in tax receipts.

As a practical matter, international markets are still in an intermediate stage. While financial capital can flow quite freely between the major industrial economies, the need to balance any net movement of capital with equal changes in current account flows (i.e., trade in goods and services) still requires significant changes in relative prices.[18] Thus, large outflows of capital would result in a significant depreciation of the currency in order to achieve a matching change in the trade account. This would be offset by a reverse appreciation in the future when the income from foreign investments flows back to the United States. These movements in the exchange rate act as a restraining influence on the capital outflow because the depreciation raises the attractiveness of investing in the domestic economy.

While the future trend is toward a more integrated world economy, the option of investing abroad should be viewed as an escape valve for the policy of increased national saving. It limits the decline in the rate of return to capital that would otherwise accompany a large surge of saving in a closed economy. Thus, the expansion of investment options actually makes a policy of increased national saving more attractive, but it changes the distributional consequences between domestic labor and capital.

FUNDING SOCIAL SECURITY

Despite the attraction of a higher rate of return, the suggestion that we might replace the current pay-as-you-go system with a full reserved system suffers from a fundamental flaw. Changing now would require the transitional generation to pay twice for retirement: their own retirement through a fully funded system and that of the currently and near-retired through the old pay-as-you-go system. The result would be a large drop in the after-tax income of the transitional group of workers. Even if the benefits to future cohorts were significantly positive, it is difficult to perceive how one could induce a transitional group to bear the costs.

However, the fact that the costs of the system, and thus taxes, are projected to rise substantially in the future raises the possibility of an intermediate policy of advance funding of the added future costs. Current workers support a smaller population of retirees for a shorter period of retirement than will be the case when they retire. This fact, combined with a lower growth in the future work force, accounts for the sharp growth in the projected dependency rate. The magnitude of the added burden on future workers could be reduced if the current work force agreed to meet the added cost of their retirement through an increase in their own saving. The result would be a larger future stock of capital and thus a large pool of income out of which their future benefits would be paid. Although contribution rates would continue to rise in the future, they would be applied to wages that would be higher than in the absence of such a program. In addition, a substantial portion of future benefits would be paid out of the interest earnings of the Social Security funds, rather than relying solely on the contributions of future workers.

Beginning with the 1977 and 1983 amendments, Congress began to move away from a pay-as-you-go system of financing toward a greater emphasis on adjustment of taxes and promised benefit levels to maintain actuarial balance between future costs and future income. Actuarial balance was defined as equality (within 5 percent) of the present discounted value of future revenues and payments over a 75-year horizon. Those calculations would be based on current legislation for benefits and tax rates. Because of the future increases in the cost rate, a focus on actuarial balance implied a degree of advance funding and a buildup of a significant reserve. Thus, each cohort of workers would pay a portion of their own retirement costs, to the extent that those costs were greater than the costs of the currently retired.

A Brookings study (Aaron, Bosworth, and Burtless, 1989) examined the economic implications of a system of partial funding in which (1) Congress would consistently adjust taxes to maintain the system in actuarial balance over the 75 year horizon, and (2) the surplus would be set aside to add to national saving.[19] That study was based on the more optimistic assumptions of the 1986 Trustees' Report. The study's most important result was to show that even the relatively small amount of advance funding implied by a rule of maintaining actuarial balance could, if saved and invested, generate increases in aggregate income sufficient to offset the added costs of OASDI on future workers and more than compensate those generations, through increases in their before-tax income, for the added taxes they would have to pay. The need to move forward the schedule of tax increases in order to maintain actuarial balance would reduce consumption in the short run, but the subsequent faster growth of incomes would allow annual consumption to return to its former level within 15 years and reach a peak increase of about 3.5 percent at the height of the baby-boom retirement in 2030. Second, the 1996 projections implied that only three adjustments in the tax rate would be required to maintain actuarial balance, increases of about 0.8 percent in the years 1999, 2027, and 2060.

Much has changed since the Brookings study was completed in 1988. The revision to the trust fund projections since 1986 has resulted in a much faster rate of growth in the cost rate, and the system has already fallen into "actuarial imbalance." The fact that the Congress has taken no action on either benefits or tax rates to restore balance implies a far smaller reserve buildup and, thus, a much smaller pool of potential saving. Thus, the first assumption of our report—that the current generation would understand the nature of the increased burden that their retirement places on future workers and that they would be willing to partially fund a portion of those costs—now seems questionable. Second, our proposal at the time also required that the current generation recognize the critical importance of setting aside the reserve, letting it add to national saving, and thereby increasing the wealth that would be inherited by future generations.

The first problem (inaction) is a serious one, because it reflects the unwillingness of public officials to take action that imposes any costs on future voters. The precedent set by the 1994 response to a looming cash shortfall in the disability program is also discouraging; Congress simply shifted funds from an OASDI program already out of long-run actuarial balance to meet a more pressing short-term need in the DI program. If public officials will take no action to maintain actuarial balance, the issue of what to do with the surplus will gradually become moot. But, in fact, we cannot conclude that inaction was the wrong answer until we resolve the second issue: Can an increase in the OASDI surplus add to national saving?

THE EFFECT ON NATIONAL SAVING

The assumption that the surpluses of the fund will "pass through" and increase national saving is critical to the notion of using partial funding of Social Security to offset the increased burden on future workers. National saving is the sum of saving in the private sector—household saving and the retained earnings of corporations—and saving in the public sector. In the period between the end of World War II and 1980, the national savings rate averaged about 8 percent of national income—a *private* saving rate of 8.5 to 9 percent offset by a *public* dissaving of 0.5 to 1 percent. More recently, the situation has deteriorated significantly. The private saving rate fell through the 1980s to an average of 6 percent in the 1990–93 period, while public sector dissaving ballooned to nearly 4 percent. The result is a low national saving rate of about 2 percent of national income (see Table 10.2).

A funded Social Security system would create a third source of national saving. However, that saving would not add to national saving if its existence led to a decline in private saving or an increase in the dissaving of the public sector.

There has long been a debate about whether the introduction of Social Security or an increase in the promised benefits would lead to an offsetting reduction in private saving. Suffice it to say that the issue has not been resolved to everyone's satisfaction. In this case, however, the choice between a funded program or a continuation of a pay-as-you-go program would have no effect on the magnitude of the promised future benefit. It is that promise, the future liabilities of the system, that should influence private saving, not the magnitude of any annual surplus of the fund. Thus, except to the extent that funding would make the future promise more cred-

TABLE 10.2. Net National Saving and Investment, 1950–1993.
(Percentage of Net National Product)

Category	1950–69	1970–79	1980–89	1990–93
National Saving	8.5	7.9	4.3	2.0
Private	8.6	8.9	7.1	5.8
Government	−0.1	−1.1	−2.8	−3.8
Investment	8.5	8.2	4.2	2.1
Domestic	8.1	7.9	6.1	3.2
Foreign	0.4	0.3	−1.9	−1.0
Statistical Discrepancy	0.0	0.3	−0.1	0.1

Source: Data from U.S. National Income and Product Accounts

ible, there is little reason to expect that partial funding would lower the private saving rate.[20]

Instead, the more critical issue involves the response of the government component. To some extent, the issue is entangled in a debate as to whether Social Security is a transfer program or a retirement program. To some, including many of it supporters, Social Security is simply a system of transfers between different groups in society, in which case there is no reason to separate it from other activities of the government. Its revenues are seen as part of general government revenues, requiring Congress to decide how to allocate its scarce resources among competing claims. The assignment of a specific category of government revenues to a specific type of expenditure is viewed as bad budget policy.

The emphasis on keeping Social Security within the budget is evident in the fact that, despite the formal movement of Social Security to the status of an off-budget agency, nearly all public analyses and discussions of the budget focus on the total, inclusive of Social Security. It is even more obvious when we note that the current proposal for a balanced budget amendment is written to include Social Security and that many in Congress seek to use the current surplus of the Social Security funds to finance other programs. While cuts in Social Security benefits may be "off the table," the same is not true of the surplus.

Yet, so long as Social Security is an integral part of the total budget, there is no reason to anticipate that a surplus in the fund would actually lead to a rise in national saving. The decision to fund a portion of the fund would be a purely internal matter, offset within the government sector as a whole.

If Social Security is a transfer program, there is a strong argument for abandoning the effort to build up additional reserves, cutting the tax rate, and reverting to pay-as-you-go financing. The existence of large reserves will simply make the future problem of Social Security worse from a political perspective. If the current generation of workers are credited with the fiction of having contributed to a retirement fund from which they immediately withdrew the proceeds to finance current consumption, they will argue that the future reserve is something meaningful which they are entitled to have returned. Income taxes on future workers would have to rise to repurchase the securities previously issued to the Social Security fund. Yet, the current generation will have simply substituted a wage tax for the income taxes that would normally be needed to finance current outlays of the operating budget. If all government revenues are to be comingled, the excess funding of Social Security simply represents a shift to greater reliance on regressive wage taxes to pay for programs formerly financed with personal and corporate taxes. Many would argue that it would be better to revert to a broader-based tax to finance these government activities.

Yet most Americans view Social Security as a retirement program and seem to agree with the policy of setting aside the surplus as a vehicle for saving. They are normally very surprised to learn that the surplus is being used to finance other programs and that the budget deficit most frequently mentioned in public discussions includes the finances of Social Security. As a retirement program it makes sense to fund a portion of the future costs, as is done with private pension plans, to reduce the burden on future generations of workers.

Thus, one part of an effective program to use Social Security as a vehicle for raising national saving must involve a change in the budgetary process to more clearly differentiate Social Security from the operating budget of the government. It will require significant changes in the way the fiscal choices are presented and in the economic concepts governing the decisions. In one dimension this has already occurred, given that the primary responsibility for short-run economic stabilization has shifted from the Congress to the Federal Reserve. That shift reflects both the observed inability of the Congress to make timely decisions and a changed perspective on the importance of fiscal policy for stabilization in a situation of increasingly integrated global capital markets. In the future, the role of national fiscal policy will be analogous to that of the states' budgetary policy within a national economy. Just as states recognized the futility of an independent fiscal policy, federal fiscal policy is becoming of reduced relevance to the short-run behavior of the United States economy.

A commitment to differentiate between the retirement accounts and the budget would require the federal government to make its decisions with budgetary rules that are closer to those of the states. Most states present their budgets in ways that exclude their retirement programs, and nearly all have sought some degree of funding of those liabilities. As the states have built up their pension reserves, they have been able to resist the temptation to increase their own borrowing as an offset. In a few states, borrowing is prohibited by the constitution, but in most it is not. Some evidence that their retirement account surpluses have added to saving is provided in Figure 10.3. While the annual state retirement fund surpluses have steadily grown to over 1 percent of the gross domestic product (GDP) in the 1990s, the nonretirement budget balance has fluctuated close to zero, with no clear tendency to rise or fall over time.[21] In fact, state retirement accounts have now grown to the point that they represent an increment to national saving of about 1 percent of national income. The ability of most states to make rational decisions about their pension liabilities should suggest that the federal government is at least capable of doing the same.

There are several options for increasing the degree of separation between the Social Security funds and the federal operating budget in ways that might reduce any temptation to use the funds' surplus as a justification for a larger budget deficit. The most direct, but not necessarily the best, approach would be to simply alter the proposed balanced budget amendment currently before the Congress to exclude the

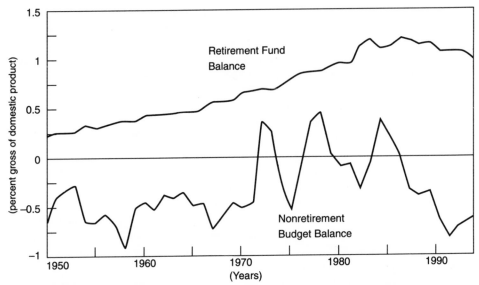

Figure 10.3. Retirement and nonretirement budget balance of state and local governments (as percent of Gross Domestic Product). *Source:* Figure based on Table 3.3 of the U.S. National Income and Product Accounts.

surplus of the Social Security fund. It would achieve the objective of saving the OASDI surplus. However, it would be part of an amendment that many view as too inflexible a rule for the budget itself.

A more practical approach, now that Social Security is administered by an independent agency, is to remove entirely its revenues and expenditures from budget documents and the annual process by which the Congress makes budgetary decisions.[22] The Congress and the administration would exercise oversight responsibilities, and the Congress might continue to exercise the power to veto changes in contribution rates and benefit formulas. The board of trustees would be assigned broader responsibilities to propose specific actions as necessary to maintain the fund's actuarial balance, and they would be held accountable for the management of the investments. While changes in the fund balances would affect the economy, the year-to-year variations would be small and of little consequence for fiscal policy. At a minimum, the change would prevent the public presentation of the budget deficit as being smaller than it actually is. And it would approximate current state treatment of their retirement accounts.

Furthermore, it is possible to devise a system in which the funded portion of the Social Security system is moved to the private sector. Workers could be offered the option of shifting a portion of their contribution to a privately managed, defined-contribution program. Such proposals raise complex, but not unsolvable problems, of how to reduce the OASDI benefit of such individuals in an actuarially correct fashion that does not worsen the financial position of the remaining fund. This is complicated both because of the redistributional elements of the benefit formula and the fact that the inflation protection built into the public program is not duplicated in private programs. Furthermore, given the observed political pressures to broaden the conditions under which existing Individual Retirement Accounts can be cashed out for nonretirement purposes, the argument could be made that this proposal would not effectively translate into added national saving.

In the typical case, the size of the private account would be small, and it may be expecting too much to believe that individuals would be willing to devote the time required to become knowledgeable about investment decisions. It might be preferable, instead, to follow the practice of some private retirement programs and allow workers to make choices between a limited number of privately managed funds with strong regulatory supervision by the Social Security system.

Ultimately, there is no means of guaranteeing that a partial funding of Social Security would lead to higher saving. But such a cynical view of the inability of the public and its elected officials to make rational decisions when the issues are put before them in a clear fashion raises questions that go far beyond a consideration of Social Security financing alone. The program itself continues to attract a high level of public support, even among those who question whether they will receive a benefit (see chapter 11). Yet a continuation of sole reliance on pay-as-you-go financing will encounter serious problems as future demographic and economic trends lower the rate of return. Those problems can easily be resolved by a shift to advance funding of a portion of the future liability.[23]

Finally, we should not use the fiscal experience of the 1980s as evidence that a surplus in the OASDI accounts cannot add to national saving. Many factors contributed to the emergence of a large fiscal deficit and the difficulties of taking action to reduce it. Mistakes were made in the early 1980s in combining an increase in defense spending with a tax reduction, and the positive benefits of supply-side economics never materialized. Furthermore, we continue to have difficulty adjusting to a situation in which the built-in growth in existing programs exceeds the growth of the economy and, thus, of tax revenues.[24] To a large extent these problems developed before the onset of a Social Security surplus. As the reserve of the OASDI funds grew in size, the overall deficit actually declined.

MANAGEMENT OF THE OASDI FUND

The creation of an OASDI reserve will also raise significant questions about investing the funds. At present, the OASDI reserves are invested in Treasury securities that earn the average rate of interest on government bonds with terms longer than four years. Rather than being purchased on the market, with the associated broker fees, the bonds are purchased directly for the Treasury in the equivalent of the private placement market for corporate bonds. Over the past 10 years, the average rate of real return has been about 5 percent, but it is expected to decline to 2 percent in the intermediate projections, more in line with the average historical yield.

It is sometimes suggested that the some of the future financing problems could be reduced if the OASDI funds were free to be invested in private securities and earn a higher rate of return. As the huge financial investment debacle in Orange County, California, demonstrates, such a recommendation should not be made lightly. There is a need for a clear understanding of its consequences.

First, from the perspective of society as a whole, the change would yield few benefits. It would make the financing position of the OASDI system appear stronger, but it would not in itself increase national income. As a simple thought experiment, imagine that the OASDI system sold off $1 trillion of Treasury securities and replaced them in its portfolio with an equal number of private securities paying a higher rate of return. The higher return would presumably reflect the higher degree of risk inherent in the private debt. However, a simple swap of public and private debt between the OASDI trust fund and the private markets would have no appreciable effect on total saving, the stock of physical capital, or output. The return, and hence the gain in national income, is given by the before-tax return on capital discussed earlier. The trust fund would report a higher rate of return, while the private sector would hold the lower-yield Treasury securities previously held by the fund. The resources out of which the consumption of future workers and retirees must be financed, however, would remain the same.

Society will not benefit from a policy that simply shifts the distribution of financial assets between the OASDI fund and the private sector unless there are barriers to portfolio diversification in private markets.[25] Modern capital markets are highly integrated, however, and investors can easily alter the composition of assets in their portfolios to achieve the mix of return versus risk with which they feel comfortable. As a result, the interest-rate differential between corporate and government bonds increases in recessions and other periods when risks are perceived to have risen. There is no discernible correlation between the yield spread and changes in the share-to-total-credit market debt accounted for by the government. As shown in Figure 10.4, the higher proportion of very low risk governments in the private-sector portfolio might induce some increase in the demand, and, hence, the price of risky equity issues. But in any global market the effect would seem small.

Instead, the significance of a policy of investing in private securities lies in the fact that the Social Security system would capture a larger portion of the return on capital for its own purposes. One's attitude toward that would presumably depend on whether the original decision to advance-fund a portion of the future liability actually translates into increased national saving. If not, the decision to invest in private securities operates much like a tax, albeit a voluntary one. A larger share of the nation's capital income would accrue to the Social Security funds in return for their agreement to assume more of the investment risk. As a result there would be a need for a smaller rise in future tax rates, given that the system would extract resources to meet retiree payments more through interest and less through taxes. It might affect future attitudes about who is truly paying for the consumption of the retired; but the total amount of resources available for consumption would remain the same. Even so, we might still agree that the current investment policy seems excessively conservative for a broad-based retirement fund with very long-term and relatively predictable liabilities and that a higher return would reduce the perception of workers that they pay all of the costs.

A more interesting situation arises in the case in which increases in the Social Security fund *do* add to national saving and the stock of wealth. Why should the fund be credited with only a 2 percent return if its actions actually add something closer to 6 percent in future income to the nation? Such a policy camouflages from public view much of the benefit of advanced funding. Furthermore, if the difference between the total return of approximately 6 percent and the 2 percent received by

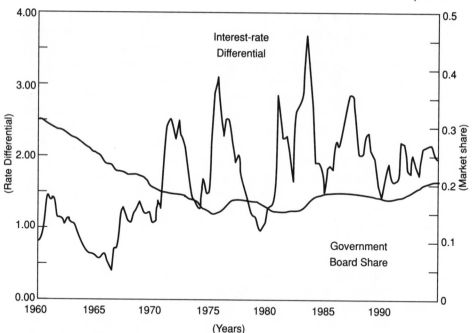

Figure 10.4. Corporate versus government bond rate differential (in percents). Interest rate differential is the corporate BAA interest rate less the interest rate on Government fixed ten-year maturity; the government share of the market is the percent of total credit market debt held publically. *Source:* Figure based on data supplied by the Board of Governors of the Federal Reserve System.

the funds is allowed to accrue to the private sector, it would presumably be consumed in the proportion in which private income is currently divided between saving and consumption, Alternatively, if the Social Security system captured a larger portion, that increment to income would presumably be saved.

Of course, if the funding rule by which the system is to be kept in close actuarial balance operated in a symmetric fashion, a higher rate of return would push the system toward an actuarial surplus and a reduction in contribution rates relative to the prior assumed path. Workers would probably save about the same portion of that gain in after-tax income as we observe for the private sector as a whole. In that case, a decision to invest in a riskier portfolio of assets would involve no net gain to the national saving rate.

But such an outcome is not required. It would be equally reasonable to allow the reserve to build up beyond the minimal level, as long as it involved no increase in tax rates, since Social Security would still be far short of a fully funded status. The result would be a far larger, but gradual, rise in the national saving rate. In the near term, the rise of private income, and thus consumption, would be postponed, with a larger portion of the benefits of increases in saving being retained for the future. It would go a long way toward eliminating any need for raising taxes on workers in the future.

Finally, if Social Security extracted a larger portion of the return on its saving, there should be no appreciable effect on investment. Business firms are largely indifferent to the source of their funds as long as the interest cost is the same. Private savers also would not be disadvantaged, since they could balance off their greater holding of the debt from the general government by combining it with a portion of assets further up the scale of risk.

Any proposal for public investment in private securities immediately raises concerns about who would make the decisions and how the capital might be allocated among competing projects. But, in the near term those concerns would be no greater than those that now exist with large state and private pension funds. Furthermore, management of the fund could be spread among a substantial number of private fund managers, with no direct control by Social Security of their investment choices. Instead, it would evaluate their performance on the basis of relative rates of return and the risks that they involve. In effect, Social Security would be investing in a broad cross section of the entire capital market. Public scrutiny and review would be beneficial in encouraging Americans to focus on these types of issues.

QUANTITATIVE MAGNITUDES

An illustration of the magnitudes of change implied by a shift to partial funding can be provided by using the intermediate projections of the trustees' report as a baseline. First, the financial position of the Social Security fund is reestimated to include a tax rate increase of 2 percentage points in 1995 to restore actuarial balance. Second, the change in the investment policy is assumed to result in a 1 percentage point increase in the assumed yield on its assets until 2060. These changes are shown in Figure 10.5. The tax increase alone would allow the fund to continue to build up its reserve until about 2023. However, it would begin to run deficits again in about 2055, and it would be exhausted near the end of the 75-year horizon.

On the other hand, if the restoration of actuarial balance were combined with a change in investment policies that allowed the fund to earn just 1 percent more than the rate on government securities, the reserve would stabilize at a level roughly equal to the taxable wage base. Given that taxable wages average 40 to 45 percent of GDP, this amounts to an increase in the long-run capital stock from about the present three-times-GDP to about 3.5. The increase in national saving would represent 3 to 4 percent of national income at its peak and about 1 to 2 percent in the long run. While there is some tendency near the end of the forecast horizon for the savings of the fund to decline as a share of taxable wages, it remains strongly positive throughout. In effect, these two changes would eliminate any problems with the Social Security fund for the foreseeable future.

I have not attempted a full economic simulation of the policy changes using the same simulation model used for the 1988 study, because of time constraints and the need to recalibrate the model to the current economic assumptions. However, the process being simulated is quite simple, and the qualitative nature of the results can be inferred. The calculations shown in Figure 10.5 make no allowance for the increase in wages, and thus benefit payments, that will result from the policy change. However, because the increase in taxable wages precedes the rise in benefits, the financial position of the funds would actually improve as a result of taking account of the effects on the rest of the economy. As shown in the 1988 study, while the

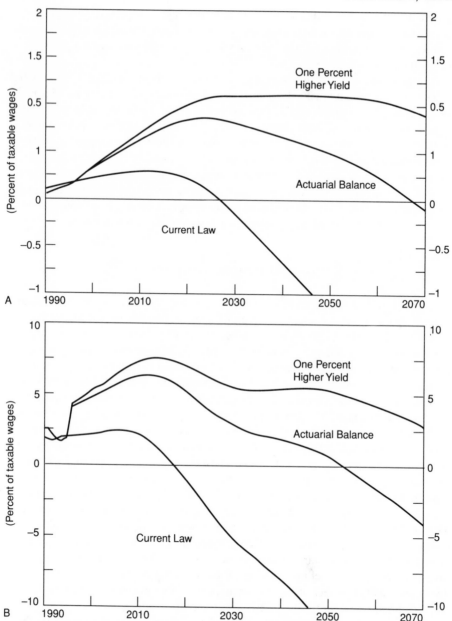

Figure 10.5. A, Assets of the OASDI trust funds with alternative investment policies (in percent of taxable wages); **B,** Saving of the OASDI trust funds under alternative investment policies. (in percent of taxable wages). *Source:* Author's calculations (explained in text).

increase in future benefit payments is substantial, the much larger rise in GDP still results in a net gain to the nonretired population.

Second, because the Social Security system captures a larger portion of income from its investments and reinvests the proceeds, the future decline in savings (which would normally follow from a rise in the cost rate against a constant tax rate) is largely eliminated. There is no apparent need for further adjustments of tax rates in future years. The differences in saving are shown in Figure 10.5b as the gap between the two lines labeled "actuarial balance" and a "one-percent higher yield." On the other hand, because the saving rate is maintained, consumption rises more slowly, and the number of years before it returns to its prior level is delayed. In effect, the benefits of saving the surplus are pushed further into the future, but ultimately they become much larger.

CONCLUSION

The deteriorating long-run financial position of the OASDI fund can no longer be dismissed as a problem of minor concern. In responding to this situation, it is important to note that the implicit yield to the average contributing worker in a pay-as-you-go system is going to fall dramatically in future years. At the same time, the success of private retirement funds has increased public awareness of the benefits of a funded retirement program. The sharply escalating cost rates in future years provide the United States with the opportunity to shift over to a partially funded program for the public portion of the retirement system without the need to impose double taxation on any transitional generation.

Furthermore, the current practice of limiting investments of the OASDI fund to government securities represents an unduly cautious investments strategy, one that hides from public view the benefits of a partially funded system. The combination of a tax increase to restore actuarial balance and a mildly more aggressive investment policy could essentially eliminate future financing problems.

Many will believe that the solution presented here is overly simplified and such small changes in funding cannot be sufficient to offset a near doubling of the future dependency rate. But such arguments fail to recognize that OASDI benefits will only increase by 2 percent of GDP between now and 2070, from 4.8 to 6.8 percent; even in the high-cost option, the increase is only 4 percent of GDP. Changes of this magnitude are less than the variations in the share of the GDP devoted to defense since the mid-1970s. While Social Security is a large share of the government budget as currently presented, it is a small element in the total economy. Given the high return from added capital formation and compounding growth rates, challenges of this magnitude can easily be met as long as society is willing to act sufficiently far ahead of the need.

ENDNOTES

1. This chapter was originally published as part of the proceedings of the 1995 annual conference of the National Academy of Social Insurance.

2. The actuarial balance is computed as the present value of future tax receipts minus the present value of future outlays, plus the difference between the initial trust fund balances and the present value of a target terminal-year reserve equal to one year's outgo. The discount rate is the interest rate earned by the funds on their invested reserves, and the calculations extend over a 75-year horizon. Close actuarial balance is said to exist if the balance is within 5 percent of discounted costs.

3. One major problem with using the alternative projections to evaluate risks to the funds is that there is no associated notion of probabilities to attach to the alternatives. The low- and high-cost alternatives, for example, do not seem equally likely relative to the intermediate projection. This ought to be a major goal in future refinements of the actuarial estimates.

4. There are many ways to define and measure dependency rates, depending on what one wishes to emphasize or analyze (see Marmor, Cook, and Scher, chapter 12; Schulz, Borowski, and Crown, 1991). The focus here is on those who pay payroll taxes to finance the the benefits paid out.

5. This is not completely true, because the benefit ratio will vary in response to changes in the length of retirement and the proportion of workers who take early retirement with an actuarial-reduced benefit. Because benefits are indexed only for price inflation, the benefit rate will decline as the average number of years of retirement rise.

6. The two major economic factors are the rate of real-wage growth and the real interest rate. A doubling of real-wage growth from the intermediate assumption of 1 percent per year would lower the actuarial imbalance over a 75-year horizon by about 1 percent of taxable wages, half the anticipated shortfall. An increase in the real interest rate from the assumed 2.3 percent would improve the balance by about 0.6 percent.

7. Not all of the funding imbalance is due to increased costs. The projections also incorporate an implicit tax cut relative to total employee compensation because of continued growth in untaxed employee benefits. The loss of revenues represents about one-sixth of the funding deficit.

8. Again, the potential variance is very wide. The required tax rate in 2030 could range between 13 percent of payroll (low-cost case) and 20 percent (high-cost alternative).

9. A wide range of proposals for adjusting taxes and benefits are discussed in other chapters of this book.

10. Hurd and Shoven (1985).

11. I would differentiate between proposals to means-test Social Security benefits and those that want to treat these benefits in the same way as private pensions for purposes of income taxation. The latter goes more to a principle that two individuals of similar circumstances should pay similar taxes to support government programs (see Kingson and Schulz, chapter 3.)

12. The normal age of retirement is the age at which those eligible can retire and receive benefits that are not reduced for early retirement.

13. Decisions to take early retirement have a limited impact on costs because the benefits are actuarial-reduced, but they do reduce the revenue of the system.

14. It has taken the United States a surprisingly long time to even complete the transition through the first generation that received benefits without having to pay for prior retirees. The Congress continued to expand the program up until the early 1970s by enriching the benefit formula and bringing additional portions of the work force into the system. Thus, there have been successive waves of cohorts who receive benefits out of proportion to past contributions. Even today's new retirees cannot claim to have spent their full work life in a mature pay-as-you-go system. The expansion of the system ended in the early 1970s, and the next few years will see a dramatic decline in the return to new retirees.

15. This was first pointed out by Paul Samuelson (1958), and the point has been made many times since in articles on Social Security.

16. The marginal effective tax rates are those for 1990 as reported in Fullerton and Karayannis (1993). The overall average return was computed using as weights the net capital stock in 1990 for the three sectors as given in Board of Governors of the Federal Reserve (1994). A similar calculation using the rate of return on nonfarm business capital, as reported by Oliner and Sichel (1994), resulted in an average yield of 6.3 percent.

17. Data on the current value of foreign direct investments and the income earned are published in the United States balance of payments. The average real rate of return since 1985 has been 8.5 percent, compared with the previously discussed corporate return of 7.8 percent on domestic investments.

18. Most empirical studies still place the price elasticity of both United States exports and imports at about unity.

19. In view of the current debate about the effect of government policies on the economy, it is interesting to note that we were actually calling for a form of dynamic revenue estimation, allowing for induced changes in future output to be included in the calculation of the benefits of a policy change. I would note, however, that the assumptions used in the 1988 study and in this chapter incorporate very conservative estimates of the benefits of increased capital formation.

20. Although young workers often respond in polls that they do not expect to receive Social Security benefits, that could be attributed to growing public cynicism toward everything involving government or any notion of a community of interest (see Reno and Friedland, chapter 11). It is notable that there is no evidence that they have acted on their beliefs by increasing their own saving.

21. Admittedly, this situation may be changing. A few state governors have discovered that they can alter the rules governing the funding status of their public pension funds in ways that allow them to reduce contributions. Other states have attempted to alter the funds' investment decisions to subsidize other activities.

22. The 1990 Budget Enforcement Act removed Social Security revenues and expenditures from the budget and from estimates of the federal budget deficit. This was done, in large measure, as a means of preventing the current annual Social Security surplus from being used to mask the federal deficit in general revenues and to remove Social Security from yearly budgetary deliberations. Despite these intentions, OASDI expenditures continue to be presented and discussed in the context of a unified federal budget.

23. We should not ignore the experiences of other countries where benefit promises exceeded the financing capabilities of the system. Such situations gave rise to strong incentives among young workers to avoid the system, and the funding crises lead to ill-conceived efforts to redefine benefits in ways that resulted in capricious redistributions of income among and within age cohorts.

24. In this respect, the current problems of the operating fund are a precursor to the future difficulties of Social Security.

25. Aaron, Bosworth, and Burtless (1989), pp. 101–104.

CHAPTER 11

Strong Support but Low Confidence
What Explains the Contradiction?

VIRGINIA P. RENO AND ROBERT B. FRIEDLAND

Opinion surveys show that Americans have a favorable impression of Social Security. They have a pretty good idea of its basic purpose and how it works, and they do not object to paying Social Security taxes to support it. At the same time, many Americans report in opinion polls that they do not have much confidence in its future. Thus, there is a contrast between public *support* for the program, which is high, and public *confidence* in it, which is low.

The low confidence Americans report in the future of Social Security becomes a matter of interest because it could translate into an erosion of support for Social Security. Social Security is unlike other forms of retirement income in that its future depends on the collective support that Americans have for it and the collective influence they exert over it. For these reasons and because it is an important American institution, it is important to explore the meaning of, and possible reasons for, the low levels of confidence in Social Security.

The chapter begins with a brief historical review of public attitudes juxtaposed with Social Security policy developments. It shows how, in the first four decades of the program, strong support for it was translated directly into policies to expand coverage and improve the adequacy of Social Security benefits. In the mid-1970s, automatic adjustments were enacted to make Social Security benefits keep pace with growth in the economy. Economic shocks required adjustments in the system, including some slowing of unintended growth in future benefits. Questions about the public's confidence in the future of Social Security surfaced and began to be measured in public opinion surveys.

The next section of the chapter reviews survey findings since the mid-1970s about the public's knowledge of, support for, and confidence in Social Security, including a discussion that compares public confidence in Social Security, private pensions, and personal savings. The third section speculates about what the reports of low confidence may mean and explores possible causes of the low confidence in Social Security. We postulate, based on our analysis of Social Security and on opinions reported in polls and focus groups, that despite Americans' basic knowledge of how Social Security works today, there are critical gaps in the information available to workers that would help them understand its value and assess its future. In particular, workers' low confidence in Social Security for their own future may reflect three kinds of gaps in knowledge. First is an understanding of the different but complementary roles that Social Security, pensions, and savings fill for individuals and for society as a whole. Second is recognition that the features that make Social Security different from pensions or savings are key elements of its security for individuals. Third is the realization that Social Security derives its sustainability from Americans' support for it. The chapter concludes that citizens need more precise information to help them understand the value of Social Security for their own future retirement and to assess various policy options.

HISTORICAL OVERVIEW OF PUBLIC SUPPORT, POLICY DEVELOPMENT, AND CONFIDENCE

1. The Early Years: General Support

In the early years, opinion surveys did not draw sharp distinctions between the means-tested Old-Age Assistance program and Social Security. As Berkowitz (chapter 2) discusses, both programs were newly created in the Social Security Act of 1935 and, at the outset, far more of the elderly received Old-Age Assistance than received Social Security. Surveys often described the benefits from both programs as "pensions," which may explain why respondents did not draw distinctions between the two. Americans often did not realize that while the assistance program was for the needy elderly, eligibility for Social Security benefits was related to workers' prior contributions, and the benefits were paid without regard to need. Nonetheless, income maintenance for the aged received overwhelming support, rising from 68 percent of the population in 1936 to 94 percent in 1944. The strong support was found in all age, income, regional, and occupational groups (Schiltz, 1970; Sherman, 1989).

2. The 1950s and 1960s: Public Support and Program Growth

In the 1950s and 1960s, public support for Social Security was demonstrated directly by the votes of elected representatives in Congress, which broadened Social Security coverage, expanded benefit eligibility, updated benefit levels to keep pace with growth in the economy and, in addition, raised the real level of benefits (see chapters 2–7).

Landmark legislation in 1950 extended Social Security coverage to most self-employed persons and to farm employees (which then were a significant part of the work force) and raised Social Security benefit levels. As Berkowitz (chapter 2) notes, these changes brought significant increases in the proportion of the elderly who received Social Security benefits. By 1955, elderly Social Security beneficiaries outnumbered Old-Age Assistance recipients by about 2 to 1—39 percent, compared with 18 percent of the elderly—although Social Security beneficiaries were still less than half of all elderly (Social Security Administration, 1994a, p. 147). Other legislation added and expanded disability insurance protection in 1954, 1956, and 1960; provided for early retirement benefits, first for women in 1956 and then for men in 1961; raised the level of widows' benefits; and, in 1965, established Medicare to provide hospital and medical insurance for the elderly.

Much of the public debate about Social Security during the economic expansion of the 1950s and 1960s centered on how large the discretionary benefit increases should be (see Moon, chapter 4). During this period, benefits were not automatically adjusted to keep pace with either price or wage growth. Since revenues from Social Security taxes rose with wage growth, surpluses built up in the Social Security trust fund.[1] These surpluses allowed Congress and the president to pass legislation increasing benefits. Such benefit increases were particularly likely in election years. Furthermore, poverty estimates, which were first developed by the federal government in the early 1960s, documented that large portions of the elderly were living in poverty or near poverty (Orshansky, 1965). Increasing Social Security benefits was viewed as an effective way to enable the elderly to share in the economic prosperity enjoyed by the working-age population.

Polls conducted during this period showed that Americans supported Social Security. In two 1952 surveys, for example, 92 percent of Americans replied that Social Security was a "good thing to do," rather than a "mistake" (Page and Shapiro, 1992).[2]

3. The 1970s: Concerns About Confidence

During election year 1972, when a Democratic Congress and Republican president were running for reelection, legislation specified an *ad hoc* benefit increase of 20 percent and provided that in 1975 and thereafter, benefits would be adjusted automatically, based on increases in the cost-of-living as measured by the consumer price index (CPI).[3]

In 1972, there was not yet reason to expect that the post–World War II prosperity of the 1950s and 1960s would not continue. The automatic-adjustment formula put in place in 1972, however, turned out to be technically flawed.[4] It resulted in higher than intended growth in benefits for new and future retirees. Long-range projections showed that the system was not sustainable without correcting this inadvertent overindexing of future benefits and that, for the first time, the Social Security trust funds were looking at serious long-range deficit.

Legislative proposals were developed by the executive branch in 1975 and 1976 and enacted by Congress in 1977 to correct the problem of overindexing in the benefit formula. As the changes were phased in from 1979 to 1986, replacement rates for new retirees, which had risen rapidly in the 1970s, declined, so that benefits for an average earner retiring at age 65 leveled off at about 42 percent of the worker's prior earnings. See Figure 11.1, which traces changes in benefit levels expressed as replacement rates (or benefits at retirement as a percentage of the prior year's earnings), for an illustrative worker retiring at age 65 in each year.

At this time, surveys began to collect information about confidence in the future of Social Security. Periodic surveys by the American Council of Life Insurance first

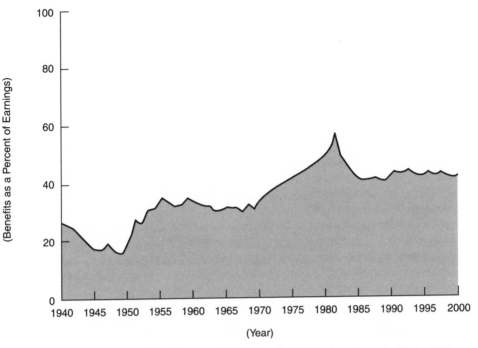

Figure 11.1. Replacement rates of average earners retiring at age 65, 1940–2000. *Source:* Office of the Actuary. U.S. Social Security Administration.

reported in 1975 that fully 63 percent of Americans were either very confident or somewhat confident about the future of Social Security, while only 10 percent said they were not at all confident (Figure 11.2). By 1978, after widespread publicity about the projected long-range insolvency, which had been addressed in the 1977 legislation, confidence in the future of Social Security had dropped precipitously. In 1978, just 37 percent of Americans reported confidence in the future of Social Security, while those not at all confident rose to 21 percent. Yet, during this period of financial concern, Americans wanted to maintain the level of benefits provided, with polls showing that 54 to 68 percent of the American people opposed cutting benefits or raising the retirement age as a way to lower benefit costs (Page and Shapiro, 1992).

4. The 1980s to Now: Policy Debates and Confidence

Just after the 1977 legislation, a new shock hit the economy, with unanticipated consequences for Social Security's short-range financing. Inflation rose at an unprecedented rate and, in fact, outstripped the growth in earnings. In the three years of 1979, 1980, and 1981, annual benefit increases, based on the CPI, were 9.9 percent, 14.3 percent, and 11.2 percent, respectively, while annual wage growth over the same three years was 9.8 percent, 9.0 percent, and 9.8 percent, respectively (Board of Trustees, 1994, table II-D-1, p. 52). Benefits rose with price growth, but trust fund revenues rose only with wage growth. This created a short-range drain on the trust funds.

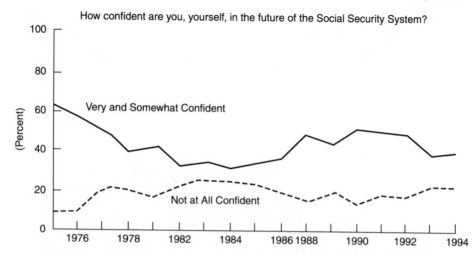

Figure 11.2. Confidence in Social Security. *Source:* American Council of Life Insurance.

While there were early signs of problems in 1980, there was little interest during an election year in tackling the difficult issue of slowing the growth in Social Security benefits, particularly for those already on the rolls. In mid-1981, the new Reagan administration came out with its proposals for abrupt and severe cuts in benefits for early retirees and disabled workers. The proposals were received with alarm and were quickly abandoned, but Social Security became a political issue in the 1982 elections, as candidates traded charges about lack of support for, or willingness to cut, Social Security.

The short-range financing problem, nonetheless, needed to be addressed. Early in 1982, President Reagan formed the National Commission on Social Security Reform, chaired by Alan Greenspan, composed of congressional leaders and private citizens, and charged with developing recommendations to remedy the Social Security financing problem. The commission's recommendations, issued in January 1983, became the blueprint for 1983 legislation to restore the solvency of the Social Security trust funds through a series of modest changes. For more detail, see the discussion in Berkowitz (chapter 2).

Although, plainly, the 1982 financing problem was far from insurmountable, the debate and media coverage that preceded action reached a fever pitch over the impending "bankruptcy" of the Social Security program. There were predictions that, if Congress failed to act early in 1983, full benefits could not be paid beginning in July of that year. It is perhaps not surprising, then, that confidence in the Social Security system plummeted to an all-time low in 1982 and 1983, and remained low in 1984 after the remedial legislation had been enacted (see Figure 11.2). Confidence in Social Security rebounded later in the 1980s as the nation enjoyed stable economic growth and low inflation and Social Security disappeared from the headlines.

In recent years, confidence may have again waned due to a new debate building about the future of Social Security.[5] While Social Security is adequately financed until about 2030, it is not adequately financed over the full 75-year projection period from 1995. As discussed in chapters 13–15, however, a combination of moderate changes could bring the program into balance. But as Marmor, Cook, and Scher point out (chapter 12), many program critics describe the future retirement of the baby boomers as an *unaffordable demographic bulge that threatens the very sustainability* of Social Security. Public response to these new financing concerns will be influenced by the public's understanding and attitudes about Social Security, the subject to which we now turn.

PUBLIC UNDERSTANDING, SUPPORT, AND CONFIDENCE

1. Americans' Understanding of the Basic Features of Social Security

Various surveys since the mid-1970s have shown that Americans have a pretty good idea of the basic purpose of Social Security and how it works. For example, most Americans know that Social Security benefits are financed by earmarked Social Security taxes, that the taxes of current workers are used to pay for current benefits, that the system pays disability and survivor benefits as well as retirement benefits, and that benefits are based on workers' earnings from which Social Security taxes were paid. And they know that benefits are not simply for the needy (Advisory Council on Social Security, 1991; Friedland, 1994b; Hart, 1980; Sherman, 1989; Yankelovich, 1985).

Americans also understand that Social Security is not meant to meet all the needs of retired people. Surveys in 1979, and again in 1991, asked respondents to choose which of two statements best described the purpose of Social Security: (a) Social Security benefits alone provide enough to meet the basic needs of retirees, or (b) Social Security benefits alone are not enough, but together with other sources should meet the basic needs of retirees. In both years a large majority (65 percent in 1979 and 73 percent in 1991) said that benefits would be enough only when combined with other sources. Despite this recognition that Social Security is meant to provide only a foundation of retirement income, the majority in both surveys said they wished the purpose was the broader one (61 percent in 1979 and 52 percent in 1991) (Advisory Council on Social Security, 1991).

2. Workers' Doubts About the Course of Future Benefits

Americans have mixed notions about the level of Social Security benefits, particularly about whether or how they increase over time. While Social Security benefits for those on the benefit rolls have been indexed to keep pace with inflation since 1975, Americans are unsure about the future course of benefits. In 1979, many Americans did not know that benefits were automatically adjusted for inflation (Hart, 1980). Other surveys during the 1980s found that Americans generally opposed cutting cost-of-living increases in benefits. It is not clear that, in the absence of prompting, they would have known that benefits were indexed in that way. Americans' views in March of 1994 about the future level of benefits are summarized in Table 11.1.

While the majority believed that benefits should increase, either with inflation or faster than inflation, most Americans who were not themselves receiving Social Security believed that benefits would actually decline or be eliminated. It is im-

TABLE 11.1. Expectations and Preferences About Future Benefit Level Changes (Persons Not Receiving Social Security Benefits, March 1994)

Future benefits changes	EXPECT to happen	What SHOULD happen
Total percentage	100	100
Increase more than the rate of inflation	3	10
Increase at the same rate as inflation	7	48
Increase for some, but decrease for others	23	25
Stay the same	12	10
Decrease	39	4
Be eliminated	17	3

Source: Reprinted, with permission, from Friedland (1994b), based on EBRI/Gallup Survey, March 1994.

possible to tell whether their low expectations about the level of future benefits reflects lack of knowledge about how Social Security is adjusted over time or pessimism about future policy developments. The course of future benefits under the current law is rather complicated, and it is not surprising that workers are unsure about it. In brief:

- Benefits for those on the rolls are automatically adjusted for inflation.
- For those not yet retired, future benefits at retirement will have kept pace with the growth in economy-wide wages, which reflect improvements in the standard of living during the retiree's working years. That is, initial benefit levels for future retirees rise by more than inflation because they rise with both inflation and real improvements in the standard of living.
- The gradual increase in the age at which full retirement benefits can be claimed in the future, however, means that those who do not delay retirement will have benefits that replace somewhat less of their pre-retirement earnings than is the case for new retirees of the same age today.

While working-age Americans have a pretty good understanding of basic aspects of Social Security, they do not understand the rather arcane provisions that affect the level and security of benefits for future retirees, including themselves. Further, they may anticipate far more significant cuts in future benefits than would be needed even if the entire long-range imbalance in the Social Security system were to be solved by benefit reductions.

3. High Support and Low Confidence

As Marmor, Cook, and Scher (chapter 12) and Myers (chapter 13) also note, Americans since the mid-1970s have consistently expressed strong support for the Social Security program, despite low levels of confidence and great uncertainty about future benefit levels. A 1979 survey by Peter D. Hart Research Associates revealed strong support for the Social Security system. In an open-ended question asking for comments about the advantages and disadvantages of Social Security, more than 90 percent of respondents volunteered statements relating to Social Security helping the elderly or the retired and providing security, particularly income security. In fact, the most common disadvantages cited were that Social Security didn't do enough and that the benefits were too low. When asked to choose between continuing or ending the program, 77 percent opposed ending it, including 67 percent who *strongly* opposed it. If given a choice, 77 percent of the American public would opt to stay in the program. As might be expected, the higher income groups were less likely to say they would stay, but a majority in every income group said they would do so.

Furthermore, Americans reported in 1979 that they did not object to the Social Security tax or to prospects for a tax increase. Asked to choose between increasing Social Security taxes and lowering benefits, 69 percent favored the tax increase over lower benefits. Further, Americans reported they found the Social Security tax much less objectionable than other federal, state, or local taxes. Yet, despite their willingness to pay taxes to support the system, respondents expressed low levels of confidence about its future, with only 42 percent reporting they were confident that Social Security would have the funds to provide their benefits (Hart, 1980; Sherman, 1989).

In 1985, in connection with the 50th anniversary of the original Social Security Act, and shortly after the financing crisis of 1982–1983, Yankelovich, Skelly, and White, Inc. surveyed the American public about their experience with the Social Security program. That survey, too, found strong support for Social Security: 92 percent said it was an important government program; given a choice between continuing or phasing out the program, 88 percent said it should continue; and many saw Social Security as relieving them of the financial burden of supporting aging parents (80 percent).

There also was little objection to the Social Security tax. The large majority (79 percent) said that they knew that taxes were used to pay for current benefits, and nearly the same proportion considered the taxes to be fair (Sherman, 1989; Yankelovich, 1985). Again, however, despite strong support and willingness to pay for Social Security, the younger respondents had relatively little confidence in the future of the program.

Support for Social Security was also reported in a 1986 survey. It found that the vast majority of Americans favored increasing (57 percent) or maintaining (40 percent) the level of Social Security benefits. Eighty-two percent said that they were satisfied that a portion of each working person's income goes to finance Social Security, and most (71 percent) said they would be willing to pay higher taxes to support benefits (Cook, 1990; Cook and Barrett, 1992).

Research suggests that public support is based on the view that society as a whole benefits from the program and that Social Security leads to independence. Even those not receiving it feel they benefit because they are connected to someone in their family who is a potential or actual recipient. For example, the son-in-law may recognize that if his in-laws did not receive Social Security, he might have to help them with financial support or ask them to move in with his family.

The 1991 Advisory Council on Social Security commissioned a survey similar to the 1979 Hart survey. It, too, found that Americans said they were familiar with Social Security (93 percent); had favorable impressions of it (73 percent); and did not mind paying Social Security taxes to support it (77 percent). The favorable impressions and willingness to pay taxes to support Social Security were dominant among all age, education, and income groups (Advisory Council on Social Security, 1991). However, this survey, too, found that many seemed to doubt that Social Security would have the money to pay their benefits; just 46 percent of those not receiving benefits agreed with the statement: "Social Security will have the money to pay benefits to me when I retire."

A 1994 Gallup poll, sponsored by the Employee Benefit Research Institute and the National Academy of Social Insurance, again found that Americans did not mind paying Social Security taxes to support the program. Those not receiving benefits were asked about "the fact that a part of every working person's income goes to support the Social Security program?" About 80 percent were either "in favor" or "strongly in favor" of this situation (a level of support similar to that found by Cook and Barrett in 1986). The 1994 poll also found that 73 percent opposed a cutback in spending on Social Security benefits. Again, a low level of confidence in future Social Security benefits was found (Friedland, 1994b).

4. More Confidence in Pensions and Savings than in Social Security

In a 1994 poll, when asked about their confidence in the future of Social Security versus employer-sponsored pensions, versus individual savings, respondents under age 55 rated Social Security the lowest. Rather surprisingly, they rated highest the source that most financial experts would say had the greatest individual risk: individual savings.[6] As Bosworth (chapter 10) and Gramlich (chapter 9) discuss, this perception contrasts starkly with the reality that the United States savings rate is extremely low, having declined from over 9 percent during the 1950s and 1960s to just 2.2 percent in 1992 (Bernheim, 1994). More directly, research indicates that the personal savings of baby boomers is, on average, below what will be needed to maintain pre-retirement standards of living (Merrill Lynch & Co., 1994; U.S. Congressional Budget Office, 1993). One study indicates that the "typical baby boom household is saving at one-third the rate required" to maintain pre-retirement living standards (Bernheim, p. 5), though this study does not include the value of housing assets.[7]

Table 11.2 shows the results of the poll that asked people to rank their confidence levels relative to whether Social Security; employer pensions, including 401(k) plans, or personal savings, including individual retirement accounts (IRAs) would be available throughout their retirement years. Social Security ranked the lowest among all age groups, except for those age 55 or older. However, people *age 55 or older* ranked Social Security the highest and pensions and personal savings the lowest of any age group. An important difference between a young worker and a 55-year-old is that 55-year-olds know how much savings have actually accumulated over their prime working years; for many, the amount is very small. Further, older persons are likely to have more fully assessed their retirement income, and, in that sense, be offering a more informed judgment.

It is striking that the proportion of Americans who have confidence that their pensions will be available throughout their retirement years is almost as high as the proportion of workers who are actually included in employer-sponsored pension plans. In 1993, about 55 percent of all wage and salary workers were covered by pension plans on their main job. For many, the only pension was a 401(k)-type plan,

TABLE 11.2. Confidence That Sources of Income Will Be Available Throughout Retirement

(in percentages)

	Total	18–34	35–54	55 and older
Social Security				
Confident	30	21	22	52
Mixed feelings	24	26	21	26
Not confident	43	52	55	16
Employer Pensions or Savings Plans				
Confident	49	47	55	42
Mixed feelings	20	27	18	14
Not confident	24	25	25	21
Personal Saving (including IRAs)				
Confident	56	60	58	50
Mixed feelings	24	26	23	22
Not confident	19	14	19	23

Source: Reprinted, with permission, from Friedland (1994b), based on EBRI/Gallup Survey, February, 1994.
Note: People were asked to rank their confidence levels, with 5 being extremely confident and 1 being not at all confident. Here, the rankings of 4–5 are confident, 3 is mixed, and 1–2 are not confident.

which bears great similarity to individual savings in that the employee makes discretionary contributions to the plan and bears all the risk of the investment returns. More traditional pension plans covered about a quarter to a third of younger workers and just under half of middle-aged workers in 1993 (Woods, 1994).

The high level of confidence workers report about their future pensions, especially their own personal savings for retirement, is consistent with earlier findings from the Hart survey in 1979 and the Advisory Council survey in 1991. In both surveys, young respondents were much more likely to believe that their employer-sponsored pensions or income from their own individual savings would be the most important source of income when they retired. While this may be what people expect, it is not what has occurred in the past. Nor is it projected to occur in the future.

As Moon's analysis (chapter 4) indicates, Social Security is the principal source of income for most retirees today: fully six in 10 elderly couples and unmarried individuals receive half or more of their income from Social Security (Grad, 1994). Dynamic simulations of retirement income that were done for the 1991 Advisory Council, too, portray a scenario for 2020 that bears much more resemblance to the situation for today's elderly than that anticipated by survey respondents. Changes in pension laws, particularly since 1974, have improved the security of employer-sponsored pensions for covered workers, and simulations project a significant increase in receipt of pensions among the future elderly. Still, Social Security is projected to continue to be the most important source of income for most retirees (Advisory Council on Social Security, 1991). The fact remains, however, that the public (especially younger adults) has less faith in the availability of Social Security during their retirement years than in the availability of either private pensions or savings.

LOW CONFIDENCE IN SOCIAL SECURITY

1. People's Expectations of Social Security

Does low confidence in the future of Social Security mean that people genuinely do not expect to receive it? The answer clearly is no. The same surveys that report low confidence that Social Security would have money to pay them benefits when they retire also show that respondents, when asked about their retirement income, say they expect to get Social Security (91 percent in 1979 and 93 percent in 1991). Further, when asked if it would be a major source or a minor source of their retirement income, many believed it would be a major source: 60 percent in 1979 and 45 percent in 1991. A smaller proportion expected Social Security to be their most important source of retirement income (37 percent in 1979 and 27 percent in 1991). People clearly do expect to receive Social Security, even though many expect it to be only a minor source of their retirement income, and they express low confidence in its future viability.

Focus groups conducted in connection with the 1985 survey found that concern about the future of Social Security was less about its being discontinued than about the adequacy of benefits it would pay in the future. Focus groups conducted by the National Academy of Social Insurance in 1994 found similar results. In focus groups with workers in their 20s and workers in their 40s, participants' views about the future of Social Security evolved over the course of the groups' discussions

> Very early in the discussion of employee benefits, someone would usually say matter-of-factly that Social Security would not "be there" in the future. Later, having the group talk about Social Security forced people to think about what they were saying. Very often participants would gain a sense of confidence about the program based on the conversation in the focus group. During that conversation it became clear that the matter-of-fact "it won't be there" statement was not based on any sort of judgment. It was simply a reaction. By the end of the discussion, participants in each focus group had begun to really think about Social Security for what seemed like the first time. (Friedland, 1994a, p. 42–43)

Daniel Yankelovich has argued that most public opinion polls do not reflect public judgment, which he defines as public opinion that has been formed after confronting the issue, struggling with the consequences of that opinion, and being prepared to make the changes implied by the opinion (Yankelovich, 1991). The distinction between "reaction" and "judgement" was borne out in the focus groups. As participants shared what they knew, or thought they knew, about Social Security, they developed a shared confidence about what it is and how it works. Sometimes their information was not accurate. Despite this, as they discussed it, they came to be much less cynical about the future of the program, and there often appeared a genuine yearning to be reassured by some expert that Social Security would, in fact, "be there" (Friedland, 1994b).

2. "Confidence" in a Restructuring Economy

Confidence in anything that is 20 to 40 years into the future may be too much to ask in an uncertain world in which many things are changing for reasons that appear to be beyond the control of individual workers. Workers may feel they have less control over their lives and the security of their jobs as they experience, personally or among peers, downsizing, plant closures, and manufacturing relocations to other parts of the country or beyond its borders. Further, the nature of work itself is changing. Workers may feel less secure about their future employment and whether the skills they have will still be needed. Low confidence in Social Security may simply reflect general insecurity that comes with change in the labor market. A restructuring economy, however, is not an adequate explanation for workers' reported low confidence in Social Security, because workers express higher confidence about other types of retirement income.

3. The Effect of Individual Optimism

As Moon (chapter 4) discusses, it is true today that income from assets and pensions is the major source of income for retirees at the top of the income distribution. Elderly income composition by levels of total income shows that for those in the top 20 percent of the income distribution, income from assets or personal savings is the largest single source. Earnings for those not yet retired and pensions are a large share (Reno, 1993). Perhaps the high expectations and confidence young workers have in these sources reflect their belief, or aspiration, that they will end up at the top of the income distribution at the end of their work life. But, except at Lake Wobegone, not everyone can be far above average. What might appear as optimism might also be denial. Too many of us may be quick to deny that we will grow older, face physical limitations, and not do as well in our careers or savings and investment decisions as we intended.

4. Confidence and Individual Discretion?

Personal savings is the source of retirement income with the greatest individual discretion (and risk); yet, it is the source in which Americans report they have the most confidence. Perhaps individual discretion brings a sense of control, which leads to a sense of security and confidence. For example, individuals actively make decisions about how much to put aside and how to invest personal savings or 401(k)-type employer plans. This wealth may be more tangible and provide individuals with a sense of control over the outcome of the investment. Without judging the validity of the view that discretion leads to control and secure outcomes, it is worth considering the connection between Americans' feeling of control and their levels of confidence in Social Security.

A feeling of lack of control may be important in understanding the low confidence Americans place in Social Security. In one sense, the lack of individual control is an important part of the strength of Social Security. Workers don't have to "do" anything to be sure they are covered by Social Security. Their contributions are deducted from their wages and matched by their employers; the earnings record they build through their lifetimes becomes the basis for their Social Security benefits. At retirement, they don't have to predict their remaining life-span and parcel out their Social Security to cover it. It is there for the duration, and it keeps pace with inflation.

In a much broader sense, however, the future of Social Security depends very much on the collective support that Americans have for it and the collective control they exert over it. The continuity of Social Security is assured solely because voters support it, see its value, and want it—for their grandparents, their parents, themselves, and their children. Workers' support for Social Security, made clear to elected officials, is their source of control over its future. If workers do not understand this distinctive feature of Social Security, and instead believe that it is in the hands of others and they have no say about it, that would contribute to low confidence in the future of Social Security.

5. The Effect of Distrust in Government

Recent opinion polls indicate Americans report a low regard for the federal government. When asked about the trustworthiness of various institutions, the federal government rated lowest, while successively higher ratings were given to private corporations, investment companies, public schools, and banks. Ratings of occupations according to their credibility gave lowest ratings to nonelected government officials, with successively higher ratings to investment counselors, accountants, and schoolteachers (Friedland, 1994b).

In the same March 1994 opinion poll, respondents were quick to agree with statements of disdain about the federal government—its inability to manage funds, assertions that elected officials or government employees are dishonest—and yet to agree that the federal government runs the best country in the world. Focus group respondents also were quick to complain about government mismanagement. But their tone was more blithe than bitter as they recounted tales of Watergate and costly Defense Department toilet seats. The right to criticize government seemed more deeply held than concerns about any particular piece of criticism. Ultimate appreciation for living in the "best place" on earth seemed more strongly felt than disappointment with any particular policy or evidence of wrongdoing (Friedland, 1994b).

6. The Impact of the Social Security Policy Debate on Confidence?

A review of Social Security policy debate since the mid-1970s shows that American's confidence in the future of Social Security dropped when debate about Social Security "reform" escalated (see Figure 11.2). While confidence rebounded somewhat after corrective action was taken in 1977, and again in 1983, each "crisis" seemed to ratchet down the steady state confidence level.

It is striking that the "reforms" enacted in 1977 and in 1983 were quite modest in relation to the high pitch of the debate that preceded enactment. Social Security seems to pose a particular dilemma for policymakers. Because it is so popular, they are reluctant to make even modest changes. The rhetoric of debate has to reach crisis proportions before they gain confidence that the electorate will support their actions. Paradoxically, the rhetoric that bolsters the confidence of policymakers tends to undermine the confidence of the electorate. While Americans continue to support Social Security, and their confidence rebounds to some degree after each "crisis," it nonetheless seems shaken by the high pitch of policy debate.

7. The Intangibility of Social Security

Individual savings and employer pensions are clearly more tangible than Social Security. With saving, there is a financial report or bank statement showing the value of that asset. Pensions are required by the Employee Retirement Income Security Act to provide annual reports to participants. Social Security does not yet have the counterpart to such statements. A new law requiring the Social Security Administration (SSA) to provide individual workers with personalized earnings and benefit estimate statements is based on the belief that making Social Security more tangible to American workers will increase their confidence in it. Senator Moynihan, the chief congressional sponsor of the new law, believes that lack of confidence in Social Security is directly related to the lack of communication between the Social Security Administration and the public:

> All of us pay into Social Security, but rarely, until we become beneficiaries, do we ever hear from Social Security. We pay our taxes to Federal, State and local governments and we hear back from them every year—reminding us to tote up how much we've paid in and how much we still owe or are due back. We receive monthly statements from our banks and credit card companies. Yet every month, in every paycheck, we see money withheld for Social Security, but we hear nary a word from the Social Security Administration. (Congressional Record, 1989, S 620–621)

With the new, individualized, benefit statements, Social Security is expected to become more tangible for workers.[8] Further, they will have something to "do" about their future benefits, in that they will be encouraged to check that their earnings record is accurate, and to correct it if it is not.

8. Inadequate Information and Low Confidence

Survey respondents often indicate that the news media is their most frequent source of information about Social Security. Newspapers and television were the most common sources cited in a February 1994 poll (Friedland, 1994b). The news media, by its nature, focuses on "news" about problems that need "reform" or on conflict among policy officials. An analysis of print media treatment of Social Security since 1980 weighed the balance of news stories in terms of the number of paragraphs devoted to various positions about Social Security policy proposals. On proposals involving reducing benefits, financial restructuring, and reducing eligibility for benefits, paragraphs supporting such proposals outnumbered those opposing such proposals by about two to one. The same analysis shows that politicians are the media's first choice for sources of information or quotes about Social Security. The president, administration officials, and party leaders in the Congress are favorite sources (L. Jacobs and Shapiro, 1994). While Social Security alone is not particularly newsworthy, what the president says about it, or disagreements between the president and opposition party leaders, is news.

Furthermore, while there is growing awareness of the need for retirement planning as the baby-boom grows older, even feature stories in the popular press that offer advice about retirement planning give very little attention to Social Security. For example, a recent weekly news magazine devoted about 20 pages to a feature series about retirement planning for the baby boomers, but mentioned Social Security only in passing and characterized both Social Security and traditional pensions in negative terms: "underneath the hype, the investment firms are saying what boomers need to hear: since companies are phasing out guaranteed pensions, workers must provide for themselves by contributing to—and wisely managing—employer sponsored savings plans such as the 401(k). Taxes will probably rise, and a stressed Social Security system may falter" (*U.S. News and World Report*, 1994, p. 86). The feature series was almost exclusively about individual investment options, with over 30 quotes from financial advisors about what was hot and what was not, along with a brief story about how pension credits can be lost without vigilant monitoring by plan participants.

Counting on the news media as the primary source of information about Social Security means that it is likely to be cast in terms of crisis, disagreement, and debate or be overlooked altogether. After the news media, Americans' next most common sources of information about Social Security, according to recent polls, were friends, neighbors, or co-workers. The Social Security Administration or other government agencies were relatively low on the list of sources that people say contributed to their understanding of Social Security. Focus groups with employee-benefit managers and financial advisers showed that they rarely discussed Social Security with their clients, except to explain how pension products they offer are integrated with Social Security. Furthermore, focus groups with workers in their 20s and in their 40s indicated they had had little or no exposure to positive information about the value of Social Security for their own future retirement (Friedland, 1994b).

While Americans report they rely mainly on the news media to learn about Social Security, they have opportunities to learn about savings options from professionals whose livelihood depends on selling their products to their customers. Pension and savings options are extremely complicated. But individual investors or employers setting up pension plans get individualized attention and a persuasive explanation of how particular retirement income products will meet their needs.

Social Security is also complicated, but there seems to be a relative vacuum in the information available to American workers about its strengths and how it fits with other sources of retirement income that are offered in the marketplace. American workers cannot be expected to learn for themselves about the nuances of future Social Security financing; its unique benefit provisions that keep pace with economy-wide economic growth before retirement and provide inflation protection throughout retirement; the ways in which it is different from, and in many ways is more secure than, individual retirement savings; and how it is distinct from other government activities. While there is a market to promote the unique features of various individual savings instruments, there is no counterpart to that forum to explain the unique strengths of Social Security.

CONCLUSIONS

Americans' consistent support of Social Security seems to be related to an understanding that Social Security promotes independence not only for beneficiaries but also for working-age families who might otherwise have a much larger personal obligation to support aging family members. Americans also are quite knowledgeable about some basic features of Social Security. They understand that it is financed through Social Security taxes, and they do not mind paying those taxes. They also understand the importance of Social Security for current retirees and are willing to support it for their parents and grandparents.

Americans' reports of low confidence in the future of Social Security seem to reflect two different themes. At one level, reports that Social Security "won't be there" appear to be a gut reaction to a pollster's question rather than a carefully formed judgment. Perhaps that reaction should not be surprising when people's main source of information is popular media coverage of Social Security as a topic of controversy and conflict among public officials. More in-depth surveys of retirement expectations, in contrast with opinion polls, find that the same workers who express little confidence that Social Security will be there, when later asked about their expected sources of retirement income, almost always say they expect to get Social Security; in fact, many expect it to be a major source of retirement income.

Focus groups showed a similar phenomenon. Discussions typically began with blithe assertions that Social Security won't be there, but then evolved into a more thoughtful discussions that ended with a genuine wish to be reassured that it would, in fact, be there. These findings are consistent with the work of Yankelovich, who argued that polls often capture quick reactions rather than informed public judgment.

At another level, the low confidence in Social Security appears to reflect important gaps in information that would help workers assess the value of Social Security for their own future retirement. The new requirement that the Social Security Administration provide personalized earnings and benefit statements to covered workers may help. In addition, however, Americans' low confidence may reflect gaps in information in three broader areas. First is a lack of understanding regarding the different but complementary roles that Social Security, pensions, and savings fill for individuals and for society as a whole. Second is the failure to recognize the features that make Social Security different from pensions or savings: that it is mandatory, universal, fully portable, and fully indexed to keep pace with the economy. These are all key elements of the security it provides to individuals. Third is the realization that Social Security, unlike pensions or savings, derives its sustainability from the Americans who support it, not from the financial returns of particular investment decisions. The future of Social Security depends directly on the collective support of Americans and the collective influence they exert over it.

Savings and pensions are important supplements to Social Security. But because of investment risk, they cannot substitute for the basic level of retirement income that comes from a public system. Strong public support is the best assurance that Social Security will be there in the future. Understanding this, as well as the unique ways in which Social Security is dynamically adjusted to grow with the economy and protect against inflation for future retirees, may be the key to raising Americans' confidence in its future.

ENDNOTES

1. Contributions did not fully keep pace with wage growth because the taxable earnings base was not indexed to keep pace with wage growth, although there were some *ad hoc* increases. However, wage increases below the wage base brought increased revenues to the trust funds.

2. Questions about public confidence in Social Security did not draw enough attention to measure them in opinion polls.

3. As inflation rose, 1973 legislation provided another *ad hoc* increase of 11 percent in 1974.

4. The formula for automatically indexing Social Security benefits for cost-of-living increases was based on historical experience that wages generally grew at about twice the rate of inflation, that is, wage growth (of, say, 4 percent) was made up of roughly equal parts *inflation* (2 percent) and *real wage*, or productivity growth (2 percent), which brought a real increase in workers' standard of living. When, however, prices rose far more rapidly than real wages, the formula overindexed future benefits for the inflation component of nominal wage growth.

5. A change in the sequence and wording of the questions in 1993 in the American Council on Life Insurance survey may also have affected the survey response.

6. A closer look at the three components of retirement income—Social Security, pensions, and personal savings—shows that they fill complementary roles. Each has strengths that the others lack. On the dimension of security, Social Security probably ranks highest, while pensions and savings, which generally are designed to supplement Social Security, offer more flexibility, discretion, and individual control, but they also pose somewhat more risk for individuals than does Social Security. Personal savings are the riskiest of the three types of retirement income because the individual must defer current consumption in order to save; the person must resist the temptation to use accumulated savings prior to retirement, for fun or for emergency; and savings are not guaranteed against loss through bad luck or bad choices in the financial markets. While there is some protection through regulation of the banking and financial industries, and federal insurance of bank deposits, there remains a high degree of individual risk. Examples abound of fortunes won and nest eggs lost by individual private savers. Even cautious investors who try to avoid market risk run the risk that their investments may not keep pace with inflation. Savings, too, are an important supplemental source of retirement income, particularly for high income workers.

7. The Congressional Budget Office reports that when housing wealth is included in the Bernheim analysis, "the index of adequacy of savings increases to 84 percent" (U.S. Congressional Budget Office, 1993, p. 43).

8. The law as amended in 1990 requires the Social Security Administration to (1) provide personal earnings and benefit estimate statement (PEBES), on request, beginning October 1, 1990; (2) provide PEBES automatically to workers age 60 and over who are not already receiving Social Security benefits and for whom a current mailing address can be determined, beginning September 30, 1994; and (3) provide PEBES automatically, annually, to all workers who are not receiving benefits and for whom a current address can be determined, beginning October 1, 1999. Statements provided to workers under age 50 are not required to include estimates of monthly retirement benefits; in the absence of such estimates they must include a description of possible future benefits.

CHAPTER 12

Social Security Politics and the Conflict Between Generations
Are We Asking the Right Questions?

THEODORE R. MARMOR, FAY LOMAX COOK, AND STEPHEN SCHER

Social Security has been, and remains, one of the most popular and successful social programs in American history. As Reno and Friedland point out in the previous chapter, polls consistently find that Americans of all age groups are nearly unanimous in their support for the maintenance of its pension benefits. Moreover, the retirement program has done precisely what its originators intended it to do: protect retirees and their families from income losses that would drastically reduce their economic well-being.[1] Against this backdrop of popularity and achievement, it is surprising to find so many policy elites fretting about the alleged unfairness of Social Security.

Is the United States allocating too large a proportion of its public resources to the elderly at the expense of the young?[2] This question, which has come to be framed as one of "generational equity," has prompted a considerable amount of comment since the mid-1980s. And it has also bred conflict between some groups and individuals claiming to represent either the young or the old. Our view is that the substantive claims underlying this conflict are largely fictive. The conflict is the product, instead, of a fundamental misunderstanding of Social Security, coupled with the broader political efforts of the most prominent critics to reduce the scope of, and public expenditures for, America's social insurance programs.

The controversy about the claimed conflict between young and old over Social Security pensions is very much a part of contemporary debate in American politics over social policy. As such, it can best be understood as an instance of a broader dialogue about the proper role and scope of the federal government. We begin then by considering the context of American political debate and continue by locating the disputes over Social Security and the welfare state within it.

195

THE AMERICAN POLITICS OF EXAGGERATION

Foreign observers from de Tocqueville to Thatcher have described American politics as unruly, combative, and feverish. Whether the question is support for cabinet nominees or the invasion of Haiti, tax increases or prayer in the schools, universal health insurance or welfare reform, disputants swat incessantly at each other. Particular constituencies and advocates obviously vary with the conflict, but there is a recurrent process. Claims of crisis are made to attract attention, followed by predictable countercharges of emotionalism and attention grabbing. Statistical aggregates (deficit levels here and abroad, or estimates of the number of homeless, disabled, fearless, or fearful) are presented in speeches or in writing as if the mere statistics were sufficient to justify a single, inescapable policy response to a complex social or political problem.

Crisis mongering and fact throwing ensure that the supply of American public "problems" will be enormous; the simple citation of facts can always establish a gap between aspiration and actuality. Moreover, there are always compelling illustrations to demonstrate the character of the difficulties and, if appropriately crafted, to suggest the right remedy. There will, of course, be difficulties, audiences are told. But, with political will and a modicum of good luck, the nation can choose the right course and move towards whatever is claimed to be the desirable state of affairs: less infant mortality, better education for the young, more effective defense, less injustice, lower medical costs, more habitable cities, more readily available therapeutic drugs, control over Alzheimer's disease, reduced levels of cancer, fairness in Social Security, or whatever.

With an emphasis on unanalyzed statistics and with the goal of identifying yet another crisis, rhetoric and ridicule supplant reasoned analysis and discussion all too often within the political arena. Indeed, what Americans learn about politics and policy choices, particularly on television but also in the print media, gives enormous weight to the simplistic analysis of problems, to vivid images of allegedly straightforward remedies, to the confusion of anecdote with social fact, and to the purveying, alternately, of doom and delight. These are the materials out of which politicians create their own, often self-serving, myths of political or social problems and of how they must be remedied. We all may agree, of course, that genuine problems exist or that "there oughta be a law," but the real issue—and the real challenge—is to determine just what law should be enacted, just what can reasonably be achieved.

In this context, what is sometimes known as America's "politics of exaggeration" tends to obscure rather than address the sources of America's social and political problems, and what must be done to ameliorate them. The complaint is not simply that reasoned debate is too rare in American politics, but that mythmakers and their calls of crisis play too prominent a role in defining what the policy debates are about. Open democratic politics must include cliches, slogans, rallying symbols, even myths of failure and of ready remedies. Nonetheless, the politics of exaggeration, when systematic, can paralyze as well as prod. All too often, elected politicians, appointed officials, pressure groups, and the media coalesce to produce a cacophony of proposal, commentary, and appraisal. Strident and superficial public debate tends to inhibit rather than enhance the formulation and implementation of effective public policy. In place of collective determination to ameliorate public problems, we end up with a deeply divided citizenry who cannot agree on either the sources of our problems or how to address them. And in place of ameliorative programs, we end up with heightened expectations and programmatic half measures. The consequences are ineffective interventions, recurrent recriminations, and, increasingly, the political disillusionment of the American public.

THE CRISIS OF THE WELFARE STATE

Current political disputes over social welfare policies have been shaped by two decades of troubled economic circumstances and declining expectations in America. For much of the 1970s and 1980s the recurrent refrain in American commentary on social policy was that of crisis. Stimulated by the quadrupling of oil prices in 1973–74, the stagflation of the 1970s occasioned dire observations about the capacity of American government to improve social conditions. Some argued that diminished public revenues made it impossible to satisfy the expectations generated by the Great Society programs of the Kennedy-Johnson years. Others claimed that the programs themselves had helped to produce the economic mess we came to call stagflation. Whatever the cause, the malaise seemed palpable. A diminished sense of what was possible, a sad or angry reaction to the earlier aspirations, and a skeptical view of governmental capacities—all of these reactions constituted the basic claim that there was a crisis in America's welfare state.

Exacerbating this sense of crisis and disorientation was the fact that America's social welfare programs were themselves adopted in response to crises, and in times of great social need; they lack a deeply rooted, widely understood ideological foundation, a common social or political vision.[3] We live, for instance, with the legacy of the New Deal's social policies, a set of programmatic initiatives for providing relief, promoting economic security, and insuring against the devastating family consequences of unemployment, widowhood, industrial accident, and the like. As Berkowitz discusses in chapter 2, from this beginning came later adaptations of the original models, extensions of Social Security and related programs to the survivors of workers (in 1939), to disabled workers (in 1956), and to the medical expenses of the elderly and the poor (Medicare and Medicaid in 1965). As a consequence, with a perceived crisis in these social programs themselves, the political consensus about the programs—their legitimacy, their viability, and their goals—is vulnerable to exaggerated fears.

Political discussions of social welfare policies have followed the same pattern of frenzied activity described in the preceding section. The facts presented, the standards invoked, the options considered—all are regularly riddled with misconception and much mischief (Marmor, Mashaw, and Harvey, 1990). There are, to be sure, excellent descriptions of American conditions, and there is an abundance of social scientific work, much of it illuminating when understood properly. But as this scholarly work is used in political disputes over social welfare policies, the nuances and uncertainties of the social scientific literature are typically lost. Assisted by a large industry of analysts who provide the requisite factual foundation in reports and studies, elected officials, lobbyists, and other participants in political debate latch onto the "explanations" and "solutions" that best fit their own political goals. The results of this process are deeply unsettling, a kind of rationalistic fantasy where elements of reasoned argument and symbol rattling coalesce into a muddle of intellectual confusion.

Amidst this confusion, however, there is a continuing and recognizable pattern, one that reflects two quite different, competing views of the goals of our social welfare programs: the residualist and the social insurance conceptions of the welfare state.[4] Each of these has its own attractions. Each has had an impact on public discussion. And each has the capacity to influence the character of America's social welfare programs, including the treatment of the young and the old.

The view of the welfare state as "residualist" characterizes social policies as a safety net. The "net" of social welfare programs is intended to rescue the victims of capitalism and to give subsistence-level relief to those unable to provide for their own needs. This view of purpose, originating as it did in the European poor laws, is found everywhere among capitalist nations. Though its popularity differs among those nations, the residualist conception has had a pervasive impact on public debates about social welfare programs. In the United States, and in Australia and Canada as well, the residualist conception is the staple not only of business and financial elites, but also of substantial proportions of middle- and lower-income populations.

Most of those who describe the welfare state as residual believe that social policy's aim should be temporary assistance, and its governance highly decentralized. In federal regimes the rallying cry of the residualists has been to diffuse authority for social programs to the states and provinces. American public assistance programs such as the federal-state Aid to Dependent Children (later Aid to Families with Dependent Children, AFDC), which was part of the original Social Security Act of 1935, exemplify the residual model. Advocates of decentralization presume that individual families will typically assure the welfare of their members. When that fails, institutions close to those families—charitable groups, then local and state programs—constitute the appropriate protection against destitution.

The metaphor of the safety net suggests the key features of residualist welfare policy. The net is close to the ground and the benefits are accordingly modest—a subsistence that might vary widely in connection with community standards of adequacy. The clientele are the down and out; the eligibility criteria, whether tests of needs or means, are designed to sort out the truly needy from the rest. There is an implicit notion of avoiding potential waste; aid should go only to those who need the net to survive. Minimal adequacy, selectivity, localism, and tests of need—these constitute the residualist's controlling notions for evaluating the welfare state.

So stated, the conception of welfare as residualist differs sharply from what is known as the social insurance model. The basic purpose of social insurance is to maintain economic well-being amidst threats to loss of family income. What links social insurance advocates is their rejection of the residualist conception of welfare as a mere safety net against destitution.

The central metaphor of social insurance is the insurance card. If the net of welfare is to catch those who have already failed, the card of social insurance symbolizes prevention against a radical decline of a family's living standards. The aim is simple: the universalization of the financial security presumed in the fringe benefits of higher civil servants and economic elites. The threats to economic security include some obvious ones—involuntary unemployment, widowhood, sickness, injury, or retirement—as well as less obvious ones such as a large family (child allowances). Welfare states have provided for these eventualities at different times, in different sequences, and with considerable variation in generosity and terms of administration. Yet, irrespective of form and levels of payment, social insurance programs have rejected as inferior the selective machinery of means-tested programs: the more universal the entitlement, the closer it is to the model.

As Thompson and Upp (chapter 1) and Ball (chapter 18) note, contributions during working life, according to the orthodox theory of social insurance, "entitle" one to "protection" against large reductions in economic status. Sometimes the contributions are payments into the larger society's general tax revenues, as is the case in Canada. Or, as in Great Britain, contributions are in the form of weekly social insurance payments. These arrangements differ from the percentage-of-payroll taxes of the United States' Old-Age and Survivor's Insurance program, the familiar FICA tax. Yet the idea is the same: to contribute while working to future financial security. The overriding goal is to protect citizens, through a social insurance program, against the predictable risks of a modern industrial society.[5]

THE CONFLICT BETWEEN THE OLD AND THE YOUNG OVER SOCIAL SECURITY

With this background in mind, we are in a position to turn to Social Security itself, with special attention to the much-touted conflict between old-age beneficiaries and younger Americans. Those younger Americans, according to the proponents of intergenerational inequity, face unfair prospects. They will either receive no Social Security retirement benefits at all, or obtain, in comparison with previous retirees, substantially reduced "rates of return" on their contributions to Social Security.[6] In the meantime, Social Security's current and projected expenditures appear to make other social programs for children and working Americans unaffordable.

What facts support this fearful picture? There is no dispute that America's older citizens receive the lion's share of the income, in cash and in services, that the nation's social programs distribute. In 1994, for example, expenditures on the elderly amounted to roughly a third of the entire federal budget.[7] Nor, as Reno and Friedland note in chapter 11, is there disagreement that a large proportion of younger Americans *fear* that Social Security pensions will not "be there" for them when they retire. Two-thirds of Americans aged 25 to 34 believe it is either very or somewhat likely that they will not receive their retirement pensions. The same proportion fears for the future of the entire Social Security program itself.[8] What underlies these fears and beliefs is fundamental uncertainty about the fiscal future of Social Security pensions. As Myers discusses in Chapter 13, current projections are that pension payments will begin to exceed the Social Security payroll and benefits tax early in the twenty-first century, and that the resulting operating deficit will deplete the Social Security trust fund by 2030. Will substantial—and unaffordable—tax increases be the only means of maintaining reasonable benefit levels and of paying the promised pensions to retirees?

Before turning to the issue of future affordability, let us begin by discussing whether it is even appropriate to conceptualize Social Security issues in terms of the young versus the old, in terms of the supposedly threatened and the supposedly indulged. "Justice between age groups," as Norman Daniels has cogently argued, "is a problem best solved if we stop thinking of the old and the young as distinct groups. We age. The young become the old. As we age, we pass through institutions that affect our well-being at each stage of life, from infancy to very old age" (1988, p. 18).

All young people anticipate, even if hazily, a time when they will be old. Their parents and grandparents are vivid examples of what it means to move through the life cycle. A social insurance system designed to deal with predictable changes in income is simultaneously a means of distributing income among particular age cohorts and a means of distributing income over the life cycle of particular people. As a normative matter, the justice of a program is a question of whether it treats people fairly as they move through stages. As a financial matter, the affordability of programs over time is whether current promises can be kept. The first matter is one that ignores time, place, and particular facts. The second is very much a matter of whether, at some future time, promises can be kept. Keeping these two issues distinct is crucially important if problems concerning Social Security are to be properly understood and addressed. Unfortunately, much of the old-versus-young debate over Social Security has disregarded this distinction and consequently confused, rather than clarified, public discussion.[9]

The foregoing analysis is quite consistent with the available survey data. Americans do not see issues of Social Security as involving an irreducible conflict between the young and the old. For example, in a random survey of 1,209, Americans, Cook and Barrett (1992) found that an astounding 97 percent favored maintaining or increasing Social Security benefits. Four out of five respondents reported they were satisfied that a portion of every working person's income goes to support Social Security. Almost two-thirds said they would pay higher taxes if the program were threatened with cuts from its current pension levels (which provide retirees, on average, about 40 percent of their pre-retirement wage and salary income). As Reno and Friedland note in chapter 11, other polls tell a similar story. The National Election Surveys and the National Opinion Research Center, which have monitored attitudes toward Social Security since 1982, provide cross-sectional data from two large national samples that substantiate high levels of support for Social Security (Cook, 1996).

At least as far as public preferences are concerned, then, there is undeniably broad support for a Social Security pension program whose goals fall well within the social insurance, rather than the residualist, conception of the welfare state. The American public appears committed to a pension program that provides retirees with reasonable income security, and at a level above that of mere subsistence. Moreover, there is only marginal support for cutting back pensions to the minimal levels preferred by residualists.

Given this continuing public support for the present Social Security pension system, one might wonder why there has been such fearfulness about the retirement program's future, both its fairness and its future affordability. Here is where specters of the future—widely disseminated—have frightened so many contemporary citizens.[10] Upon examination, however, the facts are far less frightening than they may be made to appear at first glance. Since the reform amendments were enacted in 1983, for example, the surplus of revenues over benefits and administrative expenses has been substantial (Marmor, Mashaw, and Harvey, 1990, p. 140).[11] This obvious fact led Brookings Institution economists Henry Aaron and Robert Reischauer to characterize Social Security as an "island of budgetary surplus in the midst of an ocean of red ink " (Aaron and Reischauer, 1987). In 1994 alone, the Social Security "surplus"—the excess of revenues over outlays—amounted to $44 billion.

With a cumulative surplus in 1994 of $436 billion in the Social Security pension program, the question of affordability depends only upon the prospects for maintaining current pension levels into the indefinite future. The demographic data are, in fact, already well known. The elderly of the twenty-first century have, for the most part, already been born, and their gross numbers can be estimated with considerable confidence. The elderly will almost surely constitute a larger share of the population than they do now (12.6 percent) (see Table 12.1). Nonetheless, the record of other industrialized countries provides grounds for cautious optimism. Many of these countries have been maintaining their retirement pension programs intact with proportions of the elderly far greater than the United States is projected to have in 2010 (12.8 percent).[12]

In assessing the future affordability of Social Security pensions, it is also important to determine what other changes there will be in the demands upon both the income of workers and the public treasury. What else is happening to the population that will affect the affordability of Social Security pensions and other social welfare programs? In this context, one crucially important change concerns what is known as the "dependency ratio," the percent of the population not available for productive work (children, the elderly, and the disabled). Although the number of elderly Americans is increasing and will continue to increase, the number of infants and school-age children is *decreasing* even more rapidly. By 2040, the dependency ratio is expected to be even lower than it was in 1960 (U.S. Congress, Committee on Ways and Means, 1989, Table 13, p. 89). And insofar as the dependency ratio

TABLE 12.1. Estimated Percentages of Population Age 65 and over, 1970–2020, in Selected Countries.[a]

	1970	1980	1990	2000	2010	2020
Canada	7.9	9.5	11.5	12.4	13.3	16.7
France	12.9	14.0	14.0	15.6	16.0	19.5
Germany	13.7	15.6	14.6	15.5	18.4	19.1
Italy	10.9	13.1	14.1	17.0	18.9	20.9
Japan	7.1	9.0	11.7	16.2	20.1	24.2
United Kingdom	12.9	15.1	15.7	15.4	15.8	18.2
United States	9.8	11.3	12.6	12.3	12.8	16.3

Source: Compiled by authors from data in United Nations (1993), p.p. 408–9, 462–3, 470–1, 510–11, 514–15, 660–1, 666–67.

[a]The projections for 2000, 2010, and 2020 are based on assumptions about future trends in fertility. In preparing these assumptions, the United Nations' statstical unit publishes high-, medium- and low-fertility variants but says that the medium-fertility variant projections can be thought of as "most likely" (United Nations, 1993, p. 84). Therefore, we use medium-fertility variant projections in this table.

is decreasing, the total burden upon workers to support the young and the old may also decrease as well, despite the expected growth in the number of elderly Americans.[13]

This line of reasoning does not require any particular conclusion about whether the mix of future financial demands will be more or less acceptable to future taxpayers. But it does provide a context in which "affordability" can be more reasonably assessed. If we know that the proportion of one set of claimants on public support will grow in scale and that the proportion of another will fall, it places the shape of our public household in perspective. Then the question becomes a practical one of shifting expectations, adjusting flows of taxation, and the like. The available data simply do not support the vision of a society overrun by greedy geezers. Instead, what we can project is that reasonable adjustments will need to be made in Social Security pensions and taxation levels in order to achieve the consensual and morally appropriate goal of maintaining Social Security pension support for our retired citizens. Indeed, by one estimate (Ball, 1996), a 1.9 percentage point increase in taxes on employees and employers would correct the shortfall projected for 2020.

THE DIVISIVE ISSUE OF GENERATIONAL EQUITY

We have just seen how helpful it is to distinguish between the normative desirability of, and public support for, Social Security pensions, on the one hand, and the affordability of those pensions, on the other. For example, with the goal of maintaining long-term pension levels threatened in the late 1970s and early 1980s by the retirement program's *projected* long-term deficits, Congress enacted the requisite reforms. By putting Social Security back on a firm financial foundation, the reforms of 1983 effectively ensured that the system's basic commitments would be protected for the foreseeable future.[14]

Once the 1983 reforms were enacted, one might have expected the public debate over Social Security to subside. Once again, Social Security was, or so it seemed, a politically popular, fiscally sound program with clear, broadly accepted purposes. Nonetheless, after a pause in the mid-1980s, the disputes returned and, indeed, grew increasingly strident by the end of the decade. Political conservatives remained deeply dissatisfied with the admittedly large expenditures to which Social Security is committed; motivated by residualist goals to reduce these expenditures, conservatives succeeded in re-opening the debate by changing the terms of the debate itself.

The issues raised in the 1970s and early 1980s had mostly to do with affordability. Could Social Security be maintained in an economic context of stagflation? Was "bankruptcy" its fate? The clear answer of 1983 was yes to the first question and no to the second. What, then, could be raised as a fundamental objection to a widely supported program, one regularly labeled a "sacred cow" by its critics? From the conservative perspective of welfare state residualists, a currently solvent Social Security program required reinterpretation. That reinterpretation, it turned out, involved the theme of "generational equity." And because this expression combined claims of unfairness with ones of affordability, it became a potent ideological symbol and weapon against the *status quo*.

The question of how this old-versus-young formulation took shape in the 1980s and 1990s is one on which future historians will expend ample energy. But, for our purposes, it is necessary only to outline the main features of the campaign and the policy issues they raise. Quite apart from the merits of their arguments, the purveyors of the conflict between old and young have played upon the consciousness of age within American culture. This became more politically salient when the federal government, constrained by stagflation, faced difficult allocational decisions in an environment influenced by an increasingly powerful, highly visible lobby of America's seniors.[15] In this context, residualist critics invoked the concept of generational equity, as it came to be defined in the early 1980s, as a means of creating conflict where previously there had been none: the current young should not be deprived of opportunities for economic and social well-being because of excessive allocations of resources to the old.[16]

This strategy of reinterpreting the affordability of social welfare programs for the elderly in terms of a supposed conflict between generations was very successful indeed. Even in the wake of the Social Security reforms of 1983, pundits received enormous attention and succeeded in making the conflict between young and old feel both real and pressing. In 1984, for instance, Senator David Durenberger (R-Minnesota), founded Americans for Generational Equity (AGE) to "promote the concept [of generational equity] . . . among America's political, intellectual, and financial leaders." Claiming credit for calling "into question the prudence, sustainability, and fairness of federal old age benefit programs" (AGE, 1990, p. 2), AGE's impact was, according to scholarly evaluations, considerable. One scholar of American social policy maintains that AGE, despite going out of business in the wake of Senator Durenberger's financial scandal in the late 1980s, reshaped public discussion. "All future policy choices," according to Quadagno, "will have to take generational equity into account" (1989, p. 364).

What political conservatives claimed, some academic figures supported. This was particularly true of the demographer, Professor Samuel Preston. Preston was the best known of the academic experts to support the charge that conditions had deteriorated for children and improved dramatically for the elderly. Moreover, Preston claimed that "gains for one group . . . at least in the public sphere . . . come partly at the expense of another." It was but a short intellectual step from this position to the conclusion that huge "transfers from the working-age population to the elderly are also transfers away from children" (1984, pp. 450–52). This formulation remains at the core of the charge of generational inequity, and the source of deep conflict between the young and the old.

As well befits American politics and its tendency to abuse statistics for partisan purposes, it is worth mentioning that Preston is a distinguished demographer, with considerable expertise in the determinants of large-scale population shifts. But he has no expertise in public finance, social insurance, or public policy politics. His fearful formulation, substantiated with data from the 1970s, took no account of the reforms of 1983. None of this mattered, however, to residualists looking for the evidence they needed to support the charge of generational inequity. His views spread rapidly through both academic and journalistic circles.[17]

This disconnection between the realities of program finance and the rhetoric of generational conflict has, indeed, become standard since the mid-1980s. Whereas the doomsaying of the early 1980s was occasioned by the projected deficits of the Social Security system, criticism of the Social Security system took on an altogether different cast by the late 1980s. The facts were plain. By 1989, the system's reserves had reached $163 billion and were to increase to $226 billion by the end of 1990. Ironically, such surpluses were as worrying to the critics of the greedy aged as the projected deficits had been. They constituted what one congressman called a "catastrophe waiting" to happen. Even the *New York Times* came to regard Social Security surpluses as "a crisis in trillions . . . a crisis in slow motion" (*New York Times*, 1988, A-18). This continuity of programmatic criticism and fearful forecasting, given the enormous change of fiscal facts, shows clearly the ideological character of the debate over old and young in social policy politics. When critics wring their hands whether a program is in deficit or surplus, one rightly suspects they are critical of the program's aims as such, and not simply of the program's performance.[18]

In the late 1980s political conservatives moved beyond their assault on Social Security toward a broader attack on America's welfare state. In *On Borrowed Time: How the Growth of Entitlements Threatens America's Future*, Former Secretary of Commerce Peter Peterson and the political analyst Neil Howe launched a residualist critique of entitlement programs in general. The generational equity issue was again the battering ram used against the elderly. In addition to constituting an illegitimate transfer from the young to the old, excessive Social Security disbursements were, the authors argued, "a direct cause of our federal deficit" (P. Peterson and Howe, 1988, p. 43). After the unexpected demise of Americans for Generational Equity, Peterson himself helped to found a new group, the Concord Coalition, with the same conservative policy agenda. Nominally dedicated to the purpose of educating Americans about the hard financial choices the nation will be confronting, the coalition reiterates the conservative position that government spending favors older, more affluent Americans at the expense of a younger generation that is already under financial distress (Concord Coalition, 1992). In addition to encouraging younger Americans to see themselves as needy and to see the elderly as an affluent group not deserving of public support, the coalition is not beneath the use of scare tactics. It has warned, for example, that the failure to transform Social Security may bring on a generational war. And given their own residualist political agenda, Peterson and other coalition members have been ready to lead it.

Though Peterson, Howe, and other conservative residualists portrayed themselves as defending the interests of America's children, many professionals dedicated to promoting just those interests have seen through this strategy. They recognize it as a dangerous effort to divide the young and the old, and to undercut public support for important governmental programs such as Social Security.[19] Many advocates for the interests of children have therefore made a concerted effort to quell the intentionally divisive rhetoric of generational equity. Of special importance has been their role in founding Generations United, a group whose goal is to "dispel the myth of competition for scarce resources and reap the benefits of intergenerational collaboration... and interdependence" (Generations United, 1990a, 1990b). According to David Liederman, executive director of the Child Welfare League of America, who helped to start Generations United, "What we are trying to say is that the fates of the generations are linked. Obviously, I want better programs for kids... but they should not come at the expense of seniors, especially the large number of seniors who are poor or near poor" (quoted in Pearlstein, 1993).

No one can doubt that the Social Security retirement program needed the reforms enacted in 1983 or that more reforms will be needed in the future. The 1983 reforms put Social Security back on the track to fiscal balance, and there seems little reason to doubt that a nation dedicated to the continuance of the program will again find the means and the resolve to adapt it to changing circumstances. In this context, the shrill claims of generational inequity are substantively misguided and factually unfounded. Nonetheless, interpreted within the larger residualist political agenda of reducing the scope of the federal government and of rejecting the existing goals of the welfare state, the claim of generational unfairness has proven to be remarkably newsworthy. By invoking the seemingly high moral ground of generational equity, residualists have succeeded in launching a concerted and surprisingly resonant attack upon Social Security and other programs for the aged.[20] It is important to note, however, that advocates of generational equity, despite their alleged concern for the young, have almost never made demands that public expenditures for the benefit of children be increased.

The claim of generational unfairness has proven to be a deeply divisive element in the social policy politics of the last decade. Because reasoned public debate is so difficult to sustain in the United States, this conflict will surely remain a source of tension in future discussions of programs affecting elderly Americans.

ENDNOTES

1. For purposes of this essay, Social Security refers to the retirement, disability, and survivors pensions administered by the Social Security Administration. The SSA also administers public assistance programs (AFDC, SSI) that do not depend on social insurance principles. Certain programs (e.g., Medicare, Medicaid) are administered by other agencies (e.g., the Health Care Financial Administration). It is against this broader background of social welfare policy that we will assess the character, and the distortions, of the dispute over generational equity as it relates to Social Security pensions.

2. It is not just the policy elites who are fretting. The issue of generational equity has become a prominent one in the mass media, which often stress the element of conflict between generations. Witness such newspaper articles as "America Is at War with Its Children" (*San Francisco Chronicle*, 12 October 1989); "Older Voters Drive Budget" (*Washington Post*, 15 October 1990); and "Robbing Baby Peter to Pay Aging Paul" (*Boston Globe*, 10 February 1991).

3. This contrasts with Sweden, for example, where social security programs were much more directly linked to social democratic ideological foundations (Williamson and Pampel, 1993a, 1993b).

4. To avoid any possible confusion, it should be noted that some scholars refer to this social insurance conception of the welfare state as the "institutional model" of social welfare.

5. Because of its marginal impact on both public debate and public policy, we are relegating to an endnote a third conception of the welfare state, namely, that of the radical populist. From this radical perspective, the aims of help and compensation are themselves questionable, since they constitute adjustments to the harsh realities of industrial society, not means of transforming society. The standard for the radical theorist is equalization, not equitable insurance payments or adequacy of cash payments. The aim is social change, not evening the distribution of income over the life cycle. And the mechanisms are not ameliorative social programs for the people, but income and power to the less privileged. What social insurance advocates count as generous provision is, for the radical populist, a token gesture, no more than a way to gloss over the contradictions of modern capitalism. For others on the radical left, social insurance and other social welfare benefits are a citizen's rightful wage, a benefit that workers demanded

and won through conflict with the economic elite. This entire section draws liberally from Marmor, Mashaw, and Harvey, 1990, chap. 2–3.

6. The projection of substantial declines in the rate of return on Social Security contributions creates an independent source for claiming generational inequity in relation to Social Security and Medicare. The current generation of elderly Americans has, according to this argument, received a much higher rate of return than will apply to the current cohort of working Americans. For an extended discussion of this issue, its distortions and complexities, see chapter 5 by Chen and Goss.

7. That budget was approximately $1.53 trillion (U.S. Office of Management and Budget, 1995, table 6-1). The fact that a large share of the federal budget is for programs affecting the elderly is a consequence of how the United States has structured its public household, not some sort of mistake. Medicare began as a program for the elderly, the only example in the western industrial world of public health insurance for an age group. This has the effect of highlighting the medical costs of the elderly when the fact is that elderly citizens are high utilizers of medical care in every society. Likewise, the retirement program of the SSA assumes a more prominent place in federal expenditures because the United States funds primary and secondary education from largely local sources and, unlike Western Europe, does not have a very large public housing program. In short, what should be no surprise—the prominence of the elderly in American public finance—is inappropriately treated as some sort of failure.

8. See chapter 11 by Reno and Friedland for a detailed analysis of Social Security and public opinion.

9 By focusing exclusively on Social Security retirement pensions, critics invoking the conflict between young and old have effectively ignored the federal government's established commitment to provide economic protection over the entire course of the life-span. For example, children already benefit, directly or indirectly, from a wide range of programs administered by the SSA and by other federal agencies.

10. See the later discussion of Americans for Generational Equity and the Concord Coalition, two of the most recently established groups that have resorted to crisis mongering and manipulation of statistics in an effort to undercut public support for Social Security.

11. These included raising the eligibility age from 65 to 67 by some time in the twenty-first century, increasing payroll taxes, subjecting up to 50 percent of Social Security benefits to income taxation, and instituting a surplus revenue system.

12. The projected proportion of elderly Americans in 2020 (16.3 percent) is approximately the same as Great Britain has already experienced, and without having to drastically alter its pension benefits (see Williamson and Pampel, 1993a, 1993b).

13. The image of elderly Americans as greedy geezers who are depleting the public treasury at the expense of the young is, in this context, a product of incomplete demography. There are, in fact, two measures of dependency. A narrow measure of dependency is the ratio of conventional retirees to workers. It is this ratio that is increasing and that, taken in itself, appears to support alarming projections. A broader and more helpful measure of dependency, however, is the ratio of Americans over 65 *plus* children under 18 *plus* other nonworkers such as the disabled, to workers. By taking the elderly, the children, and the disabled into account, this ratio provides a much more complete picture of those dependent upon the public treasury for support and services. It is this ratio that is decreasing and that undercuts projections that Social Security pensions will overrun the public treasury. Moreover, because the proportion of children under 18 is decreasing, the support and services this cohort requires as it moves toward adulthood will also be less than it has been in the past.

14. For example, Social Security reserves totaled an estimated $226 billion in 1990, up from $163 billion just the year before.

15. This analysis follows that of Pierson and Smith (1994, pp. 22–23 and 43–47), who also found that issues of age have little to do with the politics of social policy in Canada, where discussions are dominated by issues of class and federalism. Similarly, in an analysis of the salience of issues related to generational equity in Canada and the United States, Cook et al. found little attention given to generational equity in Canada (Cook, Marshall, Marshall, and Kaufman, 1994).

16. With the American welfare state focusing so much on programs for the elderly (such as Social Security pensions and Medicare), some critics have blamed the nation's fiscal problems on its greedy geezers. This scapegoating was an unanticipated consequence of how America has structured its public household. Canada, with an equivalent proportion of the elderly and with similar rates of medical care use, experienced comparable economic strain in the 1970s and 1980s. But because Canada's universal medical program covers everyone who is sick, and not just the elderly, there has been no widespread handwringing there about the "greying of the federal budget" (Marmor and Beglin, 1995).

17. Between 1985 and 1992, the *Social Science Citation Index* shows that Preston's writings in *Demography* and *Scientific American* were cited in 158 articles. This amount of attention classifies Preston's work as what some scholars call a "research front." Only 3 percent of all published articles in scholarly journals are cited 50 times or more (Garfield, 1984).

18. This analysis is drawn from Marmor, Mashaw, and Harvey, 1990, chap. 5.

19. For a discussion of how the conflict between young and old might be reframed, see Kingson and Williamson, 1993.

20. For an analysis of the 1995 residualist assault on Medicare, see Marmor and Beglin, 1995.

CHAPTER 13

Will Social Security be There for Me?

ROBERT J. MYERS

Currently, many people, especially those in the middle and younger ages, raise the important question, "Will Social Security be there for me when I reach retirement age?" And this is repeated frequently by financial and other columnists and public commentators. In fact, it is getting so that many do not even ask this question, because they feel certain that it will not be there! Or, at the very best, they believe that, if Social Security continues, the benefits will be much smaller relatively than now, possibly being reduced by being means-tested (or, more accurately, income-tested).

Conversely, most older people, especially those receiving Social Security benefits, or close to such receipt, have much more confidence in the future viability of the program. Whether this is because they have more mature judgement, based on study and knowledge, or because they are only self-concerned and think the program will last for at least their lifetime is, of course, arguable.

This chapter will first discuss why there is currently such a widespread lack of confidence in the long-range fiscal viability of the Social Security program (Old-Age, Survivors, and Disability Insurance, or OASDI). (The matter of how great the lack of confidence there is at present is discussed and analyzed in detail in chapter 11.) Then views will be presented as to why the confidence level should be higher, and why the OASDI program will, almost certainly, "be there" out into the far-distant future, even for all time to come! The OASDI system will be considered as a whole, even though there are two separate trust funds: for OASI and DI. Over the past years, whenever one part of the system was in substantially weaker financial condition, the combined tax rate was appropriately reallocated, and it is thus assumed that this will always be done when necessary.

REASONS FOR THE LACK OF CONFIDENCE

As Reno and Friedland discuss in chapter 11, confidence in the long-term viability of the OASDI program decreased from the mid-1970s until the early 1980s. This was due in large part to the financing crisis that led to the 1977 amendments and then the subsequent failure thereof to solve the short-run financing crisis that arose because of the unusual economic conditions in the late 1970s and early 1980s, when prices rose rapidly and much more than did wages. These amendments, however, did much (although not all necessary) to solve the long-range problem by correcting the flaw in the benefit-computation methodology.

Confidence increased from the mid-1980s to 1990, likely due to the 1983 Amendments solving the short-range financing crisis. This was done primarily through a permanent delay of six months in the cost-of-living adjustments in the benefits, increasing the employer-employee tax rates in 1984 and 1988–89, increasing the self-employed tax rates in all future years, extending coverage to more categories of workers, and subjecting a portion of the benefits of high-income individuals to income tax (with the resulting taxes reverting to the OASDI Trust Funds). As a result, significant buildup of the trust-fund balances occurred from 1983 on. These amendments were also intended to solve the long-range financing problem by gradually increasing the "normal retirement age" (the age at which unreduced benefits are first available) from 65, beginning in 2003, to 67 in 2027 and after.

The drop in the confidence level after 1990 was probably due to the rather widespread attacks on the program from a growing number of organizations. Some of these organizations, for example, the Concord Coalition, founded by former Senators Rudman and Tsongas (Myers, 1994a), have quite properly been concerned about the size of the federal budget deficit and the ever-rising national debt. They believe that cutting back entitlement programs such as OASDI will help to solve this problem.

Other persons believe that monies have been diverted from the OASDI trust funds to finance the federal deficit, and, thus, the assets are no longer there to finance future benefits (e.g., Citizens Against Government Waste, founded by J. Peter Grace). Still others argue that the program will not be there when the baby boomers retire and thereafter; or, at best, young people will not get their money's worth out of the OASDI program when they retire (e.g., American Association of Boomers, Lead— or Leave, and Third Millennium) (Myers, 1992b, 1993b).

Then, adding to the public misunderstanding, many media writers and commentators embellish upon the utterances of those organizations. It is no wonder that the American public is so uncertain about the viability of the OASDI program! After all, it is much easier to attract the public's attention by proclaiming a disaster than by dispassionately stating that all is reasonably well.

This, however, is not to say that, even though over the short run—the next 10–15 years—the OASDI program is very unlikely to have any financial problem of a cash-flow nature, there are no possibilities of long-run problems (Myers, 1993c). The intermediate-cost estimate in the 1995 Trustees' Report (Board of Trustees, 1995) shows the following events (see Table 13.1):

a. The fund balance of the combined OASDI Trust Funds becomes exhausted in 2030; the combined employer-employee contribution rate then would have to be increased from the presently scheduled 12.4 percent by 4.1 percentage points if no changes were made in the benefit structure, with further increases thereafter, to 5.7 percentage points ultimately.

TABLE 13.1. Measures of Long-range Actuarial Status of Combined OASDI Trust Funds for Various Trustees' Reports, According to Intermediate-cost Estimate.

Year of Report	Exhaustion Year[a]	Maximum Balance[b]		Maximum Fund Ratio[c]		Actuarial Balance[d]	Ultimate "Excess" Cost Rate[e]
		Year	Amount	Year	Ratio		
1983[f]	2062	2045	$20.7t	2015	544%	+.02%	2.27%
1984	2060	2044	19.0	2015	544	−.06	2.27
1985	2050	2029	12.1	2015	495	−.41	2.33
1986	2051	2031	12.8	2015	526	−.44	2.58
1987	2051	2032	12.8	2015	545	−.62	2.75
1988	2048	2031	11.8	2015	531	−.58	3.68
1989	2046	2029	11.9	2015	546	−.70	4.10
1990	2043	2027	9.4	2015	475	−.91	4.16
1991	2041	2026	8.1	2015	418	−1.08	4.52
1992	2036	2023	5.6	2014	335	−1.46	5.11
1993	2036	2024	5.0	2015	298	−1.46	4.94
1994	2029	2018	3.0	2012	241	−2.13	5.67

Source: Various Board of Trustees Reports for OASDI and *Actuarial Notes,* U.S. Social Security Administration.

[a]Year when fund balance falls below zero.

[b]Year when maximum balance at end of year in dollars is reached, in trillions.

[c]Fund ratio is the fund balance at the beginning of the year expressed as a percentage of the outgo during the year.

[d]The excess of (1) the ratio of the present value of income from payroll taxes on benefits transferred to the OASDI trust funds, plus the fund balance at the start of the period, to the present value of taxable payroll for the 75-year valuation period over (2) the ratio of the present value of outgo for benefits and administrative expenses, plus the present value of the annual outgo at the end of the period (so as to have a fund balance then of this size) to the present value of taxable payroll for the 75 year valuation period.

[e]This is the excess of (1) the outgo for benefits and administrative expenses in the last year of the valuation period (as a percentage of taxable payroll) over (2) the scheduled payroll tax rate (12.4%), plus the income taxes on benefits transferred to the OASDI trust funds (also expressed as a percentage of taxable payroll).

[f]Includes the effects of the 1983 Amendments.

b. Annual outgo exceeds income from payroll taxes, income taxes on benefits, and interest earnings of the trust funds in 2019 and each year thereafter; the fund balance thus peaks at $3.3 trillion in 2019.

c. Annual outgo exceeds income from payroll taxes and income taxes on benefits (i.e., disregarding interest earnings of the trust funds) in 2013 and each year thereafter.

d. The lack of actuarial balance over the 75-year valuation period is 2.17 percent of taxable payroll.

The actuaries in the Social Security Administration have always recognized that their estimates for as long a period in the future as 75 years could not be expected to be precise, no matter how accurately computed. So, besides the intermediate-cost estimate (or "best" estimate, based on what are believed to be the most reasonable assumptions as to each of the cost elements involved), they have prepared both low-cost and high-cost estimates.

In doing so, the assumption for each cost element, such as mortality rates, retirement rates, disability rates, price and wage inflation, and real interest rates, is varied above and below (from a cost standpoint) the assumption in the intermediate-cost estimate. For example, although all three estimates assume that life expectancy will increase in the future, the high-cost estimate assumes larger rises than does the intermediate-cost estimate, while the low-cost estimate assumes smaller rises. Such variation is selected to be reasonable, not just the largest amount that could occur.

The picture is, of course, much less favorable under the high-cost assumptions; the year of exhaustion of the fund balance is 2016, and the ultimate combined employer-employee contribution rate would have to be 14.7 percentage points higher than now scheduled. Conversely, under the low-cost assumptions, the picture is very bright; the fund balance builds up continuously over the 75-year valuation period, and no increase in the contribution rate is ever needed (in fact, the ultimate combined employer-employee rate could be 0.1 percentage point lower).

Many people are concerned about the much higher cost of the OASDI program—not merely in dollar terms but, more importantly, relative to taxable payroll—when the baby-boom cohort moves into the retirement ages (roughly in 2010–45). This is a valid concern, and one that has been recognized for years in the trustees reports, but the resulting situation does not constitute an insuperable financing problem.

According to the intermediate-cost estimate of the 1995 Trustees Report (Board of Trustees, 1995), the number of beneficiaries (including auxiliary and survivor beneficiaries) per 100 covered workers will increase from 31 at present to 51 in 2035–45, a 65-percent relative rise. The corresponding ratio for the low-cost estimate is 42 (or 35 percent higher), while for the high-cost estimate it is 61 (or 97 percent higher). It is important to note that the ratio does not decline after the baby-boom cohort passes from the scene, but rather is level or slightly increasing.

Quite obviously, the foregoing trends clearly indicate that a long-run financing problem for the OASDI program lies ahead, as was also shown by the four "events" described earlier. The next section will discuss how the problem can reasonably be solved.

Those who express doubts as to the long-range viability of the OASDI program sometimes point out that, over the years since the 1983 amendments were enacted, its long-range actuarial status has been reported to be worsening. Such views are based on data such as those displayed in Table 13.1, which shows several measures of the long-range actuarial status of the combined OASDI Trust Funds for various trustees' reports according to the intermediate-cost estimate.

One widely used measure is the year when, according to the intermediate-cost estimate, the fund balance is estimated to become exhausted. This year has been advanced from 2062 in the 1983 report to 2030 in the 1995 report. Similarly, the estimated maximum fund balance was $21 trillion in the 1983 report and is only $3 trillion in the 1995 report. Further, the long-run actuarial balance is shown as slightly positive in the 1983 report, but it is a deficiency of 2.2 percent of taxable payroll in the 1995 report. It is important to note that 14 percent of this deficiency is due to the DI portion of the program, which also represents 14 percent of the total cost of the program.

Some critics have asserted, possibly on the basis of the foregoing progressively worsening long-range, estimated experience in the estimates of recent years, that the actuarial estimates are always too optimistic. This is not necessarily immutably so. Over the years, the actuaries in the Social Security Administration have always tried to make the best and most reasonable assumptions and to use proper methodology in evaluating both the existing program and any proposed changes thereto. This has recently been given public recognition by Congress (U.S. Congress, House of Representatives, 1994).

On the other hand, the actuarial estimates could possibly be too pessimistic as to future costs. Their goal is to present the "best" estimate in the aggregate. It is likely that the actual experience may be of a higher cost nature as to some elements, and the reverse for others. So, in balance, it seems equally likely that the estimates will be too pessimistic as that they will be too optimistic. At least, that is the theory. Of course, persons who are philosophically opposed to the OASDI program will naturally tend to emphasize the unfavorable possibilities shown by the high-cost estimate.

This is not to say that the actuarial projections have always been completely accurate in portraying what the future experience will be. Let us consider two instances where the actuarial estimates turned out well, compared with the actual experience. First, the original (1935) estimate of the cost in 1980 of the Social Security retirement and lump-sum survivor benefits was 9.35 percent of taxable payroll. The actual 1980 cost for the OASI program was 9.36 percent, or virtually the same. Of course, there is some degree of noncomparability between these two figures, because benefit and coverage provisions were changed after 1935, such as the substitution of monthly survivor benefits for lump-sum ones.

Second, consider the estimates of the balance of the OASDI Trust Funds at the end of 1987 and at the end of 1993 in the various trustees' reports made after 1983 (when the very significant amendments rescuing the program from a serious financing crisis were enacted), as against the actual experience in those two years. As Table 13.2 shows, for the experience in 1983–87, the low-cost (or optimistic) estimates closely portrayed what actually occurred, while the high-cost (or pessimistic) estimate showed far too low fund balances. Thus, the 1983 low-cost estimate of the fund balance at the end of 1987 was almost exactly what transpired, whereas the corresponding high-cost estimate was only 40 percent of the actual figure.

Similarly, as to the fund balance at the end of 1993, the intermediate-cost estimate made in most years after 1983 was very close to the actual experience: generally, 5 to 10 percent higher. If it had not been for the unfavorable disability experience in 1991–1993, the comparison would have been even closer. The 1983 estimate of the fund balance at the end of 1993 was 21 percent *lower* than the actual-experience figure.

POSSIBLE SOLUTIONS TO THE LONG-RUN FINANCING PROBLEM

The long-run financing problem of the OASDI program can be solved in many different ways. The existence of this problem, which is by no means an overwhelming one, does not necessitate the abandonment or phasing out of the program. It is probably best to solve the problem about equally by reductions in benefit costs and increases in financing.

One solution based solely on increased financing would, as indicated previously, involve an increase in the combined employer-employee contribution rate of 4.1 percentage points beginning in 2029, with further gradual increases to 5.7 percent-

TABLE 13.2. Comparison of Actual Balance of OASDI Trust Funds As of End of Year 1987 and 1993 with Estimates from Various Trustees' Reports. (in billions)

Year of Report	Fund Balance at End of Period			Actual Balance as % of Estimate		
	Low-Cost	Intermediate	High-Cost	Low-Cost	Intermediate	High-Cost
Period Ending December 31, 1987						
1983[a]	$67.4	$39.7	$27.2	98%	58%	40%
1984	75.9	51.7	26.1	110	75	38
1985	62.0	47.1	27.5	90	68	40
1986	62.7	53.4	50.6	91	78	74
1987	69.9	67.0	61.5	102	97	89
1988[b]	68.8	68.8	68.8	100	100	100
Period Ending December, 1993						
1983[a]	$562.6	$300.1	$234.9	149%	79%	62%
1984	556.2	389.1	187.5	147	103	50
1985	525.5	393.3	143.1	139	104	38
1986	514.2	396.7	230.9	136	105	61
1987	526.8	408.4	212.2	139	108	56
1988	504.5	438.2	316.1	133	116	84
1989	496.6	420.0	310.3	131	111	82
1990	503.4	463.8	388.4	133	123	103
1991	430.4	413.8	378.3	114	109	100
1992	396.0	383.6	375.4	105	101	99
1993	382.3	378.3	376.1	101	100	99
1994[b]	378.3	378.3	378.3	100	100	100

Source: Various Board of Trustees Reports for OASDI and *Actuarial Notes*, U.S. Social Security Administration.
[a] Includes the effects of the 1983 amendments.
[b] Actual experience.

213

age points ultimately (based on the intermediate-cost estimate). It can be argued that this is economically sustainable, because the added cost to both employers and employees can readily be "paid for" from productivity and real-wage increases over the next three decades (which should average 1 percent per year, or even more).

Various types of benefit reductions over the long run are possible, and, in fact, some are being proposed for the short run. However, cost reductions for the short run are not necessary insofar as the OASDI program is concerned, but they are—illogically, and even erroneously—being proposed for purposes of reducing the general-budget deficits (Myers, 1994c). (Such budget-deficit reduction does not really occur, because decreased outgo from the OASDI Trust Funds merely means that the trust funds own more of the national debt, and the general public owns correspondingly less, with the national debt remaining at the same level.)

Short-run benefit reductions have been proposed in two areas: reducing the cost-of-living adustments (COLA's) below the consumer price index rise and means-testing benefits. Neither of these is desirable or necessary. COLA increases are not benefit liberalizations; but rather, they merely maintain the purchasing power of the benefits (which is particularly important for the oldest retirees, for whom needs are usually more, but the cumulative reduction effect is the greatest). As Kingson and Schulz (chapter 3) discuss, means-testing the benefits is most undesirable for many reasons, including (1) the stigmatization of the beneficiaries thus resulting will weaken public support for the program; (2) many people will reduce their saving efforts (of which the nation really needs more), because savings will only result in less OASDI benefits; and (3) significant fraud and abuse will occur, as beneficiaries conceal or transfer their assets and income, so as to avoid loss of OASDI benefits.

Instead, if benefit-cost reductions are to be made, they should be phased in gradually on a deferred basis. Many possibilities are discussed in the various chapters of this book. One of the most reasonable ways to do this is through raising the "normal retirement age" more than is currently scheduled, perhaps eventually to 70 or 72, and doing so slightly more rapidly than present law does. At the same time, disability benefits would be available for those unable to work beyond age 65 and before the new normal retirement age. This benefit-cost reduction can be viewed as not being a de-liberalization; but rather, merely keeping the normal retirement age up-to-date with increasing life expectancy (just as COLA's are not "real" benefit liberalizations).

Another such benefit-cost reduction is to lower gradually (and slightly) the general benefit level, through reducing the factors in the basic benefit formula. This is not as desirable as the foregoing change, because disability and survivor benefits would be reduced.

In balance, it is my view that the best approach is to provide about half of the necessary long-run financing through a gradual increase in the normal retirement age over what is now scheduled, with the remainder coming from higher contribution rates at some time in the long-run future.

WHY THE CONFIDENCE LEVEL SHOULD BE HIGHER

Probably, the telling argument as to why people should have confidence in the long-run viability of the OASDI program is its generally excellent financial condition at present. Its total invested assets at the end of 1994 were about $436 billion, or about 128 percent of the anticipated outgo in 1995. This compares with only $12 billion at the end of 1983 (after deducting the loan to the OASI Trust Fund from the Hospital Insurance Trust Fund).

Over the long run, it seems very likely that a financial problem may arise some two or three decades hence. However, one of the great strengths of the program is its flexibility, namely, that both benefit and financing provisions can be altered to meet changing social, economic, and demographic conditions. For example, in the 1940s, the contribution rate was frozen (i.e., not allowed to increase as scheduled), because it was believed that excessive fund balances were developing. Then, in the 1950s and 1960s (when automatic-adjustment provisions were not legally prescribed), benefit amounts and the maximum taxable earnings base were increased from time to time as gradual inflation occurred, and the actuarial estimates showed long-run surpluses developing. Further, there is the well-known example of the 1983 act, under which a variety of relatively "painless" minor changes were made, reducing benefits and increasing financing.

Note that this possibility of changes taking place is not confined to OASDI; the net premium rates for participating life insurance policies can vary depending upon experience, and the same is true for the benefit amounts under defined-contribution pension plans, which use "excess" interest to finance additional payments.

Further, the Social Security program has broad support, even though it is recognized that changes will very likely have to be made over the long run (see chapter 11 for more details). Clear and important evidence of this can be found in the words of President Reagan, certainly a reasonable conservative in this area, when he signed into law the 1983 Amendments, as follows (Reagan, 1984):

This bill demonstrates for all time our nation's ironclad commitment to Social Security. It assures the elderly that America will always keep the promises made in troubled times a half a century ago. It assures those who are still working that they, too, have a pact with the future. From this day forward, they have our pledge that they will get their fair share of benefits when they retire.

And this bill assures us of one more thing that is equally important. It's a clear and dramatic demonstration that our system can still work when men and women of good will join together to make it work."

So, today we see an issue that once divided and frightened so many people now uniting us. Our elderly need no longer fear that the checks they depend on will be stopped or reduced.

These amendments protect them. Americans of middle age need no longer worry whether their career-long investment will pay off. These amendments guarantee it. And younger people can feel confident that social security will still be around when they need it to cushion their retirement.

These amendments reaffirm the commitment of our government to the performance and stability of Social Security. It was nearly 50 years ago when, under the leadership of Franklin Delano Roosevelt, the American people reached a great turning point, setting up the Social Security System."

Today we reaffirm Franklin Roosevelt's commitment that Social Security must always provide a secure and stable base so that older Americans may live in dignity.

CONCLUSION

For all of the reasons given previously, I am convinced that the Social Security program "will be there" to provide a basic floor of protection for retirement, disability, and death of the breadwinner for all time to come. This will be true not only for today's beneficiaries, not only for today's workers, but also for youngsters who have not yet entered the labor force and even those yet unborn. The details of the program, such as retirement-age requirements, benefit amounts, and financing provisions, may be quite different from those now present. The basic characteristics of the program, however, will be unchanged.

Hopefully, public confidence in the long-range fiscal viability of the Social Security program will increase in the near future—as it rightfully should! However, if this is to occur, it will be essential for the public to understand the issues better, especially as to the self-supporting financing nature of the program and its real relationship to the general budget. Unfortunately, much misleading and incorrect information on these issues is being circulated in the public media nowadays.

To put it into a single phrase—Social Security will outlive us all!

PART III

Additional Views on the Issues

CHAPTER 14

Adequacy and Equity Issues: Another View

MICHAEL D. HURD

Many of the prior chapters are concerned partly or substantially with the redistributive aspects of Social Security. One can identify two broad types of redistribution. The first is related to the insurance aspects of Social Security. Because of the progressivity of the benefit schedule, Social Security redistributes from the well-to-do to the less well-to-do. This is an outcome of insurance: the risk of having low lifetime earnings is partly reduced by having relatively larger Social Security benefits in retirement. Because Social Security is an annuity, it insures against mortality risk, the possibility of outliving one's assets. This is redistribution from the short-lived to the long-lived. Because Social Security is indexed it insures against inflation risk, which means that one generation insures another generation.

A second type of redistribution is intended, or *ex ante,* redistribution, that is, redistribution from one group to another but not necessarily on the basis of individual need. The main example is the windfall gains to the start-up generation: both the poor and the wealthy paid in much less than they have received. In my view, these windfall gains are partly responsible for some of the controversies surrounding Social Security.

To fix ideas, consider a simple lifetime allocation of resources. Suppose someone works for 40 years and retires for 20 years. To finance a replacement rate of 40 percent, which is about what Social Security aims for on average, requires a saving rate of 15 to 20 percent of earnings under the assumption that the real interest rate equals the growth rate of earnings. Let us take the 15 percent rate as the benchmark against which to judge Social Security contributions. Currently the contribution rate for retirement and disability is 6.2 percent of earnings (on both employee and employer) up to a maximum of \$62,700 (1996), which is greater than the earnings of the great majority of workers. Thus, in steady state, where each worker pays his own retirement benefit, the contribution rates are a little too low. Even though population growth can sustain the shortfall, I think this 15 percent figure provides a good point of reference.

In the start-up generations, the contributions were much lower: an 85-year-old faced contribution rates during work life that ranged from 2 to 8.75 percent, up to a maximum earnings level that often was about the mean level of earnings. Thus, as a cohort, today's 85-year-olds probably paid in 2 to 3 percent of earnings. This conclusion is qualitatively verified in some of the studies reported by Chen and Goss (chapter 5).[1] Those very high rates of return were feasible because of the age distribution of the population; fairly low tax rates over the following generations could support large benefits because of the high ratio of workers to beneficiaries. Furthermore, the increase in benefits during the 1970s produced substantial social good: the poverty rate among the elderly, which had been about 35 percent in the 1950s, fell to about 12 percent today. Since most workers had living elderly parents, they supported increases both because the increases benefitted their own parents and because it relieved them of the burden of support.

However, the windfalls also went to the well-to-do: ordinary workers are taxed to provide transfers to retired elderly who neither need the benefit nor earned the benefit.[2] Furthermore, the well-to-do received the largest windfall gains in absolute terms, although not in relative terms (Hurd and Shoven, 1985). To see the political implications, consider four generations: the retired, the pre-retired (with ages in the late 40s to early 60s), the baby-boom group, and the young in the post-baby-boom cohorts. As a group the retired have windfall gains. The replacement rates for the pre-retired can be sustained because of the size of the baby-boom generation, who reasonably think that a fair situation is to pay in and get back about what the retired generation paid in and got back. This, however, is not feasible because of demographic changes: the post-baby-boom generation is not large enough to support such windfall gains. A reasonable conclusion by the baby-boom generation is that the retired generation got benefits that were too large. This conclusion is strengthened by the obvious and observable fact that the well-to-do retired got substantial windfall gains. Exacerbating the situation is the lack of real-wage growth since the mid-1970s and the high housing prices faced by the baby-boom generation.

A solution at one time might have been to make Social Security means-tested. This is probably not a good idea now because the well-to-do in the pre-retirement generation will not get windfall gains. In fact, because of the progressivity of the benefit schedule, the well-to-do will increasingly be the least favored. That is, in the effort to recover some of the windfall gains of the well-to-do retired cohort, the well-to-do in the pre-retired cohort, which will not receive windfall gains, would be harmed.

A middle ground is to increase the taxation of benefits. Most of the benefits have not been taxed, and under our tax law as it applies to other investments, most benefits should be. Thus, I come to roughly the same conclusion as Kingson and Schulz (chapter 3). However, my reasons are somewhat different from theirs. It seems to me that political support for Social Security has been weakened exactly because of advantageous treatment of the well-to-do in the start-up generation; reducing their benefits through taxation could lead to greater support among the working population, which correctly sees that it is paying for the unearned benefits of the well-to-do elderly.

One reason Kingson and Schulz give for opposing means-testing Social Security is their concern that it will reduce saving. This is, however, an empirical matter. To see this, consider, for example, someone with post-retirement income of $10,000 from Social Security and $80,000 from other sources, and suppose further that the optimal consumption plan for this person is to consume the same after retirement as before retirement: $90,000 both before and after. Now imagine that, through means-testing, all of this person's Social Security income is denied. An optimal consumption plan would require reducing consumption before retirement, thereby increasing saving, until post-retirement and pre-retirement consumption would again be the same. Optimal consumption could be somewhat, but not much above, $80,000 because the income from the increase in savings could finance a slightly higher level of post-retirement consumption than before.

The conclusion in this example is that saving for retirement would be increased by means-testing Social Security. In other examples, however, it could be reduced. The fact is that the aggregate result on saving depends on consumer preferences and their positions on their budget constraints. Our empirical knowledge is not adequate to answer this question.

Even if the baby-boom cohort accepts that the relationship between contributions and benefits (as specified in current law) is fair, there is considerable worry among experts about whether that relationship should be maintained and about the sustainability of that relationship. In my view, it is not enough simply to say, as do Marmor, Cook, and Scher (Chapter 12), that the experts are wrong or that we should not be concerned about intergenerational equity.

Consider the trend in poverty rates as shown in Table 14.1. The primary cause of the fall in the poverty rate of the elderly was the increase in Social Security benefits. The causes of the increase in the poverty rate of children are many, and I do not want to imply a causal link. Nonetheless the economic situation of many children has degenerated, and it is certainly reasonable to consider redistributions toward children. Whether such a redistribution should come at the expense of the elderly, the well-to-do elderly, or the working population is, of course, a separate matter.

Marmor, Cook, and Scher argue that the current situation is sustainable because the dependency ratio is actually falling. This argument is not relevant for at least two reasons. First, the choice of having children is almost completely a choice by the parents about how to allocate their own resources. Each couple earns its income and decides how to consume it, and there is little welfare loss through the tax and transfer system from their individual choices. Second, society does spend resources on children, which, just as financing programs for the elderly, requires taxation. However, the amounts spent per person are greatly different. In 1990 public spending per elderly person through OASDI, Medicare, and Medicaid (65+ only) was

TABLE 14.1. Trend in Poverty Rates.

	1970	1991
Elderly	24.6	12.4
Children	14.9	21.1

Source: Data from U.S. Department of Commerce, 1993.
Note: The poverty rate of children is the poverty rate of the household in which they live.

about 3.1 times greater than public spending per child (largely through public education). This difference in expenditures per person will increase with the growing cost of Medicare. The conclusion is that the dependency rate should be calculated over the retired-to-working population, and in that case it will increase substantially.

Medicare is not part of the Social Security retirement income system, but the taxes paid in its support reduce the availability of tax revenues to support retirement income. In my view the two should be considered together because workers realize that, when they retire, excessively high Medicare costs are likely to lead to reductions in Social Security benefits.

Table 14.2 shows that while the tax increases necessary to fund the retirement system (OASDI) are substantial, they are probably politically and economically feasible; by 2040 Social Security taxes would have to be increased by about 37 percent. However, the fraction spent on Medicare (HI and SMI) is predicted to more than triple, causing the total tax burden to more than double. I would conclude that the predicted growth in health care spending casts serious doubt about the sustainability of current benefits (both retirement income and Medicare).

Because of the progressivity of the benefit schedule, there has been considerably less controversy about intragenerational equity than about intergenerational equity. One aspect that has attracted attention is the relationship between benefits of a single person, compared with a couple. This is, of course, the topic of chapter 6 by Holden.

I will take as a given that Social Security should be earnings-based for the reasons discussed in Kingson and Schulz (it should not be a welfare program), and that it should be redistributive. That is, within the constraints imposed by the objective of redistribution, benefits should be directly related to earnings. This is the goal of equity: workers should get back what they put in.

For this discussion I will identify three broad demographic groups: single earners, one-earner couples, and two-earner couples. Consider first a two-earner couple in which both spouses earn exactly the same amount. In the Social Security system each is treated the same as a single worker who has the same earnings, thus achieving equity; identical earnings produce identical cash benefits. From the point of view of redistribution, this is not appropriate. A couple does not need twice what a single person needs. However, undoing this would require a marriage tax; two single earners that marry would have benefits reduced. I know of no support for such a marriage tax.

Now consider a two-earner couple in which the earnings of each spouse are different. In the extreme this would be a one-earner couple, which, to simplify the exposition, I will take to be the case. If each spouse receives benefits on his or her

TABLE 14.2. Social Security Funds as a Percentage of Gross Domestic Product.

	OASDI	HI & SMI	Total
1994	4.83	2.53	7.36
2020	5.95	6.49	12.44
2040	6.66	8.63	15.29

Source: Board of Trustees (1994).

earnings record, equity is achieved with respect to single earners or to two-earner couples with identical earnings. However, this creates two problems. First, because of progressivity of the benefit schedule, income will drop at retirement, compared to the situation in which each spouse earns exactly half the earnings of the single earner. This implies that there should be some redistribution toward the single-earner couple. Second, if the single-earner dies, the survivor could be poor. Thus, from the point of view of redistribution, basing benefits solely on the earnings of each spouse is unsatisfactory. This is why the system provides spouse and survivor benefits. It should be clear, however, that from the point of view of single workers, spouse and survivor benefits are a departure from equity, and holding constant total benefits, they require a reduction in the benefits of single workers (and of identically earning couples). This departure from equity is overcome by the societal desire to provide adequate support for all.

Now suppose the nonearning spouse has some small earnings. Under Social Security law family benefits do not increase because the spouse benefit is larger than the worker benefit. From the point of view of equity this is appropriate because the spouse benefit was not equitable in the first place; it was given to achieve redistribution. From the point of view of redistribution, not increasing the family benefit is appropriate. There has been no apparent change in need. Therefore, equity is improved, and redistribution is unchanged. Overall this is an improvement.

This is not the conclusion of Holden (chapter 6). The difference comes from a difference in the thought experiment. In her examples, the earnings of both spouses are changed, keeping the total constant. This leads to lower benefits for a two-earner couple than for a single earner couple, which is said to be unfair. According to my argument, however, the apparent unfairness comes from the societal desire to redistribute from singles to couples. It is the spouse and survivor benefits that are departures from equity. That is, the base situation is the single person or identically earning couple. Equity is achieved across the two types of households, and redistribution is achieved through the progressivity of the benefit schedule. If among couples the benefit derived from the earnings of a single earner is greater than the combined benefits of the couple, the conclusion should be that there has been excessive redistribution toward the single earner couple, not that the identically earning couple gets benefits that are too low.

A separate issue is the high poverty rate of elderly widows. Partly this results from widows being the long-lived survivors of couples. A fixed amount of lifetime income can only finance a certain amount of lifetime consumption, so, unless income is completely annuitized, it is almost inevitable that the oldest will be the least well off (see Moon, chapter 4). Partly the high poverty rates are the result of cohort differences; the oldest come from less well-to-do cohorts. One solution is to reallocate some of the Social Security spouse benefit to the survivor benefit. This could reduce the poverty rate of widows rather substantially with a rather small increase in the poverty rate of couples (Hurd and Wise, 1991). However, this is a result of the arbitrary relationship between the poverty line of couples and of singles. According to the relative poverty line, couples only need 26 percent more income than singles. Most estimates based on observed consumption patterns indicate that a figure closer to 40 percent is more accurate. If this is the case, there would be less to be gained from a reallocation of the spouse and survivor benefits.

In conclusion, I would say that several of the chapters understate the problem associated with an aging population because they do not mention Medicare. Indeed, it is true that several European countries have population profiles similar to what the profile will be like in the United States in 2020. These countries, however, are now alarmed about their own Social Security systems and are trying to find ways to scale back the systems.

ENDNOTES

1. I believe both employer and employee contributions should be included in rate-of-return calculations, and that life tables should be used either implicitly or explicitly. For example, it is not meaningful to discuss the length of retirement for payback of Social Security contributions without reference to a life table to find what is the likely length of life following retirement.

2. Despite the occasional letter to the editor claiming that the retired earned their benefits, this is not true in any meaningful economic sense.

CHAPTER 15

Financing and Work Issues: Another View

DWIGHT K. BARTLETT

Social Security policy discussions often revolve around issues concerning its financing and economic effects. Several chapters provide interesting insights into such issues as they relate to the future of Social Security. In commenting on these chapters, I hope to provide another view for readers. Virginia Reno and Robert Friedland (chapter 11) document very well both the continuing support for the Social Security program and the erosion of the level of confidence in its future, particularly in the late 1970s and early 1980s. They then speculate about the reasons for the erosion in confidence, contrasting it with the relatively high confidence level individuals seem to have in private pension plans, employer-sponsored plans, and personal savings.

Unwittingly, the actuaries who prepare the financial projections of the Social Security system, which are included in the annual trustees' reports, play into the hands of the media. The media treat the actuarial projections as if they were absolute statements of fact rather than somewhat tenuous projections. The dangers of relying on these projections to draw fixed conclusions about the financial condition of the system were discussed at considerable length in a landmark article by Ray M. Peterson in which he said, for example,

> The actuaries of the Social Security Administration . . . have done skillful professional work in the public interest by furnishing reliable benchmarks to test the actuarial equivalence of contributions and benefits under the Social Security Act. It is no criticism of their activities to suggest that all actuaries have a responsibility to make clear to the public the limitations of the significance of actuarial calculations. . . . The work of the actuary must not become a soothing agent that unduly quiets a legitimate concern as to the truly successful operation of programs established by one generation which will have powerful effects upon future generations. (R. Peterson, 1959, p. 812.)

In their projections in the trustees' report, the actuaries do, of course, attempt to warn readers about the dangers of excessive reliance on the projections by actually making three sets of projections based on optimistic, intermediate, and pessimistic demographic and economic assumptions. The projections based on the intermediate assumptions are those commonly referred to by the media and others in characterizing the current financial condition in both the short term and the long term. Yet, moderate changes in the assumptions do have an enormous effect on the projections. For example, on the pessimistic assumptions, the projections in the "1995 Annual Report of the Board of Trustees" (Board of Trustees, 1995) indicate that the combined Old-Age Insurance Survivors Insurance, and Disability Insurance trust funds will be exhausted in the year 2017; whereas under the intermediate assumptions, exhaustion will take until 2030. Under the optimistic assumptions, exhaustion would never occur. Nor are these assumptions set in a way that the projected trust fund ratios bracket the full range of possible outcomes. Officials who are responsible for designing and administering the system must also share in the blame for excessive reliance on the actuarial projections.

As many chapters discuss, because of the faulty method of indexing the benefits calculation that was introduced during the Nixon administration, which resulted in overly generous benefits in the mid-1970s, the trust funds were in serious danger of being depleted within a few years. That widely reported crisis undoubtedly was the most significant reason for the approximately 20 percent decline in public confidence in Social Security that occurred in the late 1970s.

These technical flaws in indexing benefits were corrected by legislation that was adopted in 1977. Actuarial projections made at that time indicated that the trust funds would not be exhausted until well into the twenty-first century. Perhaps understandably, as a result of avoiding the imminent crisis, officials made unwarranted statements. The Acting Commissioner of Social Security at the time, said, for example, in the March 1978 issue of the *Social Security Bulletin* that "With the signing of the social security amendments of 1977 into law, the Congress and the President have *assured* [emphasis added] the financial soundness of the social security program for the next fifty (50) years" (Snee and Ross, 1978, p. 4). This excessively optimistic view was reiterated by his successor in 1979.

Unfortunately, the economy performed poorly in the late 1970s and early 1980s, resulting in high inflation outstripping wage growth, and in high unemployment. The high inflation, reaching double-digit levels, rapidly increased benefits because they were indexed to compensate for inflation, while slower wage growth and high unemployment depressed tax revenues, relatively speaking. The bad economic experience fell outside the range of even the pessimistic actuarial assumptions made at the time the 1977 amendments were developed. Thus, within several years, in spite of the assurances provided by various SSA commissioners that the 1977 amendments had fixed the program for at least 50 years, there was once again the likelihood of exhaustion of the trust funds in the near term. Once again, it became necessary, on short notice, to amend the program's benefits and revenues in order to avoid exhaustion in the short run as well as to restore the long-term actuarial balance of revenues and benefits. The major elements in the long-range fix were to phase in a higher normal retirement age of 67, in lieu of 65, over the first three decades of the twenty-first century and to introduce the taxation of benefits, as well as coverage extensions and delay of cost-of-living-adjustment (COLA) benefit adjustments.

Again, the program was advertised as being fixed forever, that is, it was not expected that the trust funds would be exhausted at any time during the following 75-year period. Nevertheless, as of this date, we once again find ourselves in the position that, under the intermediate assumptions, exhaustion would occur in the year 2030. The problem is not exactly around the corner, but it is close enough to again alarm baby boomers who reasonably expect to be living at that time.

Clearly more effort needs to be made to educate both policymakers and the general public concerning the lack of certainty of the actuarial projections. Even trust fund projections over a five year or shorter period can prove to be dramatically off the mark as a result of deviations of actual experience from projection assumptions, as was analyzed in a paper by Joseph Applebaum and Dwight Bartlett (Applebaum and Bartlett, 1982).

Gramlich (chapter 9) concludes that the Social Security program does not produce major economic distortions in the United States at present and may in fact actually add modestly to net national savings and investment. He discusses, somewhat optimistically, possible future changes in the program itself or in other policy areas that would keep looming program deficits from damaging the economy. I generally concur with his analysis.

In my view, the public needs to understand better that the supportability of the program, in the macroeconomic sense, is not necessarily determined by the level of payroll taxes required (Bartlett, 1990). The payroll tax mechanism for financing the program was adopted at the program's beginning as a political device for reinforcing taxpayers' commitment by creating the illusion of the taxpayer earning his benefit right by paying a tax that effectively constituted a premium. The tax has, of course, important economic effects as to how the burden of the program is distributed throughout the economy. But the real burden of the program results from the benefits being paid, not the taxes being collected. For this reason, much more attention should be paid to the cost of the program as a percentage of gross domestic product (GDP). For some years these estimates have been included in an appendix to the trustee's report, (appendix C of the 1995 report). This projection indicates that the cost of the OASDI program is 4.78 percent of GDP for 1995. It will rise under intermediate assumptions to 6.75 percent by the year 2030, when most of the baby-boom generation will have retired, and will remain at approximately that level indefinitely into the future.

This compares with the historical costs of OASDI as shown in Table 15.1. If that projected cost is viewed as a sustainable burden, then there are a variety of ways of providing appropriate income to cover that cost. If that is viewed as an unsustainable burden, then there are a variety of ways of reducing benefits. But a discussion framed in those terms and placed in the context of other retirement income sources, such as private pensions and personal savings, is much more likely to be a rational and less emotional one than a discussion that focuses on artificial constructs such as projected fund exhaustion date and payroll tax levels required to support the program while avoiding exhaustion.

Robert J. Myers (chapter 13) takes a position I support. He states that there is no reason to be excessively pessimistic, given that relatively modest adjustments to the program from time to time can be made that will keep revenues and benefit expenses in balance over the years. I would only add a caveat to the effect that sig-

**TABLE 15.1. OASDI
Expenditures as a Percentage
of Gross Domestic Product in
Selected Calendar Years.**

Year	OASDI %
1940	0.06
1945	0.14
1950	0.36
1955	1.26
1960	2.30
1965	2.73
1970	3.28
1975	4.36
1980	4.56
1985	4.72
1990	4.56
1995	4.78

Source: Data from Office of the Actuary,
U.S. Social Security Administration.

nificant benefit changes should be made with a substantial period of advance notice. Potential beneficiaries react less negatively to the benefit reductions if they
have time to adjust their own personal financial planning to the change. Such a
change is exemplified by the relatively modest outcry when the 1983 amendments
instituted the change in normal retirement age after the turn of the century.

Myers notes in his Table 13.1 the significant change in "the exhaustion year" of
the OASDI Combined Trust Funds from the year 2062 in the 1983 report to 2029
in the 1994 report. This change in the exhaustion date parallels the change in the
75-year actuarial balance of the program measured as a percentage of taxable payrolls from +0.02 percent in 1983 to −2.17 percent in 1995. Interestingly enough,
he does not comment on the reasons for the change but simply offers it as evidence
that the financial condition of the program will vary from time to time and that
should not come as a shock to observers.

Nevertheless, it is instructive to look at the reasons for the change as determined
by the Social Security Administration's Office of the Actuary (see Table 15.2). In
support of the notion that one should not overreact to modest changes in the actuarial balance, it is noteworthy that nearly one-half of the change since 1983 is accounted for, not by changes in amendments to the system or by changes in economic and demographic assumptions justified by emerging experience, but rather
by changes in methodology used by the actuaries. I say this not to be critical of the
actuaries but to point out that over time there are changing opinions as to how the
financial condition of the program should be appraised.

I was somewhat surprised that Myers did not take the opportunity to reiterate his
previously stated opposition to the projected substantial buildup in the trust funds
until 2015, a view with which I agree. Economists argue that, everything else being equal, the buildup of the trust funds represents the potential for additional national savings, reduced consumption, and increased capital formation (see Gramlich,

chapter 9, and Bosworth, chapter 10). This additional capital would, the argument goes, make more sustainable the additional benefit costs when the baby-boom generation retires. The everything-else-being-equal scenario, I believe, is highly improbable. The national government will be far less likely to face up to dealing with the annual deficits from the balance of its programs if it can use the current Social Security surpluses to mask a significant part of those deficits. The 1995 unwillingness of the Republican leadership in the Senate to commit itself to the achievement of a balanced budget, *excluding Social Security operations*, is instructive. Even if one accepts the argument that the trust fund buildup leads to additional capital formation, it is inescapable that sometime prior to the exhaustion of the trust funds, benefit outflows will begin to exceed tax income, most likely sometime during the second decade of the twenty-first century. The trust funds consist of nothing other than IOU's from the government. The government will have to provide additional funds to pay off the IOU's, either by reducing the deficits from the balance of its operations or permitting its total deficit to enlarge. Again we see that the operation of the Social Security programs is not properly measured by trust fund operations but, rather, by the aggregate benefit levels in relation to the total economy.

In chapter 8 on the labor market effects of social security, Quadagno and Quinn review the rapid decline in labor force participation rates among older men in the United States since the mid-1960s. No one can seriously question that the maturing of the Social Security and private pension systems in this country has been the principal influence in that decline. The authors then go on to argue that the Social Security program, as presently constructed with its earnings tests, will operate to discourage persons from remaining in the work force when their participation will be needed to enlarge the national product in the face of the rapid growth of retirees. It should be noted that this view of the labor market effects of these tests is not universally held. First of all, the deferred-retirement credit for those who lose benefits because of the earnings test will be raised to a full actuarial equivalent of 8 percent

TABLE 15.2. Change in the Actuarial Balance of the OASDI Program, from the 1983 to the 1995 Trustees' Reort, Based on Intermediate Assumptions.

	Percentage of Taxable Payroll
Balance in 1983 report	+0.02
Balance in 1995 report	−2.17
Change in balance	−2.19
Reasons for change:	
Legislation	+0.10
Valuation period	−.55
Economic assumptions	−.79
Demographic assumptions	+.83
Disability assumptions	−.70
Methods	−1.07
Inclusion of beginning trust fund balance (1988 TR)[a]	+.06
Effect of present-value calculation (1988 TR)[a]	+.24
Cost of ending trust fund ratio of 100% (1991 TR)[a]	−.16
All other	−.15

Source: Data from Office of the Actuary, U.S. Social Security Administration.
[a]Change first included in that year's Trustees' Report.

per year of deferment shortly after the turn of the century. Thus, the earnings test leads, not to a loss of benefits, but merely to a deferral of benefits. The deferred-retirement credit may actually induce some of the older workers to stay in the labor market, since the 8 percent credit is based on average mortality expectations and is thus more than the full actuarial equivalent for healthier persons. Secondly, while the earnings test may discourage, at the margin, some persons from earning more than the maximum amount permitted without loss of benefits ($11,280 in 1995 for a person 65–69 years), it may have the opposite effect on those whose earnings exceed that cutoff point. Those persons will have to have greater earnings to maintain their total income in order to offset the loss of benefits. It should be noted that the Office of the Actuary, SSA, currently prepares its cost estimates for increases in permitted earnings without loss of benefits, on the assumption there will be little net effect one way or the other in aggregate earnings.

The authors also discuss the work disincentives for older persons that are incorporated in the typical private pension plan, as well as ad hoc early-out programs that employers sometimes offer as part of their downsizing efforts. Clearly, one anomaly that ought to be addressed legislatively is the Employee Retirement Income Security Act's requirement that qualified pension plans have a normal retirement age not greater than 65. If 67 is the correct normal retirement age for the Social Security program in the twenty-first century, why should it not be at least a permitted normal retirement for an employer-sponsored pension plan?

Robert L. Brown, a Canadian actuary, has recently made an ingenious proposal (R. Brown, 1995) for indexing retirement ages that would be applicable to the Social Security programs of Western nations. His concept involves the notion of wealth transfer from the working to the nonworking portion of the population, whether young, aged, or otherwise unemployed. Each segment of the nonworking population is assigned a certain relative weight as to what support is required to maintain a comparable living standard to the other nonworking portions of the population. Then as the population experiences demographic shifts over time, the Social Security system's retirement age can be changed so that the aggregate support level in relation to the working population can be maintained at a constant ratio.

Professor Brown finds that, when not just the aged population, but all components of the nonworking population, are taken into consideration in this way, the required increase in the retirement age is much less dramatic. He concludes, for example, that for the Canadian Social Security system, which is under greater stress from age and population trends than the system of any other Western nation, an increase of the retirement age to 69 by 2025 will be fully adequate.

While it may be difficult to persuade planners in the United States to ever adopt this type of thinking about its Social Security system, it nevertheless exemplifies the flexibility in thinking—free from the crisis approach we have taken in the United States—that is so badly needed.

CHAPTER 16

Institutional and Administrative Issues

Stanford G. Ross

The chapters in this volume generally reflect a belief that the Social Security program has unique characteristics that give it special importance to the society. At the same time, most of the authors give little attention to the institutional aspects of the program. As a lawyer and former government manager of the Social Security system, I would submit, however, that the defining characteristics that have made Social Security exceptional among social programs in the United States are its institutional arrangements. Consequently, this chapter will emphasize the legal foundations and administrative structures of the American Social Security program and the supportive political culture that is thereby engendered.

As the first two chapters of the book discuss, modern societies almost universally make provision for the elderly and disabled through some state-established structure. As family and community support systems break down under the strains of industrialization, government-sponsored programs of one variety or another tend to be adopted. While social insurance approaches have been prevalent in the countries of the Organization for Economic Co-operation and Development (OECD), other approaches are also extensively utilized, including universal programs, means-tested programs, mandated and regulated private programs, and private programs voluntarily created in response to tax incentives. In fact, most OECD countries utilize several of these approaches in various combinations. What distinguishes social insurance from the other approaches varies from country to country, but in the United States, the significant differences are found in legal and administrative arrangements that have developed over a period of 60 years. These arrangements continue to adapt, adjusting the program to the changing needs of the society it serves.

DEDICATED PAYROLL TAX

The central feature of the Social Security system is that it is a contributory system with its own revenue base. Payroll taxes, which supply almost the entire support for

231

the program, are a legally dedicated funding source. As the payroll tax revenues are collected by the Internal Revenue Service (IRS) for the Social Security Administration (SSA), they are automatically transferred by the Treasury Department into trust funds from which benefits are paid. The manner in which the system operates and allocates functions among the responsible agencies of the United States government is shown in Figure 16.1 and Table 16.1.

Coordination among the three agencies is achieved by representation on the governing board (Secretarial level), an SSA/IRS policy board (Executive level), written agreements in the form of SSA/IRS memoranda of understanding and extensive staff networking, including working level groups and task forces.

The financial-management pattern is now so well established in the United States that Americans tend to take it for granted. Yet in many countries, without the dedicated revenue source, the financing of Social Security is more fragile, and the program is more susceptible to the vicissitudes of current government finances.

TRUST FUND ACCOUNTING AND ANNUAL PUBLIC REPORTS

Various government officials, from the beginning, have portrayed the payroll tax as creating an earned right to benefits that inhibits changes in the program that would not be consistent with its long-term functioning. The government has also engaged since the beginning in an extensive system of public accountability. One of the most important parts of that system is the issuance of annual trust fund reports that provide projections of income and revenues for the next 75-year period. In recent years, these reports have been reduced to a plain English summary that receives wide distribution.[1]

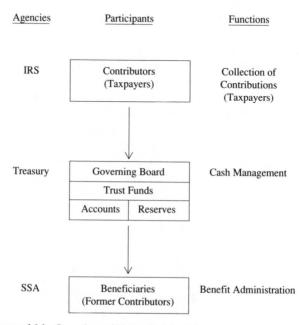

Figure 16.1. Overview of U.S. administrative process.

TABLE 16.1. Allocation of Functions to Agencies in United States System.

Treasury	IRS	SSA

Manages Funds
  Receives monies collected
  by IRS
	Collects SS Taxes
	  Assigns numbers to all
	  employer entities
	  (corporations, etc.)
		Authorizes payment of benefits
		  Assigns numbers to all
		  individuals

Transfers money to SS trust fund accounts	Sends monies to Treasury	Creates beneficiary wage records from IRS forms
Invests trust fund money and collects interest	Sends wage forms to SSA to process	Computes benefit amounts
Pays benefits to beneficiaries	Creates and maintains tax records	Sends wage information to IRS to help with compliance
Pays administrative expenses to SSA	Collects monies not voluntarily paid	Sends information to Treasury to pay beneficiaries
Coordinates with banking system	Examines all taxpayers to be sure of compliance	Issues personal earnings and benefit estimate statements to individual
	Matches records with Treasury and SSA	taxpayers
		Services beneficiaries
	Services taxpayers	
Acts as managing trustee of trust fund board that issues reports to Congress and public	Reports on collection to Congress and public	Reports on benefit payments to trust fund board, Congress, and public

The basis for the 75-year projections is that a young worker entering the work force for a substantial period, say the next 30 to 40 years, and then expecting a retirement period of 20 to 30 years, should be given a 75-year projection to cover the entire horizon of his or her involvement with the program. In recent years, the Social Security Administration has begun to issue personal earnings reports and estimated benefit statements that link the 75-year projections of the overall system to an individualized projection of the beneficiary's entitlement. These personalized reports are expected in the future to be issued to every taxpayer every year, with the expectation that they will establish a tighter personal connection between the individual and the program.

The concept of the trust funds is taken seriously by the government managers. The program, under the law, is governed by a board made up of the Secretary of the Treasury (as the managing trustee), the Secretary of Labor, the Secretary of Health and Human Services, the Social Security Commissioner, and two public trustees—one from each of the two major political parties. This board holds meetings twice a year to take necessary actions and to provide annual reports to the Congress and the public. While in recent years there has been considerable criticism of the Social Security trust funds as being illusory, such allegations are not well informed and ignore both the legal and the administrative realities surrounding the program.

TRANSPARENCY AND FIDUCIARY RESPONSIBILITIES

A principal element of the success of the American Social Security program is its "transparency." The public understands that as a contributory system there is a linkage between contributions paid and benefits received. While one can argue about whether that linkage is tight enough, there is no doubt that it does exist and that it differentiates the program from public assistance programs and any kind of non-contributory program.

A related characteristic is that government occupies a fiduciary relationship to the public with respect to this program. Present taxpayers are future beneficiaries. In this sense, it resembles a private insurance scheme, with the government as sponsor and guarantor of the financial integrity of the system. While one can argue about what responsibilities the government should have, there is no question that one responsibility is concern for its most vulnerable citizens. If social insurance programs are adopted to address this concern, the government generally takes on major responsibility as the sponsor of the program for the effective implementation of this approach.

INVESTMENT OF SOCIAL SECURITY RESERVES

One of the most misunderstood aspects of Social Security is the way monies in the trust funds are managed. Central to the structure of the current program is the fact that the excess of payroll taxes that are collected are automatically invested in United States government bonds. For most of the history of the program, financing has been on a largely pay-as-you-go basis, that is, income is roughly equal to outgo on an annual basis. But even a pay-as-you-go system requires contingency reserves to smooth out the flow of revenues and benefit payments over time. These reserves are invested to create income for the program.

As discussed in many prior chapters, reserves are currently increasing rapidly. The trust funds are presently scheduled under the law to amass reserves equal to about 300 percent of the next year's outgo. Thus, reserves of about $436 billion were accumulated as of the end of 1994 and are scheduled to grow to well over a trillion dollars by 2010.

The trustees of the funds set in 1990 a standard of a 100 percent contingency reserve ratio, that is, a requirement that there should always be at least an amount equal to one year's outgo at the beginning of each year. The reason for the contingency reserve is that if legislative change is needed or unexpected circumstances arise (e.g., a serious recession), there should be sufficient reserves to sustain the system while Congress undertakes action to bring the program back into financial balance.

The investment of reserves in United States government securities backed by the full faith and credit of the federal government provides the most secure form of investment. It also insulates the Social Security program from the kinds of political considerations that would be involved if the funds were invested in private markets. A rate of return is stipulated by statute equal to the highest long-term government interest rates, based on an amalgam of the market-based rates that the U.S. Treasury pays at any time.

In recent years, there has been considerable criticism of the investment in United States government securities because of the budget deficits. The charge is made that the surpluses in the Social Security trust fund have, in effect, helped finance the general deficit. Whether or not this is true is a complicated question of political economy. But even if it were true, the U.S. Treasury has borrowed from the trust funds and issued obligations that are the same as those held by other parties in the United States and abroad. There is no question that these bonds can be liquidated by the Social Security trust funds and used to pay benefits, and, indeed, this is projected to be done during the period 2011 to 2031.

As Bosworth (chapter 10) discusses, higher rates of return for the trust funds might be achieved by investing in private markets. However, I believe that such action would necessarily involve increased risk and, generally speaking, that it is undesirable for Social Security funds to be subjected to unnecessary risk. In many countries where social security funds have been invested in private markets, there have been losses that undermined the integrity of the system and, in some cases, led to system collapse. While it is unlikely that these worst case scenarios would ever prevail in the United States, criticism of the system might be intense in any year in which values in private markets fell and substantial losses took place. Generally speaking, investment in government securities is likely to provide a real rate of return of about 2 percent, which over the long term for which Social Security is designed, is an entirely suitable rate of return for the system.

INDEPENDENT AND COST-EFFECTIVE ADMINISTRATIVE STRUCTURE

Not only are the legal aspects of Social Security important to its particular characteristics in American society, but the administrative structures that have grown up also are critical. The Social Security Administration has recently become an independent agency within the executive branch of government. This restores the organization to the same kind of structure it had when the program was first enacted in 1935. But even when the Social Security Administration was part of the Department of Health and Human Services, it was a large agency with its own reach throughout the country. Currently, there are some 65,000 employees working in about 1,300 local offices, seven regional offices, and a national headquarters in Baltimore, Maryland.

The agency has had a particular culture based on serving beneficiaries and, at times, has been considered one of the paramount agencies of the government. In recent years, the agency has experienced administrative difficulties, but it basically provides the program with an operational capacity that is designed to provide continuity and flexibility to meet the changing needs of the American public.

Looking across the OECD countries, all successful social insurance programs have administrative structures that carry out the major functions of the program effectively. Moreover, criteria for evaluating such structures are available. Table 16.2 sets out these characteristics of social security systems. The United States ranks high with respect to every one of the functions required and, in many respects, provides

TABLE 16.2. Relationship of Major Functions to Administrative Structures and Criteria for Evaluation.

Function	Structure	Criteria for Evaluation
Revenue base	Contribution collection system	Error rates based on ratio of actual collections to those legally required
Benefit payments	Benefit payment system	Error rates based on ratio of correct payments to those legally required
Financial management	Actuarial office for projection of revenues and expenditures	Accuracy of projections in relationship to actual results
Communications	Data and information systems; computer systems	Accuracy of records, usefulness of data bases, timeliness of reports, etc.
Program policy	Office using data, information, etc. to plan programs, analyze results, etc.	Usefulness of reports, timeliness of planning, etc.
Organizational management	Top management, central head-quarters, field management	Overall level of performance, evaluation of functions, structure, policies
Field operations	Local offices	Accuracy and timeliness in performing work

a useful model for those countries of the world, such as the ones in central and eastern Europe and in the developing countries, who need to improve Social Security operations. The United States system operates with administrative costs that are less than 1 percent of benefit payments. In terms of cost-effective operations, Social Security in the United States may rank as the best in the world.

SUPPORTIVE POLITICAL CULTURE

All of these institutional elements have helped to create a political culture that has served over a period of some 60 years to enhance the program and make it popular with the public. Any program of this magnitude will, of course, change. Society's needs will change. Indeed, one of the strengths of a social insurance approach is that alterations can be made to adapt to large changes in society. Indeed, social insurance may be more flexible than private insurance arrangements in dealing with societal problems such as changing demographics, inflation, varying types of economic growth, and all kinds of social change. Adaptation is essential to the functioning of social insurance, and the American Social Security system has in fact been continually changed to meet emerging conditions.

TESTING OF THE INSTITUTIONS

Social Security is presently in a time of testing in the United States. The disability program is not functioning well (see Mashaw, chapter 7). The Medicare program, which is closely tied to Social Security but not discussed in this book, is in need of dramatic reform. OASDI itself is in need of having its long-term financing strengthened.

In a larger sense, the problems of Social Security are being created by a long-term fiscal imbalance that confronts all of the OECD countries, including the United States. While the particular configurations of the imbalance vary, depending on the individual country's demographics and design of social welfare and tax systems, the strategic problem that is presented is more or less universal. All of the OECD countries, including the United States, have "overmatched" revenue systems: the expenditures that are desired by the society far exceed any willingness to pay for those expenditures. The United States has not come to grips with the issue of whether there need to be changes in the tax system that will better support the expenditures that the public desires and needs.

Secondly, there are relatively weak political mechanisms for placing revenue and benefit systems in balance. A president has a four-year horizon and sometimes as long as eight years, and senators have six years. Members of the House of Representatives, however, have only two years. It is very difficult for these men and women in Congress to come to grips with problems that may involve a great deal of political difficulty during their two year terms. Taking needed actions may even destroy possibilities for reelection, while often the political beneficiaries are persons who have yet to run for office. Thus, there is generally a political ability to deal only with crisis-level problems. Yet Social Security requires carefully considered changes that will take place over very long periods, generally 50 years or more. Even so, historically, major problems have been attended to, although generally only at the last minute. Indeed, the Social Security system was created in 1935 in response to the Great Depression and extraordinary political developments that suggested the possibility of more radical approaches if action was not taken promptly. The remedial legislation in 1983 (see Berkowitz, chapter 2) waited to the point at which benefit checks would not have been sent out. And yet, over the long run, the political system seems sufficiently responsible to achieve needed changes.

In general, Social Security has evolved to this point by incremental changes, and it is likely that pattern will prevail in the future. From a practical standpoint, Social Security is so much a part of the structure of society in the United States that it is hard to imagine it not being maintained at roughly the present level of support. Private benefit plans generally are predicated on a Social Security system at approximately the present level. The Medicare system of health care for the aged and disabled is predicated on an income in the population that is based on Social Security. The SSI program of means-tested benefits for the elderly and disabled is designed to augment a Social Security system at the present level. Social Security is at the core of the American system of social protection and may be expected to remain so positioned.

CONCLUSION

I believe the conclusion is inevitable that Social Security will endure as long as the key institutions that have evolved to date are maintained so that the political culture surrounding those institutions continues to support the program. The Social Security system as it exists today may be inadequate in certain respects and certainly requires change. Yet, as with democracy itself, it is hard to believe that there is any alternative that is better. It is entirely feasible to make necessary changes in a responsible and commonsense way. When one looks around the world, there are no better institutions than the American Social Security system to meet the needs of the elderly, the disabled, and surviving family members in a modern society.

ENDNOTES

1. The basic document reflecting the institutional arrangements of Social Security is the "Annual Report of the Board of Trustees of the Federal Old-Age and Survivors Insurance and Disability Trust Funds." This document, along with the Annual Report of the Board of Trustees of the Federal Hospital Insurance Trust Fund and the Federal Supplementary Medical Insurance Trust Fund, is published annually (e.g., Board of Trustees, 1995). The trust fund reports are required by law to be issued to the Congress on April 1 of each year and are printed by the House Committee on Ways and Means. These annual reports contain voluminous information on the current income and outflow, and projections of the future operations, of the programs. The Summary, which in 1995 was a 14-page document, is distributed widely to congressional offices and the public.

A document with detailed information on the administrative aspects of Social Security is the "Annual Financial Statement" issued by the Social Security Administration. It contains detailed information on various aspects of the operations including processing schedules and work load data. The Government Accounting Office frequently issues detailed studies of particular operational issues, to provide oversight on how the Social Security program is being administered and how its operations in various areas can be improved.

The classic study of Social Security administrative issues is Derthick (1990). This book analyses the administrative operations within the context of policymaking by the executive branch and Congress and oversight by the Congress and the courts.

The International Labour Office (1984) contains a chapter on "Administration of Social Security," which describes administrative structures on an international basis. Information is provided with respect to collection, record keeping, and benefit payment methods used by various countries. The International Social Security Association in Geneva, whose members are the social security organizations in some 150 countries, does extensive work in the administrative area and publishes various studies, research, and occasional papers, which can be found listed in their *Catalogue of Publications*.

PART IV

The Future: Alternative Perspectives

CHAPTER 17

Social Security in the Twenty-First Century
The Need for Change

C. EUGENE STEUERLE

INTRODUCTION

Social Security has proven to be one of the most successful social programs not only in the United States, but also throughout the industrial world.[1] Social Security has removed large numbers of elderly from poverty and given them opportunities to live fuller and more complete lives in retirement. Despite this success, it is not without faults; some of its design features reflect yesterday's needs and respond inadequately to such social phenomena as longer life spans, changes in working conditions, and expansion of the number of two-earner couples in the labor market. The United States Social Security system also sustains some older political compromises, such as significant benefits for many high-income households that are well in excess of what they could have purchased from a private insurance company with the same tax dollars. These compromises reduce the program's efficiency and equity. Most importantly, the program is predetermined to grow in ways that limit its responsiveness to the evolving needs of both the elderly and the nonelderly.

There is no reason to expect that Social Security in the twenty-first century should look exactly like its mid-twentieth century ancestor, although I suspect there will be many resemblances. Adaptability of goods and services is a hallmark of economic growth.[2] This standard applies to public, as well as private, goods and services. In the broader sweep of history, the widespread availability of both public and private insurance for old age and health is a relatively recent phenomenon. Like all products, insurance policies are required over time to move toward more mature stages of development. Both public and private insurance, therefore, should respond to evolving demand; they should not be isolated from competition from newer goods and services that society may come to deem more valuable.

As other chapters discuss, the Social Security system of the twenty-first century

241

is far from being in financial balance. The Social Security trustees and actuaries have made this imbalance crystal clear for a number of years (e.g., Board of Trustees, 1995). Even under optimistic assumptions about changes in birthrates, economic growth, and so forth, Social Security will still be paying out benefits well in excess of taxes collected, while its companion program, Medicare, is in even worse shape.

The causes for the imbalances are multiple, and only a few can be noted here. The system has never adjusted for increased life spans, although a slight increase in retirement age for full benefits from age 65 to age 67 is scheduled to begin after the turn of the century. Annual benefits also increase in real terms, but at about the average rate of wage growth in the economy. Once the baby-boom population starts filling the ranks of the elderly early in the twenty-first century, and the "baby-bust" population that follows dominates the working-age population, the ratio of workers to support each elderly person will fall dramatically.[3] Medicare costs are also predicted to rise because of this demographic shift and because of the built-in cost pressures already in the United States health-care system. These conclusions are factual, not bound by political philosophy or party. They are sometimes met with one of two striking, but contrasting, conclusions: that either the system is in extraordinary crisis or all of its promises are essentially sacrosanct and can easily be met with only a bit of legislative tinkering. Neither is true. Yes, promises of benefits are in excess of promises of taxes that need to be paid. But this requirement for reform hardly makes necessary the elimination of the program itself and the denial of all benefits to future generations. This nation and all advanced industrial nations, no matter what the design of their Social Security, are committed to seeing that elderly individuals at least have a minimum level of retirement income. In addition, these societies have come to accept the notion that individuals during their working years should be mandated to pay into a retirement system. Once such a mandate is set, it would be difficult and, by many standards unfair, to deny a later retirement benefit to those who have abided by the mandate. Unless society abandons one of these goals—to maintain a decent standard of living for those in old age, to require individuals to finance part of their own retirement, and to provide some return on mandated retirement contributions—some form of Social Security is likely to survive. By the same token, there remain a variety of alternative mechanisms for meeting these fundamental goals.

Because individuals plan their retirements according to government promises of future benefits, there is an advantage to making reforms in ways that do not drastically change expectations just before they retire. The existing Social Security program, for example, has significant built-in growth, especially if one counts medical benefits under Medicare. Evolutionary, rather than revolutionary, reform might simply moderate this rate of growth, so that real benefits are not reduced over time but only cut back relative to current promises of what that growth will be.

At the same time, the problems of an imbalanced system with inconsistent promises should be addressed soon. The large demographic shifts previously mentioned are just around the corner as the baby boomers move into the retirement age population. Indeed, under current law, baby boomers born in 1946 become eligible for early retirement benefits as soon as the year 2008. Increases are scheduled in Social Security, Medicare, and other elderly benefits by several percentage points of the gross domestic product (GDP). The sooner reform is started, therefore, the easier it is to insure that drastic benefit changes do not occur from one year to the next, that is, that those retiring in 2015 do not face a drastically different benefit structure than those retiring in 2014.

Even if the significant deficits scheduled in the system were viable as a matter of social policy, they cannot be tolerated from a fiscal policy standpoint. If projected Social Security and Medicare deficits are added to other deficits already in the system, the federal government's borrowing would approach levels that by historic standards are unsustainable. Such demands would also reduce the amount of private sector saving left for investment, likely slowing down rates of growth as well.

Reform is made inevitable not simply by inconsistent promises and imbalances between long-run benefits and revenues. Other reforms discussed soon are likely to be forced by changing demographics and societal demands: adjusting benefits to eliminate the unfair treatment of secondary workers, eliminating the earnings test and other signals that society does not want the near elderly and young elderly to work, and better meeting the needs of the poorer, usually older, elderly and so on. Many existing provisions are likewise unfair and inefficient, so delay in dealing with them places unrecoverable costs on society.

The lifetime value of Social Security and Medicare benefits approaches one-half million dollars for an average-income couple retiring today. ("Lifetime value" here means the amount of money that an insurance company would demand up front if, at age 65, the couple were to ask it to provide the same amount of cash and medical benefits to them over their remaining lives.) Roughly half of this amount is due to cash benefits in Old-Age and Survivors Insurance and half to the rapidly growing Medicare program. Excluding increases due to price inflation, but including projected health cost rises in excess of general prices, the lifetime value increases toward one million dollars for a high-income couple retiring in a few decades.

It is not an issue whether society can afford these amounts; in many ways, it already is affording them. Instead, society must confront the question of whether automatically scheduled increases in lifetime Social Security and Medicare benefits represent the best way to allocate future resources, or whether they might be devoted to other important needs in society, such as helping youth (who have the nation's highest poverty rates), crime prevention, education and training. If needs among the elderly turn out to be paramount, moreover, then society must additionally ask itself whether predetermined uses of new resources in Social Security and Medicare are really being directed in the fairest and most efficient manner to this group.

Social Security and Medicare have been put on automatic pilot in ways that make them grow not only in real terms, but usually faster than the growth rate of the economy. Other government programs are not. When it comes time for legislative enactment, for example, increasing the growth rate of spending on some education programs from 0 percent to 1 percent is treated as an expenditure increase. Lowering the rate of growth of Social Security spending from 5 to 4 percent is counted as an expenditure decrease. If no agreement on change can be reached by the president and the Congress, then Social Security grows by 5 percent and the education programs by 0 percent.

Saying that taxes can always be raised does not get around the problem. Regardless of level of taxation, programs that grow automatically are still favored in a predetermined manner over other discretionary uses of funds, even before the future has arrived. Economists also argue that the distortionary costs of taxes grow significantly as the tax rate increases.[4] Hence, if one raises or uses taxes to pay for one item in the budget, it inevitably makes more difficult the raising or using of taxes for other purposes.

Many choices for today, in effect, are determined by past legislators. Without reform of Social Security and Medicare, choices will be restricted further for the citizens of the twenty-first century, and they will be constrained in their ability to spend according to their own priorities and perception of the greatest needs of society.

BASING REFORM ON PRINCIPLES

In chapter 1, Thompson and Upp present certain criteria for comparing various approaches to providing social welfare: individual dignity, coverage, distribution of benefits and costs, administrative costs, incentives, fiscal discipline, and facilitation of market adjustments. In this chapter, I would like to present a complementary, somewhat overlapping, set of principles that I find useful for discussing Social Security reform. Such reform should be based on a solid set of principles. Here I distinguish between goals and principles. Attaining a certain benefit level is a goal. Principles, however, are used to determine the appropriateness of specific goals, in both absolute and relative terms. I suggest the following principles, derived and adapted largely from the theory of public finance, as a basis for reforming the system over time.

1. Taking Care of Those Less Well-Off (Need and Progressivity)

Despite efforts to define Social Security in the language of insurance, one motivation for its creation dominated all others: the needs of the elderly. If, in the 1930s, the elderly had no special needs that were not shared by the rest of the population, there would have been no Social Security program, at least none that bears any resemblance to the program we know. From the beginning Social Security was meant to redistribute, in particular, to the poorer of the elderly. It attempted to achieve this end partly through the payment of benefits to initial generations who paid little to the system and partly through a progressive benefit formula that provided a higher rate of return on the contributions of those with lower average earnings. Proper application of the principle of relating resources to needs, however, requires continual reassessment of where needs in society are greatest among all groups, as well as of where needs among the elderly are most prevalent.

2. Ensuring a Fair Return on Contributions (Individual Equity)

The original architects of Social Security likened it to private pensions and annuities, under which benefits bear a clear relationship to contributions. Given the redistributive elements of the plan, of course, the promise of a fair or market rate of return on all contributions was a promise that could not be kept for everyone. If someone is to benefit from a redistribution, then someone must pay (see Chen and Goss, chapter 5).

The conflict between this principle and gearing the program progressively toward need was sidestepped during Social Security's first few decades. Continual increases in tax rates on younger generations were used to finance successively higher levels of benefits for retirees. As it turned out, the system went well beyond providing a fair return on contributions for these first few generations of retirees. Almost no participants retiring up to today, not even the highest earners, were required to make contributions that came close to covering the value of benefits received.

Low-income couples retiring in 1980, for example, paid into the Old Age and Survivors Insurance about $27,000 in taxes, plus the forgone interest that they could have earned on those taxes.[5] They got back $150,000, a net transfer of $123,000. High-income couples paid in about $83,000 in taxes and forgone interest, but got back $316,000, a net transfer of $233,000. Both low- and high-income retirees in 1980 also received huge transfers through Medicare, as very low rates of Medicare tax during a few working years gave them entitlement to a fairly expensive and ever-expanding health-care system in retirement.[6]

Only as we move into the twenty-first century will there be a reversal of the situation whereby substantial net transfers are made to all retirees, even those with very high incomes. Tax rates paid by current workers are a multiple of those paid by many workers of the past, thereby reducing and often making negative the amount of transfers, or the value of benefits received less taxes paid. Only by continuing to raise tax rates on current workers to support higher benefits for each succeeding generation of retirees can all new retirees also receive benefits in excess of what they put into the system. But continually rising tax rates is a mathematical impossibility at some point.

Social Security was able to avoid the day of reckoning as long as Social Security tax rates rose at approximately 3 percentage points per decade—from a combined employer-employee rate of 3.0 percent in 1950 to 15.3 percent in 1990. For the 1990s, however, there is no scheduled tax rate increase. Achieving a balance between taking care of those elderly in need and giving a fair return on contributions was an issue that was essentially dodged for retirees up to now, but it is one of the main tasks facing Social Security in the twenty-first century.

3. Treating Equals Equally (Horizontal Equity)

The principle of equal treatment of equals is pervasive throughout government policy. If you and I commit equal crimes and are equal in all other circumstances, then we should face the same penalty. If you and I have equal income and are equal in all other respects, then we should pay the same income tax. This equity principle as applied to Social Security implies that there should be equal assessments of payroll taxes on those with equal earnings, and there should be equal benefits for those paying equal amounts of taxes and having equal needs.

4. Achieving Maximum Benefit to Society from Available Resources (Economic Efficiency)

In social programs, this principle means that society ought to get the most out of its available resources by examining and comparing various social benefits and costs. The early Social Security literature, for instance, was concerned with maintaining incentives to work and tried to insure that those costs did not rise too high. The application of the principle is sometimes difficult, because all individuals do not agree as to the benefits or the costs of government programs, but the principle still compels us to try to weigh all benefits closely against all costs. Such weighing also requires that comparisons of alternatives be made for each additional dollar spent and at each margin. A program may be worthwhile on average, but parts may still be broken, leaving many dollars that could be allocated more efficiently elsewhere.

APPLICATION OF THE PRINCIPLES

These principles allow one to consider Social Security in a consistent fashion. They do not preclude other goals, although many can be subsumed under the broad headings. For example, a stable financing source is related to reducing some of the costs associated with uncertainty for recipients, taxpayers, and the government. On the other hand, one goal that has been used in Social Security's past—determining benefits as a replacement for prior wages—should not be elevated to the level of a principle. Indeed, it was the use of this goal that for decades led to net transfers, over and above Social Security contributions and interest earned on those contributions, that were larger for high-income individuals than for low-income individuals. An example of this was noted in the section on individual equity. Even though higher-income individuals received lower replacement wages than others, they often paid so little in taxes that their absolute transfer was still higher. Thus, indiscriminate use of the replacement goal led to a violation of principles; it neither related benefits to needs nor could be justified as a return on prior contributions.

These principles for Social Security do not allow one to state unequivocally the exact form that future adjustments should take. Such decisions require judgement in a variety of areas, in particular, in how much redistribution or progressivity society wants at a particular point in time, including how much redistribution it considers appropriate across different generations and how it ranks different needs among its citizens. Principles, however, do allow one to sort through options in ways that allow some ranking of both benefit and tax options. Some benefit reductions can also be found inferior (or no better) than others by almost any criterion. Some proposals for tax increases can be ranked similarly.

One of the most important means of achieving common ground is to agree that options for changing the benefit or tax sides of Social Security can and should follow logically from a basic set of principles. Those willing to commit themselves to starting with a set of principles are much more likely to arrive at partial consensus than those who start with a political agenda or advocacy of a particular constituency.

DESIGN OF REFORM

Although most of the remainder of this chapter centers on individual proposals for reforming Social Security for the coming century, it is important that each reform not be considered in isolation. For instance, one potential reform may pare back the rate of growth of benefits. Another reform, however, may change the schedule under which benefits are determined, so as to reduce the number of elderly who are poor. Because of their impact on selected groups, many reforms might be objectionable if left standing by themselves, but acceptable if considered in combination.

1. Reforms Worth Considering

To the extent that taxes must be increased or benefits reduced—and inevitably one, the other, or both must happen—the principles underlying Social Security highlight several options for consideration.

Increase and Index the Retirement Age for Both OASI and Medicare. Foremost among these changes are increases in the retirement age for both OASI and Medicare. The twentieth century has seen a vast expansion in number of years of retirement supported by government. For a couple retiring at age 62 today, Social Security benefits on average can be expected to last for 25 years, that is, until the longer living of the couple is expected to die.[7] People live many years longer and retire many years earlier than when Social Security was first created. The expansion in number of years of retirement has added substantially to the lifetime cost of Social Security. It has also reduced the total output in the economy and added to the tax rates and saving rates necessary to support retirement. On the other hand, replacement rates—annual benefits relative to earnings prior to retirement—have been much more stable.[8] In effect, much of the increased cost of cash benefits has gone to support people in years further and further from death.[9]

The Normal Retirement Age for receipt of full benefits is scheduled gradually to rise to age 67 for workers turning 65 between 2003 and 2025. The two-year increase is roughly equal to the growth in average life expectancy at age 65 projected to occur over the four decades between enactment of that increase in 1983 and when full implementation is achieved. This increase, however, does not offset any of the past growth or future growth in years of retirement support after 2025. The earliest age at which one can receive reduced OASI benefits, moreover, is scheduled to remain constant at age 62, while the age at which all persons become eligible for Medicare is left at 65.

Moon (chapter 4) discusses the economic status of older persons. As she points out, it has improved greatly. In fact, data on income and wealth distributions, adjusted for family size, reveal that the near-elderly and young-elderly in their 60s are generally better off in most economic terms than are much of the rest of the population (Hurd, 1990; Radner, 1993a; Smeeding, 1989; U.S. Bureau of the Census, 1990). And these numbers don't even take into account the potential to work of many retired near- and young-elderly. They reflect, moreover, only some of the risks to economic security that increase with age: loss of assistance from a spouse, health-care costs, inflation-based erosion of many private pension plans.

By some measures, children are now the poorest group in society. At the same time, by providing more benefits further from death, government programs have been designed in such a way as to increase automatically transfers from moderate-income young families with children to higher-income individuals among the near-elderly and the young-elderly. It is highly doubtful that a system designed initially on the principle of helping those in greater relative need should become irresponsive to shifts in relative needs within society. Indeed, the original Social Security Act was meant to meet social needs of all the population, not just the elderly.

One means of increasing the retirement age is to adjust gradually the Normal Retirement Age until it effectively provides a constant expected number of years of retirement support such as 15. Once that target is reached, the Normal Retirement Age would be indexed to grow with life expectancy, so that the years of expected support stayed constant.

Increases in the retirement age, of course, require other programs as well. There are great disparities in well-being among many of the near-elderly and young-elderly, who might be affected by such changes. Thus, disability benefits must remain available for those who become disabled before legal retirement ages. If benefits are required for the near-elderly because of reduced capacity to work, rather than more complete disability, then such benefits ought initially to be set at a lower level than at older ages, when inability to work at all jobs is more likely.

A society that for decades has come to expect more and more years of retirement support—at the cost of smaller and smaller shares of total resources for younger populations—will take time to adapt to such a change in emphasis.[10] Not only will disability programs be affected, but also unemployment programs, private retirement and insurance plans, and even seniority scales within work forces. This argues further for beginning the process of adjustment soon, so that it can take place in a gradual way that allows individuals and systems to react and adapt.

Place Greater Restriction on Early Retirement Options. While the Normal Retirement Age is at least scheduled to increase slightly, if inadequately, the early retirement age of 62 is held constant in current law. Annual benefits will be lowered for those retiring at age 62 through larger actuarial reductions as the gap between Normal Retirement Age and the early retirement age is increased.

Given the tendency of the older elderly to be relatively poorer than much of the population, as well as in need of assistance for long-term care and other problems of old age, Social Security benefits ought to be restricted for those individuals who, by retiring early, increase their probability of falling back on the public sector for more support. The current system gives the misleading signal that adequate income at age 62 will be sufficient at age 82 or beyond; often it is not. For a given amount of lifetime payments to any individual, another option might be to exchange a reduced level of benefit in the early years of retirement for a higher benefit level later.

In sum, the early retirement age of 62 should be raised or the requirements for its use should be made more restrictive. Thus, the gap between Normal Retirement Age and the early retirement age should not be allowed to expand, as is scheduled after the turn of the century under current law. With current provisions, even greater shares of benefits continue to go to those who, year after year, have more and more years until death and less and less need relative to other recipients of old-age insurance. This shifting of resources toward years of lesser need does not agree with the need-based or progressivity principle underlying much of Social Security's development.

Include All Contributions to Social Security in the Calculation of Benefits. Horizontal equity, as well as efficiency considerations, argue strongly for the inclusion of all contributions to the Social Security system, including years not now counted, contributions of partially retired workers, and all contributions of spouses, in the calculation of benefits to be received. In a progressive system, of course, not all taxes will receive the same rate of return. Nonetheless, the current system inconsistently provides a partial rate of return on the earnings of high-income individuals who work the minimum required number of years, while it provides a zero return on all the earnings of many moderate-income spouses, on the additional earnings of many elderly individuals, and on extra years of work by individuals at all income levels.[11] These disparities are the consequences of rules such as those that count a maximum of 35 years of taxes in determining levels of benefit. One must also choose between spousal benefits and a worker's benefits; the former are often so generous that no additional Social Security benefit accrues in a family that moves from one-worker to two-worker status (see Holden, chapter 6).

Among the many consequences, the current formula discriminates by providing lower benefits to the harder working among households with equal lifetime contributions to Social Security. For example, 50 years of work at $35,000 per year will yield lower benefits than 35 years at $50,000.[12] In effect, the standard of progressivity is applied inconsistently and the standard of equal treatment of equals is violated. In addition, the net tax rate on marginal work—that is the amount of taxes, less benefits, associated with additional work—is much higher than necessary to support a given progressivity goal. This raises the efficiency costs of the net tax system as a whole. Note that by adjusting the benefit formula in other ways, this proposed change can be achieved while maintaining the overall progressivity of the existing system.[13]

Remove the Elderly from Poverty.   Today most elderly have Social Security benefits that remove them from poverty or SSI benefits that at least move them closer to subsistence at a poverty level. Benefits in Social Security ought to be adjusted over time so that all elderly eventually receive some minimum that would remove them from poverty. Changes in the benefit formula provide one means of achieving this end, although the minimum would need to be adjusted so as not to give undue support to those receiving substantial pensions from other government retirement programs.[14] In addition, actuarial adjustments should be made in the benefits provided to couples so that a spouse is not left in poverty when widowed. For example, lower initial benefits (for the worker and spouse) could be exchanged for a higher survivor's benefit after one spouse dies; the adjustment could be made in an actuarial manner that did not change the lifetime value of expected benefits for the couple.[15]

Expand the Tax Base to Include All Forms of Compensation (Social Security Tax Reform).   Expansion of the tax base to include all forms of compensation has long been a goal of tax reformers seeking to reform the income tax. It is an appropriate reform also for Social Security. Failure to do so maintains the unequal treatment of similarly situated workers. For example, someone earning $30,000 in cash wages will pay substantially greater Social Security tax than someone earning $25,000 in cash and $5,000 in nontaxable employee benefits. At the same time, the current exclusion of many employee benefits from Social Security tax creates many problems of efficiency. It encourages excessive consumption of health care and other employer-provided benefits. Among the related consequences are resources unnecessarily lost to the additional administrative cost associated with excess insurance. Benefits of the existing tax treatment of health insurance, moreover, often inure to health-care providers in such forms as higher salaries rather than to those receiving the extra insurance.

The Social Security Administration today predicts that the Social Security tax base will continue to erode in the future as nontaxable employee benefits rise relative to taxable cash wages, a significant, although not dominant, reason for the long-term deficit. Even if the more complete reform suggested here is not feasible politically, the erosion should be stopped. By itself, Social Security tax reform could increase benefit outlays substantially, since more wages being subject to taxation requires higher benefit payments in the long run. Some offset in the benefit formula, therefore, may be required as well.

Expand the Income Taxation of Benefits. If the net benefits of current and near-future retirees are to be reduced, increasing the amount of benefits subject to income taxation is far preferable to many other types of cuts. Reforms in the taxation of benefits also have the temporary advantage of recapturing from current high-income retirees some of the subsidies that exceed the fair annuity value of their contributions. Currently, most high-income individuals over 65 already receive very large net transfers from the system.

Recent reforms in the taxation of benefits already make up to 85 percent of cash benefits subject to taxation for higher-income taxpayers, although no account is taken of the favorable income tax treatment of Medicare benefits. Raising the proportion to 100 percent might be a crude way of adjusting further for those Medicare benefits. For most elderly, however, tax burdens remain far below the burdens of nonelderly households at the same levels of income and with many more child-rearing responsibilities (Sammartino and Williams, 1991). This provides at least an equity argument for lowering the threshold at which taxation applies, although that threshold is already falling gradually in real terms, due to inflation.

For many future retirees, the equity of taxing OASI benefits will not follow as neatly from the principles just laid down. Lifetime redistributive patterns created by the Social Security benefit formula will at last become progressive within cohorts. That is, high-income individuals will end up contributing more to the system than they receive in benefits. Given the much higher level of overall benefits that are scheduled for future retirees, however, taxation, including some adjustment for nontaxed Medicare benefits, remains one way of modifying the net cost of the system and helping to bring it into overall balance. Straightforward adjustment of the benefit formula, of course, could achieve much of the same end. Taxation adjusts according to current income and need, while the Social Security benefit formula adjusts according to lifetime earnings. Neither adjustment is perfect. Taxation is based on total income, including private pensions and interest, and, therefore, discourages lifetime saving; the benefit formula does not adjust for current circumstances. A mixture of the two, therefore, may be a reasonable compromise.

Gradually Adjust Spousal and Workers' Benefits So All Spouses Are Treated More Equally.   Under current law, nonworking spouses of high-income workers are granted much larger benefits than are given to spouses of low-income workers and to most working spouses. A strong case can be made that spousal benefit rules should not consistently favor high-income spouses, much less provide net transfers to their households. Such a pattern of transfers cannot be justified on the basis of any of the principles listed earlier. Certainly higher-income spouses do not have greater need, and no case can be made that the benefits to nonworking spouses are related in any way to contributions made.

Any funds raised by gradually adjusting spousal benefits so that all spouses are treated more equally could be spent to help finance a related conversion suggestion: providing some marginal return or benefit for the contributions of all working spouses. Society may also wish to convert the spousal benefit into one that accounts for the needs of those who raise children. The current spousal benefit by no means meets this goal, since it goes to many who do not raise children, does not go at all to many single parents who do raise children, and implicitly rewards higher-income individuals for their child-rearing more than it does lower-income individuals.

Abolish the OASI Earnings Test and the "Health Earnings Test"—The Requirement That Elderly Workers Cannot Receive Medicare if Their Employer Provides Health Insurance to Its Workers.   Social Security has developed a complex array of rules for adjusting the benefits of those who deviate from a normal retirement age. An earnings test reduces Social Security benefits by 50¢ for every dollar earned over a basic exempt amount below age 65 and by 33¢ for every dollar earned above another exempt amount between ages 65 and 70. Workers aged 70 and older are exempt from this earnings test.[16]

To me it is clear that this earnings test is a tattered remnant of a bygone era. Even independently from its strong antiwork sentiment, it violates almost all standards of efficiency and equal treatment of equals under the law. For example, it helps maintain a tax system in which households with equal levels of income are taxed very differently: elderly workers often pay much more tax than nonelderly workers who, in turn, pay much more than elderly nonworkers.

In recent years, Social Security has increasingly provided delayed retirement credits—adjustments that raise later benefits—to compensate for reductions in benefits through the earnings test. Given enough adjustments in these credits, or in other actuarial formulas, some of the equity and efficiency problems surrounding the earnings test could be eliminated.

All of these additional offsets, however, cannot solve a more basic issue: the earnings test would remain one of the many signals that our society, as well as our government, sends to our citizens when they still have a life expectancy of as long as 15 or 20 years: "You should retire. You are old. We do not want you to work." The earnings test would remain a bad and confusing signal to many elderly individuals.

Eliminating the earnings test by itself would probably not result in a large expansion in work efforts by the elderly and the near-elderly. Instead, it must be viewed as part of a larger reform strategy that also centers around reform of retirement age rules and allows for the evolution of work patterns, particularly among the near-

and the young-elderly. Elimination of the earnings test is not sufficient to allow this evolution to occur, yet it may be one necessary component.

Note, by the way, that elimination of the earnings test in isolation could increase slightly federal expenditures on retirement and, by some measures, make the system slightly less progressive. In a broader reform package, these effects again can be offset easily in ways that would leave the Social Security System fairer, more financially sound, and equally progressive, for instance, by slight changes in the benefit formula. Thus, in a broader reform there is no reason that elimination of the earnings test needs to benefit primarily higher-income retirees.

Government should also repeal what I call "the health earnings test," the requirement that Medicare should be the secondary payor for those elderly who work for employers providing insurance to employees. Most economists believe that the worker pays for employee benefits, that is, that employers essentially count total compensation as the cost of hiring any employee. An elderly individual with a productive capability of $20,000 a year, for example, might only be paid $15,000 in cash wages and $5,000 in health benefits under the health earnings test. The health benefits, however, displace Medicare benefits, say, of $5,000 also.

In this example, the health earnings test imposes an effective tax rate of 25 percent ($5,000/$20,000), and here there is no offset whatsoever in later delayed-retirement credits. This particular test in many cases imposes a much higher tax rate on elderly workers than does the earnings test itself. If health benefits were available and mandated for all employees under some form of national health plan, note that the current test would be extended significantly, as fewer elderly employees would be able to find jobs for cash wages only.

Revise Medicare's Built-In Growth and Open-Ended Nature.   Although the focus of this book is mainly on OASDI, Medicare cannot be ignored. Indeed, the Medicare program is in greater imbalance than is OASI. Within Medicare itself, the tendency to keep premiums and deductible amounts low is less justifiable than spending this money to help the older and needier elderly, either in cash, say, through higher minimum cash benefits, or in other health benefits such as further in-home assistance for chronic impairment problems. The built-in growth and open-ended nature of Medicare violates most principles of Social Security by predetermining where expenditures would be increased without regard to need. As a matter of budget policy, open-ended expenditures are almost never sustainable.

A related problem is the tendency by policymakers to cut back on OASI as a means of paying for larger and larger amounts of in-kind health benefits. Reducing the *share* of benefits paid in cash restricts the flexibility, adaptability, and freedom of retirees. This trade-off has already begun through the paring of cash-benefit growth even while medical care expenditures are expanding rapidly. Comparison of Medicare and Social Security rates of growth makes clear that the combined system is on a dangerous track toward much greater restrictions on choice by the elderly.

Expenditure-neutral trade-offs of cash for health benefits likely would enhance the well-being of the elderly. Under the current health system, Medicare recipients are kept from being very price conscious. Accordingly, they will often demand care that is worth less to them in aggregate than a corresponding amount of cash benefits.

Treat Programs for the Elderly As a Package. A great source of confusion for the elderly, for children of the elderly put in charge of their parents' affairs, and for the public in general is the great multiplicity of programs for the elderly. This is especially true in the area of health care, with different sources of financing and standards of financial solvency applying to Hospital Insurance (HI), Supplemental Medical Insurance (SMI), and Medicaid. HI is a form of Medicare that is considered part of Social Security; SMI, a form of Medicare not part of Social Security; and Medicaid, a form of assistance not part of Medicare. Overlap and confusion are also true to a lesser extent with Social Security and Supplemental Security Income (SSI), a welfare-based system for low-income elderly.

The principal problem with this division of responsibilities is budgetary. When HI cost controls are put into place, the effect on SMI expenditures for out-patient care needs to be taken into account. When SMI provides in-home assistance for individuals, it has an impact on Medicaid. When HI trust funds spend more money than they take in, then the combined Social Security trust funds are drained. If tax rates are adjusted to deal with upcoming demographic changes in Social Security only, they will ignore related changes in costs under SMI and SSI.

This does not mean that different programs should never be divided operationally into parts, based upon administrative efficiency and other considerations. It does mean that as a budget matter, choices of expenditures among HI, SMI, Medicaid, OASDI, and SSI should be made simultaneously. Similarly, Social Security reform aimed at dealing with the upcoming retirement of the baby-boom population should try to deal with the implications for all programs, not just for Social Security. Only in that way can appropriate trade-offs and choices among types of benefits and programs be made.

2. Other Possible Options

Some options are more neutral as to whether they fall in the category of "right" or "wrong" ways to reform the system. In part, the validity of these options depends upon how much weight one puts on such factors as (1) the progressivity of the system, versus an insurance-like principle that requires equal returns on all contributions; and (2) moving beyond restoring balance in Social Security toward a more fully funded retirement system. Some movement in these directions, however, is probably required to bring the system into balance and to increase saving in society.

Consider Gradual Adjustment of Indexing So That Benefits for Higher-Income Individuals Do Not Grow So Fast. A case can be made for price, rather than wage, indexing of the benefit formula itself—so that real benefit levels stay constant over different generations of retirees, while the replacement rate falls with rising real wages. Given a choice between this type of change and increasing the retirement age, the latter is, in my view, superior because of its ability to maintain retirement income for the very old who have lower incomes than both the younger elderly and the nonelderly. I am also concerned that any permanent movement against wage indexing might make retirement incomes insufficient to meet certain needs such as long-term care. One compromise is to let benefits rise along with wages for low- and moderate-income individuals, but to provide slower rates of benefit growth (but no less than inflation) to high-income individuals.[17] Wage indexing would still apply to all benefits going to low- and moderate-income workers, so that their retirement incomes would grow in line with economic growth rates. One can also consider price indexing only for a given period of time before reverting back to wage indexing.

In general, any broad reform of Social Security, Medicare, and other programs for the elderly should begin by looking at lifetime benefits. The usual tendency is to focus too quickly on the annual benefit amounts that derive from the benefit formula. As mentioned, however, the annual benefit amount has been less the cause of past growth in expenditures for the elderly than have been increases in years of support and constantly expanding medical costs associated with both an increased level of services and medical price inflation.[18] For the future, of course, demographic changes also add to the rising burdens of the system. Focusing on lifetime benefits leads one more naturally to deal with all aspects of a household's benefits, while at the same time distinguishing growth for the household from growth due purely to changes in the age structure of the population.

As a matter of procedure, other reforms suggested here, such as counting all years of contributions in the benefit formula, could also be implemented in a way that would gradually reduce the rate of growth of both annual and lifetime benefits. Therefore, one would want to amend with the rate schedule in the benefit formula only after many of these other adjustments were made. This amendment would then focus on such goals as insuring adequate minimum incomes and determining maximum lifetime benefits, rather than simply changing a single parameter by itself, such as the index under which the benefit schedule is adjusted over time.

Reset the Tax Rate.   Among tax options, raising the tax rate might be justified by those who desire to maintain a larger Social Security system. In general, however, it is a less efficient revenue-raising option than expanding the tax base to include untaxed compensation (e.g., Social Security taxation of employee benefits). There is no magical aspect to any one particular tax rate, nor can the issue of rates be ignored. Once an appropriate benefit level is set and the tax base is adequately defined, some tax rate is necessary to pay for the program. The aging of the population in the twenty-first century also means that the relative needs of the aged, at least as a group, will rise.

Move Toward a Double-Deck System and the Funding of Retirement.
Almost all the reforms heretofore discussed are aimed primarily at getting Social Security back into balance and improving the equity and efficiency associated with particular groups such as working spouses.

Social Security generally does not save taxes paid, with the rare exception of a modest build-up between now and the retirement of the baby-boom population, and one could argue that even that modest saving is offset by higher deficits in the rest of government operations. As discussed by Bosworth (chapter 10), some believe that our retirement systems, therefore, should go beyond the reforms discussed and deal in particular with another issue: an increase in retirement saving. Closely related are proposals to convert Social Security into a system where the welfare or redistributive aspects are cleanly separated from those parts where one receives a market rate of return on contributions. Different types of proposals along these lines are sometimes called double-deck or two-tiered approaches. Once the separation is achieved, the goal is often to put the market rate-of-return contributions into a funded system that retains the savings. Remaining contributions could still be used to support some minimum benefit or a welfare-related benefit.

There are a variety of ways that these goals might be achieved, but the issues are more complex than can be covered in this chapter. If monies of current workers are put into their individual funds, for instance, then those monies are not available to support the retirement incomes of the current elderly. At the extreme, if current workers must fund all of their own retirement and support all the Social Security of current retirees, then these workers have to pay twice for one benefit.

One related possibility is to stack a layer of funding on top of most or all of the current Social Security system, for instance, through mandated private pension plans. A small portion of the current Social Security tax could also be designated for funded accounts associated with each individual. This type of reform also needs to be coordinated with rules and allowances related to private pension plans, including attempts to make private pensions portable.

3. Reforms to Avoid

Some options cannot be justified easily by appeal to any principle, that is, they can be discarded as "wrong" ways to proceed.

Do Not Remove Cost-of-Living Adjustments. As a prime example, eliminating or significantly paring cost-of-living adjustments (COLA's) tends to have its harshest impact on those for whom the system was built in the first place: those who are truly old and in need of income. If lower levels of benefits are sought, it would be better to cut back on benefits initially granted than upon the benefits received by the oldest and poorest part of the elderly population. Of course, there still is decent justification for moving to a better measure of cost-of-living changes, as the CPI is regarded by many economists as an inferior measure of general price changes.

Do Not Apply an Annual Means-Test for Cash Benefits. The Social Security benefit formula already operates as a partial means test on the basis of lifetime earnings; when lifetime earnings go up for future beneficiaries, their lifetime Social Security taxes will increase much more than will their lifetime Social Security benefits. At the same time, the income tax is a partial means-test on the basis of annual income; higher income implies increasingly higher taxes. Some would add yet another means test to Social Security, one that would convert it to a welfare-like system where all benefits were eliminated at higher incomes. This additional test would violate a number of rules of horizontal equity and efficiency, as can be seen in the following example.

Suppose taxpayers A, B, and C have equal lifetime incomes, but only A and B save for retirement, and B gives his savings to his children. Taxpayer A is rewarded for her prudent behavior by being forced to transfer money to both B and

C. This is patently unfair. Efficiency violations are severe also. By saving more, the taxpayer decreases the transfer that she will receive at retirement; by working more, she pays more taxes to support others but not to provide for her own retirement.

Annual means-testing ignores the logic behind mandating participation in a Social Security program. An analogous logic justifies requiring every car driver to buy automobile insurance or everyone to purchase health insurance. The case here is one of horizontal equity and efficiency. Mandating insurance purchase effectively requires everyone to contribute to their own benefits when they can afford it, thereby reducing the extent to which others must cover their needs through later welfare-like payments. Annual means-testing that reduces Social Security benefits to zero ignores this fundamental relationship: if individuals are mandated to participate in a retirement scheme, then some amount of retirement benefits should be made available to them.

Do Not Subject All Earnings Without Limit to Social Security Taxation. Among very high income individuals, raising the limit on taxable earnings tends to increase benefit levels far beyond where they need to be to deal with retirement needs. Although rare, it would be possible for the wealthy to receive six- and seven-figure Social Security benefits in a year. Raising this particular limit also creates great disparities between capital income earned by the self-employed and capital income earned through ownership of stocks, bonds, and savings accounts. Only the former is subject to Social Security tax, thus creating a discrimination against self-employed individuals employing capital in their businesses.

Do Not Put Social Security on a Pay-as-You-Go Basis with the Tax Rate Always Raised to Fill Any Gap.   Social Security's long-term balances can always be solved in theory by letting the tax rate rise whenever there is any additional gap between benefits and taxes. For instance, if the retirement age is not indexed for life expectancy, then pay-as-you-go tax rates would set into law continual increases in tax rates to deal with longer life spans. If tax rates must rise, such as to deal with the swelling needs of the elderly when the baby boomers retire, then the choice should be made explicit and the taxes devoted specifically to a particular problem. Taxes should never be designed to rise automatically to deal with failure to put benefits on a sustainable path. Prescheduled, automatic, tax rate increases for only some budget programs additionally puts other government programs at a disadvantage in the budgetary process. As already noted, the government's overall tax collections in recent years have been increasingly devoted to expenditures on the elderly, even while their poverty rates have fallen and those of children have risen.

CONCLUSIONS

By getting back to basics and examining fundamental principles underlying a Social Security system, it is possible to establish guidelines for how future reform should proceed. Social Security's past successes have come in no small part when policy-makers have paid adequate attention to its long-term viability and balance. Today the system must be brought back into balance, but in a way that expands society's ability to respond appropriately to future, often unknown, needs of all the population (not just the elderly).

Universal agreement, of course, is almost impossible with respect to every proposal, and few readers will agree with every suggestion I or anyone else makes. Because Social Security is so important to all members of the public, they must be made aware of the trade-offs that are required. Workers today, for instance, must come to understand that Social Security is likely to be there for them tomorrow; nonetheless, as a factual matter, the growth rate in promised benefits must be pared, tax rates raised on their children, or both. Common ground, I believe, will be found by those willing to base their choices on a consistent application of fundamental principles to the inevitable reform of one of America's most successful social programs.

ENDNOTES

1. For greater detail on many of the issues discussed here, see Steuerle and Bakija (1994) and Steuerle (1994). The author would like to thank Jon Bakija and Gordon Mermin for their research assistance, as well as Ann Guillot for her help in the preparation of this manuscript.

2. Speaking more generally of society, Douglas North stated that "it is adaptive rather than allocative efficiency which is the key to long-run growth. Successful political/economic systems have evolved flexible institutional structures that can survive the shocks and changes that are part of successful evolution" (1994, p. 367).

3. Marmor, Cook, and Scher (chapter 12) point out that the ratio of workers to young and old nonworkers does *not* fall; however, the young require fewer government resources and are most likely to represent an investment in the future.

4. This point can be displayed through a simple example. If tax rates are increased from 0 percent to 1 percent of income, they reduce a taxpayer's income by 1 percent. If tax rates are raised from 99 percent to 100 percent, they reduce the taxpayer's remaining income by 100 percent. The latter increase, therefore, is viewed as more likely to affect or distort work and other behavior, even though, in the absence of changes in behavior, both increases initially appear to raise the same amount of revenues.

5. The example here assumes an interest rate of 2 percent plus inflation.

6. For Old-Age and Survivors insurance, the net transfers peaked for those retiring about 1980 under the assumption of a real interest rate of 2 percent. High-income individuals turning 65 in 1980 received higher net transfers than high- or low-income individuals of any other generation before or since.

7. Note that this is not the life expectancy of the wife, but the number of years, on average, until both members of the couple would be expected to die. Although men usually die at younger ages, many live to older ages than their spouses, thus raising the average longevity for any member of the couple above that for a woman alone.

8. According to Robert J. Myers (1993a), former chief actuary of the Social Security Administration, the 1939 Social Security formula was set so that a worker earning the average wage and retiring at age 65 today would receive, in the absence of changes in wages and price levels, a replacement rate of approximately 40 percent. This is almost exactly the same replacement percentage as determined under the newer formulas. Of course, longer spans of participation, or more years of Social Security contributions, were also designed by formula to lead to higher Social Security benefits as the system matured past its beginnings.

9. In an insurance context, the increased cost is due not only to longer lives after age 65, but to an increase in the percentage of individuals who live to 65 and qualify for benefits.

10. See the contrasting view expressed in Marmor, Cook, and Scher (chapter 12).

11. Social Security will only give credit for the "best" 35 years of work. Additional payments of taxes in other years yield no benefits whatsoever.

12. The wages in this example are "indexed" or relative wages.

13. As a technical matter, for a typical worker retiring on OASI, the current formula essentially takes earnings subject to tax for the top 35 years and then divides by 35 to determine an average wage (to be more precise, the calculation is based upon months). Counting all years of contributions requires nothing more than adding in all contributions into the numerator. The denominator can be left at 35 or raised to any other number. The interaction between this measure and the ultimate design of the benefit formula, which need not be held constant, would eventually determine the level of benefits and their distribution. My concern in this proposal is not really with either of those latter concerns: the overall level of benefits or their distribution through means of the benefit formula. Instead, it is to insure that all contributions apply at the margin toward benefits.

14. As noted, there are a variety of ways of achieving this goal of minimum benefits. One would need to look beyond old Social Security schedules of minimum benefits or current designs of special minimum benefits. Note also that recent reforms have worked to reduce the extent to which Social Security benefits went to federal, state, and local government workers with generous pension plans but only a few years under Social Security coverage. These reforms also attempted to limit spousal benefits going to these workers whose contributions to government retirement systems substitute for payments to Social Security. These provisions would also need to be examined in determining any new minimum.

15. This proposal has been advocated for many years by Professor Timothy Smeeding of Syracuse University.

16. For a discussion of the arguments for and against the test over the years, see, for example, Schulz (1995, chap. 4) or Steuerle and Bakija (1994, chap. 9).

17. Technically this could be achieved by wage indexing the first brackets in a (probably revised) Social Security benefit schedule, but price indexing the last bracket. However, there are a variety of other ways that the goal could be achieved.

18. The causes of cost increases are multiple, but relate in part to the design of both public and private health insurance systems. The removal of incentives for individuals to care about the cost of the care they receive, for instance, leads to excessive demand for health care and the maintenance of higher prices for health-care providers.

CHAPTER 18

Bridging the Centuries
The Case for Traditional Social Security*

ROBERT M. BALL WITH THOMAS N. BETHELL

INTRODUCTION: THE FOUR PILLARS OF RETIREMENT INCOME

For 60 years, the United States has been pursuing a retirement income policy based on four pillars:

- Social Security
- Supplementary employer-sponsored pensions
- Individual savings
- A safety-net program—now federal Supplemental Security Income (SSI)—to bring the most impoverished of the elderly, blind, and disabled up to a minimum standard of living

Each pillar complements the others; each is either directly provided for through tax revenues or encouraged by favorable tax treatment. With the enactment, 30 years ago, of Medicare, the federal health insurance program for the elderly and disabled, a fifth pillar was added to the system. By far the most important parts of this multi-pillar approach to retirement income are Social Security—contributory, wage-related, and now covering just about everyone—and Medicare.

Although this chapter focuses on Social Security, the relationship of that program to the entire complementary retirement income network must be kept in mind. Little will be said here about Medicare, for example. Obviously, however, a secure retirement is impossible without protection against the unpredictable costs of health care, and although cash benefits can meet the regular and recurring expenses of daily living, only insurance can guard against the costs of a major illness.

Social Security is now just about universal; 92 percent of those aged 65 and over are receiving benefits, with another 3 percent eligible to do so when they retire. In contrast, private pensions add a supplement for only 43 percent of retired private employees (Beller and Hinz, 1995) or, in other words, for about a third of all those

---

Some of this material has appeared in similar form in the last section (of which Mr. Ball was principal author) of the report of the Advisory Council on Social Security 1994–96.

over 65.[1] Career government pensions for federal civilian and military and for state and local employees cover 85 percent of those workers (U.S. Department of Labor, 1994), and most of those plans are built on Social Security coverage.[2]

The individual savings rate in the United States is low, and, except for home ownership, accumulated savings at the time of retirement are not usually sufficient to make a significant contribution to continuing retirement income. Of those 65 and older with any income from savings, 30 percent receive less than $500 a year; only 10 percent receive $15,000 or more (Grad, 1994).

When a complementary system of retirement income programs was first envisioned in the early days of Social Security, it was frequently described as a "three-legged stool," omitting from the discussion (and the leg count) the then federal-state system of public assistance (subsequently replaced by SSI) that provided a residual safety net.

The three-legged stool was always more of a dream than a reality. When it was first formulated in the years of the Great Depression, there were very few pension plans covering workers in private industry, and the savings available to most retirees were even more meager, relative to their needs, than today. The hope was that pension plans and savings would develop into strong complements to the Social Security system. But the stool has always been wobbly, with two short legs, and remains so today.

1. Private Pensions

Private pension coverage has remained at about 50 percent of full-time private-sector workers since the mid-1970s, but the percentage covered by defined-benefit plans has declined, while the percent covered by 401(k) defined-contribution plans has greatly increased. This shift makes payment in retirement—and the amount of payment—less certain. Under 401(k) plans, lump-sum payments are common when a worker changes jobs or retires or when a company changes hands, but these lump sums may or may not be used to provide an income stream over the period of retirement. In 1994, workers over 40 receiving such lump-sum payments reported that somewhat less than half of the payments received were put into retirement savings, investments, or other savings, with the rest going to current spending (Beller and Hinz, 1995).

It may be that 50 percent coverage and 43 percent benefit receipt are the high-water marks of private pension effectiveness, although, depending on how they are counted in the future, 401(k) plans could increase or decrease these numbers. In any event, it is clear by now that most low-wage and many moderate-income workers will not receive substantial protection from private plans.

Even for those who do have such additional private pension protection, there is another problem: inflation. At the beginning of retirement the average replacement rates (the extent to which retirement income replaces pre-retirement earnings) are nearly as high for private pensions as for Social Security. But, unlike Social Security, the private pension replacement rates, measured in terms of purchasing power, decline rapidly because of the lack of inflation protection. Only about 30 percent of private pension recipients report that they have ever received a cost-of-living increase, and among those who have, the increases have averaged only 2.1 percent a year. In 1994, private-sector workers who began receiving annuities in 1990–94 had real replacement rates averaging 22 percent, but for those who began in 1985–89, the rate had slipped to 19; for 1980–84, to 15; for 1975–79, to 11; and for those beginning prior to 1975, to 9. By comparison, Social Security replacement rates for those receiving both Social Security and private pensions remained approximately the same (25 percent) throughout the period (Beller and Hinz, 1995).

To improve the three-tier system, Social Security benefit levels, at a minimum, need to be maintained, and private plans need to be extended and improved. One step that would help a great deal would be for the Treasury to issue indexed bonds that private plans could use to provide inflation protection (Munnell and Grolnic 1986). And our low rate of individual savings needs much improvement.

2. The Peaceful "Revolution"

Social Security keeps some 15 million people above the poverty line, and millions more from near-poverty. As recently as 1967, the poverty rate among the elderly was two and a half times as high as among the rest of the population; Social Security has been the key factor in bringing the rate down to below 13 percent (on a par with rates among other adults). Without Social Security, about half of the elderly would have incomes below the federal government's rock-bottom definition of poverty (Grad, 1994).

But Social Security is much more than an antipoverty program. Because Social Security benefits are not means-tested, those who are relatively well-off are able to add other income to Social Security, providing a level of living in retirement that is not too far below what they were used to while working. That is why most people approve of Social Security and are willing to pay Social Security taxes—not only to protect their parents and grandparents today, but also to build a foundation for themselves and their families tomorrow.

In a relatively short time, our multi-pillar system of retirement-and-health protection, anchored by Social Security and Medicare, has brought about nothing less than a peaceful revolution in the way that older people, in particular, are treated in this country. But as Berkowitz's review (chapter 2) of the evolution of Social Security highlights, the *method* has been anything but revolutionary; Social Security emphasizes and reinforces the conservative values of work, saving, and self-help.

The future of Social Security depends on its continuing popularity. There is no constitutional guarantee of benefit payments, as there is for interest on government bonds.[3] Nor are the benefits backed to any significant extent by accumulated funds, as is required of private insurance. Under present law, then, the future of Social Security depends almost entirely on the continued willingness of workers and voters to pay for it.

In all probability this is a much stronger guarantee than it may appear to be. Workers in the future, like workers today, will very likely continue to see Social Security as essential protection for their parents, themselves, and their children, protection that, for most people, cannot be duplicated by private savings or private pensions. Moreover, since the personal stake in Social Security increases as people grow older, any coolness toward the program among the young and unmarried tends to dissipate over time. No one stays young, and few retain forever the views held in one's youth. The polls have consistently shown that most people are willing to pay more for Social Security and to support other changes, if necessary, to keep the system viable. Clearly, public support for the program reflects broad support for the basic principles of the Social Security system.

THE NINE PRINCIPLES OF AMERICAN SOCIAL SECURITY

While discussions of the basic principles that govern Social Security often involve somewhat different terminology, most experts emphasize common features. For example, Steuerle (chapter 17) refers to "need and progressivity" as a basic principle, and Thompson and Upp (chapter 1) suggest that Social Security seeks to "redistribute towards lower-wage workers." Similarly, Myers (1993b) emphasizes the importance of providing an "adequate floor of protection." This chapter discusses this particular aspect of Social Security under the principle of redistribution (see principle 6 later).

Regardless of how one states them, however, there are nine principles that define the scope and purpose of Social Security and account for its accomplishments. Social Security is universal; an earned right; contributory and self-financed; wage-related; not means-tested; redistributive from the higher- to the lower-paid; wage-indexed at the time of benefit determination; inflation-proof during the period of benefit payment; and compulsory.

1. Universal

Although our Social Security system is virtually universal in scope today, it developed slowly. Many workers, including all self-employed people, were left out of Social Security at first (largely for reasons of administrative difficulty, for the goal has always been universal coverage). As Berkowitz (chapter 2) discusses, coverage has been extended gradually over the years, and today 96 out of 100 jobs in paid employment are covered. About 141 million persons will make contributions in 1996. They are buying more than retirement protection alone. Ninety-eight percent of children under 18 can count on the protection of a monthly cash benefit if a working parent dies, and about 80 percent of men and women aged 21–64 can count on monthly cash benefits in the event the wage earner has a severe and prolonged disability (U.S. Social Security Administration, 1996). And now that the program is just about universal, workers are guaranteed that their protection will follow them from job to job.

2. An Earned Right

Eligibility for Social Security benefits, and the benefit rate, are based on individuals' past earnings, a fact that sharply distinguishes Social Security from welfare and that links Social Security to wages, private pensions, and fringe benefits. Thus, as Thompson and Upp note (chapter 1), Social Security is more than a statutory right, it is an *earned* right: you qualify for benefits only if you have worked in covered employment or are the dependent or survivor of someone who has.

3. Contributory and Self-Financed

The fact that workers pay into the system via earmarked deductions from their wages reinforces the concept of an earned right and gives the contributor a moral claim on future benefits above and beyond statutory obligations. As the Supreme Court has said, Social Security constitutes enough of a property right to protect benefits against arbitrary or capricious reduction.

And Social Security is self-financed. Unlike many foreign plans, our system is financed by dedicated taxes deducted from workers' earnings (matched by employers, with the self-employed paying comparable amounts) plus dedicated taxes on benefits and, of course, the interest earned on the accumulated trust funds. The entire cost of benefit payments plus administrative expenses (which are only eight-tenths of one percent of benefits) is met without support from general government revenues.

This method of financing has given the system considerable protection against having to compete with other programs in the general budget. The fiscal discipline in Social Security arises not in the context of the unified federal budget but rather in the need to ensure that the total earmarked income for Social Security is sufficient to meet the entire cost of the program, both short-run and long-run.

Unless a program is specially protected, the federal budget process is inevitably competitive, determining on a year-to-year basis how to allocate spending for various purposes, depending on the income available. Social Security, on the other hand, is a very long-range program—people are paying today toward benefits that may not be due for 30 or 40 years—and should not be part of an annual allocation process. There would be no security in a retirement system that changed benefits, those being paid now or those payable many years hence, because of short-term budget considerations. Social Security's obligations and contributions can certainly be changed and have been. But the process of doing so requires careful decision making, long lead times, and consistency with the internal principles of the program. In budgetary parlance, Social Security should be "on the table" when the total obligations of the government are being considered for the truly long run, but its contributory and self-financing nature should keep it "off the table" in year-to-year budget negotiations.[4]

The contributory nature of the program not only helps to protect against benefit cuts but also guards against excessive liberalization. The public understands that every increase in benefits must be financed by increases in contributions by workers, and a balance is achieved, more or less automatically, between the desire for more protection and reluctance to pay more.

All in all, though, the contribution rates have reached a level where Congress and other policymakers are very reluctant to propose substantial increases.[5] At the same time, there has been relatively little objection to the current rates on the part of workers. Since they overwhelmingly approve of the program, they have been willing to pay for it—much more willing, in recent years, than they have been to support general, unspecified tax increases.

4. Wage-related

As the discussion by Thompson and Upp (chapter 1) also implies, relating Social Security benefits to earnings not only enhances the concept of benefits as an earned right, as discussed, but recognizes that the benefit level needed to achieve income security is related to one's standard of living. There would be little security in retirement if everyone, regardless of wide variations in living standards achieved during working years, received the same benefit based on a budgetary minimum standard. Under Social Security, the higher-paid get higher benefits, while, at the same time, the lower-paid get more for what they pay in (as discussed later).

5. Not Means-tested

In contrast to welfare, eligibility for Social Security benefits does not depend on the beneficiary's current income and assets; nor does the amount of the benefit. This is the crucial principle that allows—in fact encourages—people to add savings to their Social Security benefits and makes it feasible for employers and employees to establish supplementary pension plans. It is this principle, in short, that makes Social Security the key pillar in a multi-pillar retirement income system.

As Kingson and Schulz note (chapter 3), the absence of a means test is inextricably tied to the principle of Social Security as an earned right, with eligibility and benefits determined by past earnings and contributions, rather than by having to demonstrate individual need. As a result, the benefit structure of Social Security is almost the opposite of a welfare program. In Social Security, the higher one's past wages have been, the higher the benefit, because the system focuses on making up for wage loss; in welfare, payments ordinarily decrease as the recipient's wages rise, since the program focuses on meeting basic needs.[6]

6. Redistributive

As many authors in this volume discuss (e.g., Thompson and Upp in chapter 1 and Steuerle in chapter 17), one of Social Security's most important objectives is to provide a minimally adequate benefit to workers who are regularly covered and contributing, regardless of how low-paid they may be. If the system paid back to low-wage workers only the amount that they could reasonably be expected to pay for, the nation would require a very large-scale supplement to Social Security—in the form of a greatly increased SSI program or its equivalent—to meet basic need. Without a redistributive mechanism, millions of workers, after paying into Social Security for many years, would nevertheless end up on welfare. This would make the years of contributing to Social Security worse than pointless, since the earnings deductions would have reduced their income throughout their working years without producing in retirement any income above the welfare payment.

Accordingly, as Moon (chapter 4) and others explain, the Social Security benefit formula is weighted to give low-wage earners greater protection for what they contribute than is the case for highly paid earners. Likewise, those with dependents receive greater protection than those without. Social Security thus departs from the equity principle of strictly relating benefits to wages in favor of benefit adequacy, a principle that is at the core of the program's objectives. This principle sharply distinguishes Social Security from compulsory individual savings plans that produce benefits based directly on what each person has paid into the individual account.[7]

The weighted benefit formula plays an important role in the complementary relationship between the Social Security system and supplementary private pensions and savings, making it possible to achieve, up and down the earnings scale, the traditional retirement goal of reasonably replacing past earnings. Lower-paid earners, who generally cannot accumulate substantial savings, need to have benefits that replace a relatively high proportion of the earnings that they and their families lived on before retirement. The higher-paid are more likely to have pension coverage and to have been able to set aside substantial savings on their own, so when all sources of income in retirement are combined, there is a rough equivalency in replacement rates. There are many exceptions to this generalization, of course, but the point is that redistribution is a deliberate part of Social Security's design and vital to its relationship with the other pillars of our national retirement policy.

The highly progressive benefit formula favoring the lower-paid is the reason why Social Security is such an important antipoverty program. The formula, however, is not quite as redistributive as it appears. Differing mortality rates by income class show that those with lower incomes are, as a group, likely to die sooner, thus reducing their lifetime benefits (a fact that is sometimes used to argue, incorrectly, that minorities are disadvantaged under the program). But even after taking this differential into account, the program is still strongly redistributional (Goss, 1995a).

The program is of course redistributive in another even more fundamental sense, moving money for workers and their families from a period when they have work income to periods when they have lost all or a major part of their wages. Smoothing out lifetime income somewhat by shifting income from wages to the periods of retirement or disability, or to the family after the death of a wage earner, is the most basic program objective.

7. Benefits at Retirement Indexed to Prior Wages

Social Security benefits will be higher for workers retiring in the future than for workers retiring today. Because benefits are kept up-to-date with wages, future benefits will reflect any improvements in productivity and, thus, in the general standard of living, not just the maintenance of purchasing power.[8] Without maintaining this correlation to wages, Social Security benefits would decline over time in terms of replacing recent earnings and would thus become much less adequate in helping workers maintain previously attained levels of living.[9]

8. Protected Against Inflation

Social Security benefits, once they begin, are inflation-proof thereafter, an important principle that, except for federal retirement plans, is generally unavailable elsewhere. State and local plans, at best, offer only a partial guarantee; private plans offer none at all, nor are they obligated even to try. As noted earlier, some private plans do provide *ad hoc* increases, but they almost never keep up with inflation.

In the case of Social Security, the goal of keeping up with wages and prices had been part of the program for decades before an explicit provision was added to the law. The program was financed so as to allow for such updating from time to time, and this was accomplished, albeit with some lag. Now the legislative provision assures a timely update.

The cost-of-living adjustment (COLA), by maintaining the purchasing power of Social Security benefits, actually makes those benefits increasingly valuable to people as they grow older. The longer we live, the more likely we are to deplete whatever personal savings we may have accumulated. But our expenses continue and, particularly in the case of health care and other services, are likely to increase as we age.[10] For many older people the COLA saves the day.

No one, of course, would deliberately design any retirement plan with the objective of offering less protection as recipients get older. But a basic flaw in private plans is their inability to provide guaranteed protection against inflation.[11] The value of these plans thus declines over time. Although the COLA is not inexpensive, the fact is that the longer people live into retirement, the more they need its vitally important protection.[12]

9. Compulsory

Social Security requires all of us, provident and improvident alike, to contribute to our own future security. The program aims at preventing poverty before it occurs, rather than making payments to alleviate poverty after the fact. Among other things, this principle works to reduce the need for public assistance. In contrast, a voluntary plan would allow the improvident to escape their share of paying for their own future retirement needs, leaving the community as a whole to pay for them through some safety-net program like SSI.

Americans, by and large, believe in trying to help pay their own way, thereby earning benefits as a matter of right. They feel at least as strongly that other people should do the same thing. A compulsory program assures that this takes place. Compulsion, as Thompson and Upp point out (chapter 1), also makes it possible to provide for a redistribution of protection from the higher- to the lower-paid, and to avoid the problem of adverse selection that would occur if individuals were allowed to decide when and to what extent they wished to participate.

To the extent that Americans continue to understand these nine principles, at least broadly, it seems reasonable to expect them to remain popular and to govern our Social Security system in the future as in the past. As is true of most broad principles, if pushed to the extreme, some will be in conflict with others. For example, the redistributive principle soon merges into the traditional argument over equity versus adequacy. Thus, many policy debates in Social Security boil down to the relative weight to be attached to particular principles.

CONFLICT OVER BENEFIT LEVELS

Throughout the entire history of Social Security in the United States, essentially the same controversy over its proper boundaries has been at the bottom of most arguments about specific changes. On the one hand, what is the proper borderline with relief and assistance? On the other hand, where should the lines be drawn between Social Security, private pensions, and savings?

At the borderline of relief and assistance, the issue is one of the appropriateness of the social insurance approach in particular situations. Insurance against wage loss can go a long way toward meeting many, but not all, needs. How far should one reasonably go in a contributory, wage-related system, for example, in trying to meet the needs of those with only a weak attachment to the labor market? At what point does it become patently unfair to regular contributors as a whole (thereby jeopardizing their support) to skew the system to pay relatively high benefits not only to the lowest-paid but also to irregular contributors?

If redistribution is pushed too far, the wage-related character of the system is lost—and with it much of the basis for Social Security's popularity. Consequently, although there has been some consensus among Social Security supporters that steady full-time workers and their dependents should get high enough benefits that means-tested supplementation is unnecessary, few would argue for such a standard for those with only intermittent attachment to the system. This view leaves a significant supplementary role for SSI. (There are, of course, those who disagree, believing that the primary goal of Social Security should be to end poverty for all participants.)

At the borderline of private pensions and private savings, the major issue becomes: How far should a compulsory government system go and how much should be left to private effort? Social Security can arguably furnish protection more effectively than private plans (because of its low administrative costs, protection against inflation, portability, etc.), and can do so in ways that simultaneously promote important social goals. But the system does require the dedication of a portion of workers' earnings to one fixed set of purposes, that is, replacing earnings generally lost at retirement or because of the disability or death of a wage earner. How much is enough? How much should be left to workers to set their own priorities?

As Moon points out in chapter 4, benefits under Social Security are quite modest. As of January 1995, the average retirement benefit was $8,400 a year for individuals and $14,100 for workers with spouses. But the range is large, as would be expected in a wage-related program.[13] A key point, however, is that in a compulsory program requiring people to save for their retirement, as opposed to a voluntary retirement plan, one has to decide how much is justified, as compared to allowing individuals to save on their own for retirement or other purposes, or to spend currently. There is a public interest in helping people attain a retirement income reasonably related to previous earnings, but there is clearly a limit to the proper use of compulsion. In providing for replacement of about one-fourth of recent earnings for the higher-paid, we may have gone about as far as we should go for them, allowing for supplementary arrangements for private pensions and private savings on a voluntary basis that can provide the rest.

Over the years this issue has divided Social Security supporters. Workers themselves, at least as represented by organized labor, have in the past pushed for expansion of Social Security's role, to provide more adequate benefits at all earnings levels; while employers usually have resisted benefit increases. In recent years, workers, who are also deeply concerned about the cost of health insurance, have largely stopped advocating expansion of the cash benefit program. As for the insurance industry and others engaged in the business of private pension and benefit planning, they have given strong support to the general concept of Social Security and to universal coverage, but have also understandably pressed to keep benefits relatively low so that they could sell private retirement coverage on top.

These two arguments over borderlines—one at the bottom concerning social insurance's role in preventing poverty and the specific assistance programs designed to address poverty once it has occurred, and the other at the top between social insurance and supplementary private protection—will never be completely resolved. They don't need to be. Some will press for a bigger role for Social Security, and others will try to put on the brakes. Some will think that the program has gone too far in helping low-income people, and others will feel that still more can be done without endangering public support for the program.

OTHER BENEFIT ISSUES

However, aside from broad philosophical arguments over how much should be done by each of the four pillars of our retirement income system, there are equity problems in the Social Security benefit structure that need to be addressed. In particular, as Holden discusses in chapter 6, benefit levels for married couples are high relative to other benefit categories. Paying benefits 50 percent higher for a married couple than for a single retiree, as is currently done, probably overstates the cost of operating two-person, versus one-person, households; a one-third differential might be more appropriate.

Such a reduction in the spouse benefit would also help with the current perception that married women get little for their own contribution because, in effect, their benefit rate is whichever benefit is higher—as a spouse or as a worker. With this change, the majority of married women in the future would receive benefits as workers.

As Holden also discusses, the benefit rate for divorced women is the same as for a spouse living with a marriage partner, although it goes to a person living alone and is frequently inadequate in that situation. The benefit for the divorced spouse is important for women who have spent most of their lives maintaining a household rather than working in paid employment, yet the present benefit takes no account of the homemaker's contribution to family income.

Holden also notes the potential for introducing a system of "earnings sharing" into Social Security. However, there seem to be insurmountable transitional and technical difficulties in moving the entire Social Security system to an earnings-sharing basis.[14] On the other hand, the concept of earnings sharing at divorce (that is, combining earnings during the time of marriage and crediting one-half to the Social Security account of each) should be carefully explored. Canada has taken this approach, seeking to rectify a situation that results in a benefit that is entirely inadequate for one person living alone.

It might also be desirable to mitigate the penalties that wage earners now suffer when they leave the labor market to care for young children. Special treatment of the child-care years could be considered, protecting the level of a worker's benefit just as today's benefit levels are protected during periods of a worker's total disability.[15] Benefits for young families are also in some cases inadequate, including benefits for disabled children and for a sole surviving child. And the 1979 Social Security Advisory Council made a good case for modifying the benefit formula (by stepping up the last bracket from 15 percent to 20 percent) to improve the system for the higher-paid.

Except for the reduction in spouse benefits, these changes would cost more money. Given the perception that tax increases, even for Social Security, are likely to be unwelcome, it may well be that for now we should concentrate on restoring the long-term balance between income and expenses for the present program. It is true that benefit levels are insufficient for many of the very old, especially older women, who account for such a high proportion of the very old. This is the biggest unsolved problem in Social Security's benefit structure. Otherwise, the current benefit structure seems sensible for a basic system. One can argue for somewhat less here or somewhat more there, but by and large the program is doing well what it was designed to do.

FINANCING

But is the current program too expensive? Some seem to think so. However, Myers (chapter 13) and others maintain that only modest changes are needed to bring the program into financial balance. The Trustees of the Social Security funds estimated in 1995 that income (the sum of the revenue sources plus interest on accumulated funds) will exceed expenses each year until 2020. As Myers discusses in greater detail, the trust funds will then start to decline as investments are cashed in to meet the payments coming due. The trustees estimate that although 75 percent of costs would continue to be met from current contribution rates, in the absence of any changes full benefits could not be paid on time beginning in 2030 (Board of Trustees, 1995).

Expressed as a percent of payroll, the deficit over the traditional 75-year projection period is 2.17 percent. In other words, if contribution rates had been increased in 1995 by one-plus percentage points each on employers and employees, the system would remain in balance over the long-range period.

There is little political support today for actually increasing the rate by that much or that soon. But as Bosworth (chapter 11), Gramlich (chapter 10), Kingson and Schulz (chapter 3), Myers (chapter 13), and Steuerle (chapter 17) all indicate, there are many other ways to bring the program into long-run balance without departing from its basic principles or undermining the economic well-being of future workers and program beneficiaries. Some would rely more heavily on benefit reductions (such as retirement age increases and formula changes) and others on payroll tax increases. Still others would rely heavily on trust fund investment options and other changes not classified as either benefit cuts or contribution rate increases. The conclusion from their discussions and from the discussion in this chapter, however, is not that any one change is essential but rather that *the long-range expenses and revenues of the system can be brought into balance without drastic cuts in benefits or major increases in Social Security taxes, and without compromising the basic purposes and principles of the present program.*

As examples of possible policy directions, let us consider two approaches that would bring Social Security into actuarial balance: one based on partial advance funding and the other on pay-as-you go financing.

Both approaches are consistent with, and could build upon, extending coverage to the one-fourth of full-time state and local employees not now covered under voluntary compacts between the states and Social Security. This is the last sizable group of workers (about 3.7 million) not covered under Social Security, and it is only fair that they, like everyone else, should be part of our national Social Security program.[16] They would generally gain from being under Social Security's inflation-proof provisions and from coverage that would be combined with work outside of their current state or local employment. And spouses would benefit from Social Security's automatic protection, which is not provided for under those state plans where workers can decide to take higher benefits rather than have survivors' protection.

For Social Security, this extension of coverage saves money over both the short and long term, partly because contributions will be received for many years before benefit payments have to be made. The system also gains over the long term because, under present law, a high proportion of these state and local employees will get Social Security benefits anyway, based on other work; and, since not all their employment would be included for contribution and benefit purposes, under the weighted benefit formula their benefits will be high in relation to the contributions paid, notwithstanding the fact that this arrangement is intended for only the low-paid. By extending coverage, they will be treated like all other workers at their full earning level. This extension of coverage saves the Social Security system 0.22 percent of payroll over the long term (Goss, 1995b).

Another change that can be advocated as a matter of fairness is to tax Social Security benefits as other contributory defined-benefit pension plans are taxed. (This change is also consistent with either partial funding or pay-as-you go financing.) The application of this policy to Social Security would be to make Social Security benefits taxable to the extent that they exceed the employee's contributions.[17] Dedicating the proceeds of the tax on benefits to Old-Age, Survivors, and Disability insurance, as was done when Social Security benefits were first taxed, would reduce the long-run imbalance by 0.62 percent of payroll (Goss, 1995b).[18]

As a result of these two changes called for by the standard of fairness, the estimated long-range Social Security deficit is reduced from 2.17 percent of payroll to 1.33 percent. When combined with the correction to the Consumer Price Index announced by the Bureau of Labor Statistics in March 1996 (the CPI determines the COLA), the deficit is reduced to 1.04. The significance of this remaining deficit, and of proposals for eliminating it, varies depending on the financing method that is adopted. The two broad options—partial funding and pay-as-you-go—are discussed next to illustrate how the projected financing problem might be further addressed.

1. Partial Advance Funding

As of October 1, 1995, Social Security had a reserve of approximately $483 billion. This seems large, but in fact was equal to only 138 percent of the expected benefit payments for 1996, an amount just about sufficient for a contingency reserve (U.S. Social Security Administration, 1996). In the event of an unexpected increase in costs, a reserve of this size would tide the system over until the Congress could make appropriate changes in financing, but it contributes very little to meeting the cost of future benefits.

Under present law, reserves will build to $3.3 trillion in 2020 before they start down. This is more than enough for a contingency reserve. Because it is soon dissipated, however, it does not make much of a contribution to the financing of future benefits. What we have now is not quite pay-as-you-go, but it is also not a reasonable plan for partial funding. The fund builds up for about 25 years and then is used up over the following 10 years.

This funding pattern does not make a great deal of sense. A buildup followed by a drawdown could be defended as a way of financing the increased number of retirees accompanying the aging of the baby-boom generation *if* the costs of Social Security were expected to drop after the baby-boom retirees are replaced by the smaller generation that will follow them into retirement. But that is not the scenario. The cost of Social Security does indeed build to a new plateau as the result of the baby-boom generation's retirement, but the cost then stays at this high level (and even rises somewhat) because continuing increases in longevity will result in having to pay benefits longer, offsetting the drop in the number of retirees.

If we plan to build much more than a contingency reserve, it would make sense to maintain it so that earnings on the fund would make a significant contribution to the long-range balance. This is the method that private pensions follow over the shorter period (usually 30 to 35 years rather than 75) that they use in attempting to balance income and outgo.

However, relying on earnings from a substantial fund buildup as an important part of long-range financing raises the question of investment policy to a degree that it has not been raised before. With a contingency reserve, how the funds are invested doesn't make much difference, so there has been little challenge in the past to the long-standing policy of investing the trust funds almost exclusively in Treasury special obligations (which pay interest equal to the average interest on all the outstanding long-term debt of the United States).

With a large earnings reserve, however, it *does* make a big difference how the money is invested. If, for the first time in the program's history, an earnings reserve of substantial size is actually allowed to build up, the traditional investment policy would seem to be unduly conservative (as Bosworth discusses in chapter 10).[19] As the fund increases, it would be preferable—and still prudent—to increase the investment yield by putting a portion of the fund, such as 40 percent, in private equities. This could be done at minimum risk of political interference by requiring passive management of investments indexed to a broad market portfolio, under the guidance of an independent and expert board charged with selecting the appropriate index and portfolio managers.[20] Such a policy, although still conservative, would considerably raise the return on Social Security investments. A contingency reserve equal to 100 to 150 percent of the next year's outgo would, at the very least, be kept in government funds at all times, so the desired rates for equities would be reached gradually.

"Partial advance financing" is a phrase that covers any buildup beyond a reasonable contingency reserve and then maintenance of such a fund long enough to make a significant contribution to long-term financing. One argument for such prefunding is that we should have the baby-boomers themselves pay more of the costs of their retirement, as compared to increasing the contribution rates for the smaller generation that follows.

This is entirely feasible. Quite modest benefit reductions, if put into effect within the next few years in conjunction with additional state and local coverage and changes in the taxation of benefits, would build a large fund that, when coupled with increased earnings under the new investment policy, would completely eliminate the long-term Social Security deficit. This could be accomplished, for example, by lengthening the number of years over which average wages are computed by three or four years (see Table 18.1).

Additional changes have been suggested, including reducing the cost of benefits still more by changing the benefit formula or by further raising the age at which full benefits are first payable. While some experts disagree (see, for example Myers, chapter 13 and Steuerle, chapter 17), it may be undesirable to change the retirement age further before we have had any experience with the change from 65 to 67 that will take place under present law (instituted over the 2000–2027 period). First, the impact falls disproportionately on lower-paid and blue-collar workers, since they are generally least able to work longer (Sammartino, 1987). Second, we don't really know to what extent jobs will be available for those who want to postpone retirement. Third, we aren't sure that the basic rationale for the change is reasonable; that is, we aren't sure that because people are *living* longer and because some groups of older people may be healthier, most people can necessarily be expected to work longer. Perhaps the most that should be done now is to study what happens under the present retirement age provision as it gradually becomes effective before taking any further steps in the direction of increasing the first age at which full benefits are payable.[21]

Many other options are available.[22] Whatever changes are made, however, contribution rates for Social Security should be increased only modestly. Contribution rate increases could then be reserved largely for the Medicare Hospital Insurance

TABLE 18.1 One Approach to Bringing Social Security's Long-Range Revenues and Expenses into Balance.
(All Figures Shown as Percentage of Payroll)

OASDI deficit over 75 years as projected by 1995 Trustees' Report	2.17
Changes to reduce this long-range deficit, and their impact:	
Extend coverage to full-time state and local employees not now covered under voluntary compacts between states and SSA	−0.22
Tax Social Security benefits to the extent that they exceed what the worker paid in	−0.62
Extend the period over which average wages are computed from 35 to 38 years (resulting in an average 3% reduction of benefits for future beneficiaries)	−0.28
Correction of CPI (CPI − 0.21)	−0.29
Less adjustment for effect of interaction of above changes: 0.04[a]	
Improve Social Security's earnings by gradually investing 40% of funds in private equities	−0.82
Resulting OASDI balance over 75-year period	+0.02

Source: Stephen C. Goss, Supervisory Actuary, Office of the Actuary, U.S. Social Security Administration, Communication to author, April 2, 1996.

[a]The impact of a proposed change may be increased or decreased somewhat when combined with another. For example, a tax on Social Security benefits will have a reduced yield when benefits are reduced an average of 3 percent, as in the proposal to extend the averaging period.

(HI) Program. Medicare, after all, is just as important as cash benefits to income security, and Medicare is in need of shoring up. As currently financed, the HI program is expected to be able to continue paying full benefits on time for only a few more years, although further application of cost controls could postpone the day of reckoning until 2010. At that time, however, the surge in the Medicare-eligible population begins, and a considerable restructuring of HI will almost certainly be needed, including contribution rate increases or benefit cuts.

Medicare Part B (insurance for doctors' bills) also needs attention. At the very least, the general revenue subsidy, now three-fourths of the system's financing, ought to be taxed and the proceeds used to hold down the size of future premium increases and general revenue payments. Adding three times the Medicare premium to gross income for income tax purposes would tax the subsidy simply and fairly. The larger point, in any case, is that however its financing problems are addressed, Medicare is a crucial part of Social Security, and financing for OASDI must take Medicare into account.

2. Pay As You Go

Basically, Social Security has been financed on a pay-as-you-go basis. Historically there have been contribution schedules in the law that would have built up earnings reserves as a way of financing some future benefit costs. But as Berkowitz (chapter 2) notes, these schedules have always been changed before their effective date, and such reserves have never been allowed to accumulate. Thus, payments into the funds have been just about enough over the years to cover benefits and administrative costs and to leave a contingency reserve. From 1937, when contributions to Social Security began, through 1994, Social Security had collected approximately $4.9 trillion and paid out roughly $4.5 trillion, leaving $436 billion in the contingency reserve at the beginning of 1996 (U.S. Social Security Administration, 1996). Under present law, the funds are beginning to build beyond what is required of a pay-as-you-go system, but most of the program's future costs would be met on this basis, just as in the past. This is a safe enough way to finance Social Security, although not necessarily the most desirable way. Pay-as-you-go is unacceptable for private arrangements, because any particular enterprise or insurance company may go out of business and full funding is necessary to assure payment. With Social Security, on the other hand, the continued existence of the federal government can be assumed, and its taxing power can provide continued income for benefit payments.

It is not clear whether we will continue on a pay-as-you-go basis or turn to partial advance financing as discussed. If the philosophy of pay-as-you-go is retained, the most likely outcome between now and shortly after 2010 would be to shift part of the OASDI rate to Medicare. Such a shift would establish a contingency reserve for Medicare and put both programs on a pay-as-you-go basis.

It is not now feasible to predict what Medicare pay-as-you-go rates would be after, say, the next 15 years or so, assuming that between now and then there is a strong drive for cost containment—and perhaps the implementation of a national health plan. However, a reasonable pay-as-you-go schedule for OASDI, assuming the implementation of the coverage and benefit changes previously discussed, is shown in Table 18.2.

**TABLE 18.2. OASDI Pay-as-you-go
Contribution Rate Schedule.**

Years	Rate
2013–2019	6.40
2020–2029	7.05
2030–2049	7.60
2050–2059	7.85
2060–2070	8.20

Source: Stephen C. Goss, Supervisory Actuary,
Office of the Actuary, U.S. Social Security
Administration.

Either pay-as-you go or partial advance financing will work for Social Security. But partial advance funding as previously described will avoid the need for a contribution rate increase over the 75 years for which estimates are usually made. It is somewhat doubtful that a pay-as-you-go schedule rising to over 8 percent could be enacted now, so that pay-as-you-go financing might invite rather substantial benefit cuts instead. Moreover, if the rest of the budget is brought into balance later on without counting Social Security surpluses, the Social Security buildup would increase the national saving and investment rate and make it easier to support the retirees of the future because the future pool of goods and services would be larger (Aaron, Bosworth, and Burtless, 1989).

Investing some of Social Security's reserves in equities will give Social Security beneficiaries a fairer return for the contribution that the trust fund build-up makes to the nation's economic well-being. When a dollar of Social Security reserves is accumulated and the federal government borrows it rather than going into the private market, a dollar of private saving is released for private investment. The gain to the nation from the trust fund accumulation, therefore, is the return on all private investment, not only in equities but for all physical capital. This return has been at the rate of about 6 percent. The proposal for investing 40 percent of the trust funds in stocks attempts to recover only part of this return for Social Security—projecting, under reasonable assumptions, an overall return to the trust fund of 4.2 percent.

Also of considerable importance is the fact that pay-as-you-go will increasingly look like a bad deal for younger workers, who will pay much more for the same or, if the normal retirement age is advanced, for significantly reduced protection. Even under partial advance funding, young workers in the future can argue that they could do better making their own investments. This argument can be met convincingly only if Social Security increases its investment return by putting part of the build-up in stocks. For the long run, this too is an important reason to shift from pay-as-you-go to partial advance funding, with some of the funds invested in equities.

In every generation, by definition, a redistributional system like Social Security, viewed as a closed system, will do less well for the higher paid than a system that does not redistribute. This may not be the case, however, if one looks at Social Security in combination with the Supplemental Security Income (SSI) program. For the higher paid, whatever is lost under a weighted benefit formula will be offset to a considerable extent—perhaps wholly—by reduced reliance on SSI's means-tested supplement, which, of course, is supported by progressive taxes. The point is that those with the lowest incomes must either be subsidized under a social insurance approach, as is done today, or maintained directly. Either way, the cost will necessarily fall on the well-off, but a social insurance subsidy is both more orderly and efficient as well as more humane.

In addition to bringing the program into long-range balance, no matter how this is accomplished, it would also be desirable to include in the law protection against the possibility that the present long-range estimates understate the cost. As the assumptions governing the estimates change over the years (as they certainly will, reflecting new information on birthrates, mortality rates, immigration, and real-wage growth), forecasts will change. Later projections of the cost of the present program may turn out to be less than now predicted, or they may be higher. In the latter case we should have a way of adjusting the system without triggering the kind of public disillusionment that inevitably accompanies reports that the system is underfunded. One way to guard against this is to more than meet the system's needs, under present assumptions, by scheduling another contribution rate increase of, say, one percentage point for employees and employers in the 2050–2060 period. If, at some point in the future, changing assumptions show the system to be more costly than present estimates, the final rate would provide a cushion, and if a larger cushion were needed at some point, the effective date of the higher rate could be moved up. If not needed to make up a shortfall from changes in the estimates, this increased rate would be enough to finance the system far beyond the customary 75 years, whereas the pay-as-you-go rate of 8.2 percent in 2070 would need to continue to rise in later years.

WILL SOCIAL SECURITY IN THE FUTURE BE A GOOD DEAL?

Until recently, just about every Social Security beneficiary got much more out of the system than he or she paid into it, plus interest, because contribution rates were low during much of the working lives of those now receiving benefits. With contribution rates currently at levels close to what will be required over the long run, this advantage has been disappearing. Faced with the prospect of being treated less generously than those who came before, some young people have concluded that Social Security will not be a good deal for them. Although an individualized test of "money's worth" is not the most important criterion in evaluating a social insurance system, it is nevertheless important that young workers see their generation as being treated fairly (see Chen and Goss, chapter 5).

In fact, by moving to partial advance funding and investing a portion of the funds in private equities, as discussed above, Social Security can continue to be a good deal for today's and tomorrow's young workers, even if not as good a deal as for their predecessors. Investing 40 percent of the trust funds in private equities would increase the real rate of return from 2.3 percent to 4.2 percent (Goss, 1996a). This has the effect of substantially improving the contributions-to-benefits ratio for younger workers and future generations.

Moreover, in examining questions about Social Security's value—to individuals or to society as a whole—we must always ask: "Compared to what?" Can Social Security's total package of benefits be provided better or more cheaply some other way?

The answer is no.

The fact is that Social Security continues to be a good deal for both today's and tomorrow's workers because the protection it offers can be made available to everyone and because Social Security can deliver that protection at lower cost than anything else. It will also continue to be a good deal because of its protection of parents and grandparents, protection that is of great importance to working people and their children. And Social Security will also continue to be a good deal in the future, as in the past, because it contributes values to society that may not be readily measurable but are still critically important.

As Chen and Goss point out in chapter 5, in delivering a package of benefits, Social Security has two great advantages: extremely low administrative costs and universal coverage. The advantage in administrative costs is very large, with Social Security spending only eight-tenths of one percent of benefit payouts on administration, compared with 10 to 15 percent or more for most private insurance plans. And, as Thompson and Upp (chapter 1) note, as a result of universal compulsory coverage Social Security is able to provide important protection—both disability insurance and retirement and survivors' benefits—without adding extra premiums (as is necessary with private insurance) to guard against adverse selection and the risk of worse-than-expected claims experience.

Also, as previously noted, Social Security supplies a valuable protection that simply isn't available privately: inflation protection, automatic and complete. And Social Security also provides life insurance and disability protection, which many people could not buy privately.

In point of fact, exact comparisons between Social Security and private insurance are impossible, because there is no close approximation of Social Security's package of protection available in the private insurance market. Social Security's inherent advantages, including its universality, its ability to follow the worker from job to job with a defined benefit, and its low administrative cost, make it a good buy from generation to generation, compared to anything else that a worker could purchase. Perhaps the pertinent comparison, however, is not with private insurance but with compulsory private savings plans, as proposed by privatization advocates. This issue is discussed at the end of the chapter.

Private insurance and savings plans have had one cost advantage over Social Security; because they are prefunded, they are able to realize substantial investment returns. But this advantage will diminish if Social Security is at least partially prefunded in the future, as discussed earlier. In any case, however, Social Security's overall advantages outweigh the prefunding advantage of private plans. The cost may be close when looking solely at future benefits for a contributing worker, but when we add the current value of family protection for parents and grandparents as well as for the worker's immediate family, along with the societal values from having a Social Security system, it becomes quite clear that Social Security is indeed a good deal for each generation in turn.

But comparative analysis can be pushed too far. Public and private efforts have different goals, and they work well in a complementary relationship. It isn't that

Social Security should be taking the place of private effort or vice versa. The point is simply that there is no cheaper way of carrying out the functions of a basic Social Security system, and there is no better way to add supplementary protection to this basic system than with private plans. Each is the best way to do what it does; both are a good deal.

As Reno and Friedland's (chapter 11) review of the survey and focus group data shows, young workers, even those who think that Social Security will not be there for them, strongly support the current program. They appreciate that it is a mechanism for sharing with all other working families the burden of caring for the elderly and those with disabilities. They appreciate that because of Social Security and Medicare, no one family has to bear alone what could be the huge cost of caring for parents who are sicker than average or who outlive their savings. They understand that, as with all insurance, families pooled together are protected by paying for only the average risk (American Association of Retired Persons, 1990; Friedland, 1994b).

Because Social Security and Medicare spread the risk and because of their nearly universal coverage, relatively few older retired people have to move in with their children to make a go of it. Similarly, millions of married couples are spared the pain of periodically having to arrive at mutually acceptable decisions (not to mention decisions that must also be acceptable to other relatives) about how much of the family income should go to supporting elderly parents and grandparents, rather than being used for themselves and their children.

Social Security also provides current family protection by providing ongoing insurance against loss of family income due to death or disability. Among the 43 million Americans receiving monthly benefits in March 1995, nearly 3 million were children, mostly children of deceased workers, and some 5 million adults were being paid because of disability. (For more information on disability insurance, see the discussion by Mashaw in chapter 7.)

Social Security provides $12.1 trillion in life insurance protection, an amount that exceeds, by $1.3 trillion, the combined value of all private life insurance policies of all types in force in the United States in 1993. The protection for young families is very substantial. For example, a 27-year-old couple with one or both persons earning average wages, with two children, one aged two and one less than a year old, have survivors' protection worth $307,000. Disability protection for the same family amounts to $207,000.[23]

And Social Security has other values that are frequently overlooked. For example, Social Security is, as previously noted, keeping 15 million people out of poverty and millions more from near-poverty. Without Social Security, taxpayers would have to pump far more money into welfare.

Moreover, Social Security acts as an automatic stabilizer whenever the economy runs into difficulty. Ongoing regular monthly benefit payments help maintain the purchasing power of very large groups of consumers who, in the absence of Social Security, would be the first to stop buying. Instead, they continue to participate in, and contribute to, the economy.

Social Security is a blend of reward for individual effort and, at the same time, perhaps our strongest expression of community solidarity. Through Social Security we recognize that "we're all in this together," with everyone sharing responsibility, not only for contributing toward their own and their families' protection, but also for the protection of everyone else, present and future. Basing benefits on past work and wages reinforces efforts to work and save, and emphasizes an earned right to benefits, with special emphasis on protecting the lower-paid and those with dependents. It is hard to imagine more broadly valuable characteristics, but unfortunately the value to individuals of living in a society that has such a plan cannot be readily quantified, and what can't be measured is often overlooked. Yet all these values are part of the answer to the question of whether Social Security will continue to be a good deal. Viewed in terms of total value, and in comparison with what could be purchased privately, the answer to that question is clearly Yes—now and for future generations.

WHY THE PESSIMISM ABOUT THE FUTURE OF THE PROGRAM?

Given the financial viability of Social Security (discussed before), it is distressing to find so little public confidence in the program's future. As earlier chapters explained, when the reasons are explored, what becomes clear is that most people are mainly reacting to what they are told by the media, as opposed to making an assessment based on knowledge of policy issues and choices (Friedland, 1994b).

The media correctly report that the program, *as is*, cannot continue to pay full benefits forever, but far less attention is paid to the equally important fact that relatively minor course corrections can keep the ship well clear of the rocks that we can see on the far horizon. Instead, news reports and commentators tend to exaggerate both the size and imminence of the deficit and the difficulty of restoring balance. And when the talk is of the trust funds running out of money, young people assume there will be nothing left for them. It is not well understood that under the present pay-as-you-go financing, support for the system in later years comes mostly from contributions in those later years and not from assets stored in the trust funds.

Commentators are apt to point to the decline in the number of contributors per retiree as evidence that workers increasingly face an "impossible burden of support." And, as Marmor, Cook, and Scher (chapter 12) argue, this fact is often highlighted by some political activists and organizations (e.g., the Concord Coalition, discussed later) as part of their political strategy. But the media and such activists do *not* note that this change in the retiree/worker ratio has not happened suddenly, does not come as a surprise, and has been fully factored into proposals to bring the Social Security program into balance over the long run.

Nor, as a rule, do media commentators consider Social Security in context. In estimating the ability of a work force to support dependents, retirees are not the only dependents to be taken into account. What really counts is the *total dependency burden*, that is, the ratio of *all* nonworkers, old *and* young, to the active workers who produce the goods and services on which all must depend.[24] And, as Table 18.3 indicates, the number of dependents per 1,000 workers will never be as high as it was in 1965, when the baby boomers were children. As economist Frank Ackerman has observed, "If we could afford to live through the childhood of the baby-boom generation, we can afford to live through their retirement" (Ackerman, 1984).

Looking at the total dependency burden does not solve the political problem in-

TABLE 18.3. Total Dependency Burden, 1990–2070.

Year	Dependents per 1,000 Workers (both those 65 and over and those under 20)
1965	946
1990	700
2010	653
2040	787
2070	823

Source: Board of Trustees. (1995), Table II.H1.

volved in meeting the needs of a growing number of elderly in part by reallocating resources previously going to the support of children, particularly at a time when government programs for poor children are so inadequately funded. Yet the basic economic point is unmistakable: the picture of the worker of the future staggering under an increasing load of dependents is out of focus.

Clearly, as Reno and Friedland (chapter 11) report, another reason why people are uneasy about Social Security is that, while they may have some understanding of the basic principles and benefits, they don't have a very tangible sense of their own stake in the system. They have only a vague understanding of the kinds and amounts of protection they currently have.

Over the years the Social Security Administration has tried in many ways to increase public understanding of the value of Social Security protection to the individual, but it has never been particularly successful. There is, however, cause for hope. As Reno and Friedland discuss, Senator Daniel Patrick Moynihan of New York succeeded, a few years ago, in getting a provision added to the Social Security law that will greatly improve earners' understanding of their Social Security protection. With new technology making it possible, the Social Security Administration in a few years will be regularly sending account statements to every covered worker. This should be a great step forward in improving workers' knowledge of the protection they have under Social Security—and the more they know, the more certain it is that the great majority will favor continued support of the system.

PROPOSALS FOR FUNDAMENTAL CHANGE

Despite the fact that the present Social Security system can remain strong and solvent for the long run without major benefit cuts or contribution rate increases, confusion about the program's future has created a fertile climate for proposals for fundamental change. These usually focus on means-testing or privatization.

1. Means-Testing

The means-testing or income-testing approach has most recently been promoted by the Concord Coalition, led by investment banker Peter Peterson and former senators Warren Rudman and Paul Tsongas. The Concord Coalition contends that Social Security should not be paying benefits to people who can get along without them, and they propose to start reducing benefits for all families whose total incomes, including Social Security benefits and the cash value of Medicare protection, exceed $40,000 a year.

For the purposes of this discussion, the details of the Concord Coalition plan are not especially important, because the proposal would, of course, be modified in the legislative process if it ever got to that. What *is* important is the key principle: relating the amount of one's benefits to one's income at the time of eligibility.

No retirement system, public or private, presently takes this approach. And among retirement systems, the coalition would apply it exclusively to Social Security.[25] Moreover, although private pension plans enjoy special tax treatment, the coalition plan does not treat this public subsidy as a benefit. The target of the coalition's high, even confiscatory, "tax" on benefits is limited entirely to a defined group of explicit federal benefits, particularly Social Security and Medicare.

Of all the changes proposed for Social Security, this is the worst. First, the incentives are all wrong. Its message to young people, for example, is: "If you are a saver, and because of your prudence are able to attain a healthy retirement income on your own, you will be penalized—your Social Security benefits will be cut." A change of this sort would make individual provision for retirement counterproductive for many workers, since saving more would merely reduce the Social Security payment for which they would otherwise be eligible.

Equally important, such a system would make *everyone's* benefits vulnerable, not just the benefits of those above the arbitrary threshold initially selected. As Kingson and Schulz point out, once the Social Security system departs from objective eligibility criteria based on prior work and prior contributions, there is no good stopping point. When political leaders want more money for other purposes, why not change the exemption to $20,000 instead of $40,000—or peg it to the poverty level?

With the Concord Coalition's plan in place, nothing would remain of the two core principles that now protect Social Security against arbitrary reduction: (1) its universality, which assures that almost everyone has an important stake in the system; and (2) its relationship of benefits to past earnings and contributions so that payments are an earned right, not just a statutory right.

Changes along the lines proposed by the Concord Coalition would give higher-paid workers a very powerful incentive to get out of Social Security. Those who anticipate high incomes in retirement would know that their incomes would disqualify them from drawing more than token Social Security benefits, and it is hard to imagine them willingly continuing to contribute to such a system. If they succeeded in getting out, however, the increased burden on middle-income workers, that is, the burden of supporting a redistributional system, would rapidly become intolerable.

At the very least, the program would have to drop the weighted benefit formula. But it is this redistributional formula that makes Social Security so crucial for the lower-paid. Without it, benefits would be too low to provide minimum security, and they would have to turn to welfare for help. Welfare payments would then raise the incomes of such households to the allowed maximum, and low-income workers would get nothing extra for their Social Security contributions. At that point, those at both ends of the economic scale would have every reason to be dissatisfied with Social Security. Means-testing could trigger the disintegration of the whole Social Security plan and make welfare our only national system.

This proposal may not be a serious threat—if it is well understood. It is hard to imagine people willingly supporting a system to which they contribute over a working lifetime in anticipation of receiving retirement benefits, only to have those benefits withheld because they saved too much. Means-testing of benefits supported by general revenues is one thing, but the public would find such a test unfair in a program supported entirely by the dedicated taxes of the intended beneficiaries and their employers. A means-test or income test would change the basic character of Social Security; benefits would no longer be an earned right, nor would the program prevent poverty ahead of time and serve as the base on which everyone can build additional income.

2. Privatization

There is also considerable interest in privatizing part or all of Social Security. This has been stimulated by enthusiasm in some quarters for privatization as a panacea for the perceived ills of "big government," and, in part, by reports of the success of Chile's compulsory savings plan, which is gradually replacing that country's highly unsatisfactory social security system. Admiration for Chile's plan has been reinforced by a World Bank report advocating a similar approach for other countries (World Bank, 1994).

The idea is to compel private savings for old age that would be invested by the individual saver and held in an individual account. In the partial privatization schemes being discussed in the United States, funds for such savings would come wholly or partly from reducing Social Security contributions or benefits. Claimed advantages include, most importantly, a greater return on savings and, thus, higher benefits without higher contribution rates. And supporters argue that a savings account bearing the worker's name would be more popular than a social security plan in which the rules about contributions and benefits are all quite mysterious to the average individual.

The strengths and weaknesses of the idea vary, depending on whether the forced savings plan is intended to *supplement* Social Security or to *substitute* for the program, in whole or in part. In the first instance—that is, if the basic Social Security plan is retained and remains reasonably adequate for both low-wage workers and those with above-average earnings—the issue becomes mainly whether compulsion is justified to force people to save for retirement benefits above the Social Security level. It has always been considered desirable to *encourage* supplementary protection through tax incentives for private pensions and individual savings, but the additional step of making supplemental plans compulsory is controversial.

It is not at all certain that low-wage earners gain by being compelled to save more (or, what is the same thing, having to take more of their compensation in the form of deferred pension income promised for old age). Perhaps, instead, they should continue to be free to spend more to meet current needs. Higher-paid workers, too, may well have current needs that take higher priority than adding to basic income protection in retirement. Assuming that everyone has Social Security to meet that basic need, why not let individuals set their own priorities, while continuing to offer them (through the tax code) incentives to encourage additional saving? In recent years, at least, such freedom to choose has made sense to most policymakers.[26]

But how about *substituting* a private savings plan for part of Social Security? Some advocates of privatization (such as the Cato Institute) would go further, completely replacing Social Security with a compulsory savings plan. And some would add a savings plan to the Social Security system, maintaining the present contribution rate but reducing benefits to the amount that can be met by that rate. Most, however, propose taking part of the contribution rate that now goes to Social Security and investing it in personal savings accounts. That is the approach taken in legislation proposed by Senators Kerrey (D-Nebraska) and Simpson (R-Wyoming).

Still another approach, advocated by a group within the Social Security Advisory Council of 1994–96, would go beyond Kerrey-Simpson by replacing current Social Security benefits with a low, flat benefit, and then adding a compulsory private savings account (PSA) plan supported by five percentage points of the current Social Security contribution rate. Although the emphasis in the following discussion will be on these various approaches to partial privatization, much of the discussion applies equally, or even more so, to proposals for complete privatization.

It is important not to confuse the goal of achieving long-range financial balance for OASDI with the goal of establishing individual accounts. The partial privatization proposals have to achieve both goals, but the plans are sometimes presented as if their object was to achieve fund balance for Social Security while also contributing to balancing the general budget. But in fact partial privatization does not help to achieve a balance in Social Security or the general budget. On the contrary, it makes achieving these goals more difficult.

Privatization proponents must first shrink the Social Security program to address the currently projected shortfall (because increasing taxes for this purpose would be inconsistent with their goal of a smaller Social Security system), and then must shrink it again to permit transferring part of the contribution rate to individual accounts. The first step requires cutting benefits about 15 percent immediately, including benefits being paid to current retirees, if balance is to be achieved by benefit reductions only (Goss, May 9, 1995c).[27]

The proposal announced by Senators Kerrey and Simpson in May 1995 provides a good example of what it takes to accomplish both goals and of pitfalls associated with a variety of privatization plans. Their proposal brings the Social Security program back into balance and also shrinks it further so that it can be supported by the remaining contribution rate after the amount going to the individual accounts has been subtracted. The shrinkage would be severe. The benefits payable after the year 2030 would, on average, be 25 to 35 percent lower than those provided by present law, and in some cases would be cut much more. For example, a 66-year-old retiring in 2033 who has earned average wages would have initial benefits cut 26 percent, but because of changes that are also proposed for the COLA, benefits would actually be reduced 35 percent by age 76, and 40 percent by age 86.

By that time, of course, the individual savings accounts would be generating income, but it is difficult to predict the extent to which they would be able to make up for the cuts in Social Security. *Averages* can be predicted, of course, and, over time, *average* retirement income under this approach would in all likelihood com-

pare favorably with the income available under the present system, with its investments restricted to low-yield government obligations. But the actual income for particular people is impossible to determine. All that is known is that the amounts
would vary greatly from individual to individual.

Leaving aside for the moment the question of whether a shift from Social
Security's pooled arrangements to individual accounts is desirable, let us look at
what has to be done to get from here to there. Problems of transition are not merely
details to be worked out later; they are crucial—and daunting.

The biggest transition difficulty is what to do about current retirees and older
workers. Although proponents of privatization have said on occasion that present
retirees and older workers would not be affected by their proposals, this can hardly
be the case. Social Security cannot be stripped of two or more percentage points of
the contribution rate, for example, just because benefits for younger workers would
eventually be reduced. Because Social Security is essentially on a pay-as-you-go
basis, a contribution rate reduction of this magnitude in the absence of a major in-
fusion of income to the system would also require substantial benefit cuts for current retirees and older workers, none of whom would benefit from the individual
accounts. These cuts have to fall on this group because there simply wouldn't be
enough money available after the contribution rate cuts to pay them anywhere near
full benefits.

Proponents of the PSA approach would address this problem by raising the payroll tax by 1.52 percent of payroll. But this approach requires heavy borrowing from
the federal government. The proposed rate increase is sufficient to cover the *average* cost over the next 70-plus years, but would not be adequate to cover costs in
the first 40 years. To pay full benefits to present retirees and those retiring soon
would require borrowing about $1 trillion (in 1996 dollars), thus adding consider-
ably to the national debt for a considerable time. Payback begins 40 years in the future, and is completed 30 years later. This problem could be avoided, but only by
requiring a much higher contribution rate increase—more than 3 percent of payroll.
But that, of course, would be even more unpalatable.

It is true, at least theoretically, that if younger workers prefer, they can pay for
present retirees and older workers in another way. In Chile, the problems of transition to a savings plan are being handled through large, permanent infusions of general tax revenues to pay for a substantial minimum benefit and for credit for past
work under the old social security system. Fortunately for the success of its plan,
Chile had been running large general budget surpluses. In the United States, on
the other hand, this approach would require enactment of a major tax increase or,
in the absence of such an increase, either a sharp reduction of support for other programs beyond what is now required to balance the budget or a substantial increase
in the deficit.

As we try to work out these schemes in practice, we find that, in the absence of
new taxes, it is simply not possible to shift, say, two percentage points from Social
Security to private accounts (as proposed by Kerrey and Simpson, for example)
while protecting the current benefit rights of older people. In practice, partial privatization plans would also have to drastically cut COLAs for present retirees and
older workers and would also have to cut initial benefits, perhaps by moving up the
effective dates for raising the age when workers become eligible for full benefits.

If major benefit cuts for current retirees and older workers are to be avoided, the reduction in contribution rates needs to be at least partly postponed and the money for the individual retirement accounts obtained by *increasing,* rather than cutting, the contribution rate, as is done in the PSA plan. The problem is that with Social Security on a pay-as-you-go basis, the first generation of those covered by these savings plans has to continue to support present retirees and older workers at the same time that they are building their own savings plan. The only way to lessen their burden is to impose truly drastic and immediate cuts for current retirees and older workers. In contrast, plans to bring the program into balance without establishing individual accounts do not need to reduce benefits to current retirees, although a modest reduction, say through an increase in the tax on benefits, may be desirable. The path chosen by Kerrey and Simpson is to cut the COLA drastically. Given the political constraints and the antipathy to tax increases that have characterized the politics of the mid-1980s to mid-1990s, this is the probable route of others who would enact privatization plans. Thus, assessment of the various provisions of the Kerrey/Simpson plan provides insight into problems likely to be associated, to one degree or another, with other privatization alternatives.

Although Social Security's cost-of-living adjustments have been crucial to the program's success, Kerrey and Simpson propose to cut COLAs for present as well as future retirees in two ways: (1) the adjustment is to be reduced by 0.5 percent pending an expert study of how the Consumer Price Index should be redefined, and (2) the size of the COLA for all beneficiaries is limited to that payable to beneficiaries with Primary Insurance Amounts[28] at the 30th percentile from the bottom. (The PIA at the 30th percentile for 1995 is about $540 per month.) The two-thirds of retirees whose PIAs are higher than this amount would receive the same flat COLA. But a capped COLA would no longer come anywhere near maintaining purchasing power—the whole point of having a COLA in the first place.

The financing of the residual Social Security plan is complicated further for younger workers because of the need to maintain protection under Social Security's disability and life insurance program, or, alternatively, to set aside even larger amounts to purchase supplemental private life and disability insurance. This, too, is unavoidable, because a slowly accumulating savings plan cannot protect against these risks at younger ages. Until the worker nears retirement, current insurance protection is necessary.

If a savings program is to substitute for an important part of Social Security, before benefits are cut, the savings program should have been operating long enough and at a sufficiently high rate to produce an income stream equal, at least on average, to the part of the Social Security benefit that the worker gives up. This approach is obviously essential in a voluntary scheme and, if not followed in a compulsory scheme, would create deep dissatisfaction.

Privatization advocates, therefore, propose to have the savings plan open only to those below a given age, with older workers and the already retired continuing under a reduced Social Security system. Several plans propose using age 55 as the cutoff point. But 10 years to retirement age is not long enough to build up much of a savings plan. Accordingly, any Social Security cuts should take place gradually, in close calibration with reasonable expectations about savings accumulation. But this cannot be done if benefits have to be shrunk quickly to accommodate the loss of a part of Social Security financing. In any event, this type of calibration—a gradual reduction in Social Security benefits linked to a gradual increase in savings accounts—would be extremely difficult to explain and extremely difficult for the public to understand, with good reason.

Although major benefit cuts for present retirees and older workers are inevitable in any near-term implementation of a privatization scheme that does not involve increased taxes (and cutting COLAs seems to be the most practical way to do this), there are choices of how to obtain the very substantial benefit cuts that are required for middle-aged and younger workers in what is retained of a residual Social Security system. The choices made by Kerrey and Simpson are indicative of what would have to be done in any privatization scheme financed by cuts in Social Security contribution rates.

Kerrey and Simpson and PSA proponents would gradually increase the age at which full benefits are payable and then, as longevity increases, keep moving the age for paying full benefits automatically higher to preserve the same ratio between average lifetimes after the eligibility date and the number of years before it. Kerrey and Simpson would also (1) decrease benefits for higher earners by reducing the last step in the Social Security benefit formula from 15 percent at the margin to 10 percent; (2) reduce wage indexing for the higher-paid by 2 percentage points a year for 25 years; and (3) reduce spouse benefits from one-half of the worker's benefit to one-third. They would also make three changes supported by many who do not favor privatization: cover newly hired state and local employees now excluded; transfer from hospital insurance to OASDI all the revenues from the taxation of OASDI benefits; and invest a portion of the trust funds in equities.

Not all problems with privatization are transitional. A major difficulty is that, to the extent that funds are shifted to individual accounts, the ability to redistribute income is lost. After all, the whole appeal of changing to a savings plan is to emphasize individual equity, that is, a fair return to the individual saver, rather than adequacy for all. To take part of what the higher-paid save in order to increase what the lower-paid get would seem contrary to the spirit of such a plan.

To meet the objection of the loss of redistribution, some advocates of partial privatization propose raising benefits at the bottom and reducing them at the top in what remains of the Social Security program, keeping the same distribution as now when the residual Social Security plan and the new savings plan are looked at together. But that is not how beneficiaries would view the system. The higher-paid would see a dramatic reduction in what they get from Social Security, making participation in Social Security unappealing to those who earn above-average wages.

This "solution" is thus, in all likelihood, unstable. It is likely to lead to a situation in which the higher-paid press for the right to set aside more and more for their individual savings accounts and less and less for Social Security. Or they will want to get out of Social Security altogether. If that happens, there is no basis for continuing a redistributional wage-related program, such as Social Security is today. Thus, partial privatization could well be the entering wedge for getting rid of Social Security entirely and substituting a private savings system built entirely on individual equity principles, plus a government means-tested program like SSI. This outcome may well be acceptable to some privatization advocates, but, as a matter of public policy, this approach has all the disadvantages of means-testing, as discussed earlier. And the proportion of the population affected could be quite large. A savings plan financed as a percent of earnings will mean low accumulations for low earners (along with higher relative administrative costs for them), forcing many to turn to SSI for help. It was, of course, with the idea of avoiding this kind of problem—people paying all their lives for protection that then turns out to be inadequate—that Social Security's redistributional formula was developed in the first place.

There is also the problem of regulating and limiting the private investment vehicles for the 127 million people with individual accounts.[29] They would be subject to unremitting pressure to invest in one vehicle rather than another. Some fraudulent schemes would doubtless appear, along with others that might only be inappropriately risky. In any event, we could expect a huge surge in marketing efforts and in the employment and deployment of salespeople and advisors. The basic marketing and administrative costs, coupled with the cost of keeping track of the ins and outs of millions of retirement accounts and their investments, would be many times greater than Social Security's current 0.8 percent of benefit payments. The administrative costs of Chile's system are at least 15 percent—"at least" because, according to some studies, they are considerably higher (Diamond, 1996; Myers, 1992a).

There are also questions about whether an account in the name of an individual saver would or should be kept strictly for retirement. The fact is that retirement savings may not always be the most compelling goal of individual savers. President Clinton proposed in 1995, for example, that individual retirement accounts (IRAs)—tax-favored savings accounts presumably reserved for retirement use—be opened up for other purposes, and the Congress seemed disposed to give his and similar proposals sympathetic consideration. And 401(k) plans are available for other purposes—building a first-time house, for example (subject to payment of a 10-percent penalty and taxation of the funds withdrawn). There may be merit in allowing this leeway to savings vehicles such as IRAs and 401(k)s, but one of the advantages of Social Security is that it protects us all against having to support in old age those who would use their basic retirement savings for purposes other than retirement. Without that kind of protection—that is, if individual accounts are not reserved for retirement—the cost of SSI to the general taxpayer goes up.

Somewhat similarly, what is to be done about those who invest their savings badly or who, through no fault of their own, must come into or leave an equities or bond market or invest in annuities at a disadvantageous time? In these cases, too, the general taxpayer would be called upon to help.

Another major difficulty arises from the inherent limitations of a pure savings plan. How is the retiree to determine at what rate to withdraw the savings? Generally speaking, those who are in poor health will want to withdraw at faster rates than those in good health, but, since no one can guess the proper rate for an individual, some will end up short, while others will end up leaving more of an estate than they intended. The chances are that many people will be excessively cautious, to make sure their savings last, just as many will be cautious about how they invest their savings (and thus will not achieve the high rates of return assumed by advocates of savings plans). Others may be inclined to use up their savings in a hurry, figuring that at worst they will then become eligible for the safety-net, means-tested program accompanying the savings plan. And others might try to transfer their savings to relatives, as is done sometimes to establish eligibility for the means-tested Medicaid program.

The ordinary solution for the retiree's dilemma about how fast to spend savings is to buy an annuity, so as to receive a lifetime guarantee of regular payments based on average longevity. But annuities are a conservative investment, reducing the rate of return below what some may have enjoyed during the period of savings accumulation, and this needs to be taken into account in estimating the returns associated with privatization. Moreover, annuities necessarily require a high premium to guard against adverse selection. (As they near retirement, most older workers can guess whether their own life expectancy will be above or below average, with the result that annuity buyers are a relatively healthy group, requiring insurers to assume long life and thus provide fairly low payments.)

Because of this failure of the private annuity market to price products fairly for the average person, some advocates of savings plans would force all savers to buy a government annuity just before reaching retirement age. That would avoid the adverse selection problem, but it would create dissatisfaction among savers with relatively short life expectancies who would have to forfeit much of their accumulated savings by being required to take those savings at the rate appropriate for the person of average longevity.[30]

Given the fact that even professional money managers usually do not, over time, match, let alone beat, the index of a broad-based list of representative stocks, it is doubtful that creating individual investment choices, either within or as a supplement to the regular Social Security program, would be broadly valuable. Most people, including millions of the relatively well-off, have no experience in investing and no demonstrated interest in taking the time to acquire expertise. As a rule, those who do are at the very high end of the income scale, and for them the future well-being of Social Security is in any case a less pressing issue than for the less affluent. With Social Security as a base for retirement income, those with other resources are free to invest them as they wish. Particularly if Social Security increases its return on contributions by investing some of its funds in equities, there seems little reason to add individual options.

In short, privatization of part of our Social Security system would have many difficulties. Chile's plan replaced a system that was beset with enormous difficulties including poor administration, high cost, runaway inflation, bailouts from general revenues, and inequities in its treatment of different classes of workers. Privatization may indeed represent an improvement over what Chile, and some other nations, have had. But social security systems worldwide are not all alike, and a privatized retirement security system for the United States would create many more problems than it would solve.

The present Social Security system with its weighted benefit formula has been designed to leave room for supplementation by private plans and individual savings, and the Social Security replacement rates for the higher-paid cry out for such supplementation. Present law contains several inducements to retirement savings through IRAs, Keogh accounts, private pensions, and 401(k)s. It is not necessary to make room for a compulsory individual savings plan by reducing the one universal plan. Saving, for those who can afford it, is already made relatively easy. What we need to assure is the continuance of an adequate basic Social Security plan, paying benefits as a matter of right, and with the ability to redistribute some of the protection from the higher- to the lower-paid. Social Security is, in short, admirably suited to doing what it is supposed to; we should leave it alone.

CONCLUSIONS

Social Security is perhaps the best example of positive government as Abraham Lincoln defined it: "The legitimate objective of government is to do for a community of people whatever they need to have done but cannot do at all or cannot do so well for themselves in their separate and individual capacities."

As a basic system, Social Security has many advantages over relying entirely on private pensions and private savings. Social Security benefits are kept up-to-date with wages until the beneficiary starts to collect them and then are inflation-proof thereafter. Social Security protection is portable, following the worker from job to job, and benefits are not threatened by the failure of a business or the decline of an industry. And the benefits, defined by law, are not at the mercy of an individual's investment experience.

With Social Security as a base, those who can afford to do so are free to add other retirement income to it, with help from the tax system and without being penalized since there is no means-test. And, with adequate Social Security protection in place, supplementary plans and private savings are free to seek returns that, while comparatively risky, tend to pay off at relatively high rates.

These are freedoms, however, that argue for retaining, as a foundation, a broadly adequate national program such as Social Security that everyone can count on regardless of what may happen to the returns on individuals' supplementary savings. Social Security benefits are not now too high for this purpose, and the levels promised in present law should be retained or, at most, only very slightly reduced. Basic protection is particularly important in a dynamic, risk-taking economy such as ours, where long-established businesses may fail even as new ones are springing up and where whole industries may find themselves quite suddenly in decline. More than most, our economy rewards rapid adaptation to changing conditions. That is one reason why it functions well at the aggregate level, but the more dynamic the economy, the greater the need for individual protection against major economic hazards. We need the individual security that Social Security supplies regardless of mergers, bankruptcies, and volatile employment levels.

Over time, of course, there will be changes in Social Security, as there have been in the past—and as there should be. But the system that has never missed a payday in 60 years of existence is soundly bottomed on principles that, as polls continue to show, have broad appeal for Americans. A system founded and funded on such principles has every reason to endure—and I believe it will, in much the same form and based on the same principles.

ENDNOTES

1. This includes those who have partial protection—at best—under 401(k) plans. As Ferguson and Blackwell (1995) show, 401(k) plans, named for the section of the Internal Revenue Code that permits pretax contributions to a voluntary salary-reduction plan, are far from adequate retirement plans; they are more like employer-encouraged savings plans. To the extent that they are replacing traditional pensions, workers are the losers. From 1984 through 1991, the percentage of workers covered under defined-benefit plans dropped by 13 percent, and the percentage covered by defined-contribution plans other than 401(k)s dropped by 25 percent. Higher-paid workers frequently find 401(k)s attractive, because they allow access to the money before retirement for special needs such as buying a house or meeting medical expenses (albeit with a 10 percent penalty for early withdrawal and with the benefits taxable); they also have a say in how the funds are invested, and can stop contributing as they wish. Moderate- and low-income workers, on the other hand, are rarely able to participate in 401(k) plans. Half of all full-time, year-round workers make $26,700 or less annually and, for the most part, must focus on paying for shelter and food. Thus, while 60 percent of workers making $75,000 or more and employed in firms offering 401(k)s are participating, only 25 percent of those making $20,000 to $25,000 do so. This is in contrast to the more or less automatic coverage of traditional employer-paid pension systems. Moreover, participants often start making contributions late in their careers, frequently too late for meaningful accumulations; more than half of 401(k) participants between ages 51 and 60 have accrued balances of less than $10,000, which is not much for an annuity.

Employers have a strong incentive to promote 401(k)s. Instead of paying around 7 percent of payroll for a defined-benefit plan, they can offer a 401(k) for 1 or 2 percent of payroll (based on putting up 50¢ on each dollar put up by those employees who want to participate). It is not surprising that when the two kinds of plans are run side-by-side, the defined-benefit plan may be allowed to deteriorate and more attention is given to the "do-it-yourself" 401(k) plan. In short, 401(k)s can be valuable savings vehicles—for those who can afford to save—but they are not very good retirement plans.

2. About a fourth of all state and local employees, the only major group not covered by Social Security in the entire United States workforce, are covered only by their own plans. In 1992, of the 14 million full-time state and local employees (defined as those who earned more than $6,000 a year), 3.7 million were not covered by Social Security (estimate by Office of the Actuary, Social Security Administration).

3. As the Supreme Court said, in part, in *Fleming* versus *Nestor*, 363 U.S. 603 (1960): "The Social Security system may be accurately described as a form of social insurance. . . . The 'right' to Social Security benefits is in one sense 'earned,' for the entire scheme rests on legislative judgement, that those who in their productive years were functioning members of the economy may justly call upon that economy, in their later years, for protection." The Court went on to say that Social Security, nevertheless, can be changed by Congress, as long as the changes are not arbitrary. In the words of the Court, "to engraft upon the Social Security system a concept of 'accrued property rights' would deprive it of the flexibility and boldness in adjustment to ever-changing conditions which it demands."

4. Cutting Social Security to "reduce the deficit" or to "balance the budget" is likely to be counterproductive. If benefits were cut more than necessary to bring them into balance with the earmarked sources of support, it is unlikely that the "saving" thus produced would be sustained. The self-financed contributory nature of the program would call for reductions in income to maintain the balance within Social Security, leaving the unified budget just where it was.

5. Social Security contribution rates are currently 7.65 percent of earnings (6.2 percent for Old-Age, Survivors, and Disability insurance, plus 1.45 percent for Medicare), with the employee's contribution matched by the employer. In point of fact, most economists (e.g., Gramlich in chapter 9) hold that workers are contributing the full 15.3 percent, since the employer share actually comes out of what would otherwise be available for higher wages.

In spite of this burden, there appears to be no good substitute for employee payments. The earned right to benefits, the protection of benefit levels, and responsible benefit planning all flow, in part, from the contributory nature of the program. For the lowest-paid families, relief has been provided through the Earned Income Tax Credit: Social Security still gets the contributions, but workers get a refundable credit that offsets the Social Security tax for the lowest paid and phases out as income rises.

6. Although Social Security eligibility and benefit amounts are not affected by current income, some provisions of the program—the benefit formula and taxation of benefits—favor lower-paid over higher-paid people. This has produced some confusion over the use of the term "means-test." Taxing Social Security benefits affects the well-off more than those with lower incomes, and the benefit formula is tilted to favor those with a history of low wages. In this sense, one's "means" do affect how much one gets. But this is not a means-test as used in a welfare program. Perhaps we need different terminology to distinguish between reducing benefits because of current income and assets—the traditional welfare means-test—versus the effect of the income tax on total spendable income or adjusting benefits to the level of wages lost, and therefore to presumed need, as is done in social insurance. Until new terminology arrives, however, it would be less confusing to confine the term "means-test" to its traditional use in welfare programs.

Some observers also confuse the retirement test (or earnings test) in Social Security with a means test. The object of this test is to establish the existence of retirement before paying a retirement benefit; if earnings are below a certain amount, one is treated as retired, with benefits reduced to the extent that earnings exceed the exemption. Because the retirement earnings test does in fact reduce benefits or with-hold them altogether if earnings continue above specified levels, it is sometimes seen (incorrectly, how-ever) as an income or means-test. The main point of difference is that the retirement test is confined to earnings and is intended to test wage loss and retirement when a presumed need arises. It is not a means test in the welfare tradition. The test is now extremely generous, exempting $30,000 a year between ages 65 and 70.

Many previous supporters of the retirement test are now calling for its repeal. The provision is, of course, a disincentive to work in old age and very unpopular with those elderly people who can and want to work. Its repeal would at one time have cost a great deal, but in the 1983 amendments the law was changed so that the "delayed retirement credit," an increase in benefits for every month that retirement is postponed between ages 65 and 70, will later be the actuarial equivalent of taking benefits earlier. Thus, there will be little long-range cost to paying benefits at age 65 whether or not an individual is working. Now that it would cost very little to repeal it, policymakers are facing a real dilemma. If re-peal costs little and the provision is unpopular, why not repeal it? There is still the question, however, of whether the public would react badly to paying Social Security benefits to high-paid executives who just keep working after 65 without any loss of earnings. Perhaps, from the standpoint of public relations at least, it would be better to postpone payment until retirement even if doing so won't save money. At present, full benefits are payable as an annuity at age 70 without regard to the level of current earnings, so the public relations problem described already exists, but to nothing like the extent that it would if the earnings test were repealed.

7. Social Security benefits, and thus the replacement of prior earnings, also vary according to the num-ber of dependents assumed to draw their support from the same wage. Aside from addressing a presumed greater need, this is also a way to keep down the cost of the system. Paying the same to those with and without dependents would require paying single workers more than enough to provide an "adequate" ben-efit for them, because the benefit must also be high enough to be adequate for a family. By departing from strict definitions of equity, the system saves money in paying higher-paid and single workers less than if their replacement rates had to be high enough for the lower-paid and those with dependents.

The progressivity of the benefit formula is very substantial. For those retiring now at age 65 who earned low wages over their careers, benefits equal approximately 58 percent of recent earnings; for the workers who earned average wages, benefits equal 43 percent of recent earnings; for the maximum earn-ers, benefits equal 24 percent of recent earnings (Board of Trustees, 1995). Benefits are 50 percent higher if there is an eligible spouse. The actual benefit formula producing these results in 1995 (the formula applicable to workers born in 1930 and reaching age 62 in 1992) was 90 percent of the first $387 of Average Indexed Monthly Earnings (AIME), plus 32 percent of the next $1,946 of AIME and 15 per-cent of the rest of AIME (i.e., over $2,333); the dollar amounts in the formula are adjusted annually as wage levels rise. The way this formula works is that the very lowest paid, those with AIME of $387 or less ($4,644 per year), got a benefit of 90 percent of AIME; the replacement of AIME at the highest level to which the 32 percent weighting applies (AIME of $2,333 or $27,996 per year) is about 43 per-cent of AIME. (Note: The percentage replacements cited here differ from "replacement rates" used else-where since here benefits are measured in relation to AIME, whereas in replacement-rate calculations they are typically measured against recent earnings, i.e., the last year's earnings.)

8. For example, the worker who has been earning average wages and retires today at age 65 gets an annual benefit of $10,322, equal to 43 percent of recent earnings. A worker who retires at the normal

retirement age in 2010 will get approximately the same percentage of recent earnings (42 percent), but real wages (after inflation) in 2010 will have risen by about 10 percent under the Trustees' Economic Assumptions. Thus, the worker who has earned average wages and retires in 2010 will get 42 percent of this higher wage and, therefore, a benefit in 1995 prices of $11,293 a year, rather than $10,322. Of course, the nominal benefit will be much higher ($20,529, according to the trustees' assumptions), but the increase in real benefits is what is important. (It should be noted that the normal retirement age, now 65, rises gradually beginning in the year 2000, reaching 66 in 2009, where it remains until 2017, thereafter rising gradually to 67 in 2027).

9. Indexing of earnings serves somewhat the same function as relating benefits to the three or five years of highest earnings, a common provision in private pensions and government career plans. The Social Security approach is superior, however, in reflecting the entire working career and past contributions, thereby avoiding the inequity of treating those who move up the ladder more adequately than those who remain in a more or less stable position relative to other workers.

10. Thus, Social Security COLA is not an optional extra that can be readily reduced, postponed, or eliminated outright, as is sometimes suggested by those seeking to make an artificial distinction between the "basic benefit" and the COLA. As Berkowitz (chapter 2) notes, the COLA has been an integral part of the Social Security system for 20 years, and is included in all cost estimates.

11. They could offer such protection, however, if the Treasury were to do the guaranteeing by issuing indexed bonds for pension plan investments, as the Treasury proposed in 1996.

12. Indeed, it is hard to exaggerate the importance of the COLA. To illustrate, consider this example, using a working couple who are relatively well off: One is earning the average wage—$24,825 in 1995—and one is earning a wage halfway between the average and the maximum covered under Social Security, $43,013 in 1995. They plan to retire in 2010, when one will be 62 and the other 65. They figure that in order to maintain about the same level of living in retirement that they had while working, they will require an income that is about 70 percent of their combined earnings. In current dollars, their Social Security benefits will be $38,676 a year, and they are counting on private pensions and income from savings amounting to $49,538 to give them the 70 percent they want. Thus, when they start out in retirement their Social Security benefits account for 43.8 percent of their income, but since Social Security is indexed to prices after retirement, and private pensions and savings are not, Social Security plays an increasingly important role during retirement. When they are 72 and 75, their Social Security benefits will be $61,977, assuming an average inflation rate of 3 percent, but their other income will still be $49,538. After 20 years in retirement, Social Security will represent not 43.8 but 58.5 percent of their total income ($69,853 in current dollars). Social Security benefits will have maintained their value, in contrast to the private pension income that they were counting on to attain their overall goal.

13. For example, the single worker who has in the past always earned maximum wages, and who retired in January 1995 at age 65, would be eligible for a benefit of $14,424 a year.

14. This subject has been explored in depth several times (e.g., Fierst and Duff Campbell, 1988; U.S. Social Security Administration, 1985; Advisory Council on Social Security, 1979).

15. One such proposal would be to freeze the wage record of a parent during a year when there was a child in the home three years of age or younger and the parent had earnings so low as to not qualify for four quarters of coverage (in 1995, annual earnings of under $2,100) so that caring for the child at home could be presumed.

16. Coverage of this group can be gradually extended by first covering the newly hired. This approach, which was used when coverage was extended to federal employees, allows the employing entity to gradually absorb any increasing cost. Setting an effective date a year or two after enactment would provide time to work out the integration of Social Security with the state and local retirement systems and to either reduce or eliminate any new cost to the employer while maintaining the desired level of protection for employees.

17. Present law has special provisions protecting the benefits of persons with low incomes that go beyond the general provisions of the income tax that protect low-income people. Even without these provisions, 40 percent of beneficiaries would not pay taxes on their benefits because of the income tax rules, and ultimately it would be fair to depend on these rules to protect low-income Social Security beneficiaries. These special provisions—no taxes for beneficiaries with annual incomes below $25,000 and for couples below $32,000—should be phased out; there is no good reason for this special treatment.

18. Of the 0.62 percent, 0.31 percent would take the place of the tax on benefits now going to Hospital Insurance, Part A of Medicare. It is a peculiarity of present law that the proceeds from the taxes on OASDI benefits imposed by the 1993 amendments went into the HI fund. This came about because it would have required 60 votes in the Senate to increase income for OASDI, but this was not the case for HI. This change should not be made until later on, say 2010 to 2020, when it may be assumed that there will be substantial changes in Medicare financing in any event.

19. Barry Bosworth is the first in some time to propose a big fund buildup and investment in private equities.

20. Under this plan, the total fund would always exceed the size of the fund expected under present law, and the part of the fund invested in government securities would always be larger than a contingency reserve for a pay as you-go system. The annual stock transactions of the Social Security fund would account for less than one percent of all U.S. stocks, and even in the long run, total investment of Social Security in equities would be expected to be well under 10 percent of the value of all stocks.

The expert board would operate under a statutory fiduciary standard requiring that trust fund investment policy be solely for the economic benefit of Social Security participants and not for any other economic, social, or political objective. The board would have only three functions:

First, the board would select an appropriate passive market index (such as the Russell 3,000 or the Wilshire 5,000) to govern Social Security's investments.

Second, the board would select, through bidding, one or more of the leading passive equity index portfolio managers experienced in serving large institutional accounts. The managers would also have the function of maintaining the proportion of Social Security's total funds at roughly 40 percent in stocks and 60 percent in corporate bonds, instrumentalities of the United States such as Fannie Mae, and Social Security's traditional investment in long-term government obligations.

Third, the board would monitor portfolio management and establish mechanisms to impartially review the overall operation of the plan, periodically considering changes in the passive index or in portfolio management as appropriate.

It would also be necessary to ensure that Social Security holdings cannot be used to influence corporate policies. Perhaps it would be sufficient to simply prohibit the voting of Social Security-held stocks. Alternatively, it might be desirable for the voting of Social Security stocks to automatically be scored in the same proportion as other stockholder votes, or, if a vote on important policy such as changing management requires more than a majority for approval, perhaps the computation of the base to which the proportional vote is applied should be figured without counting shares held by Social Security. Whatever the approach the neutrality of Social Security in corporate policy matters should be established and protected.

Social Security would be the largest but not the first federal defined-benefit retirement system to invest a high proportion of its assets in the stock market. In 1995, for example, the Tennessee Valley Authority had about half of its $3.8 billion in assets invested in stocks; the Federal Reserve System had about two thirds of its $2.9 billion in assets in stocks and the Army/Air Force Exchange had about 80 percent of its $1.9 billion in assets in stocks (U.S. General Accounting Office, 1996.)

None of these federal systems has been politically influenced. Although Social Security's investments would, of course, be far larger, the principle of investing solely for the benefit of participants could be protected by requiring indexing and passive management by professional portfolio managers.

21. For more discussion about the effect of Social Security on work and retirement, see the discussion by Quadagno and Quinn in chapter 8.

22. For example, the proposal to tax Social Security benefits as other contributory defined-benefit plans are taxed includes shifting the proceeds of that part of the tax on Social Security benefits that now goes to Medicare. The proposal is to iron out this peculiar wrinkle when Medicare is refinanced, which has to take place not later than the 2010-2020 period. Although such an allocation of taxes on OASDI benefits seems to make little sense for the long run, many oppose taking anything away from the critically underfinanced Medicare program. If this reallocation is not adopted, it could be made up for in many ways.

One option is to speed up the timetable for establishing age 67 as the normal retirement age by dropping the present hiatus between 66 and 67. Another option that might be feasible over time, with experience, would be to invest much more of the funds in equities rather than the 40 percent sometimes proposed; the payoff from doing so could be large. And, on the contrary, if investment in stocks is not adopted, the program can still be brought into balance with a six-percent benefit cut and a quarter of one percentage point increase in the employee contribution rate ($25 per $10,000 of annual earnings), matched by the employer. The point is not that any of these changes is particularly desirable but that the author's illustrative plan can be changed and still yield the same financial results.

23. Estimates by the Office of the Actuary, Social Security Administration.

24. See Hurd (chapter 14) for an alternative view.

25. Mr. Peterson did include federal pensions in the proposal that he submitted, as an individual, to the Entitlement Commission in 1994.

26. Although mandated universal pensions (MUPs) were recommended by a presidential commission in the late 1970s, the proposal did not generate much support.

27. As discussed earlier, balance can be achieved without anything like such drastic benefit cuts if other steps are taken.

28. The Primary Insurance Amount (PIA) is the monthly benefit payable to a person who retires at the age of first eligibility for full retirement benefits. All other benefit amounts, such as those for a surviving spouse and dependents, are based on the PIA, and are calculated as a percentage of that amount.

29. This is the estimated number of Social Security contributors under 55 in 1998, the year when Kerrey-Simpson would become effective. Of the 145.3 million workers expected to be covered by OASDI in 1998, 126.6 million, or 85 percent, will be under 55 (Goss, 1995c).

30. Most buyers of private annuities buy policies that reduce the rate of payment in order to obtain a total payment guarantee that goes to their heirs if they die before receiving the guaranteed amount.

The PSA plan does give workers who are now young a better contribution/benefit ratio on average than they would get under a plan maintaining approximately the same benefit and contribution rates as the present Social Security system. The latter plan is known as the Maintain Benefits (MB) plan in the council report. However, with the PSA plan, many workers will get less than the average return and have poorer contribution/benefit ratios than what they would get under the MB plan. This is true because the MB plan sets contribution and benefit ratios by law so that the "money's worth" ratios are independent of investment returns. In any event, substituting a PSA approach for the present Social Security system would lose many important values in Social Security not captured by the "money's worth" criterion narrowly defined as the benefit/contribution ratio.

Young workers do somewhat better, on average, under the PSA plan almost entirely because the plan increases taxes substantially and has much more money available for investment than the MB plan. And then the PSA plan assumes that about 50 percent of the proceeds being invested will go into stocks as compared to 40 percent for the MB plan.

If the Social Security fund were built up by the same 1.52 percentage point increase in the payroll tax and 50 percent of Trust Fund accumulations were invested in stock, the MB plan could provide higher benefits and there would be little difference in the benefit/contribution ratio between the two plans.

In addition to the PSA plan, another group within the Advisory Council would establish a compulsory savings account, although a much smaller one, while cutting back on Social Security. This plan does not have a better contribution/benefit ratio than the MB plan, but the more modest appearance of this Individual Account (IA) proposal may win it more serious consideration than the PSA plan. Yet, serious criticism can also be made of the IA approach. The objections, in some cases, are the same as those to the PSA plan, and can be summarized as follows:

(1) It increases the payroll tax to 14 percent, for the one purpose of improving retirement income in old age. This will make it more difficult to solve Medicare's financial problems. If the payroll tax were to be increased by the same amount—1.6 percentage points—and directed to Medicare, this alone would move the estimated date for Medicare trust fund exhaustion from 2001 to 2017, making it quite likely that the rest of Medicare's financial problems could be solved by cost controls, with only modest reductions in protection.

(2) As stated earlier, it is doubtful that it is doing low-wage earners any favor to cut back on Social Security protection and then require them to save money individually for the one purpose of retirement income. Most such workers would be better off being allowed to spend more currently for food, clothing, shelter, and other immediate needs.

(3) All plans that cut back on Social Security and establish compulsory savings plans have in com-

mon the problem of maintaining the savings until retirement. Once the accounts are established under the names of individuals, as "their" money, people will want access to their money in emergencies and for other good purposes, and the Congress will be under great pressure to give it to them.

(4) Because the IA plan does not invest any of the central fund's accumulation in investments paying more than long-term government bonds, there is no way that the central plan could come close to competing with the advertised rate of return of the IA. The IA plan cuts back on Social Security and makes Social Security less appealing than the current system for the above-average earner. Consequently, as with the PSA plan, there is likely to be the same push for raising the amount of individual savings and reducing the role of the central plan.

REFERENCES

Aaron, Henry J. 1966. "The Social Insurance Paradox." *Canadian Journal of Economics and Political Science* 32, No. 3 (August): 371–374.

Aaron, Henry J. 1977. "Demographic Effects on the Equity of Social Security Benefits." In M. Feldstein, ed. *The Economics of Public Service.* New York: MacMillan, pp. 151–173.

Aaron, Henry J. 1982. *Economic Effects of Social Security.* Washington, DC: The Brookings Institution.

Aaron, Henry, Barry Bosworth, and Gary Burtless. 1989. *Can America Afford to Grow Old?* Washington, DC: Brookings Institution Press.

Aaron, Henry J. and Robert D. Reischauer. 1987. "Bite the Deficit, Not Social Security." *Washington Post* (December 16).

Achenbaum, W. Andrew. 1986. *Social Security: Visions and Revisions.* New York: Cambridge University Press.

Ackerman, Frank. 1984. *Hazardous to Our Wealth: Economic Policies in the 1980s.* Boston: South End Press, p. 121.

Advisory Council on Social Security. 1979. *Social Security Financing and Benefits: Report of the 1979 Advisory Council.* Washington, DC: U.S. Government Printing Office.

Advisory Council on Social Security. 1991. *A Message from the American Public: A Report of a National Survey on Health and Social Security by the Advisory Council on Social Security.* Washington, DC: U.S. Government Printing Office.

Altmeyer, Arthur. 1966. *The Formative Years of Social Security.* Madison, WI: University of Wisconsin Press.

American Association of Retired Persons, Research and Data Resources Department and The Polling Report Inc. 1990. *Social Security: An Analysis of Recent Polling Data, January.* Washington, DC: American Association of Retired Persons.

Americans for Generational Equity. 1990. *Annual Report.* Washington, DC: Americans for Generational Equity.

Applebaum, Joseph A. and Dwight K. Bartlett. 1982. "Economic Forecasting: Effect of Errors on OASDI Fund Ratios." *Social Security Bulletin* 45 (January, 1982): 9–14.

Baldwin, Peter. 1990. *The Politics of Social Solidarity.* Cambridge: Cambridge University Press.

Ball, Robert M. 1978. *Social Security Today and Tomorrow.* New York: Columbia University Press.

Ball, Robert M. 1994. Testimony Before the Bipartisan Commission on Entitlement and Tax Reform. (July 15). Reproduced.

Ball, Robert M. 1996. Personal Communication.

Ball, Robert M. and Henry J. Aaron. 1993. "The Myth of Means-Testing." *Washington Post* (November 14): C4.

Ball, Robert and Arthur Hess. 1993. "Reflections on Implementing Medicare." Monograph. Washington, DC: National Academy of Social Insurance.

Barfield, Richard E. and J. N. Morgan. 1969. *Early Retirement: The Decision and the Experience.* Ann Arbor, MI: University of Michigan Press.

Barr, Nicholas. 1992. "Economic Theory and the Welfare State: A Survey and Interpretation." *Journal of Economic Literature* 30 (June): 741–803.

Bartlett, Dwight K. 1990. "Pensions, Public and Private, Whose Burden?" *Benefits Quarterly* 6, No. 2 (2nd quarter): 16–22.

Beller, Daniel J. and Richard Hinz. 1995. *Retirement Benefits of American Workers.* Washington, DC: U.S. Department of Labor.

Berkowitz, Edward. 1983. "The First Social Security Crisis." *Prologue* (Fall): 132-149.

Berkowitz, Edward. 1987. *Disabled Policy: America's Programs for the Handicapped.* New York: Cambridge University Press.

Berkowitz, Edward. 1991. *America's Welfare State: From Roosevelt to Reagan.* Baltimore: Johns Hopkins University Press.

Berkowitz, Edward. 1995. *Mr. Social Security: The Life of Wilbur Cohen.* Lawrence, KS: University Press of Kansas.

Berkowitz, Edward and Kim McQuaid. 1991. "Social Security and the American Welfare State." *Research in Economic History,* Supplement 6: 169–190.

Bernheim, Douglas B. 1994. "The Adequacy of Savings for Retirement: Are the Baby Boomers on Track?" Paper presented at policy forum sponsored by the Employee Benefit Research Institute-Education and Research Fund, Washington, DC, May 4. Reproduced.

Bernstein, Merton C. 1990. "Social Security: Continued Entitlement or New Means Test? An Issue of Program Stability." *Research Dialogues* 26 (July): 1–8.

Bernstein, Merton C. 1995. Personal Communication (March 2).

Binstock, Robert H. 1983. "The Aged as Scapegoat." *The Gerontologist* 23 (April): 136–143.

Bipartisan Commission on Entitlement and Tax Reform. 1995. *Final Report to the President.* Washington, DC: U.S. Government Printing Office.

Blinder, Alan. 1988. "Why Is the Government in the Pension Business?" In Susan W. Wachter, ed. *Social Security and Private Pensions.* Lexington, MA: DC Heath and Company, pp. 17–40.

Board of Governors of the Federal Reserve. 1994. *Balance Sheets of the U.S. Economy* (C.9 release), data diskettes.

Board of Trustees, Federal Old-Age and Survivors Insurance and Disability Insurance Trust Funds. 1994. *1994 Annual Report.* Washington, DC: U.S. Government Printing Office.

Board of Trustees, Federal Old-Age and Survivors Insurance and Disability Insurance Trust Funds. 1995. *1995 Annual Report.* Washington, DC: U.S. Government Printing Office.

Bodie, Zvi. 1982. "Investment Strategy in an Inflationary Environment." In Benjamin Friedman, ed. *The Changing Roles of Debt and Equity in Financing U.S. Capital Formation.* Chicago: University of Chicago Press. pp. 49–64.

Borowski, Allan. 1995. Personal Communication (February 27).

Bosworth, Barry. 1996. "Fund Accumulation: How Much? How Managed?" In Peter A. Diamond, David C. Lindeman and Howard Young. *Social Security: What Role for the Future?* Washington, D.C.: National Academy of Social Insurance, pp. 89–115.

Brown, J. Douglas. 1977. *Essays on Social Security.* Princeton, NJ: Princeton University.

Brown, Robert L. 1995. "Paygo Funding Stability and Intergenerational Equity." *Contingencies* 7, No. 2 (March/April), American Academy of Actuaries: 26–32.

Buchanan, James M. 1968. "Social Insurance in a Growing Economy: A Proposal for Radical Reform." *National Tax Journal* 21 (December): 386–395.

Burkhauser, Richard. 1994. "Protecting the Most Vulnerable: A Proposal to Improve Social Security Insurance for Older Women." *The Gerontologist* 34 (April): 148–149.

Burkhauser, Richard, J. S. Butler, and Karen C. Holden. 1991. "How the Death of a Spouse Affects Economic Well-Being After Retirement: A Hazard Model Approach." *Social Science Quarterly* 72, No.3: 504–519.

Burkhauser, Richard and Andrew Glenn. 1994. "Public Policies for the Working Poor: The Earned Income Tax Credit Versus Minimum Wage Legislation." Washington, DC: Employment Policies Institute.

Burkhauser, Richard, Robert Haveman, and Barbara Wolfe. 1993. "How People with Disabilities Fare When Public Policies Change." *Journal of Policy Analysis and Management* 12, No. 2: 251–269.

Burkhauser, Richard and Joseph F. Quinn. 1983. "Is Mandatory Retirement Overrated? Evidence from the 1970s." *Journal of Human Resources* 18: 337–358.

Burkhauser, Richard and Timothy M. Smeeding. 1994. "Social Security Reform: A Budget Neutral Approach to Reducing Older Women's Disproportionate Risk of Poverty." *Policy Brief* No. 2/1994. Syracuse, NY: Syracuse University, Center for Policy Research.

Burkhauser, Richard and Jennifer L. Warlick. 1981. "Disentangling the Annuity from the Redistributive Aspects of Social Security in the United States." *Review of Income and Wealth* 27, No. 4: 401–421.

Burns, Eveline M. 1949. *The American Social Security System.* Cambridge, MA: Riverside Press.

Burtless, Gary. 1996. "The Folly of Means-Testing Social Security." In Peter A. Diamond, David C. Lindeman and Howard Young. *Social Security: What Role for the Future?* Washington, D.C.: National Academy of Social Insurance, pp. 172–180.

Burtless, Gary and R. A. Moffitt. 1984. "The Effect of Social Security Benefits on the Labor Supply of the Aged." In Henry J. Aaron and G. Burtless, eds. *Retirement and Economic Behavior.* Washington, DC: The Brookings Institution, pp. 135–171.

Carney, Terry and P. Hanks. 1986. *Australian Social Security Law, Policy, and Administration.* Melbourne: Oxford University Press.

Chakravarty, Subrata N. and K. Weisman. 1988. "Consuming Our Children." *Forbes* (November 14): 222–232.

Chater, Shirley S. 1994. "Retirement Earnings Test." Statement before the U.S. Senate Committee on Finance, May 24. Reproduced.

Chen, Yung-Ping. 1967. "Inflation and Productivity in Tax-Benefit Analysis for Social Security." In U.S. Congress, Joint Economic Committee. *Old Age Income Assurance*, Part III: Public Programs, 90th Cong., 1st Sess. Washington, DC: U.S. Government Printing Office, pp. 85–108.

Chen, Yung-Ping and K. W. Chu. 1974. "Tax-Benefit Ratios and Rates of Return Under OASI: 1974 Retirees and Entrants." *Journal of Risk and Insurance* 41 (June): 189–206.

Cleveland, Robert. 1995. Private communication regarding Bureau of the Census unpublished numbers.

Cohen, Wilbur. 1951. "Aspects of Legislative History of the Social Security Amendments of 1950." *Industrial and Labor Relations Review* 4 (January): 198.

Cohen, Wilbur. 1952. "Income Maintenance for the Aged." *Annals of the American Academy of Political and Social Science* (January): 154.

Cohen, Wilbur J. 1958. *Retirement Policies Under Social Security*. Berkeley and Los Angeles: University of California Press.

Cohen, Wilbur J., Robert M. Ball, and Robert J. Myers. 1954. "Social Security Act Amendments of 1954: A Summary and Legislative History." *Social Security Bulletin* (September): 16.

Coll, Blanche D. 1973. *Perspectives in Public Welfare*. Washington, DC: U.S. Department of Health, Education, and Welfare.

Committee on Economic Security. 1935. *Committee on Economic Security Report to the President, 1935*. Washington, DC: U.S. Government Printing Office.

Concord Coalition. 1992. *The Concord Coalition: Citizens for America's Future*. Washington, DC: Concord Coalition.

Concord Coalition. 1993. *The Zero Deficit Plan*. Washington. DC: Concord Coalition.

Congressional Record. 1989. Senator Moynihan, January 25. Washington, DC: U.S. Government Printing Office: S 620–621.

Cook, Fay Lomax. 1990. "Congress and the Public: Convergent and Divergent Opinions on Social Security." In Henry J. Aaron, ed., *Social Security and the Budget: Proceedings of the First Conference of the National Academy of Social Insurance*. Lanham, MD: University Press of America, pp. 79–108.

Cook, Fay Lomax. 1996. "Public Support for Programs for Older Americans: Continuities Amidst Threats of Discontinuities." In Vern Bengtson, ed. *Continuities and Discontinuities in Adulthood and Aging*. New York: Springer, pp. 327–346.

Cook, Fay Lomax and Edith J. Barrett. 1992. *Support for the American Welfare State: The Views of Congress and the Public*. New York: Columbia University Press.

Cook, Fay Lomax, Victor W. Marshall, Joanne Gard Marshall, and Julie E. Kaufman. 1994. "The Salience of Intergenerational Equity in Canada and the United States." In Theodore R. Marmor, Timothy M. Smeeding, and Vernon L. Greene, eds. *Economic Security and Intergenerational Justice*. Washington, DC: The Urban Institute Press, pp. 96–101.

Daniels, Norman. 1988. *Am I My Parents' Keeper? An Essay on Justice Between the Young and the Old*. New York: Oxford University Press.

Danziger, Sheldon, Robert Haveman, and Robert Plotnick. 1981. "How Income Transfers Affect Work, Savings, and the Income Distribution." *Journal of Economic Literature* 19, No. 3 (September): 975-1028.

Danziger, Sheldon, Jacques van der Gaag, Eugene Smolensky, and Michael Taussig. 1984. "Income Transfers and the Economic Status of the Elderly." In Marilyn Moon, ed. *Economic Transfers in the United States*. Chicago: University of Chicago Press, pp. 239–282.

David, Sherri I. 1985. *With Dignity: The Search for Medicare and Medicaid*. Westport, CT: Greenwood Press.

Departments of Social Security and Veterans' Affairs. 1994. *Annual Reports 1992–93*. Canberra: Australian Government Publishing Service.

Derthick, Martha. 1979. *Policymaking for Social Security*. Washington, DC: The Brookings Institution.

Derthick, Martha. 1990. *Agency Under Stress: The Social Security Administration in American Government*. Washington, DC: The Brookings Institution.

DeVroom, Bert and M. Blomsa. 1991. "The Netherlands: An Extreme Case." In Martin Kohli, M. Rein, A. M. Guillemard, and H. van Gunsteren, eds. *Time for Retirement: Comparative Studies of Early Exit from the Labor Force*. New York: Cambridge University Press, pp. 97–126.

Diamond, Peter A. 1977. "A Framework for Social Security Analysis." *Journal of Public Economics* 8 (December): 275–298.

Diamond, Peter A. 1996. "Social Security Reform in Chile: An Economist's Perspective." In Peter A. Diamond, David C. Lindeman and Howard Young. *Social Security: What Role for the Future?* Washington, D.C.: National Academy of Social Insurance, pp. 213–224.

Drazaga, Linda, Melinda Upp, and Virginia Reno. 1982. "Low Income Aged: Eligibility and Participation in SSI." *Social Security Bulletin* 45 (May): 28–35.

Duggan, James E., R. Gillingham, and J. S. Greenlees. 1993. "Returns Paid to Early Social Security Cohorts." *Contemporary Policy Issues* 11, No. 4 (October): 1–13.

Dyer, J. 1977. "Coordination of Private and Public Pension Plans: An International Summary." In Dan McGill, ed. *Social Security and Private Pension Plans: Competitive or Complementary?* Homewood, IL: Richard D. Irwin, pp. 29–40.

Eller, T. J. 1994. *Household Wealth and Asset Ownership: 1991*. Current Population Reports, Household Economic Studies, P70–34. Washington, DC: U.S. Bureau of the Census.

Employee Benefit Research Institute. 1993. *Sources of Health Insurance and Characteristics of the Uninsured: Analysis of the 1992 CPS*." EBRI Special Report and Issue Brief #133. Washington, DC: Employee Benefits Research Institute.

Families USA. 1992. *SSI Aware*. Final Report. Boston, MA: Families USA.

Feldstein, Martin S. 1974. "Social Security, Induced Retirement, and Aggregate Capital Accumulation." *Journal of Political Economy*, 82, No. 5 (September-October): 905–926.

Feldstein, Martin S. 1977. "Social Insurance." In Colin D. Campbell, ed. *Income Redistribution*. Washington, DC: American Enterprise Institute, pp. 71–97.

Feldstein, Martin S. 1987. "Should Social Security Be Means-Tested?" *Journal of Political Economy* 95: 468–484.

Ferguson, Karen and Kate Blackwell. 1995. *Pensions in Crisis*. Washington, DC: Pension Rights Center.

Ferrara, Peter J. 1982. *Social Security Reform: The Family Plan*. Washington, DC: Heritage Foundation.

Fierst, Edith and Nancy Duff Campbell. 1988. *Earnings Sharing and Social Security: A Model for Reform*. Washington, DC: Center for Women's Policy Studies.

Flint, Anthony. 1994. "GOP Makes Welfare Top Priority for Reform." *Boston Globe* (November 17): 1,8.

Freiden, Alan D. Leimer, and R. Hoffman. 1977. "Internal Rates of Return to Retired Worker-Only Beneficiaries Under Social Security, 1967–1970." In *Studies in Income Distribution*. Washington, DC: Office of Research and Statistics, U.S. Social Security Administration.

Friedland, Robert B. 1994. *When Support and Confidence Are at Odds: The Public's Understanding of the Social Security Program*. Washington, DC: National Academy of Social Insurance.

Fullerton, Don and Marios Karayannis. 1993. "United States." In D.W. Jorgenson and R. Landau, eds. *Tax Reform and the Cost of Capital: An International Comparison*. Washington, DC: Brookings Institution, pp. 333–368.

Garfield, Eugene. 1984. "The 100 Most Cited Papers Ever and How We Select 'Citation Classics.'" *Current Classics* 23 (June 4): 176–178.

Garfinkel, Irwin, ed. 1982. *Income-Tested Transfer Programs: The Case for and Against*. New York: Academic Press.

Generations United. 1990a. *Strategies for Change: Building State and Local Coalitions on Intergenerational Issues and Programs*. Washington, DC: Generations United.

Generations United. 1990b. *Promoting Cooperation Among Americans of All Ages*. Washington, DC: Generations United.

Gilman, H. 1988. "Medicare Change Prompts Pitches for Tax-Free Plans." *Boston Globe* (January 19): 35,45.

Goss, Stephen C. 1995a. "Analyses of Relationship Between Mortality and Income Levels." Memorandum to Harry Ballantyne, Chief Actuary, Social Security Administration, Baltimore, MD, March 9.

Goss, Stephen C. 1995b. "Estimated Long-Range OASDI Financial Effect of Proposal by Bob Ball." Memorandum to Harry Ballantyne, Chief Actuary, Social Security Administration, Baltimore, MD, May 5.

Goss, Stephen C. 1995c. Personal communication with Stephen C. Goss, Supervisory Actuary, Social Security Administration, May 9 and May 22.

Goss, Stephen C. and Orlo R. Nichols. 1993. "OASDI Money's Worth Analysis for Hypothetical Cohorts." Unpublished memorandum, Office of the Actuary, Social Security Administration, March 1.

Grad, Susan. 1994. *Income of the Population 55 or Older, 1992*. Washington, DC: U.S. Department of Health and Human Services.

Graebner, William. 1980. *A History of Retirement: The Meaning and Function of an American Institution, 1885–1978*. New Haven: Yale University Press.

Greenstein, Robert. 1994. "Comments on 'The Roles of Social Insurance, Tax Expenditures, Mandates, and Means-Testing.'" In Robert B. Friedland, Lynn M. Etheredge, and Bruce C. Vladeck, eds. *Social Welfare Policy at the Crossroads: Rethinking the Roles of Social Insurance, Tax Expenditures, Mandates, and Means-Testing*. Washington, DC: National Academy of Social Insurance, pp. 23–26.

Guillemard, Anna-Marie. 1991a. "International Perspectives in Early Withdrawal from the Labor Force." In John Myles and Jill Quadagno, eds. *States, Labor Markets and the Future of Old Age Policy*. Philadelphia: Temple University Press, pp. 209–226.

Guillemard, Anna-Marie. 1991b. "France: Massive Exit Through Employment Compensation." In Martin Kohli, M. Rein, A. M. Guillemard, and H. van Gunsteren, eds. *Time for Retirement: Comparative Studies of Early Exit from the Labor Force*. New York: Cambridge University Press, pp. 127–180.

Haber, Carole and Brian Gratton. 1994. *Old Age and the Search for Security*. Bloomington, IN: University of Indiana Press.

Haber, William and Wilbur Cohen, eds. 1948. *Readings in Social Security*. New York: Prentice Hall.

Harris, Richard. 1966. *A Sacred Trust*. New York: New American Library.

Hart Peter D. Research Associates, Inc. 1980. *A Nationwide Survey of Attitudes Toward Social Security*. Washington, DC. Unpublished.

Hausman, Jerry A. and David A. Wise. 1985. "Social Security, Health Status, and Retirement." In David Wise, ed. *Pensions, Labor, and Individual Choice*. Chicago: The University of Chicago Press, pp. 159–191.

Henson, Mary F. 1990. *Trends in Income, by Selected Characteristics: 1947 to 1988*. Current Population Reports, Series P-60, No. 167. Washington, DC: U.S. Government Printing Office.

Hobbs, Charles D. and Stephen L. Powlesland. 1975. *Retirement Security Reform: Restructuring the Social Security System*. Concord, VT: Institute for Liberty and Community.

Holden, Karen C. 1982. "Supplemental OASI Benefits to Homemakers through Current Spouse Benefits, a Homemaker Credit, and Child-Care Drop-out Years." In Richard V. Burkhauser and Karen C. Holden, eds. *A Challenge to Social Security: The Changing Roles of Women and Men in American Society*. NY: Academic Press, pp. 41–65.

Holden, Karen C. and Timothy Smeeding. 1991. "The Poor, the Rich and the Insecure Elderly Caught in Between." *Milbank Quarterly* 68, No.2: 191–219.

Holden, Karen C. and Pamela Smock. 1991. "The Economic Costs of Marital Dissolution: Why Do Women Bear a Disproportionate Cost?" *Annual Review of Sociology* 17: 51–78.

Holtzman, Abraham. 1963. *The Townsend Movement*. New York: Brookman Associates.

Honig, Marjorie and Cordelia Reimers. 1989. "Is It Worth Eliminating the Retirement Test?" *American Economic Review* (May): 103-107.

Howe, Neil and Phillip Longman. 1992. "The Next New Deal." *The Atlantic Monthly* (April): 88–99.

Hurd, Michael D. 1989. "The Economic Status of the Elderly." *Science* 224, No. 12: 659 – 664.

Hurd, Michael D. 1990. "Research on the Elderly: Economic Status, Retirement, and Consumption and Saving." *Journal of Economic Literature* 28, No. 2: 565–637.

Hurd, Michael D. and Michael J. Boskin. 1984. "The Effect of Social Security on Retirement in the Early 1970s." *Quarterly Journal of Economics* 99, No. 4: 767–90.

Hurd, Michael D. and John B. Shoven. 1985. "The Distributional Impact of Social Security." In D.A. Wise, ed. *Pensions, Labor and Individual Choice*. Chicago: University of Chicago, pp. 192–221.

Hurd, Michael D. and David A. Wise. 1989. "The Wealth and Poverty of Widows: Assets Before and After the Husband's Death." In David Wise, ed. *The Economics of Aging*. Chicago: University of Chicago Press, pp. 177–199.

Hurd, Michael D. and David A. Wise. 1991. "Changing Social Security Survivorship Benefits and the Poverty of Widows." Paper presented at the NBER-JCER Joint Conference on the Economics of Aging, Hakone, Japan, September, 1991.

International Social Security Association. 1984. *Catalogue of Publications*. Geneva: International Social Security Administration.

International Labour Office. 1984. *Introduction to Social Security*. Geneva: International Labour Office.

Ippolito, Richard A. 1990. "Toward Explaining Early Retirement After 1970." *Industrial and Labor Relations Review* 43, No. 5: 556–569.

Jacobs, Klaus, M. Kohli, and M. Rein. 1991. "Germany: the Diversity of Pathways." In Martin Kohli, M. Rein, A. M. Guillemard, and H. van Gunsteren, eds. *Time for Retirement: Comparative Studies of Early Exit from the Labor Force.* New York: Cambridge University Press, pp. 181–221.

Jacobs, Larry R. and Robert Shapiro. 1994. *The News Media's Coverage of Social Security, 1977–1994.* Washington, DC: National Academy of Social Insurance.

Jacoby, Sanford M. 1993. "Employers and the Welfare State: The Role of Marion B. Folsom." *Journal of American History* 80: 525–556.

Kaus, Mickey. 1994. "The Case for Means-Testing Social Security." In Robert B. Friedland, Lynn M. Etheredge, and Bruce C. Vladeck, eds. *Social Welfare Policy at the Crossroads: Rethinking the Roles of Social Insurance, Tax Expenditures, Mandates, and Means-Testing.* Washington, DC: National Academy of Social Insurance, pp. 117–124.

Killingsworth, Charles C. and Gertrude Schroeder. 1951. "Long-Range Cost Estimates for Old-Age Insurance." *Quarterly Journal of Economics* (May): 199–213.

Kingson, Eric R. 1984. "Financing Social Security Agenda-Setting and the Enactment of the 1983 Amendments to the Social Security Act." *Policy Studies Journal* (September): 131–155.

Kingson, Eric R. and Edward D. Berkowitz. 1993. *Social Security and Medicare: A Policy Primer.* Westport, Ct: Auburn House.

Kingson, Eric R. and Regina O'Grady-LeShane. 1993. "The Effect of Caregiving on Women's Social Security Benefits." *The Gerontologist* 33: 230–239.

Kingson, Eric R. and John B. Williamson. 1993. "The Generational Equity Debate: A Progressive Framing of a Conservative Issue." *Journal of Aging and Social Policy* 5, No. 3: 31–52.

Kiplinger's Personal Finance Magazine. April 1994.

Kollmann, G. 1993. "Social Security: The Relationship of Taxes and Benefits for Past, Present, and Future Retirees." CRS Report for Congress. Washington, DC: Congressional Research Service, The Library of Congress.

Kotlikoff, Laurence J. and D. A. Wise. 1989. *The Wage Carrot and the Pension Stick.* Kalamazoo. MI: W. E. Upjohn Institute for Employment Research.

Laczko, Frank and C. Phillipson. 1991. "Great Britain: The Contradictions of Early Exit." In Martin Kohli, M. Rein, A. M. Guillemard, and H. van Gunsteren, eds. *Time for Retirement: Comparative Studies of Early Exit from the Labor Force.* New York: Cambridge University Press, pp. 222–251.

Latimer, M. W. 1929. "Old Age Pensions in America." *American Labor Legislation Review* 19: 55–66.

Leavitt, Thomas D. and James H. Schulz. 1988. *The Role of the Asset Test in Program Eligibility and Participation: The Case of SSI.* Publication # E-2. Washington, DC: Public Policy Institute, American Association of Retired Persons.

Leff, Mark. 1984. *The Limits of Symbolic Reform: The New Deal and Taxation, 1933–1939.* New York: Cambridge University Press.

Leff, Mark. 1998. "Speculating in Social Security Futures." In Gerald Nash, Noel Pugach, and Richard F. Tomasson, eds. *Social Security: The First Half-Century.* Albuquerque, NM: University of New Mexico Press. p. 268.

Leiby, James. 1978. *A History of Social Welfare and Social Work in the United States.* New York: Columbia University Press.

Leimer, Dean R. 1978. "Projected Rates of Return to Future Social Security Retirees Under Alternative Benefit Structures." In U.S. Social Security Administration, Office of Research and Statistics. *Policy Analysis with Social Security Research Files: Proceedings of a Workshop Held March 1978 at Williamsburg, Virginia.* Washington, DC: U.S. Government Printing Office, pp. 235–267.

Leimer, Dean R. and Selig D. Lesnoy. 1982. "Social Security and Private Saving: New Time Series Evidence." Journal of Political Economy 90, No. 3 (June): 606-629.

Leonesio, Michael V. 1990. "The Effects of the Social Security Earnings Test on the Labor-Market Activity of Older Americans: A Review of the Evidence." *Social Security Bulletin* 53, No. 5: 2–21.

Leonesio, Michael V. 1991. "Social Security and Older Workers." Working Paper No. 53. Social Security Administration, Office of Research and Statistics, December.

Leonesio, Michael V. 1993. "Social Security and Older Workers." *Social Security Bulletin* 56, No. 2 (Summer): 47–57.

Levy, Frank. 1987. *Dollars and Dreams: The Changing American Income Distribution*. New York: Russell Sage Foundation.

Lewin-VHI, Inc. 1994. "Labor Market Conditions, Socioeconomic Factors and the Growth of Applications and Awards for SSDI and SSI Disability Benefits: Background and Preliminary Findings." March. Reproduced.

Lubove, Roy. 1961. *The Struggle for Social Security: 1900–1935*. Cambridge, MA: Harvard University Press.

Marmor, Theodore. 1973. *The Politics of Medicare*. Chicago: Aldine.

Marmor, Theodore R. and Julie Beglin. 1995. "Medicare and How It Grew—To Be Confused and Misjudged." *Boston Globe* (May 7).

Marmor, Theodore R., Jerry L. Mashaw, and Philip L. Harvey. 1990. *America's Misunderstood Welfare State: Persistent Myths, Enduring Realities*. New York: Basic Books.

Mashaw, Jerry L. 1983. *Bureaucratic Justice: Managing Social Security Disability Claims*. New Haven, CT: Yale University Press.

Mashaw, Jerry L. Charles Goetz, Frank Goodman, Warren Schwartz, and Paul Verkuil. 1978. *Social Security Hearings and Appeals*. Lexington, MA: Lexington Press.

Matusow, Allen. 1984. *The Unraveling of America: A History of Liberalism in the 1960s*. New York: Harper and Row.

Mechanic, David and David Rockefort. 1990. "Deinstitutionalization: An Appraisal of Reform." *Annual Review of Sociology* 16:301–27

Meier, Elizabeth L. 1986. "Employment Experience and Income of Older Women." *American Association of Retired Persons*, Publication #8609. Washington, DC: AARP Public Policy Institute.

Menefee, John A., Bea Edwards, and Sylvester Schieber. 1981. "Analysis of Nonparticipation in the SSI Program." *Social Security Bulletin* 44, No. 6 (June): 3–21.

Merrill Lynch & Co., Inc. 1994. "Savings and the American Dream: An Economic and Public Opinion Study." Merrill Lynch & Company.

Meyer, Charles W. and N. L. Wolff. 1987a. "Intercohort and Intracohort Redistribution Under Old Age Insurance: The 1962–1972 Retirement Cohorts." *Public Finance Quarterly* 15, No. 3: 259–281.

Meyer, Charles W. and N. L. Wolff. 1987b. "Intercohort and Intracohort Redistribution Under Social Security." In C. Meyer, ed. *Social Security: A Critique of Radical Reform Proposals*. Lexington, MA: DC Heath, pp. 49–68.

Meyer, Charles W. and N. L. Wolff. 1993. *Social Security and Individual Equity*. Westport, CT: Greenwood Press.

Mitchell, D. and F. Gruen. 1995. "The Role of Targeting in Rethinking Social Security." In *Social Security Tomorrow: Permanence and Change*. Geneva: International Social Security Association.

Mitchell, Olivia S. 1991. "Social Security Reforms and Poverty Among Older Dual-earner Couples." *Population Economics* (Spring): 281-293.

Mitchell, Olivia. 1992. "Trends in Pension Benefit Formulas and Retirement Provisions." In John A. Turner and D. J. Beller, eds. *Trends in Pensions: 1992*. Washington, DC: U.S. Government Printing Office, pp. 177–216.

Moffitt, Robert A. 1984. "Trends in Social Security Wealth by Cohort." In Marilyn Moon, ed. *Economic Transfers in the United States*. Chicago: The University of Chicago Press, pp. 327–347.

Moffitt, Robert A. 1987. "Life Cycle Labor Supply and Social Security: A Time Series Analysis." In Gary Burtless, ed. *Work, Health, and Income Among the Elderly*. Washington, DC: The Brookings Institution.

Moon, Marilyn. 1993. *Medicare Now and in the Future*. Washington: The Urban Institute Press.

Moon, Marilyn and Janemarie Mulvey. 1995. *Entitlements and the Elderly: Protecting Promises, Recognizing Realities*. Washington, DC: Urban Institute Press.

Munnell, Alicia H. 1977. *The Future of Social Security*. Washington, DC: The Brookings Institution.

Munnell, Alicia H. 1982. *Economics of Private Pensions*. Washington, DC: The Brookings Institution.

Munnell, Alicia H. and C. N. Ernsberger. 1989. "Public Pension Surpluses and National Saving: Foreign Experience." *New England Economic Review* (March/April): 16–38.

Munnell, Alicia H. and Joseph B. Grolnic. 1986. "Should the U.S. Government Issue Index Bonds?" *New England Economic Review* (September-October): 121.

Musgrave, Richard A: 1968. "The Role of Social Insurance in an Overall Program for Social Welfare." In William G. Bowen et al., eds. *The American System of Social Insurance*. New York: McGraw Hill, pp. 23–40.

Myers, Robert J. 1979. "Commentary" on William C. Hsiao, 'An Optimal Indexing Method for Social Security' and Lawrence H. Thompson, 'Indexing Social Security: the Options.' " In Colin D. Campbell, ed. *Financing Social Security*. Washington, DC: American Enterprise Institute.

Myers, Robert J. 1992a. "Chile's Social Security Reform, After Ten Years." *Benefits Quarterly* 8, No. 3: 41–55.

Myers, Robert J. 1992b. "Is the Social Security Sky Falling Again?" *Contingencies* 4 (July/August): 53–54.

Myers, Robert J. 1993a. "Is the 85-Percent Factor for Taxing Social Security Benefits Perpetually Correct?" *Tax Notes* (March 15): 1545–1546.

Myers, Robert J. 1993b. *Social Security* (4th edition). Philadelphia: University of Pennsylvania Press.

Myers, Robert J. 1993c. "Social Security's Financing Problems: Realities and Myths." *Journal of the American Society of CLU and ChFC* 47 (March): 38–45.

Myers, Robert J. 1994a. "Should Social Security Benefits Be Means-Tested?" Issue Paper. Fairfax, VA: The Seniors Coalition.

Myers, Robert J. 1994b. Testimony before the Bipartisan Commission on Entitlement and Tax Reform, July 15. Washington, DC: Reproduced.

Myers, Robert J. 1994c. "The Role of Social Security in the Smoke-and-Mirrors Budget Deficit." *Benefits Quarterly* 10 (First Quarter): 17–21.

Myers, Robert J. 1995. Personal communication (January).

Myers, Robert J. and B. D. Schobel. 1992. "An Updated Money's-Worth Analysis of Social Security Retirement Benefits." *Transactions of the Society of Actuaries* 44: 247–287.

Myles, John. 1988. "Postwar Capitalism and the Extension of Social Security into a Retirement Wage." In Margaret Weir, A. Orloff, and T. Skocpol, eds. *The Politics of Social Policy in the United States*. Princeton, NJ: Princeton University Press, pp. 265–299.

Myles, John and Jill Quadagno. 1995. Generational Equity and Social Security Reform." *Aging Research and Policy Report,* Florida Policy Exchange Center on Aging, Vol. 3, No. 5, pp. 12–16.

National Academy of Social Insurance. 1988. *The Social Security Benefit Notch*. Washington, DC: National Academy of Social Insurance.

National Academy of Social Insurance. 1994. *Preliminary Report of the Disability Policy Panel*. Washington, DC: National Academy of social Insurance.

National Commission on Social Security Reform. 1983. *Report of the National Commission on Social Security Reform*. Washington, DC: U.S. Government Printing Office.

New York Times. 1988. "Trillions, Trillions All Around." Editorial in *New York Times* (April 11): A-18.

Nichols, Orlo. 1994. "Do People Get Their Money's Worth from Social Security?" *OASIS* 40, No. 12 (December): 20–21.

North, Douglass. 1994. "Economic Performance Through Time." *American Economic Review* 84, No. 3 (June): 359–368.

Oliner, Stephen D. and Daniel Sichel. 1994. "Computers and Output Growth Revisited: How Big Is the Puzzle?' *Brookings Papers on Economic Activity, 2–1944*. Washington, DC: The Brookings Institution, pp. 274–334.

Organization for Economic Co-operation and Development. 1992. *Employment Outlook*. Paris: Organization for Economic Co-operation and Development.

Orshansky, Mollie. 1965. "Who's Who Among the Poor: A Demographic View of Poverty." *Social Security Bulletin* (July): 3–32.

Page, Benjamin I. and Robert Y. Shapiro. 1992. *The Rational Public: Fifty Years of Trends in Americans' Policy Preferences*. Chicago: The University of Chicago Press.

Pearlstein, Steven. 1993. "The Battle over 'Generational Equity': Powerful Spending, Tax Choices Have the Young Calling for the Old to Get Less." *Washington Post* (February 17).

Pechman, Joseph A., Henry J. Aaron, and Michael K. Taussig. 1968. *Social Security: Perspectives for Reform*. Washington, DC: The Brookings Institution.

Peterson, Peter G. 1994. "Entitlement Reform: The Way to Eliminate the Deficit." *New York Review of Books* XLI, No. 7 (April 7): 3–19.

Peterson, Peter and Neil Howe. 1988. *On Borrowed Time: How the Growth in Entitlement Spending Threatens America's Future*. San Francisco: Institute for Contemporary Studies.

Peterson, Ray M., 1959. "Misconceptions and Missing Perceptions of Our Social Security System (Actuarial Anesthesia)." *Transactions of the Society of Actuaries* Vol. XI, pp. 812–851.

Phillips, Martha. 1996. Paper presented at 42nd Annual Meeting of the American Society on Aging, Anaheim, California, March 16–19, 1995.

Pierson, Paul and Miriam Smith. 1994. "Shifting Fortunes of the Elderly: The Comparative Politics of Retrenchment." In Theodore R. Marmor, Timothy M. Smeeding, and Vernon L. Greene, eds. *Economic Security and Intergenerational Justice*. Washington, DC: The Urban Institute Press, pp. 21–51.

Preston, Samuel H. 1984. "Children and the Elderly: Divergent Paths for America's Dependents." *Demography* 21, No. 4: 435–457.

Quadagno, Jill. 1988. *The Transformation of Old Age Security: Class and Politics in the American Welfare State*. Chicago: The University of Chicago Press.

Quadagno, Jill. 1989. "Generational Equity and the Politics of the Welfare State." *Politics and Society* 17, No. 3: 353–376.

Quinn, Joseph F. 1991. "The Nature of Retirement: Survey and Econometric Evidence." In Alicia H. Munnell, ed. *Retirement and Public Policy*. Dubuque, IA: Kendall/Hunt Publishing, pp. 115–137.

Quinn, Joseph F. and R. V. Burkhauser. 1990. "Work and Retirement." In Robert H. Binstock and L. K. George, eds. *Handbook of Aging and the Social Sciences*. San Diego: Academic Press, pp. 307–327.

Quinn, Joseph F. and R. V. Burkhauser. 1994. "Retirement and the Labor Force Behavior of the Elderly." In Samuel H. Preston and L. G. Martin, eds. *Demography of Aging*. Washington, DC: National Academy Press, pp. 50–101.

Quinn, Joseph F., R. V. Burkhauser, and D. A. Myers. 1990. *Passing the Torch: The Influence of Economic Incentives on Work and Retirement*. Kalamazoo, MI: W. E. Upjohn Institute for Employment Research.

Radner, Daniel B. 1993a. "An Assessment of the Economic Status of the Aged." *Studies in Income Distribution*. No. 16 (May). U.S. Social Security Administration, Office of Research and Statistics. Washington, DC: Superintendent of Documents.

Radner, Daniel. 1993b. "Economic Well-being of the Old-Old: Family Unit Income and Household Wealth." *Social Security Bulletin* 56 (Spring): 3–18.

Radner, Daniel B. 1995. "Incomes of the Elderly and Nonelderly, 1967–92." *ORS Working Paper Series*. No. 68 (October). Washington, DC: U.S. Social Security Administration, Office of Research and Statistics.

Rawls, John. 1983. "A Contrarian Theory of Justice." In Tom L. Beauchamp and Terry P. Pinkard. *Ethics and Public Policy: An Introduction to Ethics*, 2nd ed. Englewood Cliffs, NJ: Prentice Hall, pp. 148–159.

Reagan, Ronald. 1984. *Public Papers of the Presidents of the United States, 1983*. Washington, DC: U.S. Government Printing Office.

Reno, Virginia P. 1993. "The Role of Pensions in Retirement Income: Trends and Questions." *Social Security Bulletin* (Spring): 29–43.

Robertson, A. Haeworth. 1981. *The Coming Revolution in Social Security*. McLean, VA: Security Press.

Rostenkowski, Dan. 1994. "The Social Security Trust Fund Will Be There When You Retire." Reproduced.

Ruggles, Patricia. 1990. *Drawing the Line: Alternative Poverty Measures and Their Implications for Public Policy*. Washington DC: The Urban Institute Press.

Ruhm, Christopher J. 1995. "Secular Changes in the Work and Retirement Patterns of Older Men." *Journal of Human Resources* 30, No. 3: 362–385.

Sammartino, Frank J. 1987. "The Effect of Health on Retirement." *Social Security Bulletin* 50 (February): 31–47.

Sammartino, Frank and Robertson Williams. 1991. "Trends in Income and Federal Taxes of the Elderly." Paper presented at the thirteenth annual research conference of the Association for Public Policy Analysis and Management, Bethesda, MD, October 24–26. Reproduced.

Samuelson, Paul A. 1958. "An Exact Consumption-Loan Model of Interest with or Without the Social Contrivances of Money." *Journal of Political Economy* 66 (December): 467–482.

Sandell, Steven H. and Howard Iams. 1994. "Caregiving and Women's Social Security Benefits: A Comment on Kingson and O'Grady-LeShane." *The Gerontologist* 5, No. 34: 680–684.

Schlitz, Michael E. 1970. *Public Attitudes Toward Social Security 1935–1965*. U.S. Department of Health, Education and Welfare, Office of Research and Statistics, Research Report No. 33. Washington DC: U.S. Government Printing Office.

Schulz, James H. 1984. "SSI: Origins, Experiences, and Unresolved Issues." In U.S. Senate, Special Committee on Aging. *The Supplemental Security Income Program: A 10-Year Overview*. An Information Paper. Washington, DC: U.S. Government Printing Office.

Schulz, J. 1991. "The Buffer Years: Market Incentives and Evolving Retirement Policies." In John Myles and J. Quadagno, eds. *States, Labor Markets and the Future of Old Age Policy*. Philadelphia: Temple University Press, pp. 295–308.

Schulz, James H. 1995. *The Economics of Aging* (6th edition). New York: Auburn House.

Schulz, James H., A. Borowski, and William Crown. 1991. *Economics of Population Aging: The "Graying" of Australia, Japan, and the United States*. New York: Auburn House.

Schulz, James, Guy Carrin, Hans Krupp, Manfred Peschke, Elliott Sclar, and J. Van Steenberge. 1974. *Providing Adequate Retirement Income: Pension Reform in the United States and Abroad*. Hanover, NH: New England Press for Brandeis University Press.

Schulz, James H. and John Myles. 1990. "Old Age Pensions: A Comparative Perspective." In R. H. Binstock and L. K. George, eds. *Handbook of Aging and the Social Sciences*. San Diego, CA: Academic Press, pp. 398–411.

Sherman, Sally R. 1989. "Public Attitudes Toward Social Security." *Social Security Bulletin* (December): 2–16.

Skocpol, Theda. 1990. *Protecting Soldiers and Mothers: The Political Origins of Social Policy in the United States*. Cambridge, MA: Harvard University Press.

Smeeding, Timothy. 1982. *Alternative Methods for Valuing In-Kind Transfer Benefits and Measuring Their Impact on Poverty*. U.S. Bureau of the Census, Technical Report 50. Washington, DC: U.S. Government Printing Office.

Smeeding Timothy. 1986. "Nonmoney Income and the Elderly: The Case of the 'Tweeners." *Journal of Policy Analysis and Management* 5 (Summer): 707–724.

Smeeding, Timothy M. 1989. "Full Income Estimates of the Relative Well-Being of the Elderly and the Nonelderly." In Daniel J. Slottje, ed. *Research on Economic Inequality* Vol. 1. Greenwich, CT: JAI Press, pp. 83–122.

Smeeding, Timothy M. 1994. "Improving Supplemental Security Income." In Robert B. Friedland, Lynn M. Etheredge, and Bruce C. Vladeck, eds. *Social Welfare Policy at the Crossroads: Rethinking the Roles of Social Insurance, Tax Expenditures, Mandates, and Means-Testing*. Washington, DC: National Academy of Social Insurance, pp. 97–108.

Snee, John and Mary Ross. 1978. "Social Security Amendments of 1977: Legislative History and Summary of Provisions. *Social Security Bulletin* (March): 3–20.

Solow, Robert M. 1956. "A Contribution to the Theory of Economic Growth." *Quarterly Journal of Economics* (February): 65-94.

SSI Modernization Project Experts. 1992. *Supplemental Security Income Modernization Project: Final Report of the Experts*. Baltimore: U.S. Social Security Administration.

Steuerle, C. Eugene. 1993. "Taxation of Social Security Benefits." Statement before the Senate Committee on Finance, 103rd Congress, First Session, May 4. Reproduced.

Steuerle, C. Eugene. 1994. "Implications of Entitlement Growth." Statement before the Bi-partisan Committee on Entitlement and Tax Reform, 104th U.S. Congress, Session July 15. Reproduced.

Steuerle, C. Eugene and Jon M. Bakija. 1994. *Retooling Social Security for the 21st Century: Right & Wrong Approaches to Reform*. Washington, DC: The Urban Institute Press.

Stone, Deborah A. 1984. *The Disabled State*. Philadelphia: Temple University Press.

Svahn, John A. and Mary Ross. 1983. "Social Security Amendments of 1983: Legislative History and Summary Provisions." *Social Security Bulletin* (July): 3–48.

Thompson, Lawrence H. 1983. "The Social Security Reform Debate." *Journal of Economic Literature* 21, No. 4: 1425–1467.

Thompson, Lawrence H. 1994. "The American Approach to Social Welfare." In Robert B. Friedland, Lynn M. Etheredge, and Bruce C. Vladeck, eds. *Social Welfare Policy at the Crossroads: Rethinking the Roles of Social Insurance, Tax Expenditures, Mandates, and Means-Testing*. Washington, DC: National Academy of Social Insurance, pp. 9–20.

Turner, John A. and Daniel J. Beller, eds. 1989. *Trends in Pensions*. Washington, DC: U.S. Department of Labor.

United Nations. 1993. *World Population Prospects: The 1992 Revision*. New York: U.N. Department for Economic and Social Information and Policy Analysis.

U.S. Bureau of the Census. 1988 *Measuring the Effect of Benefits and Taxes on Income and Poverty: 1986*. Washington, DC: U.S. Government Printing Office.

U. S. Bureau of the Census. 1989. *Projections of the Population of the United States, by Age, Sex, and Race: 1988 to 2080*. Washington, DC: U.S. Government Printing Office.

U.S. Bureau of the Census. 1990. "Household Wealth and Asset Ownership: 1988." *Current Population Reports*, P-60, no. 22. Washington, DC: U.S. Government Printing Office.

U.S. Bureau of the Census. 1992. "Money Income of Households, Families, and Persons in the United States: 1991." *Current Population Reports*, P-60, no. 22. Washington, DC: U.S. Government Printing Office.

U.S. Bureau of the Census. 1992. *Statistical Abstract of the United States: 1992*. Washington, DC: U.S. Government Printing Office.

U.S. Bureau of the Census. 1993a. "Money Income of Households, Families, and Persons in the United States: 1990." *Current Population Reports,* Series P-60, No. 174. Washington, DC: U.S. Government Printing Office.

U.S. Bureau of the Census. 1993b. "Poverty in the United States: 1990." *Current Population Reports,* Series P-60, No. 175. Washington, DC: U.S. Government Printing Office.

U.S. Congress, House of Representatives. 1994. "Conference Report on H.R. 4277." H. Rept.103–670. Washington, DC: U.S. Government Printing Office, pp. 96–97.

U.S. Congress, House Committee on Ways and Means. 1989. *Background Material and Data on Programs Within the Jurisdiction of the Committee on Ways and Means*. Washington, DC: U.S. Government Printing Office.

U.S. Congress, House of Representatives, Committee on Ways and Means. 1991. *Overview of Entitlement Programs: 1991 Green Book*. Washington, DC: U.S. Government Printing Office.

U.S. Congress, House Committee on Ways and Means. 1994. *1994 Green Book: Background Material and Data on Programs Within the Jurisdiction of the Committee on Ways and Means*. Washington, DC: U.S. Government Printing Office.

U.S. Congress, Senate Special Committee on Aging, in conjunction with the AARP, the Federal Council on Aging, and the U.S. Administration on Aging. 1991. *Aging America: Trends and Projections: 1991 edition*. Washington, DC: U.S. Government Printing Office.

U.S. Congressional Budget Office. 1989. *The Economic Status of the Elderly*. Washington, DC: U.S. Government Printing Office.

U.S. Congressional Budget Office. 1993. *Baby Boomers in Retirement: An Early Perspective*. Report. Washington, DC: U.S. Government Printing Office.

U.S. Congressional Budget Office. 1994a. *The Economic and Budget Outlook: Fiscal Years 1995–1999*. Washington, DC: U.S. Government Printing Office.

U.S. Congressional Budget Office. 1994b. *Implications of Revising Social Security's Investment Policies*. Washington, DC: U.S. Government Printing Office.

U.S. Department of Health and Human Services. 1992. *The Social Security Disability Insurance Program: An Analysis "109 Report."* Washington, DC: The Department.

U.S. Department of Labor. 1994. *Pension and Health Benefits of American Workers, New Findings from the April 1993 Current Population Survey*. Washington, DC: U.S. Government Printing Office.

U.S. General Accounting Office. 1991a. *Canadian Health Insurance: Lessons from the United States*. Washington, DC: U.S. Government Printing Office.

U.S. General Accounting Office. 1991b. *Social Security: Analysis of a Proposal to Privatize Trust Fund Reserves*. Washington, DC: U.S. Government Printing Office.

U.S. General Accounting Office. 1994. *Social Security: Disability Rolls Keep Growing While Explanations Remain Elusive*. Washington, DC: U.S. Government Printing Office.

U.S. General Accounting Office. 1996. *Federal Pension Data*. Washington, DC: U.S. Government Printing Office.

U.S. News and World Report. 1994. "Wake Up, Baby Boomers." *1994 Retirement Guide* (June 13): 84–122.

U.S. Office of Management and Budget. 1993. *Budget of the United States Government—Fiscal Year 1994—Analytical Perspectives*. Washington, DC: U.S. Government Printing Office.

U.S. Office of Management and Budget. 1995. *Analytical Perspectives, Budget of the United States Government, Fiscal Year 1996*. Washington, DC: U.S. Government Printing Office.

U.S. Social Security Administration. 1979. *Changing Roles of Men and Women*, Washington, DC: Social Security Administration.

U.S. Social Security Administration. 1985. *Report on Earnings Sharing Implementation*, Committee Print 99–4. Washington, DC: U.S. Government Printing Office.

U.S. Social Security Administration. 1993. *Annual Statistical Supplement, 1993*. Washington DC: Social Security Administration.

U.S. Social Security Administration, Office of Research and Statistics. 1994a. *Income of the Aged, Chartbook, 1992*. Washington, DC: U.S. Social Security Administration.

U.S. Social Security Administration. 1994a. *Annual Statistical Supplement, 1993*. Washington DC: Social Security Administration.

U.S. Social Security Administration. 1994b. *Information Bulletin*. No. 94–7. Washington, DC: Social Security Administration.

U.S. Social Security Administration, Office of the Actuary. 1995a. *Advance Estimate*. April 1995.

U.S. Social Security Administration, Office of the Actuary. 1996. "Fact Sheet on the Old Age Survivors and Disability Insurance Program," January 31.

U.S. Social Security Administration. 1995b. *Annual Statistical Supplement, 1995*. Washington, DC: Social Security Administration.

U.S. Social Security Administration, Office of the Actuary. 1995c. "Estimated Operations on the Basis of the President's Fiscal Year 1996 Budget," Table 2, February 6.

Walker, David. 1994. Testimony Before the Bipartisan Commission on Entitlement and Tax Reform, July 15. Reproduced.

Weaver, Carolyn. 1981. *Understanding the Sources and Dimensions of Crisis in Social Security: A First Step Toward Meaningful Reform*. Arlington, VA: Fiscal Policy Council.

Weaver, Carolyn L. 1994a. "The Current Status and Future Prospects of Social Security: An Alternative View." Washington, DC: American Enterprise Institute. Mimeo.

Weaver, Carolyn L. 1994b. "Social Security Investment Policy: What Is It and How Can It Be Improved?" Washington, DC: American Enterprise Institute. Mimeo.

Weinberg, Daniel and Enrique Lamas. 1993. "Some Experimental Results on Alternate Poverty Measures." Paper presented at the 1993 winter meetings of the American Statistical Association. Reproduced.

West, Jane, ed. 1991. *Americans with Disabilities Act: From Politics to Practice*. New York: Milbank Memorial Fund.

Williamson, John B. and Fred C. Pampel. 1993a. *Old-Age Security in Comparative Perspective*. New York: Oxford University Press.

Williamson, John B. and Fred C. Pampel. 1993b. "Paying for the Baby Boom Generation's Social Security Pensions: United States, United Kingdom, Germany, and Sweden." *Journal of Aging Studies* 7, No. 1: 41–54.

Witte, Edwin E. 1963. *The Development of the Social Security Act*. Madison, WI: University of Wisconsin Press.

Woods, John R. 1989. "Pension Coverage Among Private Wage and Salary Workers: Preliminary Findings from the 1988 Survey of Employee Benefits." *Social Security Bulletin* 52 (October).

Woods, John R. 1994. "Pension Coverage Among the Baby Boomers: Initial Findings from a 1993 Survey." *Social Security Bulletin* (Fall): 12–25.

World Bank. 1994. *Averting the Old Age Crisis: Policies to Protect the Old and Promote Growth*. Washington, DC: World Bank.

Yankelovich, Daniel. 1985. *A Fifty-Year Report Card on the Social Security System: The Attitudes of the American Public*. New York: Yankelovich, Skelly and White.

Yankelovich, Daniel. 1991. *Coming to Public Judgment: Making Democracy Work in a Complex World*. Syracuse, NY: Syracuse University Press.

Yelin, Edward. 1992. *Disability and the Displaced Worker*. New Brunswick, NJ: Rutgers University Press.

Young, Howard. 1995. Personal communication. May 30.

Index

Note: The term Social Security is abbreviated in many of the the entries below as SS.

307